THE LIFE AND TIMES OF

‘ALÍ IBN ‘ÍSÀ

AMS PRESS
NEW YORK

THE VICES OF AL-MUQTADIR

Drink *Music*

The unique portrait-*dínár* of the Kaiser-Friedrich Museum, Berlin
Legend on obverse—*al-Muqtadir bi'llah*

Photographed from a cast

THE LIFE AND TIMES OF
ʿALÍ IBN ʿÍSÀ

'The Good Vizier'

BY

HAROLD BOWEN

CAMBRIDGE
AT THE UNIVERSITY PRESS
MCMXXVIII

Library of Congress Cataloging in Publication Data

Bowen, Harold.
The life and times of ‘Alí ibn ‘Ísà, ‘the Good vizier’.

Reprint of the 1928 ed. published by The University Press, Cambridge, Eng.
Includes bibliographical references and index.
1. ‘Alí ibn ‘Ísà, Abbasid wazir, 859-946.
2. Islamic Empire—History—750-1258. I. Title.
DS38.4.A53B68 1975 909'.09'7671 [B] 77-180320
ISBN 0-404-56215-9

Trim size of AMS edition of this book is 5 1/2 x 8 1/2.
Original edition is 5 3/4 x 9.

Reprinted from the edition of 1928, Cambridge
First AMS edition published in 1975
Manufactured in the United States of America

AMS PRESS INC.
NEW YORK, N.Y.

Testimonials, ancient and modern, to the good character of 'Alí ibn 'Ísà

AṢ-ṢÚLÍ (a poet and historian of the fourth/tenth century):

I do not know that there has served the Banú'l-'Abbás a Vizier like him for honesty, asceticism, memorisation of the *qur'án* and knowledge of its significations, clerkship, a capacity for calculation, alms-giving and good works; nor do I know that I ever spoke with anyone more deeply versed in poetry. They have seen no one more abstemious, or gentle-spoken, or chaste. He would fast by day, and stay up at night....

From the Arabic—quoted in the Irshád of Yáqút, the History of adh-Dhahabí, the Kitáb al-Fakhrí, etc.

AL-KHAṬÍB (a historian of the fifth/eleventh century):

He was learned and virtuous and wise, and devout and just and righteous, honest in office, of a good repute in the Vizierate, and well conducted in his life. He was much given to good works and charity, to reading the *qur'án*, and to prayer and fasting; admired and was generous to the learned; and was well known for his discretion and probity and goodness and piety....

From the Arabic—quoted in the Mir'át az-Zamán of Sibṭ Ibn al-Jawzí.

A. VON KREMER (nineteenth century):

Er ist der letzte und glänzendste Vertreter der so wenig bekannten und beachteten staatsmännischen Schule von tüchtigen, kenntnissreichen Verwaltungsbeamten der besten Zeit der Abbasiden, ohne deren Dienste das damalige arabische Weltreich schon viel früher in Stücke gegangen wäre....

Ueber das Einnahmebudget des Abbasidenreichs.

A. MÜLLER (nineteenth century):

Ali ibn Isa war ein ehrlicher Mann, ein tüchtiger und humaner Beamter, die Steuerkraft der Unterthanen zu schonen und ihre Leiden zu mildern beflissen; nicht eben von heldenhaftem Muthe, für welchen in den Kreisen der damaligen Verwaltung sich wenig Platz fand, daher drohenden Gewittern, so gut er irgend konnte, ausweichend, aber stets bereit, dem Staate seine Arbeitskraft zur Verfügung zu stellen, wenn er es ohne Gefahr für sich thun zu können meinte.

Der Islam im Morgen- und Abendland.

L. MASSIGNON (twentieth century):

Kátib, il est visiblement l'idéal des divers *kottáb* qui nous ont laissé l'histoire de son temps: c'est un secrétaire d'Etat modèle, homme de bon conseil....

Al-Hallaj.

PREFACE

THE material for the biography of the "hero" of this book, 'Alí ibn 'Ísà, is exceptionally ample. I doubt whether more is to be discovered about any other minister of the Caliphs. For though numerous works on the lives of the Viziers were composed in early 'Abbásid times, little of them remains; and of one of the most detailed, Hilál aṣ-Ṣábí's *kitáb al-wuzará'*, only that part survives that is concerned with the doings of 'Alí ibn 'Ísà and of his chief rival in office. No period of the Caliphate, moreover, is more abundantly chronicled than that in which he lived.

Nevertheless 'Alí ibn 'Ísà has not received much attention from European writers. Von Kremer used the *kitáb al-wuzará'* in his *Ueber das Einnahmebudget des Abbasidenreichs*, but was concerned in that monograph chiefly with 'Alí ibn 'Ísà's statesmanship, only secondarily with him himself. Weil in his *Geschichte der Califen*, Müller in his *Islam*, and De Goeje in his *Carmathes*, have all given space to him, as have also more recently Amedroz in his edition of Hilál, M. Massignon in *Al-Hallaj*, and Professor Margoliouth in the introduction to his *Eclipse of the Abbasid Caliphate*; but he has generally been undervalued, I think, by being contrasted with his rival Ibn al-Furát. Certainly Ibn al-Furát had more vigour than 'Alí ibn 'Ísà, and owned the effrontery he lacked; but he cannot, it seems to me, be justly extolled as a statesman, since his ruthless opportunism was responsible as much as anything for the ruin of the Caliphate. Besides, with his dishonesty and self-seeking, Ibn al-Furát was typical of his class; whereas 'Alí ibn 'Ísà, with his integrity and foresight, stands out from the prevailing villainy of the age as *par excellence* "the good Vizier."

It will be seen from the "Key to References" and from various foot-notes to the text what works I have used as authorities, also which of them have been published and which remain in manuscript. I must note that there are two pertinent histories that I have been unable to consult, the *awráq* of aṣ-Ṣúlí and the *kitáb al-'uyún*, of which the MSS. are preserved in Cairo and Berlin respectively. However, De Goeje in his edition of 'Aríb gives extracts from the latter, and Professor Margoliouth in his edition of Miskawayh numerous extracts from both. So I hope that I may not have missed any very important points.

As regards spelling, except where they possess established English forms, all names are transliterated systematically from the Arabic, as are also such Arabic words as, since they have no exact equivalents in English, it has been necessary to use. Examples of English forms are Mecca for Makkah, Edessa for Ruhá, the Yemen for al-Yaman, Caliph for *khalífah*. Persian names are given their Persian, as opposed to their Arabic, forms, e.g. Níshápúr and not an-Naysábúr, Ray and not ar-Rayy, Dínavar and not ad-Dínawar. In the case of Arabic names prefixed by the article *al-*, when they are used in such constructions as require an antecedent "the," I have usually dropped the *al-*: e.g. the Baṣrah road, for the road to al-Baṣrah; the Mukharrim quarter, for the quarter of al-Mukharrim; the Mádhará'ís (meaning the persons called each al-Mádhará'í).

As regards names, the term for a name prefixed either by the word Abú, Father (of), or by the word Umm, Mother (of), is *kunyah*. The *kunyah* is used in the Arabic-speaking world instead of the name proper for politeness. In the histories some people appear as a rule under their *kunyahs*, some under their names proper, probably because, in the scarcity of surnames, the need was felt for some means of distinguishing between the many people that shared one name and patronymic. I have followed this precedent in, for example, the cases of the adventurer Abú 'Abd Allah (al-Barídí) and the judge Abú 'Umar, on the one hand, and of 'Alí ibn 'Ísà himself and his uncle Muḥammad ibn Dá'úd, on the other. Family names, or surnames, of a kind existed at the period of this history, but were far from general. They were formed either from patronymics, e.g. Ibn al-Jarráḥ, al-Kháqání (from Ibn Kháqán); from place-names, e.g. aṭ-Ṭabarí (man of Ṭabaristán); from occupation-names, e.g. al-Barídí (postmaster), *al-khazzáz* (raw-silk merchant); from a combination of two of these types, e.g. Ibn al-'Alláf (son of the fodder-man); or, in the case of a freedman, from his master's "surname" or title, e.g. al-Jarráḥí (from Ibn al-Jarráḥ), al-Muqtadirí (from al-Muqtadir).

In the hope of making the details of dating easier to follow, I append a list of the Muḥammadan months in order, showing the number of days in each.

I have to thank Mr J. Allan of the British Museum for his kindness in having casts made of the coins chosen for illustration, and for obtaining a cast of the portrait-*dínár* of al-Muqtadir from Berlin. I have also to thank Professor R. A. Nicholson for his help in the interpretation of some verses.

H. B.

COLWORTH

September 1927

THE MONTHS OF THE MUḤAMMADAN YEAR

al-muḥarram, 30 days.
ṣafar, 29 days.
rabí' al-awwal, 30 days.
rabí' al-ákhir, 29 days.
jumádà'l-úlà, 30 days.
jumádà'l-ákhirah, 29 days.
rajab, 30 days.
sha'bán, 29 days.
ramaḍhán (the Fast), 30 days.
shawwál, 29 days.
dhú'l-qa'dah, 30 days.
dhú'l-ḥijjah (the month of the Pilgrimage), 29 days.

In some years a day is intercalated at the end of *dhú'l-ḥijjah*.

CONTENTS

INTRODUCTION . . . . *page* 1

PART ONE 25

Chapter I. *The accession of* al-Mu'tadhid. 'Ubayd Allah ibn Sulaymán. *The brothers* Ibn al-Furát *and their employment of* 'Alí ibn 'Ísà *and his uncle* Muḥammad.

Chapter II. 'Alí ibn 'Ísà, *and his family, the* Banú'l-Jarráḥ.

Chapter III. Badr. *New employments, and promotion, for* 'Alí *and his uncle.*

Chapter IV. *The* Carmathians. Egypt *recovered.*

Chapter V. *The accession of* al-Muktafí. *The Vizierate and death of* al-Qásim. *The war of the Secretaries.*

Chapter VI. Al-'Abbás ibn al Ḥasan *as Vizier. The defeat of the* Banú'l-Jarráḥ.

Chapter VII. *The* Báb al-Bustán. *The learned and literary circle of* 'Alí ibn 'Ísà.

Chapter VIII. *The death of* al Muktafí. *The accession of* al-Muqtadir. *The conspiracy of* Ibn al-Mu'tazz.

Chapter IX. *The fate of the conspirators.*

PART TWO 99

Chapter I. Al-Muqtadir *and his mother. The Vizierate of* Ibn al-Furát, *and his fall.*

Chapter II. 'Alí ibn 'Ísà *in* Mecca. *The Vizierate and fall of* al-Kháqání.

Chapter III. 'Alí ibn 'Ísà *in the Vizierate. His appointments and reforms. The* qádhís Abú 'Umar *and* Ibn al-Buhlúl.

Chapter IV. 'Alí's *reforms (continued). His secretarial skill. His economies and consequent unpopularity.*

Chapter V. 'Alí's *negotiations with the* Carmathians. *The foundation of the* Fáṭimid Anti-Caliphate, *and the attack on* Egypt.

Chapter VI. *The consequences of the* Egyptian *campaign—the revolt of* Ibn Ḥamdán. 'Alí's *growing unpopularity; his misfortunes and fall.*

Chapter VII. *The second Vizierate of* Ibn al-Furát, *and his fall. The elevation of* Ḥámid ibn al-'Abbás, *and the appointment as his Assistant of* 'Alí ibn 'Ísà.

Chapter VIII. *The trial of* Ibn al-Furát.

Chapter IX. *The rivalry of* Ḥámid ibn al-'Abbás *and* 'Alí ibn 'Ísà. Ḥámid's *contract, and its consequences.*

Chapter X. *Medical questions:* Sinán ibn Thábit; ar-Rází. 'Alí *and* al-Ash'arí. Aṭ-Ṭabarí *and the* Ḥanbalites. 'Alí *as a* Ṣúfí: ash-Shiblí; al-Ḥalláj.

Chapter XI. *The machinations of the* Furát *faction. The disgrace of* Umm Músà. *The embarrassments and fall of* 'Alí ibn 'Ísà.

Chapter XII. 'Alí *on trial.*

Chapter XIII. *The violence of* al-Muḥassin *and its results.*

PART THREE 223

Chapter I. *The "Year of Perdition."*

Chapter II. 'Alí ibn 'Ísà *on his travels.*

Chapter III. *The end of* Ibn al-Furát.

Chapter IV. *A comparison. The Vizierate ill-filled.* 'Alí *given a new post, and later recalled to* Baghdád.

Chapter V. *The second Vizierate.*

Chapter VI. *The alarum of the* Carmathians. 'Alí's *despair and his disgrace.*

Chapter VII. *Further tribulations of* 'Alí ibn 'Ísà. *The second deposition of* al-Muqtadir.

Chapter VIII. *The destruction of the* Maṣáffís. *The breach between* al-Muqtadir *and* Mu'nis. Al-Muqtadir's *manœuvres.*

Chapter IX. *The Vizierate of* Sulaymán. Al-Muqtadir *triumphant.*

PART FOUR 305

Chapter I. *The conversion of* Daylam *and its first results. The final estrangement of* Mu'nis. *A new champion for* 'Alí ibn 'Ísà.

Chapter II. *The end of* al-Muqtadir.

Chapter III. *The accession of* al-Qáhir. *The last of the* Lady. *The fate of* Mu'nis.

Chapter IV. *The triumph and fall of* al-Qáhir. *The accession of* ar-Rádhí. *Employments for* 'Alí.

Chapter V. *The* Buvayhids *and the* Barídís.

Chapter VI. *The manœuvres of* Ibn Muqlah. 'Alí ibn 'Ísà *in trouble. The administration of* 'Abd ar-Raḥmán. *The* "Emir of Emirs," *and the ruin of the Vizierate.*

Chapter VII. Bachkam. *The fate of* Ibn Muqlah. *The death of* ar-Rádhí.

Chapter VIII. *The accession of* al-Muttaqí. *The* Barídís *in* Baghdád. *The last employment of* 'Alí ibn 'Ísà.

Chapter IX. *Further vicissitudes of the Emirate.*

Chapter X. *The* Image *of* Edessa. Túzún. *The second flight and the fate of* al-Muttaqí. Al-Mustakfí.

Chapter XI. *The* Mu'izz ad-Dawlah.

CONCLUSION 396

INDEX 399

CORRIGENDA

p. vii	omit reference to Margoliouth's *Eclipse of the Abbasid Caliphate*
xvii	*for* At-Tannúkhí *read* At-Tanúkhí
„	for *farj* read *faraj* (and so throughout notes), and for *al-farj* read *al-faraj*
4, line 9 from bottom	*for* a third *read* another
12, line 5	*for* was *read* were
26, line 3 from bottom	for *baná'* read *biná'*
59, line 6 from bottom	for *ath-thuráyá* read *ath-thurayyá* (and so in Index)
111, line 6	*for* sherbert *read* sherbet
„ line 12 from bottom	*for* al-Khidḥr *read* al-Khaḍhir
145, line 11, and elsewhere	*for* Farjawayh *read* Farajawayh
156, line 15, and elsewhere	*for* al-Ḥawwárí *read* al-Ḥawárí
192, line 3 from bottom	*for* annihilation *read* absorption
251, line 15	*for* invited him, to *read* invited him to,
388, note 2	for *nazila* read *nazala*

SKETCH MAP
of
AL-'IRÁQ
with parts of the
JIBÁL and KHÚZISTÁN

ILLUSTRATIONS

PLATES

I. The Vices of al-Muqtadir . . . *Frontispiece*

II. *Dirham* and *dínár* of al-Muqtadir . . *to face page* 99

III. The Triumph of al-Qáhir 331

IV. The Commanders of the Commander of the Faithful 392

MAPS

Sketch map of al-'Iráq with parts of the Jibál and Khúzistán . . . . . . *to face page* xv

Sketch map of the 'Abbásid Caliphate in the IIIrd/IXth century . . . . . . *at end*

KEY TO REFERENCES

'A.	'Aríb, ed. De Goeje.
An. *nuz.*	Al-Anbárí: *nuzhat al-alibbá'*, Cairo, 1294/1877.
Ath. (Búláq)	Ibn al-Athír: *History*, Búláq, 1290/1873.
Ath. (Tornberg)	— — ed. Tornberg.
Bal.	Ibn al-Balkhí: *fárs-námeh,* ed. Le Strange and Nicholson.
Dh. *t.*	Adh-Dhahabí: *ta'ríkh al-islám,* MS. B.M. Or. 48*.
Dh. *ṭab.*	Adh-Dhahabí: *ṭabaqát al-ḥuffáḏẖ*, ed. Wüstenfeld.
Ḏẖáf.	Ibn Ḏẖáfir (Jamál ad-Dín): *ad-duwal al-munqaṭi'ah*, MS. B.M. Or. 3685.
Eut.	Eutychius (Sa'íd ibn al-Baṭríq), ed. Pococke.
fakh.	*kitáb al-fakhrí*, ed. Ahlwardt.
Faq.	Ibn al-Faqíh al-Hamadhání, ed. De Goeje.
Fid.	Abú'l-Fidá': *History*, Cairo, 1325/1907.
fih.	*kitáb al-fihrist*, ed. Fluegel.
H.	Hilál aṣ-Ṣábí': *kitáb al-wuzará',* ed. Amedroz.
Ḥ. Kh.	Ḥájjí Khalífah: *kashf aḏẖ-ḏẖunún,* ed. Fluegel.
Ḥam.	Ḥamzah of Iṣfahán: *Annals*, Book x, ed. and trans. (Latin) Gottwaldt.
Ham. *jaz.*	Al-Hamadhání: *jazírat al-'arab*, ed. Müller.
Ham. *tak.*	Al-Hamadhání: *takmilah ta'ríkh aṭ-ṭabarí,* MS. Paris, Arabe, 1469.
Ḥaw.	Ibn Ḥawqal, ed. De Goeje.
Isfan.	Ibn Isfandiyár: *History of Ṭabaristán*, trans. Browne.
Iṣṭ.	Al-Iṣṭakhrí, ed. De Goeje.
Jaw.	Ibn al-Jawzí: *al-muntaḏẖam*, MS. Paris, Arabe, 5909.
Khald.	Ibn Khaldún: *History*, Búláq, 1284/1867.
Khald. *Pro.*	— *Prolegomena,* trans. (French) De Slane.
Khall.	Ibn Khallikán: *wafáyát al-á'yán*, trans. De Slane.

Kin.	Al-Kindí: *kitáb al-wulát*, ed. Guest.
M.	Miskawayh: *kitáb tajárib al-umam*, ed. Amedroz and Margoliouth, and trans. Margoliouth in *Eclipse of the Abbasid Caliphate*.
Maq. *it.*	Al-Maqrízí: *itti'ádh al-ḥunafá'*, ed. Bunz.
Mas. *murúj*	Al-Mas'údí: *murúj adh-dhahab*, ed. and trans. (French) Barbier de Meynard.
Mas. *tan.*	Al-Mas'údí: *kitáb at-tanbíh wa'l-ishráf*, ed. De Goeje.
Muq.	Al-Muqaddasí: ed. De Goeje.
Qaz.	Al-Qazwíní: *Cosmography*, ed. Wüstenfeld.
Qif.	Al-Qifṭí: *ta'ríkh al-ḥukamá'*, ed. Lippert.
Quḍh.	Al-Quḍhá'í: *i'táb al-kuttáb*, MS. B.M. Or. 6641.
Qush.	Al-Qushayrí: *risálah*, Cairo, 1287/1870.
Rus.	Ibn Rustah, ed. De Goeje.
S.J.	Sibṭ Ibn al-Jawzí: *mir'át az-zamán*, MS. B.M. Or. 4619.
Ṣaf.	Aṣ-Ṣafadí: *al-wáfí bi'l-wafáyát*, various MSS. Each indicated in reference.
Sub. *ṭab.*	As-Subkí: *ṭabaqát ash-sháfi'iyyah*, MS. B.M. Or. 6521.
Ṭab.	Aṭ-Ṭabarí: *History*, ed. De Goeje and others.
Tagh.	Ibn Taghríbirdí (Abú'l-Maḥásin): *an-nujúm az-záhirah*, ed. Juynboll.
Tan. *farj*	At-Tanúkhí: *kitáb al-farj ba'd ash-shiddah*, Cairo, 1903–4.
Tan. *nish.*	At-Tanúkhí: *nishwár al-muḥáḍharah*, ed. Margoliouth.
U.	Ibn Abí Uṣaybi'ah: *ṭabaqát al-aṭibbá'*.
Yáq. *mu'jam*	Yáqút: *mu'jam al-buldán*, ed. Wüstenfeld.
Yáq. *ud.*	Yáqút: *irshád al-aríb* (*mu'jam al-udabá'*), ed. Margoliouth. Second ed. of vols. I and II used.

Encyclopédie refers to the *Encyclopédie de l'Islam*, still incomplete, of which the first numbers appeared in 1913, published Leyden and Paris.

Kin.	Al-Kindí: *kitáb al-wulát*, ed. Guest.
M.	Miskawayh: *kitáb tajárib al-umam*, ed. Amedroz and Margoliouth, and trans. Margoliouth in *Eclipse of the Abbasid Caliphate*.
Maq. *it.*	Al-Maqrízí: *itti'ádh al-ḥunafá'*, ed. Bunz.
Mas. *murúj*	Al-Mas'údí: *murúj adh-dhahab*, ed. and trans. (French) Barbier de Meynard.
Mas. *tan.*	Al-Mas'údí: *kitáb at-tanbíh wa'l-ishráf*, ed. De Goeje.
Muq.	Al-Muqaddasí: ed. De Goeje.
Qaz.	Al-Qazwíní: *Cosmography*, ed. Wüstenfeld.
Qif.	Al-Qifṭí: *ta'ríkh al-ḥukamá'*, ed. Lippert.
Quḍh.	Al-Quḍhá'í: *i'táb al-kuttáb*, MS. B.M. Or. 6641.
Qush.	Al-Qushayrí: *risálah*, Cairo, 1287/1870.
Rus.	Ibn Rustah, ed. De Goeje.
S.J.	Sibṭ Ibn al-Jawzí: *mir'át az-zamán*, MS. B.M. Or. 4619.
Ṣaf.	Aṣ-Ṣafadí: *al-wáfí bi'l-wafáyát*, various MSS. Each indicated in reference.
Sub. *ṭab.*	As-Subkí: *ṭabaqát ash-sháfi'iyyah*, MS. B.M. Or. 6521.
Ṭab.	Aṭ-Ṭabarí: *History*, ed. De Goeje and others.
Tagh.	Ibn Taghríbirdí (Abú'l-Maḥásin): *an-nujúm az-záhirah*, ed. Juynboll.
Tan. *farj*	At-Tannúkhí: *kitáb al-farj ba'd ash-shiddah*, Cairo, 1903–4.
Tan. *nish.*	At-Tannúkhí: *nishwár al-muḥáḍharah*, ed. Margoliouth.
U.	Ibn Abí Uṣaybi'ah: *ṭabaqát al-aṭibbá'*.
Yáq. *mu'jam*	Yáqút: *mu'jam al-buldán*, ed. Wüstenfeld.
Yáq. *ud.*	Yáqút: *irshád al-aríb* (*mu'jam al-udabá'*), ed. Margoliouth. Second ed. of vols. I and II used.

Encyclopédie refers to the *Encyclopédie de l'Islam*, still incomplete, of which the first numbers appeared in 1913, published Leyden and Paris.

Introduction

The events that I have set out to chronicle took place between the years 279 and 335 of the Hegira, that is, between A.D. 892 and 946. The chief power in Islam at this time was that of the third, the 'Abbásid, dynasty of Caliphs, or Successors of the Prophet Muḥammad, whose capital was Baghdád, the City of Peace. The 'Abbásids had overthrown the 'Umayyads of Damascus rather more than a century before the beginning of this period, and so had succeeded to the government of all the lands (except Spain) that had ever been conquered by the Muslims. Not long after their establishment they had lost Morocco, and later Sindh, but the rest of this immense empire was still theirs in 279. In some parts of it, however, their sovereignty was now only nominal; for the Caliphate was but just recovering from a spell of anarchy, in which the authority of its rulers had been dangerously shaken.

The causes of this anarchy can be traced back to a difference of religious opinion that had appeared when Islam was first carried beyond the limits of Arabia. As long as the new religion was confined to its native land, the most serious difficulty it encountered was the indifference, common among the Arabs of the desert, to religion in general—the unbelief cursed by the Prophet—an indifference that continued to distinguish the majority of Arab converts from the minority, the Zealots, chiefly town-settled. But as soon as it came to make its way in the countries conquered from the Greeks and Persians, after Muḥammad's death, Islam encountered a difficulty of another and a much more formidable kind in the rivalry of foreign religious and philosophical ideas. The many inhabitants of these countries that were converted, having these ideas in the back of their minds, in receiving Islam could not but twist it to fit in with them. There was now added, therefore, to the Arab Indifferents and the Zealots a third type of Muslim, the Foreigner.

The capture of the Caliphate by the 'Umayyads marked the triumph of the Indifferents, of the pagan Arab spirit. It dismayed not only the Zealots, but also the Foreigners, since they found that their being Muslims did not excuse them, in the eyes of the ruling caste, for not being Arabs. They were continually made to feel their inferiority, and since they were generally far more civilised than the wild Arabs that lorded it over them, they bitterly resented their subjection. The Zealots and the Foreigners were thus united in misfortune: their joint aim became the overthrow of the 'Umayyad dynasty. This was eventually brought about in the revolution that gave the Caliphate to the House of al-'Abbás. The 'Abbásids came to power as champions of the primitive piety and the equality of all Muslims without regard to race.

The Arab dominance now vanished for ever (though occasionally Persians and other foreigners thought it worth while to forge a genealogy proving them descended from some desert tribe); and the bond that held them together once dissolved, the Zealots and the Foreigners soon discovered that they had very little else in common. The former—among whom were included of course multitudes of non-Arabs—were only concerned to believe what the first Muslims had believed. They looked with horror on the cultivation of the foreign philosophy and sciences, which they saw led their students away down strange paths from the simplicity of True-Belief. The latter—or rather those among them that had kept their foreign outlook, together with such pure Arabs and persons of mixed blood as shared it—found that to believe they must somehow reconcile the tenets of Islam with a measure of reason; and so they developed an elaborate system of explaining difficulties away—its exponents were known as *Mu'tazilites*, "Seceders".[1]

Certain of the earlier 'Abbásid Caliphs favoured these rationalists—the reign of the Caliph al-Ma'mún, the son of Hárún ar-Rashíd, saw their influence at its greatest; but the people of their new-founded capital, Baghdád, refused to follow them and clung to the teaching of the strictest literalists. At one time al-Ma'mún subjected the old-fashioned theologians to an inquisition. Consequently he and his Court became exceedingly unpopular. For this reason al-Ma'mún's successor, al-Mu'taṣim, to secure his safety enrolled a body-guard of Turks from the eastern limits of the empire. But this only made matters worse; the Turks soon took to quarrelling so violently and frequently with the people of Baghdád, that the Caliph was obliged, for the sake of peace, to remove himself and them to a new capital—to Sámarrá, about seventy miles up the Tigris.[2]

Here, however, the Turkish officers of the guard began to see how powerful they were, or might be. When al-Wáthiq, al-Mu'taṣim's son, died, it was they that chose his successor, al-Mutawakkil; and from that time on they began to play an ever more preponderating part in affairs of State. Al-Mutawakkil found himself in a vexatious situation. His predecessors had had to call in the Turks to protect themselves from subjects that resented their religious views; but he himself was in perfect agreement with the bigoted populace of the capital, who applauded his actions. For he held the rationalists in as much detestation as they did; had prohibited the study of philosophy and the sciences;

1 Cf. Goldziher: *Le Dogme et la Loi de l'Islam*, 79 *et seqq.*
2 Cf. Herzfeld: *Samarra*, 56.

and revived the long-obsolete sumptuary laws against Jews and Christians. The services of the Turks as a guard were now therefore superfluous; but he found that he could not get rid of them if he would.

Yet it is possible that the disorders that followed his death might have been avoided if al-Mutawakkil had not taken it into his head to prefer his second son, al-Mu'tazz, for the succession over his eldest, al-Muntaṣir. For the latter refused to accept his decision: with the chief Turks as his accomplices he contrived his father's murder, and seized the throne for himself. But he had only enjoyed it for six months when he died, perhaps by poison; whereupon the officers, not daring to promote al-Mu'tazz on account of the hand they had had in al-Mutawakkil's murder, chose as Caliph a cousin, al-Musta'ín. Their subordinates, however, were determined to keep the throne in the family of al-Mutawakkil; and in the end they were successful, when al-Musta'ín, after being besieged by his rival in Baghdád, to which he had fled from Sámarrá, was deposed and killed. Al-Mu'tazz, Caliph at last, hoping to put an end to the tyranny of the Turks, instigated the Berbers (who also formed part of the body-guard) against them. But when his intrigues ended duly in the assassination of one of the Turkish officers, the others avenged him by engineering a riot of the troops for their pay, which resulted in the deposition and killing of al-Mu'tazz himself. On this, a third Turk, by name Músà ibn Bughá, now the most powerful of all the officers, hurried back to Sámarrá from the campaign on which he had been engaged, intent on avenging al-Mu'tazz. And it was not long before he quarrelled with the new Caliph (al-Muhtadí, a son of al-Wáthiq); deposed and killed him in turn; and set up a third son of al-Mutawakkil under the title *al-mu'tamid 'alà'llah* (Relying upon God).

These events, of which the details are bewilderingly

complicated, from the murder of al-Mutawakkil to the accession of al-Mu'tamid, occupied just nine years (247–256/861–870). The power of the Caliphs seemed likely to succumb finally amid the anarchical rivalries of the guard. Yet after al-Mu'tamid's accession the Turkish officers caused scarcely any further disturbance. Músà ibn Bughá had no equal among them; and since the Caliph was of his own choosing, there was no more occasion for strife at Court. Moreover, owing to the paralysis of the central Government during the times of disorder, rebellions had broken out in several provinces of the empire, so that the soldiery were fully occupied in attempting to subdue them.

Several of these rebellions were of the Shí'ah, the Sect, i.e. those who support the claim to the Caliphate of the 'Alid family, the descendants of the Prophet through the marriage of his daughter Fáṭimah with his first cousin 'Alí ibn Abí Ṭálib.

This most unhappy family had never succeeded in making these claims good. If the hereditary principle had been clearly recognised from the beginnings of Islam by all believers, its right to the Caliphate would of course have been unassailable; but it had not been so recognised, except by a minority. The chieftainship of an Arab tribe often descended from father to son, but was conferred only with the consent of the tribesmen and might be withdrawn if they so wished. Muḥammad left no instructions as to who should lead the Faithful on his death; in any case he had no son, and the choice of such a leader was therefore determined, on tribal precedent, by the agreement of the leading Muslims. 'Alí, the father of Muḥammad's only grandsons, eventually became Caliph, but only fourth in succession; and these same grandsons of the Prophet, al-Ḥasan and al-Ḥusayn, were excluded from the Caliphate by the usurpation (as they and their adherents considered it) of the 'Umayyads. Later, al-

Ḥusayn, and with him some of his relatives, was killed by order of the second 'Umayyad Caliph at Karbalá (a tragedy still very much alive in the hearts of the Shí'ah). Other members of the 'Alid line were also persecuted by the dynasty, till to the Shí'ah the 'Umayyads came to embody all that was impious and loathsome. When the 'Abbásids were canvassing support for their revolt, the 'Alids were duped into thinking that its success would give the Caliphate to them, and joined eagerly in. But on the triumph of the 'Abbásids they were of course disappointed; and their only hope remained in rebellion.

The Shí'ite theory of the Caliphate differed from that of the Orthodox. Another term for Caliph, also used by the Orthodox, was *imám*: as Caliph—*khalífah*—he was the Successor of the Prophet; as *imám* he was the Leader of the Faithful. The Shí'ah applied to whatever member of the 'Alid House they regarded as their sovereign, not the term *khalífah*—which was too definitely appropriated by the Orthodox Caliphs—but the term *imám*, which had a less temporal connotation. But whereas the Orthodox held their Caliphs to be merely temporal rulers, the Shí'ah believed each of their Imáms to be divinely appointed, sinless, and an infallible guide to right conduct. The whole sect was more or less agreed on these points, though there were on the one hand moderates that looked askance at the belief in supernatural graces, and on the other extremists that worshipped in the Imám an incarnation of the Godhead. What they were continually differing about was the identity of the Imám at any given moment. All admitted that the first three Imáms were, in order, 'Alí ibn Abí Ṭálib, al-Ḥasan and al-Ḥusayn; but over the fourth and still more over the later holders of the office opinion was divided.[1]

To-day the great bulk of the Shí'ah belong to the

1 Goldziher: *op. cit.* 164–74.

party known as the *ithnà 'ashariyyah*—Believers in Twelve Imáms, Twelvers. This, for example, is now the State religion of Persia. But in the third century A.H. there were two other parties quite as important: the *sab'iyyah*—Believers in Seven Imáms, Seveners (also called Ismá'ílís)—and the Zaydites. The Seveners were at one with the Twelvers over the first six Imáms, but held to a seventh and final Imám of their own—of them more later. The Zaydites concurred with the other two parties over the first five Imáms, but opposed a great-grandson of al-Ḥusayn, a certain Zayd ibn 'Alí (whence their name), to their sixth Imám. The Zaydites were also distinguished by their conception of the Imámate. For whereas the two other parties maintained that it must always remain in the line of al-Ḥusayn, the Zaydites held that any descendant of 'Alí ibn Abí Ṭálib was eligible, provided—and in this again their attitude was peculiar—provided that he strove to establish his own temporal power by force of arms.[1]

This last doctrine naturally made the Zaydites more prone to fight for their rights than the rest of the Shí'ah; and accordingly we find that it was they that caused the 'Umayyads and the 'Abbásids most trouble. During the decade of anarchy preceding the accession of al-Mu'tamid, one Zaydite pretender revolted, though unsuccessfully, at al-Kúfah; another, of the line of al-Ḥasan, set himself up as an independent ruler in Ṭabaristán; whilst the formidable rising of the *zinj*,[2] the Negro slaves, which broke out at about the same time in the south of al-'Iráq, was stirred up and led by yet a third adventurer of the party.

But it was not only pretenders of the Shí'ah that took advantage of the Caliphs' embarrassment. Such

1 Goldziher: *op. cit.* 200–1.

2 To follow spelling adopted by Massignon: *Al-Hallaj*. The name is also spelt *zanj* and *zang*.

spiritual claims as theirs were by no means necessary for the heading of a revolt. For some time already two provinces of the empire had virtually been free of 'Abbásid control. In each there was established a dynasty descended from a governor originally appointed from Baghdád, but independent except for its acknowledgement of the Caliph as suzerain. One was the Aghlabid dynasty of Ifriqiyyah (the convenient Arabic name for the parts of North Africa now included in Algeria, Tunisia and Tripoli, or Libya). The other was the Ṭáhirid, of eastern Persia and Transoxania (the lands beyond the River Oxus, now Russian Central Asia). In 253 (867)—during the decade of anarchy—the authority of the Ṭáhirids was challenged by a brigand, who had succeeded in gaining control of the whole province of Sístán—Ya'qúb ibn al-Layth, known as *aṣ-ṣaffár*, the Coppersmith. The Ṭáhirid ruler attempted to buy him off with a governorship, but this only encouraged him to more ambitious enterprises. By the time of al-Mu'tamid's accession the greater part of south-eastern Persia was in the Coppersmith's control; and it was clear that he had every intention of adding to his dominions as much as he could.

Of these rebellions, the Zaydite in Ṭabaristán, the Coppersmith in Persia, and the Zinj in al-'Iráq, the latter was by far the most formidable, indeed it was the most formidable that the 'Abbásids had ever had to deal with. The Zinj were Negroes that had been imported for generations from Africa as slaves; they abounded in the province of al-Baṣrah. The Zaydite pretender gained their support by declaring that God had decreed their manumission; and they flocked to join him. They took al-Baṣrah in the first year, and al-Ahwáz in the second year, of al-Mu'tamid's reign; and though they were unable to hold the latter for long, they established themselves firmly about the former. Whenever the 'Abbásid forces were too weak to prevent them they pushed northwards; from bases in the swamps of the lower Euphrates they raided up the Tigris, once reaching to within a short distance of Baghdád. They were gradually driven back, till they had lost everything but their new-built capital in the neighbourhood of al-Baṣrah; yet it was fourteen years before their leader was finally defeated and killed and his followers dispersed.

The adventure of the Coppersmith threatened also to be dangerous at one moment, when Ya'qúb advanced into al-'Iráq at the very height of the Zinj war, and was only defeated at a few stages from Baghdád itself. And it had more lasting effects than the Negro rebellion, since by momentarily conquering Khurásán Ya'qúb put an end to the Ṭáhirid Government. He also drove the Zaydite from Ṭabaristán, and so allowed the 'Abbásids to regain for a time their control of it; and finally he prepared the way for the rise to greater influence than it had hitherto enjoyed of the House of Sámán in Transoxania. This family, which claimed descent from a Sasanian king (and so was as Persian as it was Muslim), had served the Ṭáhirids for some generations. A member of it was first given Transoxania in fief by al-Mu'tamid in 261 (874–5), and from that time it grew rapidly in importance.

The defeat of these two formidable rebellions—and the consequent rescue of the 'Abbásid Caliphate from an untimely extinction—was due chiefly to the energy and resource of a remarkable man, the Emir al-Muwaffaq. Al-Muwaffaq was a younger brother of al-Mu'tamid;—but he was his opposite in character. The Caliph took very little interest in State affairs: he concentrated his attention on love and food. But al-Muwaffaq was a born commander and even more a statesman; and from the first al-Mu'tamid appears to have invited his participation in matters of government. From the second year of his reign at least al-Muwaffaq began controlling appointments and, to some extent, policy. As time went on he gradually ousted his brother from all but the titles of sovereignty. On taking the field against the Negroes, he assumed as of right the chief command of the armies. His only possible rival among the officers, the Turk Músà ibn Bughá, seems to have raised no objection to his ascendancy, and as long as he lived co-operated with him loyally.

Al-Muwaffaq's one important failure in statesmanship occurred in his dealings with Aḥmad ibn Ṭúlún, the governor of Egypt. This Ibn Ṭúlún was of Tartar origin—his father had been presented as a slave to al-Ma'mún. He had first been sent to Egypt, as deputy governor, only two years before al-Mu'tamid's accession; but he quickly acquired such wealth and influence as aroused the jealousy of the governor of Syria, who instigated al-Muwaffaq against him by alleging that he was meditating rebellion. Ibn Ṭúlún succeeded in mollifying the Emir by sending him valuable presents; but later, when al-Muwaffaq demanded payment of the Egyptian taxes, Ibn Ṭúlún refused to recognise his authority. Al-Muwaffaq sent an army against him; but it mutinied on the way, and as he was so hard pressed at home, he could not spare more troops to follow it up. He was therefore obliged to conciliate Ibn Ṭúlún by giving him the government of the Frontier Provinces. But this was to invite Ibn Ṭúlún to annex Syria as well; and on the death of his rival, the governor, in 264 (877–8), he did so. The final breach with Baghdád, however, occurred only when al-Muwaffaq discovered that his brother the Caliph was plotting to flee from al-'Iráq and his tutelage and join Ibn Ṭúlún in Damascus. From that moment Egypt and Syria were definitely cut off from the Caliphate, till, in 279 (892–3), Ibn Ṭúlún's son and successor Khumárawayh offered again to acknowledge the Caliph as his suzerain.

Al-Muwaffaq's discovery of the plot to which his brother had been party naturally led to a final breach between them also. For the rest of his reign al-Mu'tamid was kept in a not too disagreeable confinement with his son, whilst al-Muwaffaq ruled the Caliphate without any pretence of partnership.

I have made no mention of the relations of the Caliphate with the outside world because at this time they were unimportant to its (the Caliphate's) welfare as a whole. On its land frontiers, in Asia Minor and in Central Asia, where its neighbours were infidel, it was often at war with them; but seldom lost or gained anything by these campaigns. Every summer, when the melting of the snows in the mountains of Asia Minor allowed of the movement of troops, the Muslims raided into Byzantine territory, laying waste the countryside, and carrying off a booty of slaves, cattle and merchandise—this was a holy occupation; the Byzantines retaliated: and the only interruptions of the foolish warfare were periodical truces for the exchange of prisoners. The heathen Turkmáns (Oghuz and Qarluq) on the eastern and northern borders of the Caliphate were not yet so active as they became in the next century. Here the most that happened was an occasional foray.

Within the Caliphate infidels abounded. Christians, Jews, Magians, Sabians, these were the "People of Scripture", towards whom, provided that they offered no opposition to the Muslims, tolerance was enjoined. Of the Christians the Nestorians were the most numerous and powerful. They had enjoyed the favour of the Sasanian Court because they had been driven as heretics from the Byzantine Empire; and the 'Abbásids had encouraged both them and their rivals the Jacobites for the same reason. At the time of the conquests a working arrangement between the Muslims and the "People of Scripture" had been arrived at, by which the latter paid a poll-tax in return for which their life, their freedom, and to a certain extent their property, was respected by the former; and by this arrangement their relations continued to be guided. To certain bigots among the Caliphs, however—notably the one pious 'Umayyad, 'Umar ibn 'Abd al-'Azíz—it seemed preposterous that there should be no more distinction between infidels and believers than this; and accordingly they issued decrees compelling the adherents of the tolerated religions to wear special garments, to ride only on asses with wooden saddles and to follow only certain callings, and forbidding them to build new houses of worship or display in public the symbols of their faith. In his general aversion to tolerance al-Mutawakkil re-enacted these sumptuary laws, which had fallen into abeyance under his predecessors. Afterwards, in the times of anarchy, they had again, no doubt, been somewhat relaxed; but at this time the "People of Scripture" were definitely worse off than they had been earlier in the century. From time to time, sometimes in response to public agitation, the Government felt impelled to revive these measures of repression. The Jews, however, continued to be indispensable to True-Believers as bankers, and the Christians (as also, though in smaller numbers, the Magians and Sabians) as physicians; both Jews and Christians, moreover, were employed in government offices as clerks and accountants.[1]

Among the unbelievers the strictly Orthodox counted also the students of philosophy; indeed in their eyes the philosophers were almost worse than unbelievers, they were heretics whose views might much more easily contaminate Islam. The Mu'tazilites

1 Von Kremer: *Culturgeschichte*, II, 165–8, 172–6.

(whom I have mentioned) merely brought foreign philosophical ideas to bear on the Faith. That was bad enough; still, they remained Muslims. But these philosophers, if they regarded Islam at all, sought, not to make philosophy agree with it, but it with philosophy. In a way, however, the philosophers were less open to attack than the Mu'tazilites; they formed no school, and the nature of their thought was less easily grasped and reprehended. In the reaction, accordingly, they did not at first suffer a persecution.[1]

In spite of the continual conversion of unbelievers to Islam, their number was always kept up, if not increased, by the slave-trade. For the Muslim laws regulating slavery forbade the enslavement of believers, although the conversion of slaves did not entail their manumission. Children borne by a slave-woman to a father other than her master were themselves slaves, her master's property (whereas the master's own children by a slave-mother were free). But religion and custom strongly encouraged the freeing of slaves: consequently their numbers always tended to diminish and had to be made up by the capture and enslavement of non-believers from outside the limits of the Caliphate (since non-believers inside had made a sacred contract with the State). The chief sources from which slaves were drawn were Central Asia, the Caucasus, Asia Minor, the Mediterranean coasts and Africa.

As well as free and bond, there were persons in intermediate stages: for example, slave-women that had borne children to their masters. Such a woman, known as an *umm walad*, the mother of a child, could not be sold, and became automatically free on her master's death. (The Lady Shaghab, who plays such an important part in this history, was an *umm walad*.) Then there were slaves that had partially bought their free-

1 See *Encyclopédie*, II, 51 (art. *falsafa*); Von Kremer: *Culturgeschichte*, II, 465.

dom, who again might not be sold. And there were slaves that their masters had agreed to free at a certain date. Absolute slaves were chattels, having no legal rights whatever; but again the hardness of their lot was mitigated by the general observance of *qur'ánic* injunctions to treat them kindly. At the other end of the scale, a slave that had received his full freedom was even then not entirely cut off from his former master. He still had to him the relationship of client to patron; and this added probably to the attractions of manumission, which might otherwise have brought with it homelessness and destitution.[1]

The government of the State was autocratic: all authority emanated from the Caliph. But, theoretically at least, the Caliph's power was not unlimited: it was bound by the sacred Law. The Law, which directed every activity—there was no distinction made between secular and religious affairs—was built up of precepts drawn first from the *qur'án*, secondly from the *sunnah* (the Custom of the Prophet as recorded in Tradition), and thirdly from what was agreed to be general usage. It was interpreted by *qádhís* (judges) and *faqíhs* (jurists), of which there were four schools. Their rulings had to conform with precedent, or be drawn from it by analogy; and in so far they were independent of the Caliph's wishes. But this independence was at least modified by the fact that these functionaries held their places and received their salaries at the Caliph's pleasure.

The Caliph exercised his authority through a minister, the Vizier (Arabic, *wazír*). The designation Vizier, of Persian origin, had been introduced by the 'Abbásids, who had modelled their Court procedure as closely as possible on that of the Sasanians, the 'Umayyad Caliphs having employed merely a secretary, a much humbler official. Al-Máwardí, who wrote a treatise on government in the eleventh century, dis-

1 *Encyclopédie*, 1, 16 *et seqq.* (art. '*abd*).

tinguishes two kinds of Vizier.[1] One merely carried out orders issued by the Caliph; the other, being invested with absolute powers as long as he remained in office, acted on his own initiative. In practice, however, the Vizier seems to have done one at one time and one at another; and the unwise exercise of such delegated authority, since it might always be repudiated, was often the cause of a fall. The advantages of the system fell chiefly to the Caliph, since he might always attribute an unpopular move to his Vizier. But the Vizier also benefited occasionally in putting off the insistent by pleading the necessity of an appeal to the Caliph.

The Vizier in turn delegated his routine duties to various secretaries, each of whom controlled a *díwán*, or office, in which a number of subordinate clerks were employed. The Vizier was usually chosen in the first place from amongst the secretaries, who were themselves promoted from amongst the subordinate clerks. Among the most important of the *díwáns* were the *díwán al-kharáj* (Revenue) and the *díwán an-nafaqát* (Expenditure), each controlled by its *zimám*, or Registry. There were also the *díwán ar-rasá'il* (Correspondence), the *díwán at-tawqí'* (Great Seal), the *díwán al-jaysh* (War), the *díwán an-nadhar fi'l-madhálim* (Court of Appeal) and the *díwán al-baríd* (Posts). All appointments to provincial governorships were likewise made by the Vizier. Each district had its governor, tax-collector, military commandant, religious dignitary, judge, postmaster and chief of police. According to the size and importance of a place, these offices were divided between several persons, or all given to one.[2]

The Vizier was very largely occupied with finance —the *díwáns* of Revenue and Expenditure were the

1 Mawerdi: *Les Statuts Gouvernementaux...traduits et annotés par E. Fagnan*, 43 *et seqq.*

2 Von Kremer: *Ueber das Einnahmebudget des Abbasidenreichs*, 18.

most important of all; and one of his chief concerns was the proper receipt of the taxes and their frugal allotment. Originally the taxes had been collected by salaried officials, but gradually this system had been superseded by that of farming, which now prevailed in most parts of the empire still under the direct control of the central Government: that is to say that contracts were given for the collection of taxes, the contractor undertaking to furnish yearly such and such a sum for a district in return for the right to extract as much as he could from its inhabitants. Unless the province was important enough to have a governor (*amír*), the tax-farmer was generally the chief official, and so derived a considerable income from presents and bribes. Nevertheless, contracts were far from always being profitable, and their failure frequently led contractors into defying the Government rather than face a loss.[1]

Ever since the first conquests the revenues of the Caliphs had gradually but steadily declined. Recurrent wars and rebellions were partly responsible for this, partly this very system of tax-farming, under the oppression of which the peasantry everywhere groaned. The land-tax (*kharáj*) and the poor or property tax (*ṣadaqah*) were the main sources of income, and from time to time desperate efforts had been made to enhance their yield. But in vain: the Vizierate and subordinate offices were seldom for long in the hands of any that had a regard for the feelings of the subject, or the wit to understand that just government was the best policy. Other taxes were the poll-tax on tolerated infidels, dues on mints, mills, factories and ships, and excises on salt-digging and fisheries.[2]

The coinage of the Caliphate was taken from the Byzantine. At this time about fifteen silver *dirhams* (drachmae) were equal to one gold *dínár* (denarius).

1 Von Kremer: *op. cit.* 15.
2 Von Kremer: *Culturgeschichte*, I, 278.

At first the provinces conquered from the Sasanians had paid their taxes in silver, whereas those conquered from the Byzantines had paid theirs chiefly in gold. By now, however, the gold coinage had attained a general currency throughout the Caliphate, and all taxes not paid in kind were paid in *dínárs*.[1]

As I have noted, the 'Abbásids came to power as the champions not only of the Zealots but also of the oppressed foreigners .They found their strongest support in the Persians; the revolution was above all a triumph of the Persians over the Arabs. In moving his capital to Baghdád—away from the Arabs towards the Persians, for Baghdád was only a few miles from the former Sasanian capital—the second 'Abbásid would seem to have acknowledged this. From its beginnings the 'Abbásid Court was Persian in character; its manners, its ceremonies, the buildings in which it was housed, were all Persian. The Caliph lost more and more the nature of an Arab chieftain—a first among equals—and, as he retired behind his factotum, the Vizier, took on more and more that of an inaccessible Chosroes. The officials of the Court and the provincial governments were most of them Persians, converts or the descendants of converts—often their ancestors had actually served the Chosroes as they were now serving the Caliph.

The army, on the contrary, remained chiefly Turkish—even after the influence of the officers had declined. As long as Islam was still growing and there were new lands to conquer, the armies, mostly Arab, had been kept on their old footing: they had been paid only in booty. But afterwards the Caliphs were obliged to keep forces under arms even when there was no war on hand, against eventualities and for police; and these had to be paid regularly out of the ordinary revenue.

1 Von Kremer: *Ueber das Einnahmebudget*, 6–8. In the next thirty years the value of silver was to decline.

Such a system, however, offended all the instincts of the Arabs; and they seem for the most part either to have returned to their desert raids, or, if they settled, to have abandoned arms altogether. Contingents from desert tribes were sometimes impressed to fight on special occasions, but only when there was a hope of booty. Neither the Persians nor the Aramean populations of Syria and al-'Iráq were naturally warlike. They would only fight for their religious opinions. Up to the reign of al-Mu'taṣim there were still two corps of Arab lancers in the Caliph's army, and one of Persians from Khurásán; but their numbers decreased with his enrolment of Turks, Berbers and Negroes, till the soldiery was almost entirely drawn from the latter races. The army was organised on the pattern of the Byzantine. The Muslims used the same weapons: short swords with shields, lances, bows and arrows, and for sieges catapults, battering rams and Greek fire; and they had abandoned the original Arab battle line for the Roman-Byzantine square. In one respect they had the best of the Byzantines—they used camels for transport instead of horses and mules.[1]

At the period of which I am writing the various elements of which the 'Abbásid civilisation was composed were ready to fuse into a whole. Religion from Arabia, thought from Greece, manners and government from Persia, vigour from the Turks; working in harmony (as they did for a short time), "they made Baghdád in the Xth century of our era the intellectual centre of the world"; this was "the unique epoch of the blossoming of Islam".[2] It was al-Muwaffaq's merit as a statesman that he placed these elements in an equilibrium. It is the tragedy of the Caliphate that this equilibrium was not longer preserved.

1 Von Kremer: *Culturgeschichte*, I, 219–20, 223–5, 230, 252, 253–5; Massignon: *Al-Hallaj*, 203.

2 Massignon: *Al-Hallaj*, xii.

BAGHDÁD

Although Sámarrá remained officially the royal residence, during his conduct of the campaign against the Zinj al-Muwaffaq had made Baghdád his headquarters, so that the empire actually came to be governed once again from the older capital. Moreover, after al-Muwaffaq's death al-Mu'tamid returned not to Sámarrá but to Baghdád, which was henceforth capital in name as well as in fact. In the first years of its life Sámarrá had grown, with the additions made at fabulous expense by al-Wáthiq and al-Mutawakkil, into an enormous city stretching for miles down the Tigris. But with its abandonment by the Court it fell into a slow decay, shrinking till it became only a small town. Baghdád, on the other hand, which had suffered severely during the siege of al-Musta'ín, revived at the change; and in a few years grew to a size, and attained a beauty, never surpassed in later ages.

Baghdád had been founded by al-Manṣúr, the second 'Abbásid. He had built the original Round City with its triple walls as a fortress; for he lived in perpetual terror of assassination, and here he need meet no one but tried courtiers. He had chosen the site for its convenience and its reputed salubrity. It was already occupied by a number of villages, inhabited it seems, chiefly by Aramean Christians, clustered round several large monasteries. One of the villages was already called Baghdád or something like it. All were gradually absorbed in the great city as it grew.[1]

The exact topography of the ancient city is still the subject of controversy. So few remains date from this period that the sites of even the chief places can for the most part only be guessed at. Contemporary and fairly minute accounts of the streets and waterways exist; but the authorities do not agree on the way in

1 *Encyclopédie*, I, 574 *et seqq.* (art. *Baghdād*).

which they should be interpreted.[1] The following details, however, are not disputed.

The city lay on both banks of the Tigris; and the two parts were connected by two, or at times three, bridges of boats. The Round City was situated on the right, or west, bank, surrounded by, and already half lost in, huge suburbs, of which the chief were al-Karkh to the south-east and al-Ḥarbiyyah to the north-west. The largest quarter of the left, or east, bank was al-Mukharrim, facing al-Karkh, and above it to the north-west lay ash-Shammásiyyah and ar-Ruṣáfah.[2] Each half of the city was enclosed by a bastioned and moated wall, in which there was a number of gates, barred up at night.

The river, which is here deep and swift and green, described a course through the city like a flattened M tilted to the right. It was bordered by thick palm and fruit orchards above and below the walls, and by brick embankments and the bare walls of houses within. It was the main thoroughfare; so that every great man had his barge, whilst for the generality boats plied for hire. Every springtime, when the snows melt in the mountains of Asia Minor, the Tigris rises with alarming rapidity, and the country about Baghdád is preserved from flood only by dykes. It is this sudden tempestuous rise that has always precluded the building of a masonry bridge. The bridges of boats can be cut in time and suffer no damage.

As well as directly from the river, the city was watered by a number of canals, which wound about among the buildings and were crossed by brick cul-

1 See Massignon: *Mission en Mésopotamie*, II. Criticisms of the conclusions of Le Strange: *Baghdad during the Abbasid Caliphate*.

2 There is some divergence of opinion about the relation of ar-Ruṣáfah to the other quarters. It is certain that the al-Mu'aḏhḏham of to-day formed part of ar-Ruṣáfah; and it is possible that it was always a suburb apart from the rest of East Baghdád. See Massignon: *Mission*, II, 77, 96.

verts. The canals on the east bank all branched from the great artificial waterway known as the Nahrawán, which took off from the Tigris about eighty miles above Baghdád and irrigated most of the plain between the river and the eastern hills. All but one of the canals of the west bank, on the other hand, derived their water, by means of the Nahr 'Ísà, from the Euphrates.

When al-Mu'tamid settled again in Baghdád he found none of the former royal palaces fit for habitation. Those on the west bank had fallen into ruin after the first siege of the city (which led to the accession of al-Ma'mún); whilst the two palaces of the east bank had likewise been destroyed in the second siege—that of al-Musta'ín by al-Mu'tazz. He took up residence, therefore, in a private mansion, which had been built originally by Ja'far the Barmecide (the Vizier of *The Thousand and One Nights*), by whom it had been presented to al-Ma'mún. Al-Ma'mún in turn had given it to his Vizier, al-Ḥasan ibn Sahl; and for this reason it was known as the Ḥasaní Palace. It is related that al-Ḥasan's daughter Búrán (who had married al-Ma'mún) was still living when al-Mu'tamid decided on the return to Baghdád. She had the palace repaired throughout and furnished luxuriously; engaged a whole retinue of slaves, girls and eunuchs; then retired herself to a more modest habitation; and presented the palace and all it contained to the Caliph.[1] The Ḥasaní Palace was situated in al Mukharrim, on the river bank. It was to form the centre of a huge mass of buildings, constructed by al-Mu'tamid's successors, which were added to one another till they formed a small city within a city.

The architecture of al-'Iráq under the early 'Abbásids, derived immediately from the Sasanian, was plain and solid. The houses of Baghdád were built

1 Salmon: *Introduction Topographique à l'Histoire de Bagdâdh*, 130; Yáq. *mu'jam*, I, 808; Le Strange: *Baghdad*, 248–9.

either of mud or of bricks crude or burnt. For the most part they were of two stories, the rooms below being vaulted and sometimes sunk half underground against the heats of summer. Those above were ceiled with timber and covered with flat terraced roofs for summer nights. To the streets the houses presented blank walls, only broken by high gateways, the lower parts of these walls being occupied in the markets by shops.[1] They were generally built round one or more courtyards, in the midst of which there were often pools or fountains. The mosques also consisted of courtyards, surrounded by colonnades, the colonnades being deepened on the side facing Mecca that all turn to in prayer. Their minarets were of brick, probably round and thick,[2] with a platform for the *mu'adhdhin* near the top. The pale brown of dried mud, the yellow of brick, the white of plaster made up the colours of the city, with the grey green of the date palms and the river, the blue green of fruit trees, the bright green and scarlet of the pomegranate, and shining high above the house-tops the green of the great tiled dome of the Palace of the Round City. Only the narrow winding streets and the tall shafts of innumerable minarets cut with sharp shadows through the little-varied surfaces.

Inside, walls were generally covered with stucco, flat expanses being decorated with moulded repetitive designs, left white or coloured red and blue; or sometimes they were lined with glass mosaic.[3] Stone and marble, and to some extent woodwork, were imported ready worked from Syria for the Caliphs' palaces at Sámarrá,[4] and presumably also for those of Baghdád;

1 To judge by those of Sámarrá. See Herzfeld: *Die Ausgrabungen von Samarra*, I, 1–2.

2 See, however, Diez: *Persien*, 76. Before the end of the fourth/tenth century there was no settled type of minaret in the eastern parts of the Caliphate. In eastern Persia, for instance, some were built as heavy square towers.

3 Herzfeld: *Samarra*, 14, 73.

4 *Ibid.* 60.

the marble being used for the dadoes of walls and, in at least one of the Baghdád palaces, for columns.[1] The houses of the rich imitated the magnificence of the palaces. Simple outside except for a high ornamental doorway that must admit a mounted lancer, they were all glorious within. Fountains of marble and gold, gold and silver ornaments and utensils, doors of precious woods, crystal chandeliers, Chinese porcelain and lacquer, thick-woven carpets, satin cushions and embroidered hangings; from saloons filled with such objects cool arcades led out to enclosed gardens brilliant with exotic flowers. And their owners' luxurious tastes were shown equally in their clothes—of silk, satin, velvet or fine linen, woven or embroidered in patterns, often with gold or silver thread; in their jewellery, with which they weighted their women till they could hardly stand unsupported; in their perfumes, with which they anointed themselves and censed their guest-rooms; and in their food and drink. They delighted to offer their visitors and enjoy themselves dishes of exquisite flavour, concocted of the rarest ingredients. The Prophet's ban on wine seems frequently to have been no ban to them; though for the scrupulous they provided a variety of delicious and unobjectionable draughts: date-wine, beer and sherbets.[2]

The climate of Baghdád was then probably much what it is to-day; only the larger area under cultivation, the greater number of palm-gardens, may have mitigated the violence of the winter winds and prevented the occurrence of the sand-storms that now sweep in upon the town from the enveloping plains. The winters, then, were cold and gusty, and under the heavy rains the mud of the streets soon turned to a cloying slush. In the summer for some weeks the heat

1 Yáq. *mu'jam*, I, 809.
2 Von Kremer: *Culturgeschichte*, II, 194–5, 204–18.

was very great, so that midday was given over to repose and only the narrowness or covering of the markets made business possible. In the spring, and sometimes in the autumn, the days were of a temperate warmth, delicious and a theme for poets.[1]

1 Authorities for the historical matter of the Introduction, where no others are cited are: Weil: *Geschichte der Chalifen*; Müller: *Der Islam in Morgen- und Abendland*; Huart: *Histoire des Arabes*; Browne: *Literary History of Persia* (vol. 1); and the Arabic chronicle of aṭ-Ṭabarí.

Part One

CHAPTER I

The accession of al-Mu'tadhid. 'Ubayd Allah ibn Sulaymán. *The brothers* Ibn al-Furát *and their employment of* 'Alí ibn 'Ísà *and his uncle* Muḥammad.

Although the unfortunate Caliph al-Mu'tamid had been altogether deprived of his rights by his dominant brother, he was destined to outlive him. Yet even so neither he nor his son Ja'far could recover much of the influence he had forfeited: for al-Muwaffaq also had a son Aḥmad, already entitled *al-mu'tadḥid bi'llah* (Seeking Support in God); and when al-Muwaffaq succumbed in 278 (892) to gout, al-Mu'tadḥid inherited all his power.

Officially al-Mu'tamid's heir was his own son: al-Muwaffaq formerly, and now al-Mu'tadḥid, only came second. But al-Mu'tadḥid was not long to be satisfied with this arrangement; and although he did his best to compensate the Caliph and his son for their disappointment by making them valuable presents, he soon contrived to have himself proclaimed heir direct. When therefore six months later al-Mu'tamid expired, probably from eating a poisoned dish, al-Mu'tadḥid succeeded him unopposed.[1]

Al-Mu'tadḥid was the son of a Greek mother, who had been a slave. His father was of a very mixed descent: the blood of the 'Abbásids, once pure Quraysh, was no longer even mainly Arab, but part Greek, part Persian, Armenian, Turkish and even Negro,[2] a mixture

1 Ṭab. III, 2123, 2131, 2133; Mas. *murúj*, VIII, 110–11; Tagh. II, 75–6.

2 For example, the Prince Ibrahím ibn al-Mahdí, whose mother was a Negress, was black himself. See Khall. I, 17.

due to their forefathers' catholic taste in concubines. He was now thirty-eight years of age.[1] In appearance he was upright and thin; and on his head was a white mole, which, since white moles were not admired, he used to dye black. His expression was haughty. In character he was brave—a story was told of his killing a lion with only a dagger. Although in his youth he was not altogether successful in warfare, he had inherited all his father's energy, and cultivated a reputation for prompt action. He was of an excessively hasty temper, being "swift to shed blood"; but he was scrupulously just. If he thought that a fault had been committed by mistake, he took no offence; he was easily touched by generous dealing in others; and when bereft of a favourite slave-girl, he showed himself positively tender-hearted. But once his righteous wrath was aroused, he would indulge a veritable passion for cruelty; and delighted to put his victims to death in the most atrocious ways. He would cheerfully inflate them with bellows and set them up as targets for his bowmen, or half bury them head-downwards in a pit. He had specially constructed below his new palace a range of torture-chambers, over which he appointed an expert official. Hardly less marked than his cruelty was his avarice: it was said that he would examine petty accounts such as a commoner would scorn to consider. But this vice was of great benefit to the dynasty: the Privy Purse, empty at his accession, contained ten million *dínárs* at his death. According to al-Mas'údí, however, his two ruling passions were *an-nisá' wa'l-baná'*, women and building; and for the indulgence of both he had ample opportunity.[2]

1 So al-Mas'údí in the *kitáb at-tanbíh*, 370. But in the *murúj*, VIII, 113, he gives the alternative age of thirty-one as well.

2 Mas. *murúj*, VIII, 113–16; Tagh. II, 132; Jaw. fol. 19 b *et seqq.*; S.J. fol. 20 b *et seqq.*; S.J. (B.M. Or. 4618), fol. 253 b; Ḍháf. fol. 132 a–b.

At the time of his father's death al-Mu'tadhid's relations with him had been anything but happy—his father had actually thrown him into prison, where he lived in daily fear of his life. This estrangement between them had been brought about by al-Muwaffaq's Vizier, a certain Ismá'íl ibn Bulbul; and al-Mu'tadhid was left in Ibn Bulbul's charge whilst al-Muwaffaq was away from Baghdád on his last campaign, in Azarbayján. When al-Muwaffaq returned, suffering tortures from his disease, which the comforts of a specially prepared litter had done little to relieve, Ibn Bulbul, seeing that he could not live, hastily summoned the Caliph and his son from their confinement. But the party that favoured al-Mu'tadhid was too strong for him, moreover the people of Baghdád were all for al-Mu'tadhid: so that when al-Muwaffaq died, the young prince, who had been released from his prison to see his father on his death-bed, at once became all-powerful. The people sacked Ibn Bulbul's house; and three days later al-Mu'tadhid dismissed him, cast him into a dungeon, and maltreated him so severely that he died within two or three months. At the same time he arrested and imprisoned such of his subordinate officials as he could lay hands on.[1]

As I have stated, the Vizier had the appointing of all his assistants in office, and it was the practice for him to choose for these posts those whom he knew to be his friends. Every past or prospective Vizier was thus surrounded by his faction, or clique of supporters. When he rose to power, they expected to rise too; and when he fell, they were prepared to save themselves as best they might from the disgrace, and the actual persecution, that was then the whole party's lot. It was customary at such a time to exact an indemnity from each official that was caught: he was forced, often

1 Ṭab. III, 2120–2; Mas. *murúj*, VIII, 105–8; Tagh. II, 86; S.J. (B.M. Or. 4618), ff. 252 b–253 b.

under torture, to sign a bond in satisfaction, and then kept in confinement until at least a certain proportion of the sum was paid. One who aspired to become Vizier would often give a guarantee to the Caliph that if appointed he would extract a definite sum from the fallen faction. In times of financial stress this was often the Caliph's only resource: and not seldom he would consent. On the death of Ismá'íl ibn Bulbul, his gold and silver plate was melted down, minted, and distributed among the troops.

Al-Mu'tadhid appointed, first as his secretary, and then, after he came to the throne, as his Vizier, 'Ubayd Allah ibn Sulaymán ibn Wahb. This 'Ubayd Allah came of a family originally Christian, which had served the State not only in 'Abbásid times, but throughout the 'Umayyad period as well. His father Sulaymán had become secretary to the Caliph al-Ma'mún at the early age of fourteen; and after attaching himself in turn to two of the Turkish generals, he had been confirmed by al-Mu'tamid in the Vizierate, to which he had first been raised by the latter's predecessor.[1] 'Ubayd Allah himself had acted for a time as Vizier to al-Mu'tamid after his father's death; and it was perhaps the natural opposition to Ibn Bulbul in which he was thereby placed that now prompted al-Mu'tadhid to rely on him. In the event the Caliph had not to regret his choice, although more than once in his sudden fits of anger he resolved on dismissing him.[2] 'Ubayd Allah had the rare and precious qualities of honesty and devotion; but he seems to have had no great gift for statesmanship. We find him, at first contact, in an administrative quandary.

The victories of al-Muwaffaq had not been achieved without the expenditure of much accumulated treasure; important parts of the empire, moreover, were still in

1 Khall. I (trans.), 596 *et seqq.*
2 Qudh. fol. 83 a *et seqq.*

the hands of rebels, who, though they were no longer a menace to the existence of the 'Abbásid power, furnished at most a precarious tribute. Ibn Bulbul had taken to exacting the revenues of the *sawád*, that is, the rich plains surrounding the capital, twice in one year. 'Ubayd Allah now found himself, in consequence, with a formidable list of daily expenses, and less than enough to meet them with. A very thorough knowledge of the resources of each district on which a toll might be levied was necessary to arrive at a method of bridging the difference. But it was just this, on account of his having been out of office, that 'Ubayd Allah lacked. He consulted his secretaries, only to find that they could conceive of no solution to the problem. One day, however, a visitor to his assembly, to whom he poured out the tale of his woes, offered him counsel, which, though it involved asking the Caliph to pardon certain prisoners (always a perilous course), still pointed a way of escape. Among the supporters of Ismá'íl ibn Bulbul were two brothers, Aḥmad and 'Alí Ibn al-Furát, who had hidden on the fall of their patron, but had been discovered and thrown into prison. Aḥmad at any rate had been tortured so that he retained the scars to the end of his life; and they had both agreed to pay a heavy fine, but were still languishing in chains. It seems that they had already heard of 'Ubayd Allah's perturbation; but even if the visitor in question had not been sent for the express purpose, he was anxious to do them a good turn. The brothers, so he told the Vizier, had all the knowledge he required, from their recent employment. He was sure that if only 'Ubayd Allah could persuade the Caliph to pardon them and consent to their rehabilitation, within three days they would discover a way out of his financial difficulties.

The Vizier summoned the prisoners, and 'Alí ibn al-Furát was brought into the assembly. He was dressed in a filthy shirt, his hair was matted and his beard was untrimmed; heavy chains caused him to shuffle in walking. "Allah, Allah!" he cried, and moaned complaints of what had befallen him and his brother, till the Vizier soothed him and bade him sit down. Yet when the problem was explained to him, he forgot his tribulations; and spoke with such authority on financial practice, and displayed such knowledge and ingenuity, that 'Ubayd Allah was delighted. The Caliph, when he sought his permission to employ the brothers, supposed that he was being imposed upon; and very naturally feared the consequence of confiding his exchequer to people he had so villainously and recently maltreated. But when 'Ubayd Allah assured him that the brothers would be fully conciliated by the return of their confiscated estates, he gave his consent: they were forthwith released; and within the appointed time they had arranged with a tax-farmer a contract for the daily supply of the necessary sums against the revenue of certain districts.[1]

The brothers Ibn al-Furát—or, to use a more convenient expression, the Banú'l-Furát[2]—came originally from a village in the Upper Nahrawán district, where they had numerous relatives. They were the first of their family to be employed in high office. We are not told the age of Aḥmad, the elder; but 'Alí, the younger, was at this time thirty-eight. They had been left well off by their father, before they took to State service: thus they had been able to keep a troop of mounted retainers, and used to come up to Baghdád periodically to enjoy themselves. Aḥmad had an extraordinary

1 H. 8–22, 219; Qudh. fol. 87 a. The date of 'Ubayd Allah's appointment of the brothers is somewhat uncertain. Two passages in H., pp. 10 and 11, suggest that it was very soon after al-Mu'taḍhid's accession; but another, H. 76, states that it was eighteen months later, when 'Ubayd Allah had been Vizier two years.

2 *Banú* being the plural of *ibn*.

knowledge of all four schools of the sacred Law; and he found this acquirement so useful that he always regretted having wasted three years studying Euclid instead. He had also an exceptionally reliable memory for poetry, and was something of a poet himself. Aḥmad had first won the approval of Ismá'íl ibn Bulbul by pointing out defects in a circular written by another secretary. Ismá'íl had given him the best of the *díwáns*, the *díwán as-sawád*; and the two brothers were considered the ablest officials in his administration.[1]

Aḥmad was now made Deputy Vizier, and soon became 'Ubayd Allah's right-hand man: indeed he and his brother won so absolute an ascendancy over the Vizier that a verse, originally applied to the Caliph al-Mu'tazz, comparing him to a parrot in a cage between two of his Turkish monitors, was now quoted to describe 'Ubayd Allah, whose every word was supplied by one of the two secretaries.[2] 'Ubayd Allah was only once known to reject Aḥmad's advice, and when rallied on his subservience, cheerfully admitted that he felt no shame in being "captive to any competent adviser".[3] Aḥmad won also the high approval of al-Mu'taḍhid, by pointing out that one of his building projects would involve him in an unnecessary loss of income.[4]

The administration of the finances seems to have been left entirely to Aḥmad, as Deputy Vizier; and he managed them so ably that the *sawád*, for instance, yielded now a larger revenue than it had done for more than two hundred years.[5] In order, presumably, to simplify the task of supervising the various *díwáns* that dealt with financial affairs, he formed a new office. It was called, probably because it was situated either in

1 H. 8, 144, 192, 193, 201; *fib.* 168; Quḍh. fol. 86 a.
2 H. 219. 3 H. 255–6. 4 H. 258.
5 H. 188–9.

the Vizier's or in the Caliph's own residence, the *díwán ad-dár*, or Office of the Palace. His brother acted as his assistant, and he engaged several secretaries for the new *díwán*. Among them were a certain Muḥammad ibn Dá'úd and his nephew 'Alí ibn 'Ísà.[1]

1 H. 131.

CHAPTER II

‘Alí ibn ‘Ísà, *and his family, the* Banú’l-Jarráḥ.

Abú’l-Ḥasan ‘Alí ibn ‘Ísà ibn Dá’úd ibn al-Jarráḥ was at this time thirty-five years of age. He had been born on Friday 8th *jumádà’l-úlà* 245 (11th August 859), two years before the assassination of al-Mutawakkil, when his world was on the brink of upheaval. His family—I may call them the Banú’l-Jarráḥ—came from Dayr Qunnà, a small town grown up about a large Nestorian monastery a mile east of the Tigris about forty miles south-east of Baghdád. But whether or not ‘Alí ibn ‘Ísà was born at Dayr Qunnà nowhere appears. The family certainly maintained its connection with Dayr Qunnà, for ‘Alí himself continued to own an estate at aṣ-Ṣáfiyah in the neighbourhood, to which both he and one of his brothers were severally banished;[1] but it is just as likely that he was born at Baghdád, or at Sámarrá where the Court then was. His father ‘Ísà was in Government service; but although in one passage[2] he is referred to as one of the chief secretaries, he never reached real eminence, and no mention is made of his whereabouts or of that of his household at the time of ‘Alí’s birth. As we hear no more of him, we may conclude that he died whilst ‘Alí was still a child or a young man; he certainly died before ‘Alí first became Vizier, because al-Mas‘údí omits ‘Alí ibn ‘Ísà from his list of those that attained the Vizierate in their fathers’ lifetime.[3] ‘Alí’s grandfather Dá’úd served likewise in the Secretariat under al-Mutawakkil and al-Musta‘ín,[4] having charge of the

1 H. 134; ‘A. 165; M. I, 221, 325.

2 S.J. fol. 137 b.

3 Mas. *tan.* 379.

4 Ṣaf. (Paris Arabe 2064), fol. 40 a, passage published in M. I, 200; Tan. *farj.* I, 50; *fih.* 128.

Family tree of the Banú'l-Jarráḥ

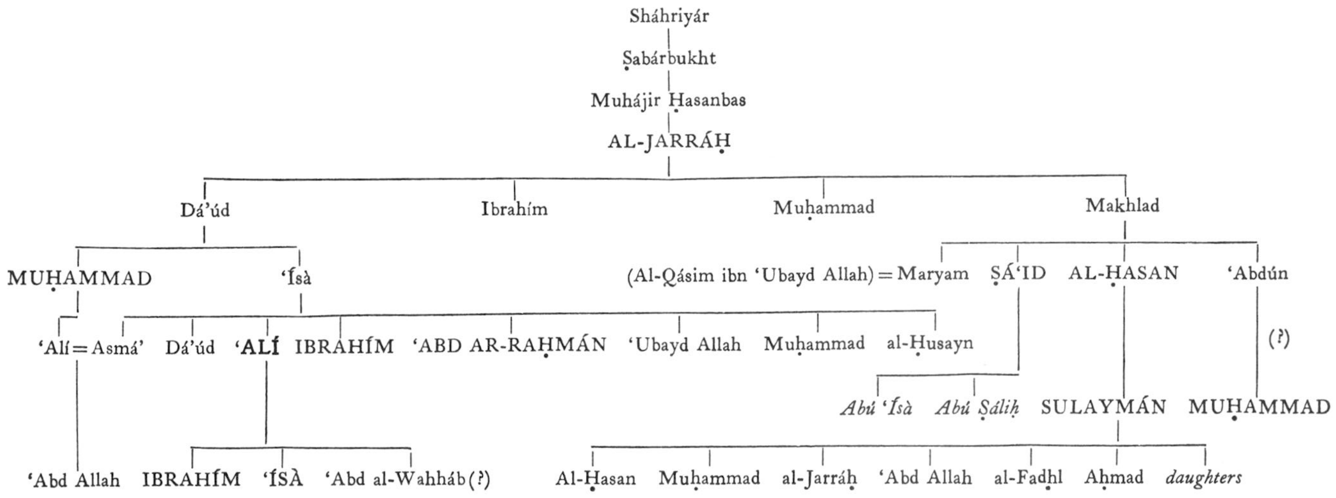

Registry under the former; and he was still living at this time. Of al-Jarráḥ, the great-grandfather, we learn nothing; only his genealogy is carried back several generations by aṣ-Ṣafadí,[1] as follows: al-Jarráḥ, son of Muhájir Ḥasanbas, son of Ṣabárbukht, son of Sháhriyár. These names confirm what this author also states, that the family came originally from Fárs: and we may safely conjecture that it was Magian by religion before its conversion to Islam. Their Persian origin seems to have been a source of interest to the Banú'l-Jarráḥ rather than one of shame, as it was to some "foreigners". 'Alí, at any rate, would afterwards retail information that he had received from his father, who had received it from his, about the ancient Persians and their ways.[2]

Dayr Qunnà, on the other hand, provided a Christian background: for besides the monks in their cells—refreshingly described as each having its fruit-trees and a separate stream—many of the townspeople were Christians, engaged in a trade illicit for Muslims, the making of wine.[3] Moreover at least one member of the family appears actually to have been a Christian himself. 'Alí ibn 'Ísà was afterwards renowned for his piety, and he was pious in a strictly orthodox way; but withal he was tolerant of differences in faith, and this may have been due in part to an early acquaintance with another religion, or the consideration that his own near ancestors had held strange tenets.

Most of the family had an accomplishment also characteristic of the "foreigner". They were men of letters, that is, historians and writers of treatises, not poets. 'Alí himself must early have moved in a literary society, and when he was once established in the Government his house became a rendezvous for the

1 Ṣaf. *loc. cit.*

2 Yáq. *mu'jam*, IV, 847.

3 Yáq. *mu'jam*, II, 688–9; Le Strange: *Lands of the Eastern Caliphate*, 37.

learned. Even more were the Banú'l-Jarráḥ a family of clerks and Secretaries of State. 'Alí's father and grandfather, as I have noted, both served in this way, although neither was especially eminent. Two of his cousins, however, al-Ḥasan and Ṣá'id the sons of Makhlad ibn al-Jarráḥ, had risen to the Vizierate; and though al-Ḥasan in particular seems to have been an abandoned opportunist, their advancement no doubt reflected honour on all their relatives. Al-Ḥasan had acted twice as Vizier to al-Mu'tamid: but on the first occasion he was forced, after only seventeen days of office, to flee away owing to the arrival at Court of an influential enemy; and on the second, the all-powerful al-Muwaffaq objected to his appointment, and forthwith revoked it.[1] His brother Ṣá'id, on the contrary, who was renowned for his piety and charity,[2] owed all his advancement to al-Muwaffaq. He was his Vizier during the long campaign against the Negroes, and was afterwards sent himself with an army against the Ṣaffárids in Fárs. On his return, however, he showed such arrogance that al-Muwaffaq's favour turned to wrath: and Ṣá'id was arrested and destituted of all his wealth—it was now that al-Muwaffaq took Ismá'íl ibn Bulbul as his secretary. Ṣá'id had died, still in prison, four years before al-Mu'taḍhid's accession. His mansion, which was one of the most magnificent in Baghdád, became State property, and was used to house particularly distinguished guests of the Caliphs.[3]

It was a brother of al-Ḥasan and Ṣá'id, 'Abdún by name, that was a Christian.[4] It appears that their father Makhlad had been converted to Christianity, presum-

1 Ṭab. III, 1915, 1926, 1927; *fakh.* 297; H. 71.
2 Jaw. fol. 5 b.
3 Ṭab. III, 1988, 2083, 2106, 2109, 2122, 2144, 2146; Mas. *murúj*, VIII, 39.
4 Mas. *murúj*, VIII, 258–9.

ably from Zoroastrianism; and Ṣá'id himself seems to have turned Muslim only a short time before becoming Vizier, when he was taunted with showing the inordinate enthusiasm of a recent convert.[1] 'Abdún had a son Muḥammad.[2] Al-Ḥasan had a son Sulaymán. I shall often have to mention both of them.

Abú 'Abd Allah Muḥammad ibn Dá'úd, 'Alí's uncle, who was given at the same time a place in the *díwán ad-dár*, was his senior by only two years. He was afterwards considered to be "one of the most accomplished men of his time". "He had been brought up under the tuition of the ablest masters in eloquence, poetry and the sciences." By profession he was a coypist, "and transcribed a great number of works, the copies of which he always read over after to correct whatever faults he might have made."[3] He was also the author of several books that were very highly thought of. The best known of these was his *History of the Viziers*, which, though it has not, alas, survived, is often mentioned and quoted by later authorities; and three others dealt with poetry and the lives of the poets.[4] He seems also to have interested himself in music. One of his freedmen, at any rate, a certain Qaríṣ, called after him al-Jarráḥí, was a noted singer and writer on musical subjects.[5]

The first time that we hear of Muḥammad ibn Dá'úd he is visiting the celebrated poet Ibn ar-Rúmí, seeking distraction from the cares that oppress him, for he is out of work. He meets there a down-at-heel but clever writer called Ibn 'Ammár, invites him, at Ibn

1 Mas. *murúj*, VIII, 122–3.

2 It is my conjecture that Muḥammad ibn 'Abdún was the son of this 'Abdún. He was very much attached to the Banú'l-Jarráḥ. But the name Muḥammad is impossible for the child of a Christian. Perhaps 'Abdún was later converted, like Ṣá'id, to Islam.

3 Khall. I, 25, note 6—translated by de Slane from *fih.* 128.

4 *fih.* 128; Khall. II, 361.

5 *fih.* 156.

ar-Rúmí’s suggestion, to his house; and makes a lasting friend of him.[1] Muḥammad’s appointment to the *díwán ad-dár* was evidently not his first employment, for at the time of this visit he had been keeping his house, after the manner of officials in disgrace. Probably he had served before under Ṣá‘id ibn Makhlad. He and ‘Alí were to remain for many years companions in office.

‘Alí himself was one of a large family; and though none of his brothers were especially to distinguish themselves, we shall often have to do with them. ‘Abd ar-Raḥmán, who was his constant companion, rose indeed to the Vizierate, but only because ‘Alí stood behind him. Ibrahím also took a certain part in affairs; but neither Muḥammad, called al-‘Aramram, nor ‘Ubayd Allah, nor Dá’úd, nor al-Ḥusayn came to the fore. There was also at least one sister, Asmá’, who married her first cousin, ‘Alí the son of Muḥammad ibn Dá’úd,[2] and bore him a son, ‘Abd Allah.

Of ‘Alí’s early life we learn very little, and nothing direct. We may suppose him as a boy to have sat in the cool arcades of mosques at the feet of various masters; and may judge how well schooled he was by the devotion and learning he afterwards displayed. Of these masters two were al-Ḥasan ibn Muḥammad az-Za‘faráni and Aḥmad ibn Shu‘ayb an-Nasá’í.[3] With both of them ‘Alí “heard Traditions”, for they were both eminent “Traditionists”.

These almost technical terms, “Tradition” and “Traditionist”, need explanation. Whenever the *qur’án* gives no certain lead for action or belief, the authority to which Islam appeals is the *sunnah*, the Custom of the Prophet; and record of this Custom is preserved in Traditions handed down through series of witnesses. At first these Traditions had been transmitted only by

1 Yáq. *ud.* I, 226. 2 H. 147; *fih.* 129.
3 Tagh. II, 312.

word of mouth; but by the third century a number of written collections had been made, six of which (one of them the compilation of this very an-Nasá'í that was 'Alí ibn 'Ísà's master) were eventually to be regarded as a canon by the Orthodox. Yet partly because copyists were liable to make errors (especially with the still unperfected Arabic alphabet), partly because usage had consecrated the system, anyone that set up as a Traditionist was bound still to receive his knowledge verbally from accredited masters. A compromise between oral and written transmission was made only when in a gathering of his pupils before a doctor one of them would read from his works and the doctor correct mistakes and interpret difficulties. In the perfect Traditionist two faculties were requisite—he must memorise easily and correctly, and he must grasp correctly the purport of the Tradition.

The Tradition itself consisted of two parts—the matter reported and the series of the authorities that vouched for its truth. The perfect Traditionist must judge how reliable each member of the series might have been, and classify the Tradition accordingly. For Traditions might be "sound", "fair", "weak", "impure", or "rejected". Or they might be classified by the number of separate channels down which they had been conveyed, or by their subject-matter. Great numbers of accepted Traditions were certainly spurious, having been invented after the conquests to provide a sanction for beliefs and actions generally considered laudable. Each sect supported its views with appropriate Traditions; and some Tradition-mongers actually confessed to having fabricated their wares in what they considered a good cause. The influence of the Tradition system of conveying information was such that all items of secular as well as religious history—and even trivial anecdotes—came to be reported in this way: with their series of authorities leading back to the eye-witness. But the term "Tradition" without qualification refers to the sacred *sunnah*.

'Alí must have studied young with az-Za'faraní, for the latter died when he was only fifteen. Az-Za'faraní had been a companion of the Imám ash-Sháfi'í,[1] the founder of one of the four Orthodox schools of law, called after him the Sháfi'ite. Every Orthodox Muslim adopts the view of the Law's obligations as taught by one of these schools. The difference between them lies in their relative strictness or liberality. The most liberal of the four is that of Abú Ḥanífah, the Ḥanafite; the strictest is that of Ibn Ḥanbal, the Ḥanbalite, founded in opposition to the former. Abú Ḥanífah allowed rulings to be arrived at by analogy from those of the *qur'án* and the *sunnah*, admitting thus a certain secularity. Ibn Ḥanbal countenanced no such tampering with the sacred word, of which he allowed only the most strictly literal interpretation. In theology his views came sharply into conflict with those of the Mu'tazilites; and during their days of power he himself and others that agreed with him had had to suffer persecution at their hands. Ash-Sháfi'í, who had taught chiefly in Egypt, modified the code of Abú Ḥanífah to bring it more into accord with pietist sentiment, but he avoided anything like the illiberality of Ibn Ḥanbal. The fourth school of law, and the oldest, is that of Málik ibn Anas (the Málikite), more strictly pietist than the Ḥanafite and the Sháfi'ite, but yet not fanatical like the Ḥanbalite.

I incline to think that 'Alí ibn 'Ísà was a Sháfi'ite,[2] partly on account of his early connection with az-Za'faraní, partly because one of his closest friends, a member of his household, was a later light of the same school. If not, he must surely have been a Ḥanafite;

1 Tagh. II, 34.

2 Although Massignon, *Al-Hallaj*, 210, puts him down as a Ḥanafite.

the conflict in which he found himself more than once with the intolerant, and since the reaction pugnacious, Ḥanbalites is enough to show that at least he was not of them. One of the points controversy had raged about, during the war between the Muʿtazilites and their adversaries, was the nature of the *qur'án*, the Muʿtazilites holding that it was created, the Ḥanbalites and those that thought as they did, that it had existed from all eternity. Az-Zaʿfarání maintained stoutly that it *was* created, so stoutly at Níshápúr in Khurásán that the town became too hot for him.[1] ʿAlí may have imbibed such Muʿtazilite notions from him: indeed he seems to have been distinctly sympathetic to Muʿtazilite ideas. Later he greatly admired a prominent Muʿtazilite doctor, Muḥammad ibn Baḥr of Iṣfahán,[2] and he was also attacked by the celebrated theologian that was to combat and eventually destroy Muʿtazilism, Abú'l-Ḥasan al-Ashʿarí.[3]

My chief reason for supposing that ʿAlí was taught by an-Nasá'í early in his life is that ʿAlí himself makes no mention of him at a later date, in enumerating the famous Traditionists that had met at his house. Another is that an-Nasá'í died in 303 (915–16) at an advanced age, having spent the latter years of his life far away in Egypt.[4] An-Nasá'í's fame rests upon his collection of Traditions, which, as I have mentioned, is one of the six books that were afterwards to make up a kind of unofficial Muslim canon.

ʿAlí also heard Traditions from his father,[5] who must therefore have survived till he was of responsible age. Perhaps it was through his father's influence that he first got employment in the Government service. This, if we may take the statement literally that he

1 Tagh. II, 226. 2 *fih.* 136; Yáq. *ud.* VI, 420.
3 Spitta: *Zur Geschichte Abu'l-Ḥasan al-Aśʿarî's*, 79.
4 Dh. *t.* fol. 21 b; Tagh. II, 197.
5 Qudḥ. fol. 89 b; Yáq. *muʿjam*, IV, 847.

served the State seventy years,[1] was when he was nineteen or twenty, in 264 or 265 (877–9), a date that would accord well with what was said of him afterwards, that he had "worked in the *díwáns* ever since he grew up".[2] With his cousins al-Ḥasan and Ṣá'id both so powerful, there can have been no difficulty in finding him a place; but where he worked and with whom, in the fifteen years that elapsed between that and his employment by 'Alí ibn al-Furát in the *díwán ad-dár*, it is impossible to say.

Wherever 'Alí may have spent the years of his youth, he must early have grown used to riots, burnings, pillagings, the movement of armies: the world into which he was born was a world turned upside down. The miseries of disorder were impressed upon him young. Their stamp remained on his mind.

1 Yáq. *ud.* v, 280; Ṣaf. (B.M. Or. 6587), fol. 133 a.
2 M. I, 107; H. 290.

CHAPTER III

Badr. *New employments, and promotion, for* 'Alí *and his uncle.*

Fate was later to place the Banú'l-Furát and the Banú'l-Jarráḥ in opposition. But as long as Muḥammad ibn Dá'úd and his nephew sat in the assembly of 'Alí ibn al-Furát, whom, as subordinates a superior, they addressed as *ustádh*, "Master",[1] their relations were of the most amicable. Both acquitted themselves so well that Ibn al-Furát commended them to his brother, Aḥmad. An occasion was soon to arise for their advancement.

During al-Mu'taḍhid's reign a good deal of fighting went on in eastern and northern Persia between the 'Abbásid forces and various adventurers (Ṣaffárids, partisans of the Zaydites, etc.), and also among these adventurers themselves. Its outcome was the re-establishment of the Caliph's authority over almost the whole country. Only the Sámánid prince of Bukhárá emerged stronger from the wars, being now possessed not only of Transoxania but of Khurásán and Gurgán as well.

These campaigns were conducted for the most part by the Commander-in-Chief, Badr. This Badr was the son of a freedman of al-Mutawakkil. He himself had served al-Muwaffaq's Master of the Horse; and had been raised to the chief command of the armies on al-Mu'taḍhid's taking offence at the conduct of his former Commander, who had tactlessly purchased a concubine recently sold by the Caliph himself.[2] Al-Mu'taḍhid had greater confidence in Badr than in anyone else, and with justice.[3] He married one of his sons to

1 H. 131. 2 Mas. *murúj*, VIII, 219–20. 3 *Ibid.* 114.

Badr's daughter.[1] His charity could be elicited only by Badr's mediation.[2] It fell to Badr more than once to turn away his wrath from 'Ubayd Allah ibn Sulaymán. For he was fast friends with the Vizier; and their friendship was very valuable to the State.[3] The absence of friction between the civil power and the military fostered the recovery of the Caliphate. It completed the temporary fusion of the various elements in the 'Abbásid civilisation that I have spoken of. It was said afterwards that there had never been such a quartet, Caliph, Vizier, Commander, and Chief of the *díwáns*, as al-Mu'taḍhid, 'Ubayd Allah, Badr, and Aḥmad ibn al-Furát.[4] When their collaboration was dissolved by death it was seen to have been very precious.

Al-Mu'taḍhid did not take part in person in any of the campaigns in remoter Persia; but on several occasions he issued forth on expeditions nearer home. In 281 (894–5), the third year of his reign, a rebellion broke out in Mosul,[5] in consequence of a combination of certain religious fanatics and Kurds; whilst almost at the same time a dispute over the succession, in which al-Mu'taḍhid thought fit to intervene, arose between two members of the semi-independent house of Abú Dulaf in the Jibál, the westernmost province of Persia. The Caliph undertook the suppression of the rebellion at Mosul in person, and easily effected it; but after advancing some distance into the Jibál, he himself retired, leaving his son 'Alí (afterwards al-Muktafí) at Ray (near the modern Teheran) to co-operate with General Badr[6] in reducing the defiant rivals.

On his return to Baghdád the Caliph sent out the Vizier 'Ubayd Allah ibn Sulaymán to join al-Muktafí. He was to supervise matters of civil government in

1 S.J. fol. 19 b.
2 Mas. *murúj*, VIII, 220.
3 Qudh. fol. 83 b; H. 180.
4 H. 189.
5 Properly al-Mawṣil.
6 See H. 261.

the territories they hoped to recover from the divided family. 'Ubayd Allah wished to have at his disposal all the information available concerning their former status and revenues. He therefore resolved to take with him an experienced secretary, to search the records and compare former with current practice. He applied for one to Aḥmad ibn al-Furát; whereupon Aḥmad advised him to take Muḥammad ibn Dá'úd, because, as he said, "he has charge of that department of the *díwán ad-dár* concerned with the conquests in the east, and in which are the old accounts". Muḥammad accordingly accompanied 'Ubayd Allah to Ray.[1]

The rival claimants made no serious opposition to the advance of the 'Abbásid forces. Nevertheless it was more than three years before 'Ubayd Allah had settled affairs in the province to his satisfaction; and for the greater part of that time he, and presumably Muḥammad ibn Dá'úd with him, was away from the capital. In his absence his duties were performed by his son, al-Qásim ibn 'Ubayd Allah. When therefore al-Mu'tadhid determined on another campaign in 285 (898–9), it was with al-Qásim as chief adviser that he set out. Their goal on this occasion was Ámid, capital of the province of Diyár Bakr, over two hundred miles to the north-west of Mosul, where, the governor having lately died, his son had attempted to set himself up in independence. Al-Qásim was now faced likewise with the need of a secretary. He also applied to the *díwán ad-dár*; and was furnished with 'Alí ibn 'Ísà. Just as Muḥammad ibn Dá'úd had had control of eastern business in the office, so had 'Alí managed affairs concerning the western provinces. His appointment was therefore peculiarly appropriate.

Ámid,[2] which was surrounded then as now with its

1 H. 132.

2 Now called Diar Bekir, Turkish for the former name of the whole province.

famous black stone walls of Roman construction, capitulated after a short siege; and on this occasion al-Mu'tadhid showed himself unusually clement to the vanquished. Whilst he was still at Ámid an embassy arrived from Hárún ibn Khumárawayh, grandson of Ibn Ṭúlún, the ruler of Egypt, offering the restitution of western Mesopotamia, which had hitherto remained with Syria in his control. The Caliph thereupon removed to ar-Raqqah on the middle Euphrates, the chief town of this province, to receive its submission; and having done so, he returned to Baghdád. It is not clear whether or not 'Alí accompanied him; but if so, he certainly visited ar-Raqqah later.[1] Probably he was obliged to go there from time to time on departmental business.[2]

Meanwhile Muḥammad ibn Dá'úd, who was by now back again in Baghdád with the Vizier, had so far gained his favour and affection, and had made such an impression on him for worth and capacity, that it had been arranged for Muḥammad to marry 'Ubayd Allah's daughter. And at the same time, in recognition of his talents as a secretary, the Vizier decided to separate his office from the *díwán ad-dár*, and entitle it *díwán al-mashriq*, or Office for the East. Al-Qásim urged that 'Alí was no less deserving than his uncle, and that in the course of their travels "he had witnessed of his ability and knowledge and secretaryship and promptitude what enlarged him in his eyes". 'Alí was therefore given the corresponding Office for the West, the *díwán al-maghrib*. Uncle and nephew remained, of course, subordinate to Aḥmad ibn al-Furát, as Deputy Vizier. But they were now the equals of his brother 'Alí, and free of his tutelage.[3]

1 H. 361; Ṭab. III, 2221.
2 Ṭab. III, 2185–8; Mas. *murúj*, VIII, 134 *et seqq*; S.J. ff. 15 b–16 b.
3 Ṭab. III, 2190; H. 132; Yáq. *ud*. I, 226.

We observe that 'Alí was not offered a wife, perhaps because he had one already—although that of course would have been no obstacle. Indeed it seems likely that, whether simultaneously or in succession, he had two at least. In the single passage where a wife is referred to directly, she is described as the mother of his younger son Abú'l-Qásim 'Ísà. Presumably, therefore, the mother of his elder son, Abú Naṣr Ibrahím, was somebody else. But each (if two there were) was kept from her male contemporaries, like their own wives, in a seclusion so decently absolute, that they knew nothing about her, and consequently have handed nothing on.[1] In times of trouble 'Alí was occasionally constrained to ask the protection of eminent friends for her (or them); but she (or they) is even then mentioned only by implication, as among "his people".

This same single passage discloses the fact that 'Alí —like his master an-Nasá'í, who had not only the full legal number of wives, but concubines as well[2]—was amorously inclined; and that his amorousness continued till he was of an age at which the young 'Ísà considered it improper. But this, of course, was very much later in 'Alí's life than the point at which we have arrived; for 'Ísà was not even born till 302 (914–15).[3] Ibrahím, on the other hand, appears to have been his brother's elder by many years, and may well have been in existence already. It seems likely, in fine, that 'Alí made a first marriage as a young man, and a second in middle age.

An incident is chronicled which shows us the *díwán ad-dár* in working. A dispute had arisen between the farmers of the land above the great bridge of Dimimmá on the Nahr 'Ísà and the traders who used the canal for transporting their goods from the Euphrates to the

1 H. 347. 2 Dh. *t.* fol. 21 b; Tagh. II, 197.
3 Dh. *t.* fol. 227 a.

Tigris. Al-Mu'tadhid therefore assembled to adjudicate upon the case a commission including al-Qásim, 'Alí ibn al-Furát, Muḥammad ibn Dá'úd, 'Alí ibn 'Ísà, and a number of other officials, judges and notaries. They all proceeded to the place and took evidence from numbers of interested persons. The traders accused the farmers of bribing the engineers so to narrow the arches of the bridge as to dam up the water for their benefit without regard to the fact that boats and coracles were thereby prevented from passing through. The evidence, however, was so contradictory that there was nothing for it but that the commissioners should measure the boats and so arrive at a proper width for the arches. In the end the traders were placated by the widening of the great central opening, and the cultivators by the conservation at their actual size of the rest.[1]

Soon after his establishment in the *díwán al-maghrib*, 'Alí was charged with the drawing up of a report on the finances of the recently pacified districts of Mosul and the Upper and Lower Záb rivers. And in doing so he came into conflict with Aḥmad ibn al-Furát, to whom, as Chief of the *díwáns*, 'Ubayd Allah showed the report when it was ready. 'Alí wished to be scrupulously fair towards the tax-payers. He would not encourage the State money-changers to squeeze the people by including their profits in the revenue accounts. To do so, in his eyes, was, if the money were really the State's, to exact the sum twice over—he said it was like "taking from the hem to patch the sleeve". Or if it were really the tax-payers', it was pure robbery. Aḥmad, however, who cared more to produce an immediate yield than to work for a problematical increase in the future, had no such scruples. He insisted that the profits must be shown.[2]

1 H. 256–7. 2 H. 255.

This is the first occasion we hear of, on which ‘Alí advocated the adoption of a principle that he was afterwards to follow himself. Just, even lenient, dealing with tax-payers, in the expectation of ultimately increasing the revenue, was to be a cardinal point of his policy as Vizier.

CHAPTER IV

The Carmathians. Egypt *recovered.*

In the year 286 (899–900) the name Carmathian (Arabic, *qarmaṭí*, plural, *qarámiṭah*), which was afterwards to become so terribly familiar to the people of Baghdád, was first brought to the attention of their rulers. In this year the commandant of al-Baṣrah received news that greatly alarmed him from al-Baḥrayn, the province (now known as al-Ḥasá) lying next to the south and bounding the Persian Gulf on the west.[1] A certain bandit of those parts, by name Abú Sa'íd al-Jannábí, had gained control of a wide district, which he had ravaged with an ever-increasing band of followers; and was now advancing northwards. The commandant appealed to Baghdád, and received instructions to wall the city about; but as the insurgents continued their manœuvres, he was not content with this, and next year demanded reinforcements. An army was thereupon sent out under a general, who had instructions to carry the war into the enemy's country. He met al-Jannábí not far south of the city; but in a two days' fight he was completely defeated, and himself taken prisoner. Al-Jannábí did not, however, advance upon al-Baṣrah; but instead turned south again, took the provincial capital Ḥajar (the modern Ḥufúf), and established himself as a local potentate. From this time forth it became evident to the 'Abbásids that the Carmathians were a power to be reckoned with.[2]

How much was known about them in Baghdád at this time is by no means clear. Fearsome rumours got

1 The name al-Baḥrayn is now, of course, applied to the group of islands in the gulf, off the coast of the province formerly bearing it.

2 Ṭab. III, 2188, 2192, 2193, 2196–7.

about of their blasphemous tenets and immoral conduct; but it was not until some years later that historians began to compile from this material, true and false, accounts of their doctrine and history. Such of these accounts as have come down to us are mostly Sunní polemics. Yet they have been generally believed, until quite recently an acute Orientalist[1] has shown them to be utterly unreliable, and has checked what truth there is in them from Shí'ite sources.

The doctrine appears in reality to have been a fitting of Hellenistic (chiefly Neo-Platonic) theosophical conceptions into a Muḥammadan Imámite framework. Just as the impact of Hellenistic thought on Orthodoxy had produced Mu'tazilism and Muslim "Philosophy", so its study by certain doctors of the Shí'ah produced, towards the end of the second century A.H., what developed later into the teaching of the Carmathians. But whereas Mu'tazilism was in favour with the early 'Abbásid Caliphs, this teaching was doubly reprehensible in their eyes, on the one hand for being, like the notions of the "philosophers", too little distinctively Muḥammadan, and on the other for being of Shí'ah parentage. Its sponsors were obliged therefore to keep it secret; and to do so they adopted a system of initiation by degrees into its tenets, modelled on the ancient Greek and Manichaean. The doctrine was theosophical: the adept would learn at length that life consists of a series of events, repeated endlessly by cycles in exactly the same way. At the beginning and end of each cycle the Divine Essence alone exists. Everything else is evolved from it through four principles. The first principle, the Primary Agent, engenders on the one hand the second and third principles, the Universal Intellect and the Soul of the World; and on the other the fourth principle, Passive Matter,

1 L. Massignon. See for this and what follows *Encyclopédie*, II, 813–17 (art. *Ḳarmaṭes*).

which is modified in turn into the material universe. Out of the Universal Intellect and the Soul of the World are moulded the minds of Prophets, Imáms and the Elect—all other minds being only phantoms of non-existence; and it is here that the doctrine first takes on a distinctively Muḥammadan tinge. For it is by the teaching of the prophets and Imáms, of which in the present epoch Muḥammad and the 'Alids are the representatives, that the minds of the Elect are led back to merge again in the Divine Essence, and a cycle completed.

The promulgators of the doctrine were of the Sevener, or Ismá'ílí, branch of the Shí'ah—it was called Ismá'ílí because its adherents believed the seventh Imám to be a certain Ismá'íl, son of Ja'far aṣ-Ṣádiq, the sixth Imám of both Seveners and Twelvers. But though they used for their own political ends the sectaries' devotion to this line of the 'Alids, they held in fact that the Imámate, far from being the exclusive prerogative of its members, may be conferred by spiritual illumination on any man chosen of Heaven for the function. Yet Carmathian pretenders to the Ismá'ílí Imámate found it expedient at least to claim 'Alid birth; and such claims generally sufficed to gain them the support of the uninitiated, though the Orthodox were often able to disprove their validity. To adherents once initiated into the teaching their validity would of course be indifferent.

It would appear to be a contradiction that the Ismá'ílís counted only seven Imáms, all of them dead, and yet claimed the office for one living. The explanation is that the Imámate was not supposed by them to have come to an end with Ismá'íl's death, but either to be still held by him though he was no longer in the body, or to have passed to a mysterious son of his, Muḥammad—whose very existence was disputed—and from him to his descendants. The Carmathians subscribed to the latter doctrine, and claimed for their Imáms descent from this Muḥammad ibn Ismá'íl. But they were still considered as of the Seveners, since only seven of their Imáms had been manifest, the rest being hidden till one should come forth and lead them to victory.

The limitation of the Imámate to seven and twelve respectively by the two branches of the Shí'ah was due in each case to a historical accident. There was no reason to limit the number at all: the Zaydites recognised no such restriction. In each case there was a confusion over the succession, which resulted in the belief that the Imám had withdrawn from the world, but still directed its fate and would reappear in the fullness of time. The last Imám of the Twelvers (who had disappeared as recently as 260 (873–4) at Sámarrá) was known as the *Mahdí*; and this title came to be commonly applied among all branches of the Shí'ah to the Imám that should be their Saviour.

The new teaching, although it had been evolved long before, first began to make considerable headway in the fifties and sixties of the third century. The repressive measures taken by al-Mutawakkil against the unorthodox must have hastened its dissemination by stirring up the latent hostility of the Shí'ah to 'Abbásid rule; moreover the Zinj rebellion showed how successfully an 'Alid revolt might be launched, and how favourable a ground was the south of al-'Iráq for such an enterprise. Already in 264 (877–8), while the Zinj were still unsubdued, the *da'wah*, the Ismá'ílí propaganda, had won many adherents among the peasants and workmen of these parts. A powerful secret society was forming, whose members shared their possessions in common and graduated by initiation in the knowledge of its aims. Its local organisers were a certain Ḥamdán Qarmaṭ (from whose surname the term Carmathian is derived) and his brother 'Abdán;

that is to say, they were the public agents of the real heads of the movement, the Imáms to be. For the present the latter remained in hiding and were only referred to by mysterious titles such as *ṣáḥib adh-dhuhúr*, He that shall Appear, or *ṣáḥib an-náqah*, the Man with the She-Camel. From the headquarters of the new sect missionaries travelled far and wide with the gospel, and established centres in al-Baḥrayn—where al-Jannábí received his commission from the Man with the She-Camel, in Khurásán, Syria, the Yemen and North Africa. The year 290 (902–3) seems first to have been fixed for the manifestation of the Mahdí and a general rising—al-Jannábí's excursion near al-Baṣrah had been no more than a local manœuvre. His victory, however, encouraged the Carmathians of the Kúfah district to rise at once; and though their attempt was easily suppressed, when in 289 (902) al-Mu'taḍhid died, as I shall have to relate, and was succeeded by al-Muktafí, the Imám judged it best to delay no longer, and gave the long-expected signal.

By this time both Ḥamdán Qarmaṭ and 'Abdán were dead. The Lieutenancy in Mesopotamia had passed to a man named Dhikrawayh, who had been preparing for the rebellion by engaging certain tribesmen of the middle Euphrates to take up arms and raid into northern Syria. The Man with the She-Camel then proclaimed himself as the Imám, publishing his descent from Muḥammad ibn Ismá'íl, and led the sectaries in person, till he was killed this same year in a fight at the gate of Damascus. His brother, called *ṣáḥib al-khál*, the Man with the Mole, succeeded him; but he too was defeated, captured and executed with abominable cruelty in Baghdád in 291 (904).

The early death of the promised Imám seems to have damped the enthusiasm of the other Carmathian groups. None of them, at least, joined in the insurrection at the appointed time. It is especially remarkable that al-

Jannábí made no move, in spite of his recent success and of the valuable aid he might have rendered the Imám by distracting his opponents. After the execution of the Man with the Mole the revolt was carried on by Dhikrawayh alone. He made desperate attempts to encourage his bedouin warriors by allowing them to attack and loot the Pilgrimage caravans as they passed on their way back from Mecca to al-'Iráq; but although the sectaries spread terror through the Euphrates territory and made the name of Carmathian fearful in the ears of the Orthodox, their vigour was on the wane. At length in 294 (907) Dhikrawayh was wounded in battle and taken prisoner. He died of his injuries on the way to the capital. On this, finding themselves leaderless, their numbers woefully reduced and their cause apparently hopeless, the rebels disbanded.[1]

The 'Abbásids benefited from the Carmathian rising in that it led to the reconquest of Egypt and Syria from the Ṭúlúnids. Ibn Ṭúlún's son Khumárawayh had submitted to al-Mu'taḍhid as his suzerain; but had continued to govern as a vassal, through his own officials. When making his submission, however, he had beggared himself to present the Caliph with what he considered a fitting gift.[2] Ever since the finances of Egypt had shown a deficit. His son Jaysh, who succeeded him, attempted to rehabilitate them by mulcting his officers. But this so disgusted them that they deposed and killed him, and set up his brother Hárún in his stead. The army, however, remained dangerously disaffected; and when the Carmathians first raided into northern Syria its people complained that the Ṭúlúnids afforded them no protection. After fighting as allies with the 'Abbásid forces against the

1 Ṭab. III, 2217–20, 2221–2, 2224–6, 2230–2, 2237–47, 2255–66, 2269–75.

2 Mas. *murúj*, VIII, 118–19; Tagh. II, 95; S.J. fol. 1 a.

sectaries, certain Ṭúlúnid officers were prompted to propose to the victorious 'Abbásid general, one Muḥammad ibn Sulaymán, a joint invasion of Egypt and the removal of Hárún ibn Khumárawayh from the throne. In 292 (904–5), accordingly, Muḥammad ibn Sulaymán led an army through Syria into Egypt and succeeded in accomplishing his object without the least difficulty: Hárún was killed in the fighting, and Egypt became once more a province of the 'Abbásid empire.[1]

1 Ṭab. III, 2248–9, 2251–2; 'A. 5–6, 7–8; Tagh. II, 97, 102, 111–12, 116, 119, 144–5; Mas. *tan.* 373.

CHAPTER V

The accession of al-Muktafí. *The Vizierate and death of* al-Qásim. *The War of the Secretaries.*

'Alí ibn 'Ísà early saw the Carmathians at close quarters: for he was in ar-Raqqah when they made their first descent on it, led by the Man with the She-Camel, on their way to Syria. The commandant went out against them, but his men were scattered and he was killed. The Carmathians, however, did not stop to enter the town, but passed on to Damascus, where they were again victorious. It fell to 'Alí to write a despatch to the capital, announcing the event. Soon after he appears to have returned there himself.[1]

Not only was there now a new Caliph, there was also a new Vizier. 'Ubayd Allah ibn Sulaymán had died, greatly regretted, almost exactly twelve months before al-Mu'taḍhid, and had been replaced in office by his son al-Qásim. Al-Qásim was a very different person from his father. He had inherited neither his probity nor his loyalty; and though he may have been shrewder in furthering his own interests, his conduct of affairs in his father's absence had earned 'Ubayd Allah's disapproval.[2] Al-Mu'taḍhid, who had observed al-Qásim to be of a jealous and intriguing disposition, at first wished to dismiss and fine him in the accepted way, and to appoint Aḥmad ibn al-Furát Vizier in his place. But General Badr, out of affection for the memory of 'Ubayd Allah, dissuaded him; and al-Qásim made an opportune appeal to the Caliph's greed by offering a large sum of money in return for the appointment.[3] Once in power, however, he planned to avenge the slight that had been put upon him. He would have

1 Ṭab. III, 2221. 2 H. 188. 3 *fakh.* 303.

the Caliph assassinated, and see to it that the throne passed to another branch of the 'Abbásid family. The plot failed because in order to win the support of the soldiery, which was essential to its success, al-Qásim again confided in Badr. But he reckoned without his devotion to al-Mu'tadhid: Badr rejected the proposal with indignation; and al-Qásim found himself in an exceedingly awkward position.[1] Happily for him, however, Badr was away from Court; and before he returned al-Mu'tadhid died. Al-Qásim appears to have been innocent of any part in bringing about his death, although rumours got about of his having been poisoned.[2] Al-Mu'tadhid was no more than forty-six years of age; but his health had been undermined by years of dissipation, and the hardships and exertions of his last campaign, in Cilicia, prostrated him.[3] His physicians found it impossible to treat him.[4] He refused to follow their prescriptions, and gave one of them a kick in the stomach that killed him.[5] He died in the Ḥasaní Palace in *rabí' al-ákhir* 289 (March–April 902), leaving four sons and a large number of daughters.[6]

To disguise his former intentions al-Qásim now judged it best to support al-Muktafí for the succession. And in order to avoid any dissension, he even shut up certain rival princes till the new Caliph was securely seated on the throne.[7] His next care was to dispose of the now dangerous Badr; and this by complicated scheming he quickly contrived to do. The unfortunate general was enticed away from his supporters with a treacherous safe-conduct, and murdered in cold blood on an island in the Tigris.[8]

The Vizier was bent on gaining an absolute ascendancy over the young Caliph. The chief obstacle in his

1 Ṭab. III, 2209.
2 S.J. fol. 25 a.
3 Mas. *murúj*, VIII, 197.
4 Jaw. fol. 64 b.
5 Tagh. II, 133.
6 S.J. fol. 25 b.
7 Tan. *farj*. I, 89.
8 Ṭab. III, 2209–14.

way was al-Muktafí's affection for a certain Christian, who had been for many years his secretary and confidant; but al-Qásim successfully surmounted it by turning the Caliph against him. Though the Christian attempted to retaliate by showing al-Muktafí the Vizier's true character, it was of no avail. He was first deprived of his offices, which were given to al-Qásim's sons; and later banished from Court.[1] Soon after, al-Muktafí conferred on al-Qásim a title, the first of a kind later to be very widely used, particularly in Persia and India: *walí ad-dawlah* (Champion of the Dynasty).[2] At the same time he gave his consent to the betrothal of his son, still a child, to al-Qásim's little daughter.[3]

Al-muktafí bi'llah (Content with God Alone) was twenty five years of age when he came to the throne. His mother, now dead, had been Turkish. He was remarkably good-looking; his complexion was fair, his hair and beard black and abundant, his figure upright and slender.[4] He had none of his father's ferocity, and at once earned popularity by pulling down his prisons and allowing the site to be used by the people. But neither had he his determination, and was easily swayed, especially by his Viziers and by his favourite, Fátik.[5] One thing he inherited from al-Mu'tadhid: a love of building. Al-Mu'tadhid had built two palaces, called the Pleiades (*ath-thuráyá*) and the Paradise (*al-firdaws*), and had laid the foundations of a third, the Crown (*at-táj*): al-Muktafí completed the Crown, and erected a new "Friday" Mosque in the palace area, whose site is still marked by a later minaret.[6] He also inherited all his father's greed of money, and was

1 Ṭab. III, 2140, 2224, 2230. 2 Qudh. fol. 89 b.
3 Ṭab. III, 2248. 4 Jaw. fol. 63 b; Tagh. II, 172.
5 Mas. *murúj*, VIII, 215.
6 The minaret of the Súq al-Ghazal, dating probably from the fifth/eleventh century; see Massignon: *Mission*, II, 43, note 6.

excessively parsimonious to boot. During his short reign he contrived to add another five millions to al-Mu'taḍhid's hoard.[1] The Caliphate seemed in his days almost to have regained its former glory, especially after the defeat of the Carmathians and the recovery of Syria and Egypt. But his health from childhood had always been wretched; death carried him off untimely; and the days of promise came all too soon to an end.

Whilst al-Qásim was weaving his intrigues, the Secretariat was divided by a quarrel into two camps—the Banú'l-Furát were pitted against the Banú'l-Jarráḥ. The feud seems to have dated from the time when 'Ubayd Allah ibn Sulaymán was away with Muḥammad ibn Dá'úd in the Jibál. While there he used to receive letters denouncing the Banú'l-Furát; but these complaints made not the least impression on the Vizier, and when he got back, he showed them to Aḥmad and his brother.[2] Who were the authors of these denigrations we are not told. But it is certain that the ringleaders of the opposition to the Banú'l-Furát were 'Alí's brother Ibrahím, his uncle Muḥammad ibn Dá'úd, and his cousin, another Muḥammad, son of the Christian 'Abdún ibn Makhlad. For some reason, perhaps on account of these very attacks, the brothers Ibn al-Furát had a grievance against Ibrahím ibn 'Ísà; and when, still during the Vizierate of 'Ubayd Allah ibn Sulaymán, they had a chance of injuring him, they took it.

At one time Ibrahím had held a post as revenue-agent on the Upper Záb River, as deputy for 'Alí. Then later (perhaps when 'Alí was given the *díwán al-maghrib*) Ibrahím held it direct, and so came under the immediate control of the Banú'l-Furát. In any case Aḥmad soon dismissed him, and instructed his suc-

1 Mas. *murúj*, VIII, 225–6; 'A. 22; Tagh. II, 172.
2 H. 72.

cessor, in securing the fine due from him to the Treasury, to imprison and treat him with severity. Muḥammad ibn Dá'úd happened to be present when he gave these instructions; and at once offered to help his nephew in paying the required sum. But when he was gone, Aḥmad cautioned the new official that he was on no account to accept this alleviation, but was to pursue Ibrahím with all rigour.

After a time, through 'Alí's influence, Ibrahím was given another post, and in the course of his duties convicted the Banú'l-Furát of withholding dues on their estates in the district and adding Government lands to their own. Al-Qásim, now Vizier, was overjoyed at this; for he had long detested Aḥmad ibn al-Furát, of whom he was mortally jealous. He had several reasons for detesting him. First, when his father 'Ubayd Allah had left him in charge of affairs, Aḥmad had so outshone him in ability, that al-Mu'taḍhid had given orders for no bill of al-Qásim's to be passed by the Treasury officials unless countersigned by Aḥmad.[1] Secondly Aḥmad had won the favour of al-Qásim's victim, Badr;[2] thirdly, he had all but supplanted al-Qásim himself in the Vizierate. When, therefore, he had reason to suspect the brothers of other misappropriation in the district of Wásiṭ, al-Qásim again set Ibrahím to investigate the matter, in the hope that his spite might find some cause for impeaching them.

It was only now that Ibrahím discovered with what malice the brothers had pursued him before. For the official whose duty it had been to extract the fine from him was now one of his own staff; and Ibrahím naturally showing a certain lack of cordiality, the official began to fear for his place, and told him the whole story. Ibrahím, consequently, set about the enquiry with all the zest of vengeance. He found easily enough that the Banú'l-Furát had misappropriated huge sums;

1 H. 188. 2 H. 179–80.

for with all Aḥmad's ability as a secretary, he had, in fact, no scruples about enriching himself at the State's expense.[1] Ibrahím brought Aḥmad to book before the Vizier, and prosecuted him so successfully that he won al-Qásim's warmest admiration. Al-Qásim resolved to arrest the brothers and fine them; but just then the Carmathian raids began: he was occupied altogether with military matters, and even had to accompany the Caliph to the scene of war himself.[2]

Then, soon after he returned, towards the end of 291 (904), Aḥmad died suddenly; on which al-Muktafí, remembering his father's high opinion of the two brothers, insisted on his offices being given to 'Alí, the younger. Aḥmad's death might have been expected to assuage the hatred of their enemies; but far from its having any such result, their hatred was merely concentrated on his brother. Al-Qásim, indeed, was only emboldened by the death of Aḥmad, of whose superior intelligence he had been somewhat in awe, to resume the prosecution of 'Alí ibn al-Furát alone. The Banú'l-Jarráḥ pressed him to do so; and neither the favour in which the Caliph evidently held Ibn al-Furát, nor the Vizier's own health, which was so bad that he could hardly get through his daily business, were enough to deter him.

To begin his examination al-Qásim drew strength from smelling-salts. But the effort was too great for him: he almost fainted, and though rose-water was sprinkled upon his face to revive him, the assembly broke up. He guessed that he would not live, and retired to his house. But from there he busied himself with the choice of a Vizier to succeed him, and on the last morning of his life wrote his advice to the Caliph. In choosing he seems for once really to have had the interests of the Caliphate at heart. He seems to have foreseen that if al-Muktafí were to appoint as Vizier

1 H. 171, 254. 2 H. 132–4.

any one of the secretaries now engaged in the fight of factions, he might very well perpetuate their division, and so injure beyond repair the instrument of government recreated by al-Muwaffaq and al-Mu'tadhid. Of the five secretaries eligible three were thus ruled out: Ibn al-Furát, Muḥammad ibn Dá'úd, and Ibn 'Abdún. The choice lay between the official now in charge of the *díwán at-tawqí'*, the Great Seal, a certain al-'Abbás ibn al-Ḥasan, and 'Alí ibn 'Ísà.

From their first acquaintance al-Qásim had been favourably impressed with 'Alí—perhaps it was that, being shifty himself, he found 'Alí's straightforwardness attractive; and now, when he knew death to be upon him, it was in 'Alí that he sought a protector for his children. 'Alí, in return, had a care for his soul; and earnestly begged him to repent of his sins, persisting until he was assured of a sincere contrition. This accomplished, al-Qásim dictated to al-'Abbás ibn al-Ḥasan a letter to al-Muktafí. In it he commended first 'Alí and then al-'Abbás in terms of almost equal approval. Entrusting it to 'Alí, he bade them both hurry to the palace, that he might learn the Caliph's decision before he died. So the two set off, 'Alí wondering greatly at so tenacious an interest at such a time in the "things of this world". As they were crossing the courtyard, however, al-'Abbás astonished him even more. He suggested that if 'Alí were to decline the Vizierate, he, as Vizier, would yet defer to him in the conduct of affairs. But 'Alí made no comment on this proposal. He left the future, piously, to God.

Al-Muktafí wept at their intelligence; and at once showed by his treatment of 'Alí that he required no further reflection to decide in his favour. "You, 'Alí," he said, "have been in my mind since you were at ar-Raqqah. I know your history and remark your gifts. Affairs are now in your hands: my choice has fallen upon you." But 'Alí excused himself. "O Commander of the Faithful," he said, "I am a man of small ability: my insistence and quick temper would ill become the holder of the office." And though they argued for a long while, 'Alí persisted in his refusal. He warmly commended al-'Abbás, saying that he well understood al-Qásim's methods in government. He himself would remain in his present position and from there use his knowledge and influence for the good guidance of ministers; but for the Vizierate the Caliph must be content with his colleague. Al-Muktafí reluctantly called for pen and paper and wrote the answer to al-Qásim with many a protestation. Finally, "I shall not reject your choice," he said, "but shall promote whomsoever you advise. As for your women and children, they are my women and children; and long may Allah guard them with your life and save us with your person."

The two ministers left the palace. Mindful of their promise, they hastened by boat to the house of the Vizier. As they made the landing-stage, the physician, at the anxious entreaty of his patient, looked out for their return from an upper window; and on seeing them, turned back into the room. But as they reached the private staircase, a woman's voice sounded from above, shrill in a first wail of lamentation.[1]

1 H. 360–2.

CHAPTER VI

Al-'Abbás ibn al-Ḥasan *as Vizier.* *The defeat of the* Banú'l-Jarráḥ.

We are nowhere given a description of 'Alí's appearance. But we may hope that he was more beautiful than al-'Abbás ibn al-Ḥasan. The poet Ibn Bassám was given to satirising his enemies in savage terms; yet presumably his portrait of al-'Abbás is founded on fact:

A Vizier with a wrinkled face, like a nose-bag;
A back adorned with two humps, and a head like a cucumber.[1]

Al-'Abbás was invested with the cloak of office on the morrow of al-Qásim's decease. The people were greatly astonished at the Caliph's choice of him, for he was by some years the youngest of the five Secretaries of State; but as well as al-Qásim's recommendation he had had behind him the influence of al-Muktafí's foster-mother, a personage of importance, for whom he had acted as secretary.[2]

The reconquest of Egypt, which occurred soon after the elevation of al-'Abbás to the Vizierate, appears to have given 'Alí ibn 'Ísà at the *díwán al-maghrib* a heavy task. It may be even that he was obliged at about this time to visit Syria. In any case he drew up a report on the finances of that province, similar to his earlier report on the Mosul and Záb districts, in collaboration with the victorious general, Muḥammad ibn Sulaymán. We learn this from an incidental reference in the geographical work of Ibn Ḥawqal, who states, further, that this report was made in 296 (908–9).[3] It is probable, however, that the date given

1 Mas. *murúj*, VIII, 261.
2 H. 229, 363.
3 Ḥaw. 128.

should really read 292 (904–5), the year of the victory in Egypt. Muḥammad ibn Sulaymán is known to have travelled through Syria in that year. He cannot have done so later; nor was 'Alí any longer in a position to make such a report in 296. Muḥammad ibn Sulaymán was a queer colleague for 'Alí. *He* was far from respecting the rights of the subject. In the few months during which he had remained in Egypt after the conquest he had made himself generally abhorred by the Egyptians. He had robbed them unmercifully, in the name of the Caliph, but largely for his own benefit. He was qualified to assist 'Alí in that he had originally served a Ṭúlúnid general as secretary, and so was familiar with Ṭúlúnid practice. But it seems that their collaboration was cut short. For whilst at Aleppo Muḥammad ibn Sulaymán was suddenly arrested at the Caliph's order, and cast into prison for his misdeeds in oppressing the Egyptians and robbing the State. He was then brought to Baghdád, where he remained four years in confinement.[1]

Al-Qásim's death had interrupted the proceedings against 'Alí ibn al-Furát. It was not long, however, before his enemies saw to it that they were resumed. 'Alí ibn 'Ísà, though he was importuned "with conversations both secret and open", refused to join them; but the new Vizier was more amenable, and promised that if he could persuade the Caliph to agree to it, he would move against Ibn al-Furát. A chance came when he and the Caliph were riding alone with Khafíf the Chamberlain on a hunting expedition at Sámarrá. Al-'Abbás then asked leave, without mentioning their names, to examine certain defaulting clerks; and the Caliph consented. Khafíf, however, was an astute person, and versed in Court intrigues. He guessed that al-'Abbás had Ibn al-Furát in mind: and when once the Vizier had left them he reminded al-Muktafí of the

1 Tagh. II, 119, 145–6.

high esteem in which his father had held the brothers; with the result that the Caliph sent him hurrying after the Vizier with a warning that the authority he had just granted was not to be applied to Ibn al-Furát. The Chamberlain took care to earn the gratitude of Ibn al-Furát by informing him, as soon as possible, of the danger he had so narrowly escaped, and of his own skill in averting it.[1]

The Caliph's regard for Ibn al-Furát was thus marked enough. Nevertheless the schemers did not despair of bringing about, if not his ruin, at least his dismissal; and when the Court returned from Sámarrá, Muḥammad ibn Dá'úd and Ibn 'Abdún contrived to persuade al-'Abbás ibn al-Ḥasan to make another attempt.

'Alí was approached by both parties. Ibn al-Furát complained bitterly of his relatives' conduct. 'Alí, deeply shocked, advised him to win over the Vizier with a bribe. He suggested that 50,000 *dínárs* would not be too much; and offered his own money in aid. Ibn 'Abdún, on the other hand, attempted to enlist 'Alí's help in *his* scheme, and was ill advised enough to hint that the Caliph would only agree to Ibn al-Furát's dismissal if 'Alí would replace him in office. This was a proposal to arouse all 'Alí's indignation: and Ibn 'Abdún retired in discomfiture.

The Vizier thought to tempt al-Muktafí with the promise of a large sum to be paid into the Privy Purse from the confiscation of the riches that Ibn al-Furát was supposed to have amassed illegally. But the Caliph valued, so he said, his talents more than his money, and declined once and for all to admit his disgrace.[2]

Ibn al-Furát presented the bribe, as 'Alí had suggested, to al-'Abbás ibn al-Ḥasan; and at the same time, to assure his position, he paid into the Treasury a sum

1 H. 230. Cf. H. 143. 2 H. 136.

large enough to cover his peculations.[1] The bribe had all its expected effect and more: not only was the Vizier won over from his attempts (which he had now seen were useless) to ruin Ibn al-Furát, he definitely changed sides in the secretaries' war. One day he sent for Ibn al-Furát to speak with him in private. The Court were convinced that Ibn al-Furát was to be arrested and disgraced: what was their surprise therefore when the Vizier, on issuing from their interview, seated the minister beside him and ostentatiously showed him every mark of respect and affection. At this same interview al-'Abbás had repeated the move he had tried before with 'Alí—he had offered to relinquish the Vizierate in favour of Ibn al-Furát. Ibn al-Furát had of course refused; whereupon al-'Abbás had charged him to watch over his family in case he should die, and had ended by embracing him and swearing eternal friendship.[2]

Al-'Abbás would now praise Ibn al-Furát in public for his generous nature—contrasting him to his advantage with the Banú'l-Jarráḥ.[3] Whatever Ibn al-Furát asked him to do against his opponents he did. When 'Alí's brothers Ibrahím and Muḥammad tried once again to convict Ibn al-Furát of robbing the State by withholding dues on his properties, the Vizier took his side and turned the plea against Muḥammad. He even allowed 'Alí himself to suffer by this change of policy. When Ibn al-Furát complained that 'Alí was subjecting his brother Ja'far to an unjust inquisition, the Vizier at once removed Ja'far from 'Alí's jurisdiction.[4] He even went so far as to humiliate 'Alí by putting his office, the *díwán al-maghrib*, once again under Ibn al-Furát's supervision.[5]

Against Ibn 'Abdún Ibn al-Furát appears to have

1 H. 135–6 and 230.
2 H. 231–2.
3 H. 220–1.
4 H. 236–7.
5 H. 232.

contented himself with storing up hatred for a day when vengeance might be possible. Against Muḥammad ibn Dá'úd his retaliation, if such it was, consisted in having him put in charge of the War Office, the *díwán al-jaysh*. This was a post that Ibn al-Furát himself had held for some time and long wished to relinquish.[1] Muḥammad had hitherto held a minor position in this same *díwán* (whilst still controlling the *díwán al-mashriq*). After he had held his new office for a while, Ibn al-Furát brought a charge against him of having expended certain sums without making out proper bills for registration. Muḥammad acknowledged his mistake, but maintained that the transaction had taken place whilst Ibn al-Furát was still in charge and that therefore he was not responsible. The Vizier, when the point was referred to him, again took sides with his new favourite. He ordered that no bill of Muḥammad ibn Dá'úd's was to be passed without the countersignature of Ibn al-Furát.[2]

His control of the *díwán al-jaysh* brought Muḥammad ibn Dá'úd into close contact with the Carmathians. He took charge of it after the execution of the Man with the Mole, but before the last campaign of Dhikrawayh. In attacking the Pilgrimage caravans Dhikrawayh was only following the example of desert bandits, who twice in recent years had done the same.[3] But perhaps because he carried out the exploit so much more thoroughly and successfully (stripping and slaying thousands), perhaps because he was already regarded as the arch-enemy of society, news of the disaster caused the most fearful dismay in the capital, where there was a public outcry for vengeance on the miscreant. The Vizier at once ordered Muhammad ibn Dá'úd to proceed to al-Kúfah, where he was to get together forces to go out and attack the enemy. Four

1 H. 232. 2 H. 235–6. Cf. H. 261.
3 Ṭab. III, 2183, 2191.

days later Muḥammad set out with a large store of treasure for paying the troops.[1] It was as a result of his exertions that Dhikrawayh was taken. It also fell to him to examine the Carmathian prisoners, who were brought for the purpose into his assembly; and it is from the information about the campaign that he collected by questioning them, that aṭ-Ṭabarí put together his account of it.[2]

1 Ṭab. III, 2273. 2 *Ibid.* 2127, 2256, 2259, etc.

CHAPTER VII

The Báb al-Bustán. *The learned and literary circle of* 'Alí ibn 'Ísà.

Being firmly settled in the Ministry and a person of consequence, 'Alí purchased soon after al-Qásim's death part of his mansion, which he converted into a house for himself. It was situated in the Mukharrim quarter and lay on the river bank not far below the main bridge by the Garden of Záhir, whence it was known as *báb al-bustán* (the Garden Gate).[1]

The Báb al-Bustán, as had been 'Alí's former abode, was regularly the scene of learned gatherings; for, as aṣ-Ṣúlí reports, "Whilst he was at the *díwán al-maghrib* a number of erudite persons used nightly to attend his table."[2] Unfortunately he omits to state who these erudite persons were, or what were the subjects of their conversation. But in another passage it is reported that as an older man 'Alí used to point to places in his Assembly where certain famous men had sat—and as it was only during his present employment that such meetings were held at his house, perhaps we may conclude that it was now that they sat in them.[3]

If so, he and his guests must often have occupied themselves with the Sacred Science, the science of Tradition—for the persons he mentions were all eminent Traditionists. "Al-Baghawí used to recite Traditions to us here," 'Alí would say, pointing to one corner, "and Ibn Ṣá'id, here," pointing to another, and so on.

1 H. 187; Yáq. *ud.* v, 279.
2 Yáq. *ud.* v, 278; Tagh. II, 313; Dháf. fol. 139 b.
3 S.J. fol. 88 a.

Al-Baghawí[1] was one of the most reliable Traditionists. He composed two Dictionaries of the Prophet's Companions, and a work on the schools of the jurists. His utterances were few, but like the "driving of a nail into teak".[2] Ibn Ṣá'id,[3] who was one of al-Baghawí's masters, and whose comprehension was as remarkable as his memory, had travelled all over Islam in search of Traditions, and had also composed a manual on the *sunnah*.[4]

'Alí was asked why he had made no mention of Ibn Abí Dá'úd of Sístán,[5] one of the most notable Traditionists and jurists of his day, and one whom he was known to have studied with. He answered that Ibn Abí Dá'úd had always allowed him to go to his house for their meetings—but in saying so he appears to have been passing over an old scandal. Ibn Abí Dá'úd had had a reason for not frequenting 'Alí's assembly—he was on the worst of terms with Ibn Ṣá'id: probably he was jealous of his reputation, which was superior to his own. Later, when 'Alí was powerful, he once caused the two old Traditionists to meet at his house, and tried to patch up a peace between them—but in vain. "O Abú Bakr," he said to Ibn Abí Dá'úd, "Abú Muḥammad is your elder, but you do not rise to him." "Nor shall I," answered Ibn Abí Dá'úd; and when 'Alí went on to persuade him of Ibn Ṣá'id's worth, he cried: "This *shaykh* belies the Apostle of God!... You think that I shall give in to you for the sake of the allowance that I receive at your hands. By God, I shall take nothing at your hands!" And Ibn Abí

1 Abú'l-Qásim 'Abd Allah ibn Muḥammad, b. 214 (829–30), d. 317 (929–30).

2 Dh. *ṭab.* Series x, No. 82; S.J. fol. 95 a; *fih.* 233.

3 Abú Muḥammad Yaḥyà ibn Muḥammad, b. 228 (842–3), d. 318 (930–1).

4 Dh. *ṭab.* Series x, No. 109; S.J. fol. 98 a; Tagh. II, 241.

5 Abú Bakr 'Abd Allah ibn Sulaymán ibn al-Ash'ath, b. 230 (844–5), d. 316 (928–9).

Dá'úd kept so strictly to the letter of his oath that for the rest of his life his allowance had to be sent to him direct from the Caliph by a eunuch.[1]

I can only guess at the other members of 'Alí's circle. The great historian and commentator aṭ-Ṭabarí was probably one of them, at least after the year 290 (903), when he returned to Baghdád from a brief visit to his native Caspian. At any rate he would have been a very welcome guest, with his great beard and his exquisite table-manners; and as he composed a short work on jurisprudence for al-'Abbás ibn al-Ḥasan during his Vizierate, he was evidently well known at this time in ministerial society.

Aṭ-Ṭabarí[2] had shown peculiar promise as quite a small child—at seven he knew the *qur'án* by heart, at eight he recited the public prayers, and at nine he was already writing Traditions. He was renowned for his extraordinary industry—on his death it was said that he had written forty pages a day for forty years. He was reputed to know as much as a specialist in many and diverse branches of learning—unlike 'Alí's Traditionist friends he was versed not only in the *qur'ánic* sciences, but, of the native, in Poetry and Grammar, and of the foreign or Greek sciences, in Arithmetic, Algebra and Logic. Yet throughout his life he kept this characteristic from his early training in the Sháfi'ite school: he would never accept public office. He was loath indeed to accept any kind of gift or reward, unless he could return the donor its equivalent; and once when he had given al-Muktafí expert advice on drawing up the deeds of a pious foundation, the only recompense he would consider was an order that on Fridays beggars should be kept out of the court-

1 S.J. fol. 88 a; Dh. *ṭab*, Series x, No. 108; *fih.* 232; Tagh. II, 235.

2 Abú Ja'far Muḥammad ibn Jarír, b. 224 or 225 (839), d. 310 (922–3).

yard of his mosque. It is, of course, to aṭ-Ṭabarí that we owe a great part of our knowledge of the early history of Islam.[1]

Aṭ-Ṭabarí was a pupil of az-Za'faráni,[2] possibly a fellow-pupil of 'Alí ibn 'Ísà. He was certainly well acquainted with 'Alí later in their lives,[3] as I shall have occasion to report. And so was his devoted reader and pupil Aḥmad ibn Kámil, sometime *qádhí* of al-Kúfah, who may likewise have been present at these gatherings. For Ibn Kámil, who long survived them both,[4] afterwards vouched for the details of 'Alí's income, both when he was in and when he was out of office.[5] Another follower of aṭ-Ṭabarí's, but one of whom nothing else, as far as I know, is recorded, dedicated a treatise to 'Alí. His name was 'Alí ibn 'Abd al-'Azíz ad-Dúlábí.[6]

A man notable in the society of Baghdád, with whom 'Alí was acquainted, was the *naqíb al-ashráf*, the Chancellor of the Nobility, a certain Ibn Ṭúmár.[7] The *naqíb* was the official head of the Prophet's family, to which he bore the relation of a chief to his tribe. Sometimes there was one *naqíb* for the 'Abbásids and one for the 'Alids; but Ibn Ṭúmár was *naqíb* for both. The man chosen for the office was usually the noblest and most respected of the whole family. His office was to keep a register of all its living members, noticing punctually all births and deaths among them; to see that all members conducted themselves as became their high

1 Yáq. *ud.* VI, 423 *et seqq.*; *fih.* 234; Sub. *ṭab.* I, fol. 252 a–b.

2 Yáq. *ud.* VI, 433.

3 Cf. Yáq. *ud.* VI, 461–2, where 'Alí sends a physician to attend him.

4 He died in 350 (961–2).

5 Ath. (Tornberg), VIII, 399; *fih.* 32, 35, 235; Yáq. *ud.* VI, 423 *et seqq.*; Dh. *t.* fol. 289 a.

6 *fih.* 235.

7 Abú'l-'Abbás Aḥmad ibn 'Abd aṣ-Ṣamad (or 'Abd al-'Azíz), the Háshimite, b. about 219 (834–5), d. 301 (914). 'A. 40, 47; Ham. *tak.* fol. 14 a.

station, and that members' widows married their equals; to judge criminal cases in which members were involved, and civil cases arising between them, admonish but not punish corporally those proved to be in the wrong, and support and represent members engaged in ordinary litigation. He had also to supervise the administration of pious bequests made in the family's favour, administer the estates of members minor, and care for such as were insane or otherwise incapable.[1] At this time Ibn Ṭúmár was already an old man of about seventy, but he was to hold his office for some years yet. It was he that was able later to state, when asked, why 'Alí ibn 'Ísà, after he had become Vizier, no longer held these gatherings at his house.[2]

'Alí wrote at least three, perhaps four, books; and in one of them, a treatise on the significations and vocalisation of the *qur'án*, with a commentary, he collaborated with two persons that must certainly have frequented his assembly.[3]

The more celebrated of the two was the Chief Reader (of the *qur'án*), Abú Bakr Ibn Mujáhid.[4] Ibn Mujáhid's knowledge of the sacred text, on which he had written several works, was considered by a famous grammarian of the time to be unequalled by that of any contemporary; his feeling for grammatical points was of the most refined. His classes, for the conduct of which he employed forty assistants, were attended by three hundred eminent scholars; and he was high in favour for his piety with the Royal Family. He was also an extremely amiable companion. He was a skilled musician and singer. Moreover, despite the solemnity of his calling he had a marked bent for joking—he declared gravity at a garden party to be no less out of place than levity in a mosque. It was only when his

1 Von Kremer: *Culturgeschichte*, I, 448–50.
2 Yáq. *ud.* v, 279. 3 *fih.* 129; Yáq. *ud.* v, 277.
4 Aḥmad ibn Músà, b. 245 (859–60), d. 324 (935–6).

professional supremacy was assailed that he grew fierce. Then he could be very sarcastic with upstarts that claimed to be Readers. Later he secured the adoption, as the sole permissible version, of the *qur'án* of the Caliph 'Uthmán; and procured the condemnation of two doctors that preferred readings from other older texts.[1]

The humbler of 'Alí's collaborators—yet the one to whom the work owed most—was a certain Abú'l-Ḥusayn, known as *al-khazzáz* (the raw-silk merchant) of Wásiṭ.[2] This personage was a grammarian by profession, having studied in both the rival schools of al-Baṣrah and al-Kúfah. 'Alí employed him as a tutor for his sons—'Ísà, the younger, later communicated Traditions on his authority.[3] He was also a caligraphist and the author of some eight books. Four of these seem to have been on linguistic subjects, three on religious and one, composed for a friend of 'Alí's,[4] historical.[5]

'Alí's other books, apart from his letters, which were published, were: first, a collection of prayers; second, a work entitled *The Book of Secretaries, the Governance of Kingdoms and the Lives of the Caliphs*; and third (if this was really his), a geographical treatise on the province of Fárs.[6] None of his writings appear to be in existence.

Other members of 'Alí's household, both recognised Traditionists, were Abú Sahl al-Qaṭṭán and Abú Bakr

1 Yáq. *ud.* II, 116 *et seqq.*; *fih.* 31; Tagh. II, 278; Khall. I, 27, note from the *tabaqát ash-sháfi'iyyah*; An. *nuz.* 338 *et seqq*; S.J. fol. 112 b; Dh. *t.* fol. 162 b; Massignon: *Al-Hallaj*, 241 *et seqq.*

2 'Abd Allah ibn Muḥammad, d. 315 (927–8) or 326 (937–8).

3 It is possible, but improbable, that 'Alí's father and not his son is here meant by 'Ísà ibn al-Jarráḥ, but see S.J. fol. 116 b.

4 Abú'l-Ḥusayn, son of the *qáḍhí* Abú 'Umar.

5 *fih.* 82; Ath. (Tornberg), VIII, 254; Dh. *t.* fol. 169 a; S.J. fol. 116 b.

6 *fih.* 129; Yáq. *ud.* V, 277; Ṣaf. (B.M. Or. 6587), fol. 132 b; Ḥ. Kh. V. 509–10.

ash-Sháfi'í. The former, Abú Sahl[1]—originally from al-Mattúthah, a place between Wásiṭ and al-Ahwáz—was a man of exemplary piety: tireless in fasting and watching and praying and in receiving and handing on Traditions, he had repeated the *qur'án* from end to end so often that it was as if a copy lay open perpetually before him. But his piety was somewhat marred in the eyes of the Orthodox by an inclination to Shí'ism; and it was also said that Abú Sahl had a defect of character—he was unscrupulous where relics of holy persons were concerned. He wrote verse, but of what sort we are not told. At present he was poor; but later with 'Alí's help he grew rich and went to live in a handsome house in the Dár al-Qaṭan on the west bank—whence, presumably, his surname.[2] Abú Bakr ash-Sháfi'í,[3] so called from his being a light of the Sháfi'ite school, was the son of a money-changer or banker. He was one of the chief Sháfi'ite theologians and dialecticians of his time, being held by the school to have surpassed in his knowledge of the fundamentals of religion everyone but its founder, ash-Sháfi'í, himself. He was an admirable writer, with (at the time of his death) five books to his credit, all on theological subjects. He was firmly attached to 'Alí ibn 'Ísà, and appears actually to have lived with him for many years.[4]

Here I may add the names of two persons that are reported to have heard Traditions from 'Alí: Abú Ṭáhir al-Hudhalí and Abú'l-Qásim Sulaymán ibn

1 Aḥmad ibn Muḥammad, b. 259 (872–3), d. 350 (961–2).

2 Tagh. II, 357; Yáq. *ud.* VI, 306, *et seqq.*; Yáq. *mu'jam*, IV, 412; Tan. *farj.* II, 14; H. 347; S.J. fol. 138 a; Dh. *t.* ff. 224 b and 289 a–b.

3 Muḥammad ibn 'Abd Allah. Not to be confused with another Sháfi'ite of precisely the same name and *kunyah*, of whom notices are given by as-Sam'ání: *kitáb al-ansáb*, fol. 326 a, Dh. *t.* (B.M. Or. 48), fol. 41 b, and Dh. *ṭab.* Series XII, No. 1. 'Alí's Abú Bakr died in 330 (941–2), whereas the other, who was a Traditionist, born in 260 (873–4), died only in 354 (965).

4 *fih.* 213; Sub. *ṭab.* fol. 269 b. See H. 224, 330, 334; and Tan. *nish.* 47–8, 225.

Aḥmad aṭ-Ṭabarání.[1] I have been unable to discover anything about the former. Aṭ-Ṭabarání (his surname means man of Tiberias) was the author of a Dictionary of Traditionists that appeared in three editions. He died at Iṣfahán in the year 360 (971).[2]

But adept as all these guests of 'Alí's were in the rehearsal of Traditions, the subject cannot always have engaged their attention. Aṭ-Ṭabárí, as I have mentioned, was equally well versed in various branches of what were known as the foreign, or Greek, sciences; and there is evidence to show that 'Alí was interested in them himself—and also in what was equally outside the purview of the narrowly Orthodox: foreign religions. 'Alí had at least one friend that was a notable translator of medical and philosophical works, the physician Abú 'Uthmán Sa'íd ibn Ya'qúb of Damascus,[3] to whom when first in power he confided the care of a hospital. Moreover, he afterwards caused his own son 'Ísà to be instructed in all the "Greek" learning, so that the latter became celebrated for his proficiency in these subjects, particularly in Logic.[4] From a passage in Yáqút's *Dictionary of Learned Men*[5] it might be concluded that 'Alí himself was schooled in Logic—but I do not feel sure that it is he, and not another 'Alí ibn 'Ísà (perhaps ar-Rummání),[6] that is there referred to. A short work on Logic was certainly composed for him, probably some years later, by the Egyptian Ibn ad-Dáyah.[7] As for his interest in strange religions, it is recorded that a learned Jew, the author of a translation of and commentary on the Pentateuch, used to dispute on matters touching their faith with his co-

1 Tagh. II, 312.
2 Khald. *Pro.* II, 159.
3 *fih.* 298.
4 Qif. 244; Ath. (Tornberg), IX, 119; Dh. *t.* fol. 227 b.
5 Yáq. *ud.* III, 102.
6 A Mu'tazilite grammarian, b. 296 (908–9), d. 384 (994–5). *fih.* 63–4; Yáq. *ud.* V, 280 *et seqq.*
7 Aḥmad ibn Yúsuf, d. about 340 (951–2). Yáq. *ud.* II, 160.

religionists in 'Alí's assembly;[1] and also that a friend of 'Alí's, when *qádhí* at Ḥarrán, caused an Arabic version of a work explaining the so-called Sabian religion to be prepared for his special benefit.[2]

But whatever the theme of discussion, before long it must generally have been interrupted by what the Arabs, or speakers of Arabic, are ready to illustrate anything with—poetry. Aṣ-Ṣúlí states that he could remember no one more profoundly versed in poetry than 'Alí ibn 'Ísà.[3] 'Alí was an occasional poet himself. He must certainly have counted poets among his visitors.

Al-Buḥturí,[4] for many years official panegyrist, most famed for his anthology, the *Ḥamásah*, but still a respectable poet, had written many an ode in praise of 'Alí's cousins, al-Ḥasan, Ṣá'id and 'Abdún, the sons of Makhlad.[5] But by now, by the late eighties and early nineties of the third century, al-Buḥturí was dead, as was also the poet friend of Muḥammad ibn Dá'úd, Ibn ar-Rúmí. The most illustrious of living poets, and indeed one of the most illustrious of the whole 'Abbásid period, was a first cousin of al-Mu'taḍhid himself, the Prince 'Abd Allah, son of the unlucky Caliph al-Mu'tazz. His *díwán*,[6] that is, his collected poems, is extant and contains many charming pieces, including one that is peculiar as being the only attempt at an epic in the language. In it he praises, in a form (unusual in itself) approximating to the rhymed couplet, the deeds of al-Muwaffaq in restoring the empire; his favourite theme, however, was wine and its drinking. To a fine and original talent and a cultivated taste Ibn al-Mu'tazz (he is generally known by this

1 Mas. *tan.* 113. 2 *fih.* 327.
3 Yáq. *ud.* v, 278; Dháf. fol. 139 b.
4 Abú 'Ubádah al-Walíd ibn 'Ubayd, b. about 204 (819), d. 284 (897).
5 See his *díwán*, ed. Constantinople, 1883.
6 Ed. Cairo, 1891.

name) had added a profound learning, acquired in part from the two best grammarians of the age; his style combines eloquence with simplicity. Besides his poems he wrote a book on verse, and chose an anthology of wine poetry; and he was also a composer of musical pieces. In appearance he was long-faced, of a deep tawny complexion, with a beard dyed black. He was an intimate friend of the Banú'l-Jarráḥ; and the fortunes of Muḥammad ibn Dá'úd were to be all too closely bound up with his.[1]

Another poet of 'Alí's acquaintance was Abú Bakr aṣ-Ṣúlí,[2] whose estimate of his poetical knowledge I have just noted. Aṣ-Ṣúlí was a man of many talents; as a poet he was chiefly concerned to produce occasional Court pieces. He was deeply learned in literary matters and delighted also in the appearance of books; in his library he had the volumes bound in various coloured leathers, red, blue or yellow, according to their contents. He was the author of at least two historical works, of which one has survived as a whole and the other in the quotation by other writers of many passages. His family, which was originally from Gurgán, a province on the east coast of the Caspian Sea, where his ancestors had been kings, had been connected with the 'Abbásids ever since the foundation of the dynasty. Though he had been at Court since the reign of al-Mu'tamid, he first made his fortune with al-Muktafí by beating the latter's favourite player at chess. His play became famous—a later Caliph declared that it was more beautiful to behold than the loveliest garden of the palace; and he wrote a book on the game, in which he enumerated six different kinds of boards and methods of play. Both his grandfather and great-uncle had been prominent at Court; and the latter, when he held a post in an

1 Khall. II, 41 *et seqq.*; *Encyclopédie*, II, 431, *s.v.*
2 Muḥammad ibn Yaḥyà, d. 335 (946–7).

administration, had engaged 'Alí's grandfather Dá'úd and *his* great-uncle Ibrahím, as well as his cousin al-Ḥasan ibn Makhlad, to act as his secretaries. I have quoted aṣ-Ṣúlí's general opinion of 'Alí, given of course much later, at the beginning of this book.[1]

There were two other poets of the time with whom 'Alí had relations, but relations less definitely amicable. The first of these was the satirist Ibn Bassám,[2] a most irritable and dangerous person. Satire had always been cultivated by the Arab poets—in desert life a tribe used the utterances of its satirist (if it was lucky enough to own one) as weapons in feuds with its neighbours, the poets of rival tents competing in vituperation. Ibn Bassám's method, suited to a more civilised society—of course he was only following the example of others—was to intimidate the great, by making them look foolish or seem hateful, into giving him money or employment; and though on one occasion he narrowly escaped having his tongue cut out by al-Qásim ibn 'Ubayd Allah, he was generally successful. Afterwards, more than once, 'Alí was to come in for his share of abuse from Ibn Bassám. At present, however (whilst 'Alí had comparatively little favour at his command), the poet seems to have been well disposed.[3]

The other poet was the blind Abú Bakr ibn al-'Alláf;[4] and in connection with him a story is told of 'Alí that seems quite incredible, so little characteristic of him does his part in it appear. 'Alí, we are told, had a slave-girl, whom a page of Ibn al-'Alláf's fell in love with and ravished. 'Alí then slew them both and stuffed their bodies with straw. Ibn al-'Alláf, stricken

1 *fih.* 150–1, 156; Mas. *murúj*, VIII, 220, 238, 311, 339; Fid. II, 96; An. *nuz.* 344; Dh. *t.* fol. 230 a; S.J. fol. 139 b.

2 'Alí ibn Muḥammad ibn Naṣr, b. 230 (844–5), d. after 306 (919)?

3 *fih.* 150; Mas. *murúj*, VIII, 216, 256 *et seqq.*; Yáq. *ud.* v, 318 *et seqq.*; Dh. *t.* fol. 19 a.

4 al-Ḥasan ibn 'Alí, d. 318 (930–1).

with grief, composed an elegy on the loss of his favourite; but since 'Alí had acted in a way perfectly proper and permissible, he was obliged to mask its real meaning by seeming to bemoan not a man but a cat. Ibn al-'Alláf's reputation as a poet rests chiefly on this Elegy to the Cat (he was even nicknamed the Cat after it). 'Alí's murder of his page, however, is only one of four pretexts suggested for its composition. The poet himself declared that he was mourning a real cat that neighbours had killed for stalking their pigeons; but afterwards first Ibn al-Mu'tazz, and later Ibn al-Furát's son, al-Muḥassin, was said to be the victim alluded to.[1]

The ground in front of the Báb al-Bustán sloped unevenly and muddily down to the water's edge; whereas the houses on either side were provided with new brickwork dykes that formed a convenient landing place for river travellers. Al-Mukharrim being one of the busiest parts of the town, every yard of these dykes was rented by boatmen, who in the scarcity of bridges and the habitual use of the river as a thoroughfare, plied a busy trade, and kept their skiffs moored alongside. To Ibrahím it was a source of sorrow that his brother's new residence should not reap the profit of such an embankment, and he besought him to undertake its construction. But 'Alí, to whom expenditure of any kind was apt to seem unnecessary, prevaricated: when an estimate of the cost had been made out, he would see. The estimate was soon forthcoming; but 'Alí doubted whether he could afford it at present. His estates, however, soon yielded the required amount; Ibrahím was sure of his dyke, and came to urge its setting up before the spring floods. 'Alí laughed, and turning to his steward he said, "O Abú'l-Qásim, tell him the tale of the property we have bought, and how

1 Fid. II, 75; Dh. *t.* fol. 112 b; Khall. I, 398 *et seqq.*

it excels in profit that building whose architect God would have increased only in reprobation and banishment!" To his brother's vexation 'Alí had characteristically squandered the amount on deserving members of the Prophet's family and indigent believers.[1]

1 H. 287–8.

CHAPTER VIII

The death of al-Muktafí. *The accession of* al-Muqtadir. *The conspiracy of* Ibn al-Mu'tazz.

Late in the spring of the year 295 (908), at the early age of thirty-two, the sickly Caliph fell very seriously ill; and it soon became evident that he had but a short time to live. He had no less than nine sons,[1] but none of them was of an age to ascend the throne. The question of the succession, therefore, was even less straightforward than usual.

It had been a fatal moment for the 'Abbásid Caliphate when 'Alí ibn 'Ísà refused the Vizierate on the death of al-Qásim ibn 'Ubayd Allah. For the choice of a new Caliph lay in practice with the Vizier: and now, consequently, it fell to al-'Abbás ibn al-Ḥasan, who was utterly unprincipled, to make the all-too-momentous decision. Again it had been a fatal moment when in the foolish war of the secretaries al-'Abbás sided with Ibn al-Furát. For now al-'Abbás, having himself no definite views about the succession, consulted indeed all the Secretaries of State, but hearkened only to the advice of his favourite.

He began by consulting them singly, as each day one of them accompanied him from his house to the palace; and discovered that whereas Muḥammad ibn Dá'úd and Ibn 'Abdún favoured one of the eligible princes, Ibn al-Furát favoured another. 'Alí for the present kept his own counsel: he insisted only that the Caliph must be one that feared God and respected the precepts of religion. Muḥammad ibn Dá'úd and Ibn 'Abdún wished for the promotion of their friend, the poet-prince, 'Abd Allah ibn al-Mu'tazz; and this

1 'A. 21.

not only for personal reasons, though these no doubt were strong, but because Ibn al-Mu'tazz might indeed be expected, versed as he was in finance and statesmanship, to make an exemplary Caliph. But the very reasons that prompted them to support him, prompted Ibn al-Furát to oppose him. Not only was a prince that sided with them likely to side against him; his very accomplishments, especially his experience of business, were not all to the minister's taste. His ideal was a Caliph that would do as he was told, that would refrain from interference and importunate enquiry. And just such a prince was to hand in al-Muktafí's thirteen year-old half-brother, al-Mu'tadhid's son Ja'far.

Ibn al-Furát was perfectly frank with al-'Abbás ibn al-Ḥasan, and pointed out that their interests were identical. If al-'Abbás wished indeed to rule, he had only to set up Ja'far. At first Ja'far would be so delighted at being excused from learning his lessons, that he would think of nothing else; and by the time that he was old enough to assert himself, al-'Abbás would have made himself so beloved that he would be indispensable. On the other hand, Ibn al-Furát reminded the Vizier that he had every reason, just as Ibn al-Furát had himself, for fearing the elevation of Ibn al-Mu'tazz. For years the prince had been asking them favours, and they had ignored them: if he were now to become Caliph, the least they could expect was neglect.[1]

To begin with, al-'Abbás seems to have fallen in with the plan of Muḥammad ibn Dá'úd. He and others that Muḥammad had won over to his point of view even appear to have approached Ibn al-Mu'tazz, and to have sworn allegiance to him in secret.[2] The prognostications of Ibn al-Furát, however, filled the Vizier with alarm, and he began to repent of what he had done. He doubted indeed the wisdom of placing

1 H. 114–15; M. 1, 2–3. 2 'A. 25.

a sovereign so young as Ja'far on the throne; but there were other princes, of a more suitable age, that yet bore him no grudge. Once, when al-Muktafí lay unconscious, al-'Abbás went so far as to enter into an understanding with one of these princes, a son of al-Mu'tamid; but al-Muktafí made a temporary recovery, and not long after the Caliph-to-be, enraged at the way in which he was addressed by the Chief of Police, had a fatal apoplectic seizure. The Vizier had no better fortune with another candidate, a son of al-Mutawakkil: and the only result of these subterranean negotiations was to make al-Muktafí suspicious.[1] He was particularly anxious that the Caliphate should remain in his father's branch of the Royal Family. He hoped to ensure its doing so by summoning the chief *qádhís*, and causing them to witness that he formally elected Ja'far his heir.

After three months of alternate relapse and recovery al-Muktafí definitely took a turn for the worse; and now al-'Abbás was constrained to discuss the matter of the succession with the four principal secretaries in his assembly, after the day's work was over. At length one afternoon, when it seemed certain that the Caliph could not survive the coming night, the Vizier announced that they must not part without having come to a decision. He therefore invited each of the secretaries in turn to speak his mind. Muḥammad ibn Dá'úd had never relinquished any of his fervour in the cause of Ibn al-Mu'tazz. He again urged the appointment of a capable Caliph. And now 'Alí supported him, arguing that though they were all creatures of al-Mu'tadhid and after him of al-Muktafí, the choice of

1 M. I, 4 states that this occurred after Ja'far's accession, when al-'Abbás repented of having made him Caliph; but 'A. 21 gives the month of its occurrence as *ramadhán*, and this can only be that of the year 295. Al-Muktafí had fallen ill the month before. By *ramadhán* of the next year al-'Abbás was no longer alive.

a Caliph was a matter of religious principle. Let them choose "this *shaykh*", he said, referring to Ibn al-Mu'tazz, that had made the Pilgrimage and was known for his righteousness and zeal, to address whom as "Commander of the Faithful" would be no exaggeration. Ibn al-Furát, however, held no less to his original idea. He again put forward his plea for a puppet Caliph, tempting the Vizier with the prospect of absolute power.

The shamelessness of his opportunism shocked the pious 'Alí. When they were leaving, he overtook Ibn al-Furát in a by-street and seized him by the hand. He swore that he himself was only seeking to do right, whereas Ibn al-Furát had clearly a less estimable object in so counselling al-'Abbás. Ibn al-Furát admitted that he had been guided by worldly considerations; but maintained that with a too knowledgeable Caliph none of them would be safe. 'Alí retorted prophetically: "By God, if the matter end thus and be so arranged, not you alone shall suffer in the dire consequence, so beware!"[1]

Al-'Abbás, however, was far from being shocked by the arguments of Ibn al-Furát: he found them most persuasive, and when the time came for action, he accepted them. What he most feared in the idea of promoting Ja'far was the people's probable objection to his youth (for no Caliph had ever succeeded so young); but Ibn al-Furát had reassured him. All would be well, he said, if the people were presented with an accomplished fact. He had only to send one of al-Mu'tadhid's retainers, who were all interested in bringing about the accession of Ja'far, to fetch him privately to the palace from the House of Ṭáhir, the mansion across the river where the young princes were lodged, and there proclaim him. Any opposition would be stifled by an opportune distribution to the

1 H. 126–7.

troops of the money customarily given them on an accession.[1]

The task of escorting Ja'far secretly to the palace was entrusted to al-Mu'tadhid's most confidential servant, the Chief Eunuch and Keeper of the Harem,[2] Ṣáfí. Al-Muktafí died in the evening, and whilst it was still night Ṣáfí crossed the river and took the young prince into his barge. To reach the palace they had to pass the house of the Vizier; and as they came within hail of it in the darkness, his men-at-arms cried out to the boatman to turn in. Ṣáfí, however, feared that the Vizier had once again changed his mind; and being determined to effect the accession of Ja'far, drew his sword and threatened to behead the boatman, unless he rowed straight on to the palace. It thus came about that Ja'far was made Caliph, with the title *al-muqtadir bi'llah* (Mighty in God); and that when the Vizier reached the palace with his son, he found that there was no longer any choice to be made.[3]

Ja'far was Caliph; but Ibn al-Furát's prophecy, that the distribution of the accession money would check all opposition, failed to come true. All the secretaries were confirmed in their positions under the new *régime*; but this, if it was intended to do so, did not conciliate Muḥammad ibn Dá'úd and Ibn 'Abdún. They were enraged at the Vizier's treachery in breaking his oath to Ibn al-Mu'tazz, and setting up Ja'far; yet they did not despair even now of gaining their end,

1 H. 116.

2 I take *ḥuramí* or *ḥaramí* to mean this. Cf. Tagh. II, 183–4: "Nadhír *al-ḥaramí* was then put as deputy over the harem in the Caliph's palace". See also Tan. *nish.* 140, where it is Ṣáfí that accompanies al-Mu'tadhid to the harem. H. 116 gives the honour of bringing Ja'far to the palace to Mu'nis. But the passage occurs in a tale told long after, when Mu'nis was famous and Ṣáfí, who died in 298 (911), forgotten. The time-table of this tale, moreover, is clearly inexact.

3 M. I, 3–4; 'A. 22.

and began plotting for Ja'far's deposition. Ibn al-Mu'tazz was still ready to play his part. He only stipulated, as indeed he had done from the first, that his accession should be brought about without bloodshed. 'Alí, for his part, was no more than lukewarm in his enthusiasm for the project. As one of the family, however, he certainly lent his support.

The conspirators calculated that whereas Ja'far's strength lay only in the retainers of al-Mu'tadhid, they had behind them the public opinion of Baghdád. In any case their chances were improved by the foolish behaviour of the Vizier. Al-'Abbás had grown quite insupportable in his new omnipotence. He offended the courtiers by his arrogant manner and the pomp he affected; he alienated the people by neglecting to hear their complaints. Also he won for the conspirators a valuable ally in al-Ḥusayn ibn Ḥamdán, an Arab chieftain of Mosul and an experienced officer, by attempting an intrigue with his favourite slave-girl.

Besides Muḥammad ibn Dá'úd and Ibn 'Abdún, a ringleader in the plot was a certain *qádhí* known as Abú'l-Muthannà;[1] and Abú 'Umar, the son and colleague of the Chief *qádhí*, was also with them. They had won over to their view a number of important officers and officials;[2] and their intentions were kept safely secret. At length, when al-Muqtadir had reigned some four months, the first move was made. As they were riding to his garden outside the city, the Vizier and a companion who attempted to defend him were set upon and killed by a number of the officers, led by al-Ḥusayn ibn Ḥamdán. The assassins then made off as fast as they could for the polo-ground under the walls, where they expected to find the young Caliph at play. By this time, however, the alarm was up: Ja'far raced for the palace at the first warning, and was soon secure behind locked doors.

1 Ṭab. III, 2282. 2 Lists are given in H. 88 and 235.

Al-Ḥusayn wasted no time by trying to force his way in. Instead he galloped off to the conspirators' rendezvous in al-Mukharrim. Al-Muqtadir's deposition was forthwith declared; and Ibn al-Mu'tazz was brought from his house across the river, and proclaimed Caliph in the Palace of the Viziers. He at once appointed Muḥammad ibn Dá'úd as his Vizier, and gave the *díwáns* to 'Alí ibn 'Ísà, and their Controls, or Registries, to Ibn 'Abdún. A proclamation of his accession was issued for the provinces, and Ja'far was instructed to quit the Ḥasaní Palace and make room for his successor.[1]

It was noticed, when all the partisans were gathered together, that neither 'Alí ibn 'Ísà nor Ibn al-Furát was present. Ibn al-Mu'tazz supposed that 'Alí hung back from base prudence. "'Alí ibn 'Ísà holds back from us," he said, "that he may pass over to Ja'far. If *he* wins, he will save his uncle; if *we* win, his uncle will save him." The absence of Ibn al-Furát he accounted very ominous for disaster.[2] When news of the revolution was brought to aṭ-Ṭabarí, and he learnt that Muḥammad ibn Dá'úd was to be Vizier and Abú'l-Muthannà Chief *qádhí*, he sat silent a while, thinking. Then he said, "This is an affair that will not succeed": he considered both judge and minister advanced beyond their deserts, and inadequate, in such a time of political stress, to their tasks.[3]

Ja'far was prepared to accept his deposition and agreed to leave the palace next day. His retainers, however, were unwilling to give in without a fight. When therefore al-Ḥusayn came down next morning to take charge, his entry was opposed, and though he and his men fought till noon with the defenders, their position in the fortress was so unassailable, that in the end he decided to give up the attack and withdraw.

1 M. I, 5–6; 'A. 27.
2 H. 137.
3 Tagh. II, 174.

Without warning the conspirators, he assembled his family and followers, and fled from the city towards his native Mosul.

A chief part in the defence of the Ḥasaní had been taken by one of al-Mu'taḍhid's eunuchs, Mu'nis by name; and now he lost no time in following up this advantage. Ibn al-Mu'tazz was giving audience in the Palace of the Viziers all unaware of the course events had taken, when some of his courtiers, who were enjoying the air outside on the embankment, were suddenly astonished to perceive a swarm of small war-boats descending upon them. Before they could give the alarm they were enveloped in a hail of arrows, and in a moment the whole palace was thrown into the utmost confusion.

Unlike the adherents of Ja'far, those of Ibn al-Mu'tazz gave up all for lost forthwith. The conspirators fled each to his own retreat without even waiting for Mu'nis and his men to land. Only Muḥammad ibn Dá'úd and the Chamberlain remained with the Pretender, and after hurriedly taking counsel, they decided to make from the city in the direction of Sámarrá, in the hope that their armed supporters would follow them. They set out, but it soon became clear that any such hope was empty. Muḥammad ibn Dá'úd accordingly dismounted at his house, whilst Ibn al-Mu'tazz fled on foot to the Tigris, and took a boat to the house of a rich man he knew to be his friend.

In the general confusion Ibn 'Abdún and 'Alí ibn 'Ísà, who had put in a belated appearance at Court on the second day, escaped together and sought refuge with a greengrocer. Their choice of a protector, however, was unhappy, for the man afterwards betrayed them to the mob. The mob handed them over to one of al-Muqtadir's eunuchs that was passing by, and the eunuch set them together on his pack-mule. The people jeered and hooted at them, as they were driven to the palace in this ignominious position; and on their arrival they were confined, both in a state of abject terror, with such others of the faction as had not pleaded coercion as an excuse for their share in the plot.[1]

It thus came about that the obstacles to al-Muqtadir's Caliphate were for a second time overcome. Ibn al-Athír reflects on the strange failure of the conspiracy. "All the people," he writes, "were determined on the deposition of al-Muqtadir and the succession of Ibn al-Mu'tazz. Yet was that not brought to pass, but rather the contrary of their wish. So was God's will fulfilled."[2] The people, however, made the best of this reversal of their hopes—if such indeed it was—by looting with equal zest the houses of the murdered al-'Abbás ibn al-Ḥasan and the fallen Muḥammad ibn Dá'úd.

1 'A. 27–8; M. I, 6–7; H. 88, 235.
2 Ath. (Búláq), VIII, 6.

CHAPTER IX

The Fate of the Conspirators.

The most urgent need was now for a new Vizier: and Ibn al-Furát, as the only one of the four secretaries that had taken no part in the plot, was clearly the most suitable person for the position. A messenger was accordingly sent to fetch him; but he had hidden himself so effectually from the conspirators, whom he still supposed victorious, that it was evening before he could be found and brought to the palace. He was invested next morning by the young Caliph, and rode home in his robes of office. At the same time money was again distributed among the troops as if for a second accession.

Al-Muqtadir's triumph was completed by the capture of Ibn al-Mu'tazz. The unfortunate prince was betrayed by a eunuch of the household in which he had taken refuge. He was at once arrested and taken to the palace; and there, in the night, he was killed. Next day his body, wrapped in a horse-blanket, was handed over to his relations; and it was disingenuously given out that he had died a natural death.[1]

Muḥammad ibn Dá'úd hid successfully for some time. Ibn al-Furát offered a large reward for his capture; but Muḥammad soon had occasion to discover that the new Vizier, generously forgetting their difference in his present misfortune, was in reality well-disposed. An acquaintance, with whom he had passed a night, betrayed his hiding-place; but before setting the police to surround the house, Ibn al-Furát contrived to warn him, and he was able to escape. This magnanimity encouraged Muhammad to approach him,

1 'A. 28–9; M. 1, 7–8; H. 23.

and he succeeded in conveying a note to his assembly. In answer he received a message by word of mouth (writing being dangerous in these times), counselling him to remain hidden for at least four months till the excitement had died down. The Vizier would then work for his pardon with the Caliph.

Muḥammad was disappointed with this advice. He foolishly suspected that Ibn al-Furát was after all seeking to harm him, and in his dejection he fell the more easily into a trap that had been laid for him. He had two eager enemies at Court, to wit, the Chief Eunuch, Ṣáfí, and the Chamberlain, Sawsan; and they had prevailed with threats on a certain near friend and fellow-townsman of Muḥammad's, a Christian, to deliver him into their hands. It appears that this Christian was cowardly enough to persuade Muḥammad of the Chamberlain's goodwill, and that in his despondent mood Muḥammad believed him. He came openly to the Chamberlain's quarters, and was at once arrested —or, according to another account, he was waylaid as he set out.

He was confined in a prison with the two *qáḍhís* that had joined in the plot, Abú 'Umar and Abú'l-Muthannà. The room was divided in three by wooden partitions to form cells, into one of which each of them was locked. The chinks in the woodwork allowed them to talk, and they speculated miserably on their chances of life. All day they expected death; but when night fell and outside noises were stilled, they took hope. At length in the small hours they heard the sound of distant keys turning in locks, and in a moment the prison was brilliant with the light of torches. The door of Muḥammad's cell was opened: he was dragged out and made to lie down. He expostulated with the jailer at being allowed no chance of expiating his crime with payments. "Will you cut my throat like a sheep's?" he cried. But the man would not listen to his pleas, and without more ado struck off his head. His body was then stripped and thrown into the well. The party marched off and the prison was left once again in darkness.

Of the two *qádhís*, Abú'l-Muthannà, who refused to recant his conviction that Ja'far was too young to be Caliph, suffered a like fate; but the sight of the two executions, which he watched from his cell, so unnerved Abú 'Umar, that he admitted his error and was saved to tell the story. When he looked at himself afterwards in a looking-glass at the *ḥammám*, he saw that his hair had turned white from terror.[1]

Next day when he was in his assembly one of his retainers came in and whispered to Ibn al-Furát that Muḥammad ibn Dá'úd had been executed. At this the clerks observed that the Vizier fell silent and was sad; but at length he spoke. "In spite of his enmity towards me," he said, "he was a wise and much-gifted man....He was kind and generous, and in killing him a grievous thing has been done." He cursed the Christian that had betrayed him, saying, "The friendship between them was well known: but he has saved himself and killed his friend."[2]

Sawsan the Chamberlain appears to have borne a grudge against 'Alí as well as his uncle: he went about saying that they had been of one mind over the conspiracy. However, the half-hearted way in which 'Alí had taken part in it now stood him in good stead, since it provided Ibn al-Furát with an excuse for mitigating his punishment. 'Alí and Ibn 'Abdún were confined together; and from their prison they made a

1 Tan. *farj.* I, 120–1.

2 The account of Muḥammad ibn Dá'úd's capture and execution in *fih.* 128, retailed by Khall. II, 361, conflicts with this version, which is drawn from M. I, 9–12 and H. 25–6. It states that Muḥammad relied on Mu'nis the eunuch to save him, but that Ibn al-Furát feared him and insisted on his death.

joint petition to the Vizier, in the hope of moving his indulgence. But the answer that he returned, though it delighted 'Alí, terrified Ibn 'Abdún—for it was addressed only to the former. Ibn al-Furát expressed his affection for 'Alí and his determination to obtain his release; but his silence reminded Ibn 'Abdún of their ancient enmity, which it was clear the Vizier had neither forgotten nor forgiven. Ibn al-Furát assured the Caliph indeed that they had both been forced to take what part they had in the conspiracy: but whereas 'Alí was let off with a light fine, a very heavy one was imposed on Ibn 'Abdún; and though they were both banished from the capital, whereas 'Alí was sent only to Wásiṭ, Ibn 'Abdún was removed as far as al-Ahwáz. A very strict watch was kept on Ibn 'Abdún in his exile: he was permitted neither to send nor to receive letters. 'Alí, on the other hand, was treated by the governor of Wásiṭ, at the Vizier's command, with every consideration, and his wants were supplied at the Vizier's expense. Moreover, lest Sawsan should continue his campaign of calumny against 'Alí, Ibn al-Furát presented him, on 'Alí's behalf, with a substantial bribe.

Wásiṭ, which the caprice of the Tigris in changing its course has now reduced to absolute ruin, lay about a hundred and forty miles to the south-east of Baghdád, and was at this time the third most important city of al-'Iráq. 'Alí, however, was not to make it his abode for long, for within a short time of his arrival, he was dismayed by news from Baghdád, which caused him soon after to travel still farther afield. He learnt to his amazement that Ibn 'Abdún had been arrested for plotting—and for plotting with no less a personage than Sawsan the Chamberlain, who had already been executed.

Under al-Muktafí Sawsan had shared with al-'Abbás ibn al-Ḥasan the chief influence at Court; but on the accession of al-Muqtadir, when al-'Abbás became all-powerful, Sawsan, much to his annoyance, was thrust into the background. He had therefore engaged in the conspiracy of Ibn al-Mu'tazz in the hope of becoming Chamberlain to the Pretender; but on its temporary success he was disappointed, and while there was yet time went over again to Ja'far. With Ja'far's rehabilitation Sawsan was confirmed as Chamberlain, but he now found Ibn al-Furát in the place of al-'Abbás, and himself no better off than before. His only hope in this case was to bring about the fall of the new Vizier, and to set up in his place someone that he could count upon to obey him.

Sawsan had pursued Muḥammad ibn Dá'úd with such fury because he had supposed that it was through Muḥammad's influence that Ibn al-Mu'tazz had rejected him: and he appears to have disliked 'Alí ibn 'Ísà chiefly because he was Muḥammad's nephew. Ibn 'Abdún's, however, was a more distant relationship: and Sawsan was drawn to Ibn 'Abdún on account of his long-standing feud with Ibn al-Furát. Ibn 'Abdún was, to be sure, in exile at al-Ahwáz: but in the hope of preferment he would probably risk escape. Sawsan accordingly sent letters to him secretly; and Ibn 'Abdún, in his anxiety to be restored to favour, accepted his proposal.

At this point, however, Ibn al-Furát got wind of the conspiracy; and he had little difficulty, since there was every proof of it, in showing up Sawsan's guilt to al-Muqtadir. He described to him not only the aims of the present plot (which included the assassination, perhaps of the Caliph, certainly of the Vizier), but also Sawsan's share in the attempt of Ibn al-Mu'tazz. The young Caliph was greatly alarmed, and at once gave his consent to Sawsan's execution. In the meantime Ibn 'Abdún had made his escape from al-Ahwáz across country to the Tigris. But Ibn al-Furát was prepared for him: he was caught as he neared Baghdád, and imprisoned in the palace.

It was the news of his capture that so greatly perturbed 'Alí. As far as he knew, he might be in but little better odour himself. Wásiṭ seemed so uncomfortably near the capital, an ex-minister so uncomfortably conspicuous. At once he wrote to the Vizier a letter of excuse and entreaty. He repudiated any firm attachment to Ibn 'Abdún, but supposed him to have been innocent of any malicious design. If such a design there was, Sawsan, he was sure, must have been wholly responsible for it. He himself was eager only to retire from public life and be forgotten at Court. Let him depart from Wásiṭ and betake himself to Mecca. His reputation might then recover, as his piety would flourish.

His mediation arrived too late to take effect. Ibn 'Abdún had already been consigned to the Chief of Police: and some days later his dead body was found outside his house by his relations. But 'Alí's request for himself was answered. He was put in the charge of a guardian, one Ḥabashí ibn Isḥáq the Jailer, and sent first to al-Kúfah. From there, it seems, he sent for his ascetic friend, Abú Sahl al-Qaṭṭán, to accompany him;[1] and when the season of the Pilgrimage came round, all three joined the caravans, and made their way to the holy city by the Baṣrah road.[2]

1 Tan. *farj.* II, 14; S.J. fol. 138 a; Tagh. II, 312.
2 M. I, 8, 12–13; H. 23–4, 26–7, 137–9.

END OF PART ONE

PLATE II

dirham (silver) minted at Baghdád in A.H. 304 (A.D. 916–17), when 'Alí ibn 'Ísà was Vizier

dínár (gold) minted at Baghdád in A.H. 307 (A.D. 919–20), when 'Alí ibn 'Ísà was Assistant to the Vizier Ḥámid ibn al-'Abbás

The legends, alike in both, run:

OBVERSE	REVERSE
There is no god but	*To God*
God alone	*Muḥammad*
With him is no Copartner	*Is the Apostle*
Abú'l-'Abbás[1] *son of*	*Of God*
The Commander of the Faithful	*Al-Muqtadir bi'llah*

Photographed from casts of coins in the British Museum

1 Abú'l-'Abbás, i.e. al-Muqtadir's eldest surviving son, afterwards ar-Rádhí, included here as *walí al-'ahd,* Heir to the Throne.

Part Two

CHAPTER I

Al-Muqtadir *and his mother. The Vizierate of* Ibn al-Furát, *and his fall.*

One day in the last year of his reign al-Mu'tadhid was walking with Ṣáfí through the women's quarters to the apartments of his concubine Shaghab, who had attained the status of an *umm walad* by bearing him a son, Ja'far. They came at length to an archway draped with a curtain, where, hearing young voices, the Caliph paused, and spied through a gap in the folds the room beyond. On the carpet sat Ja'far, then five years old, and round him in a circle a number of his little friends. It was the season when grapes were a delicacy, and the children were passing a large bunch from one to the other, biting off each a grape, till the whole was consumed.

Ṣáfí was astonished to observe that his master was deeply shocked and angered by the scene. Abandoning his visit to Shaghab, the Caliph returned to his own rooms, and there indulged a mood of dejection. He held it an evil omen for the future that Ja'far should share his fortune on equal terms with his friends. "O Ṣáfí," he said, "if it were not for the Fire and the Reproach, I should kill the boy this day; and his death would be a boon to the people." Al-Muktafí, he knew, could not long outlive him, and the people, in seeking, as they were sure to seek, a Caliph of his family, would find none older than Ja'far. Ja'far, a minor, would be a tool in the hands of the Harem, and would squander with his boon-companions, as he now squandered the luxuries of the palace, the wealth that al-Mu'tadhid had so zealously amassed.[1]

The prophecy of al-Mu'tadhid came true in every detail, so true that we may even suspect Ṣáfí of having invented it after the fact. Ja'far fell completely under the sway of his women, of his mother Shaghab in particular, who was henceforth known as *as-sayyidah*, the Lady, and of her *qahramánahs*,[2] or ladies in waiting, especially one Umm Músà. In a few years he squandered the vast private fortune of his father, to which his brother al-Muktafí had added, and for the rest of his unprecedentedly long reign—for as he came younger to the throne than any of the 'Abbásids before him, so he sat longer upon it—he was perennially in straits for money.[3]

He is commended by one historian for restoring the ancient splendour of the Caliphate, for collecting, for example, a retinue of eleven thousand black and white eunuchs. But almost in the same breath he is condemned for dispersing "in the shortest time" the whole treasure of jewels, many of them reputed to have belonged formerly to the Chosroes, from whom they had passed to the 'Umayyads and from them to the 'Abbásids. The *chefs-d'œuvre* were a ruby ring bought by Hárún ar-Rashíd for 300,000 *dínárs*, and a pearl, *al-yatímah*, the Non-Pareil, as it was called, weighing three *mith-*

1 Tan. *nish.* 140; Jaw. fol. 83 b.

2 I can think of no quite satisfactory translation for *qahramánah*. The *qahramánahs* (of whom there seem to have been three or four at a time) were officials. Jaw. fol. 86 a defines their duties by saying that each "had in her hand the pay of great and small". "Stewardess", a common translation of the word, is too nautical, "housekeeper" too humble; perhaps "paymistress" most nearly expresses the meaning. "Ladies in waiting" is hardly official enough, but emphasises the fact that the *qahramánahs* were free-born:—Umm Músà, for example, was a Háshimite: of the Prophet's family. The word *qahramán*, the masculine form, was also used of a man; and can be well translated by "steward".

3 Mas. *tan.* 378.

qáls.[1] Al-Muqtadir presented the Non-Pareil to one of his numerous concubines.[2]

From the moment of his accession he was indulged in every way, and in the course of this indulgence he acquired a taste which was to have a further unhappy effect on his character. A coin is extant of his reign which shows him on one face holding a wine-glass, and on the other holding a lute. Wine-drinking is of course forbidden in Islam, and the playing of musical instruments is looked upon as a disgraceful action. Further, the portrayal of human or animal figures is reprehended by the Prophet's own example. The coin embodies therefore a combination of indecencies.[3]

It is inexplicable that a Caliph should have chosen to advertise his failings in this way—for it cannot be said that in the change of manners drinking and lute-playing were no longer considered failings. But for whatever reason the coin was struck, it faithfully records al-Muqtadir's tastes. His drinking bouts came to form part of Court routine, and were prepared for with extravagant care.[4] Afterwards 'Alí ibn 'Ísà gave it as his opinion that five days of sobriety would have shown al-Muqtadir to be as sagacious as his father.[5] In spite of his heavy drinking, however, his health was remarkably good. The Court physician stated at his death that during his whole reign he had been sick only thirteen days.[6] In his sober intervals he was much given to praying and fasting, and his zeal for extirpating heresy was exemplary. Soon after his accession he forbade the employment of Jews and Christians as Government clerks, again putting into force the sumptuary laws against them,[7] and later he instituted an

1 That is, about 153 grams (metric).
2 *fakh*. 305; also Dh. *t*. fol. 76 a.
3 See *frontispiece*.
4 Tan. *nish*. 144.
5 Dh. *t*. fol. 122 a.
6 Dháf. fol. 138 a. Cf. S.J. fol. 59 b.
7 S.J. fol. 41 b; Tagh. II, 174; 'A. 30.

inquisition of persons suspect in their religion. Al-Mas‘údí has left us a description of al-Muqtadir's appearance when he grew up. He was of middle height, inclining to shortness; with a wide face, round but well-shapen; thick fair hair and beard; a high colour, pink and white; and little round bright black eyes.[1] In later life he became fat and unwieldy, and his hair began early to turn grey.[2]

His mother, the Lady Shaghab, a Greek by birth, had been bought as a concubine by al-Mu‘tadhid from a dame of Baghdád.[3] She had been freed, as an *umm walad*, on al-Mu‘tadhid's death; and now she soon became the most influential person at Court. Ja‘far treated her with the utmost reverence: he would always rise to greet her, embrace her and kiss her head, seat her at his side and address her with "O my Lady!" He was inclined to think that her asking for anything rendered it *ipso facto* worthy to be granted.[4] Her influence, however, was generally considered pernicious. She certainly spoiled Ja‘far outrageously, and encouraged his vices and extravagance. But the Lady seems to have been foolish rather than wicked. In a conventional way indeed she was extremely devout, and spent most of her large income in good works.[5]

At the beginning of his Vizierate, Ibn al-Furát was in high favour with the Lady, who considered, and pointed out to Ja‘far, that he was twice beholden to Ibn al-Furát for his throne. Ibn al-Furát now profited himself by the advice he had given to al-‘Abbás ibn al-Ḥasan in the matter of choosing a Caliph. He was encouraged by the Lady, who looked on admiring from behind a curtain, to treat Ja‘far almost as a son, kissing him on the head and taking him on his knee. When Ja‘far gave public audience, Ibn al-Furát would

1 Mas. *tan.* 377. Cf. S.J. fol. 37 b; Jaw. fol. 80 b.
2 Fid. I, 76; Dh. *t.* fol. 122 a.
3 Jaw. fol. 80 b.
4 Jaw. ff. 85 b–86 a.
5 Dháf. fol. 138 a.

stand at his side and speak in his name. He felt himself to be in a strong position, and determined to profit by it. According to aṣ-Ṣúlí, his income before he took office was one million *dínárs* a year. He was reputed to own in coin, paper, estates and furniture as much as ten millions' worth.[1] Nevertheless he had no scruples about enriching himself still further out of the public funds, and drew on the Caliph's private treasure to make up the deficit.[2] He began also to enlarge the Palace of the Viziers at vast expense,[3] and gave all the best places in the ministry to his relatives, who were all clamorous for recognition.[4] He saw, however, that the favour of the Caliph alone was not enough, particularly since he was obliged to share it with others: Ja'far was quite as much indebted to Ṣáfí and Mu'nis, for example, as to him. Ibn al-Furát was anxious, therefore, to make himself generally popular at Court. To win friends, he presented members of the Royal Family with pensions, which he afterwards increased, and at the same time abolished various dues that the people objected to, never pausing to reflect how the resources of the Treasury would bear the strain.[5] To conciliate enemies he used diplomacy, as with the late conspirators. In the house of one of them certain papers had been discovered, containing the names of all those implicated in the plot; and these, when they had been brought for examination to Ibn al-Furát, he had refused to look at, and had had publicly destroyed.[6]

The influence of Ṣáfí the Chief Eunuch it was impossible to combat. (In any case he fell ill in 298 (911) and died.[7]) But Ṣáfí was himself jealous of Mu'nis, and ready to abet the Vizier in driving him from Court: Mu'nis had been trained to arms; and it was not long

1 'A. 37.
2 H. 79, 116–17, 140; M. I, 13.
3 H. 23.
4 'A. 34; H. 178.
5 M. I, 13.
6 H. 119–20; M. I, 14; *fakh.* 313.
7 S.J. fol. 52 b; Ham. *tak.* fol. 9 a; Tagh. II, 183.

before Ibn al-Furát found a pretext for sending him on an expedition. For want of a more urgent call on his services, Mu'nis was first put in command of the summer raid over the frontier into Byzantine territory;[1] then later he was recalled to take part in pacifying the province of Fárs. His conduct of the latter operation, however, aroused the suspicions of Ibn al-Furát, who suddenly sent out another officer to replace him. Mu'nis was consequently offended, and returned to Baghdád in a mood of resentment.[2]

This was the more unfortunate for the Vizier in that the Caliph's affection for him and gratitude for his past services were in the meantime being put to the proof. An intrigue had been set on foot against him by a certain Muḥammad ibn 'Ubayd Allah al-Kháqání, who hoped to replace him in the Vizierate. Al-Kháqání's father had been a celebrated Vizier (first to al-Mutawakkil and later to al-Mu'tamid); but he himself, though he had once managed a *díwán*, had of late years been relegated to a post-mastership in an out-of-the-way province. His son, 'Abd Allah, had served for a long time under Muḥammad ibn Dá'úd; and it is probable that both father and son were definitely attached to the Banú'l-Jarráḥ, since they were compelled to hide after the failure of the conspiracy.[3] Al-Kháqání enlisted the help of another of al-Mu'taḍhid's *umm walads*—a kind of step-mother to the Caliph: in return for a bribe of 100,000 *dínárs* she was to urge his deserts with al-Muqtadir and the Lady; and to make himself the more acceptable in their eyes, al-Kháqání began to display a quite remarkable piety on all occasions, continually keeping Court messengers waiting whilst he finished his prayers or completed a rosary. This caused his patroness to feel that she was furthering Heaven's interests as well as her own; and

1 'A. 31. 2 M. I, 18–19; 'A. 32–3.
3 H. 261.

Ja'far himself was deeply impressed with these evidences of godliness. He seems even to have given al-Kháqání to understand that he would sooner or later make him Vizier; but he dreaded the possibility of another civil disturbance, and was evidently reluctant to move at once. Al-Kháqání perceived that if he was to succeed, he must put Ibn al-Furát in the wrong.

By the third year of his Vizierate the lavish expenditure of Ibn al-Furát had brought about what was henceforward to be the usual state of the finances, a shortage of funds. The 10th *dhú'l-ḥijjah*, the month of the Muhammadan year during which the ceremonies of the Pilgrimage are performed at Mecca, is known as *yawm an-naḥr*, the Day of Oblation.[1] Camels, sheep and goats are slaughtered on that day at a point outside the city of Mecca itself, and throughout Islam every Muslim able to buy an animal is supposed to celebrate the occasion in the same way. Now it was the Vizier's duty to provide these victims at the 'Abbásid Court for the troops and various categories of the palace servants. But Ibn al-Furát, in 299 (912), found that he had absolutely no money for the purpose. He applied therefore as usual to the Caliph for a loan from the Privy Purse. For the first time, however, the Caliph refused him. Ibn al-Furát despaired of surmounting the difficulty, till one of his secretaries suggested that the animals might be bought cheap at al-Kúfah. On this he at once gave orders for an official to go out and buy them. The man was provided with an escort, which he sent ahead with his litter, intending to overtake it outside the walls.

Now al-Kháqání was kept informed of all that passed by spies, for Ibn al-Furát had discovered his intrigue and forced him to go again into hiding; and

1 Also as *al-'íd al-kabír*, the Great Feast, and *'íd al-adḥḥá*, the Feast of Sacrifice.

when he heard of the preparations for the Feast made by the Vizier, he saw at once how he might lend them a suspicious air. As well as his friend the *umm walad*, whose assistance had been so expensive, he had another sponsor in the Harem, the *qahramánah* Umm Músà. This lady, who was herself of the royal blood, had only lately been given her influential post, on the death of a predecessor that had been drowned in the Tigris, when attempting to pass in a boat under the bridge on a windy day.[1] Umm Músà was eager to engage in politics: and al-Kháqání knew that his story would be safe in her hands.

An empty litter, so the story ran, was this day being sent to al-Kúfah, whence it would fetch a relative of the infamous Carmathian Dhikrawayh. Ibn al-Furát, in despair over the confusion resulting from his mismanagement, had resolved once again to depose al-Muqtadir and set up this personage in his place.—The Caliph had only to send out an officer, to be certain that the report was true. An officer was in fact sent out, and he duly reported the departure of an empty litter with an escort of the Vizier's men. The threat of deposition, which thus seemed to be confirmed, was of course especially alarming to Ja'far and his mother; but before making a decision they consulted her brother Gharíb (Gharíb the Maternal Uncle, as he was called) and Mu'nis. Mu'nis was in no mood to defend the Vizier, and the Uncle was equally hostile: they decided in consequence on his arrest.

Etiquette secured his freedom to a Vizier for the remainder of any day on which he had had audience of the Caliph. Arrests therefore had usually to be made at the victim's house. In this case, however, the Caliph, who was in the utmost trepidation over the whole affair, feared that the soldiery might side with

1 M. I, 20.

Ibn al-Furát against him, if he were taken at home. Every effort was made to conceal what was afoot; but an unwonted stir, and a secret meeting from which, against wont, he was excluded, were reported to Ibn al-Furát by his spies. He was filled with foreboding, and next morning, when his secretary remarked on his air of dejection, Ibn al-Furát confessed that he expected a fall. Yet an hour later he set out for the palace. He was received as usual; but was arrested before reaching the Presence.

On the dismissal of a minister it was customary for his property to be seized: and in carrying out this duty the police usually took what they could for themselves. On this occasion Mu'nis put a guard about the Palace of the Viziers, but Ibn al-Furát's private dwelling was sacked with exemplary zeal. The women were driven out and exposed to the abuse and licence of the soldiery; and when all the movables had been carried off, even the teak-wood of the roofs and doors was torn down and taken away. The hooligans of the city were thereby encouraged to pillage on their own account: for three days Baghdád was in an uproar; and order was restored with difficulty.

But al-Kháqání, meanwhile, had been invested with the cloak of office.[1]

1 H. 28 9, 264 5; 'A. 36 7; M. I, 20.

CHAPTER II

‘Alí ibn ‘Ísà *in Mecca. The Vizierate and fall of* al-Kháqání.

The caravan from al-‘Iráq was the largest and the most important of all the pilgrim caravans, for it was made up not only of the pilgrims from that province, but also of those from Persia and the East. Moreover with the caravan from al-‘Iráq was sent yearly to Mecca a present from the Caliph, the covering for the Ka‘bah, the sacred cube that stands in the midst of the great mosque.

For the needy travelling was woefully hard, particularly when, as in the year of ‘Alí's banishment, the month of Pilgrimage fell at the very hottest time of the year.[1] Some had to trudge on foot the whole way across the desert; others rode mules or horses on hard wooden saddles, or shared a camel with a fellow. Pilgrims with some means could buy a place on a camel laden with soft bales, or make weight with a companion in two baskets slung across a camel's back, with movable screens against sun and wind. For the rich and influential, such as ‘Alí ibn ‘Ísà, every effort was made to mitigate the discomforts of the journey. They too depended on camels, but with them the baskets had become palanquins, litters padded with satin upholstery, and surmounted by curtained canopies that shut them off from both the weather and the outside world. At halts in oases on the way magnificent tents were pitched for them by slaves, so that in the twinkling of an eye the bare plain was covered with a whole canvas town. The walls and roofs of these movable palaces were hung within with silken panels,

1 *Dhú'l-qa‘dah* 296 = July–August 909.

and the harsh ground beneath them spread over with layers of carpets.[1]

During the times of anarchy, the precincts of the great mosque in Mecca had fallen into a scandalous decay. In an insurrection of the Shí'ah the gold with which the doors of the Ka'bah were plated had been removed and minted down; and later the sacred enclosure had been severely damaged by winter floods, owing to the choking by fallen masonry of the torrent bed in which, inconveniently enough, the mosque is situated. For many years now a certain 'Ajj ibn Ḥájj had been governor of the holy city. He had appealed for help to al-Mu'taḍhid early in his reign: and the Caliph had responded generously by providing for the digging out of the offensive obstruction. At the same time he had removed the litter of old buildings adjoining the mosque to the north of the Ka'bah, leaving in front of it an open space; and he had constructed on the rest of their emplacement a hall with a gilt ceiling, which opened into the enclosure with twelve doorways. On al-Muqtadir's accession a party among the inhabitants of Mecca had refused to recognise his rights, and whether or not because the mosque wall was again damaged in the disturbances that followed, and the torrent bed again encumbered, two years later, after 'Alí's arrival, the floods rose so high that the Ka'bah stood in a lake of water.[2] 'Alí was much impressed with the need for improvements: and when later he was in a position to carry them out, he delighted to do so.

He was kept under surveillance in Mecca for almost three years, during which he was confined to his house and forbidden to move about as he pleased. But in 299 (912) two of his brothers, 'Abd ar-Raḥmán and 'Ubayd Allah, came with the caravans to perform the

1 Von Kremer: *Culturgeschichte*, II, 22–3.
2 Wüstenfeldt: *Chroniken der Stadt Mekka*, I, 342–4, IV, 206–9.

Pilgrimage and visit him; and 'Abd ar-Raḥmán, who arrived first, brought with him a letter from Ibn al-Furát dismissing 'Alí's guardian and permitting him to take part in the ceremonies.

The fall of Ibn al-Furát occurred not long after the brothers' arrival; and news of it was conveyed to 'Alí by a miracle—one of several by which during his sojourn in the holy city there was manifested on earth the high favour in which he was held in Heaven. An old black slave of his grandmother's was the first to hear the good news, from an acquaintance in the body-guard; and he at once hurried to the mosque to break it to his masters. 'Abd ar-Raḥmán, whom he found resting in the shade after the exertions of devotion, was beside himself with delight: he ran across to where 'Alí was sitting telling his beads, and repeated the story. But 'Alí was loath to believe it; and 'Ubayd Allah, who had been one of the last to leave Baghdád, dismissed it as a baseless rumour. The news was spread about the city, yet no confirmation of it was forthcoming; and it was not till the caravan with the brothers was on its way back, that they met a courier who told them it was true. In spite of the apparent impossibility of such rapid communication over so great a distance, they had learnt of Ibn al-Furát's dismissal on the very morning of its occurrence.[1]

Once that he was free of his jailer, 'Alí doubtless took part with especial zest in the ceremonies of the Pilgrimage. But even at other times he was tireless in his devotions. One day, when he had been performing his circumambulations about the Ka'bah with a vigour ill-suited to the heat of midsummer, he returned ready to collapse, exclaiming, "Would to God I might drink iced water!" Abú Sahl, his companion, pointed out that ice was the last thing that Mecca in the dog days could possibly provide. What was his surprise,

1 H. 141.

therefore, to observe before many minutes had passed a cool breeze spring up, the sky lower with clouds, thunder and lightning, and at last a fall of hail or snow. The freezing substance was at once gathered up in every receptacle that could be found, and many varieties of sherbert were prepared with it. 'Alí was fasting, so he might not yet partake of them himself, but he spent the hours before sunset in distributing the delicious liquids to the poor and pious of the mosque. Only when he and Abú Sahl had returned after dark to their lodging, could 'Alí be prevailed upon to drink a little that remained. And even then his thought was: "I would that my wish had been for the forgiveness of my sins!"[1]

These stories were related of 'Alí, probably long afterwards, by his relatives and friends, who were anxious to credit him with the supernatural gifts of a saint. Yet 'Alí was far from denying such spiritual favours himself, if we may believe another of his companions. The latter was three times accosted in the mosque by a venerable *shaykh*, who spoke to him of 'Alí in a mysterious way. For some reason 'Alí was persuaded that this was no real man, but an apparition of the Prophet al-Khidhr, a mysterious being liable to be seen in holy places, supposed to be of the family of Noah and to have been living since the age of Abraham, and sometimes identified, strangely enough, with Saint George.[2]

He also supposed the vision to be premonitory: for very soon after, almost exactly a year after his release, Mu'nis's chamberlain Yalbaq arrived from Baghdád with a retinue of three hundred mounted men and a convoy of fifty camels, bringing a letter from the Caliph to 'Ajj ibn Ḥájj commanding 'Alí's return. 'Alí, however, was about to take part again in the rites

1 H. 363–4; Tan. *farj.* II, 14; Tagh. II, 312; S.J. fol. 138 a.
2 S.J. fol. 138 a–b.

of the Pilgrimage; and from this nothing but a summons from Heaven would deter him. The chamberlain Yalbaq joined him, therefore, in his devotions, and delayed their setting out till these were fulfilled.

'Alí's recall was necessitated by the complete breakdown, after only twelve months, of al-Kháqání's administration. The Vizier had entrusted his son 'Abd Allah with most of his duties; but 'Abd Allah, who was a drunkard, was quite as incapable as his father, who, in spite of his cunning, appears to have been a fool. They confided the receipt and despatch of all letters to the care of subordinate clerks, and allowed even the most pressing to remain for days unread: with the result that arrears of business accumulated past overtaking. Nor were they merely incapable, they were actively dishonest. 'Abd Allah was ready to take bribes from any place-seeker, and in return give him an office already filled. Thus in one district a fresh governor was appointed for every month of al-Kháqání's Vizierate, and in another seven were appointed simultaneously. Under these circumstances it is no wonder that the Caliph, or the powers behind him, should soon have begun to think of replacing him.

At the time of his fall all the affection with which the young Caliph had been taught to regard Ibn al-Furát was eclipsed by his fears of a second deposition. But in the course of his examination for the customary fine, Ibn al-Furát was so harshly used that it was not long before that affection was restored. The official responsible was a certain Ibn Thawábah, whom al-Kháqání had charged with the fining of the whole faction. With beatings and shacklings Ibn Thawábah wrung from the smaller fry a large sum, but he was forbidden at first to apply force to the fallen Vizier, and could not in consequence obtain as much from him as al-Kháqání required. At length al-Muqtadir was persuaded to have him put to the question: but Ibn Thawábah applied the torture so mercilessly (it consisted in exposing the victim to the noon-day sun wrapped in a woollen cloak soaked in gelatine),[1] that Ibn al-Furát almost expired. In remorse for what he had allowed, Ja'far thereupon removed Ibn al-Furát from the hands of al-Kháqání altogether, and caused him to be confined in the private apartments.

But although the Caliph felt for Ibn al-Furát, to the sufferings of others he appears to have been indifferent. In spite of his indiscretion Ibn Thawábah was not dismissed; and since his methods of extracting money were eminently successful, as al-Kháqání's influence diminished, his increased. He had an ally in Umm Músà, who was finding the uncertain state of affairs very favourable to her ambitions; and though her first attempt to raise a client to the Vizierate had been unsuccessful, it succeeded so nearly that several other aspirants promptly bribed her to help them. Umm Músà and Ibn Thawábah were enjoying their new-won power, when a riot of the soldiery precipitated a crisis.

Al-Kháqání had no money for their pay, which was already long past due: he was therefore forced to ask a gift from the Privy Purse. The Caliph reluctantly consented; but at the same time he decided that al-Kháqání was to be tolerated no longer. His inclination was to restore his favourite Ibn al-Furát to office—he had already taken to visiting him secretly for advice. But Mu'nis, whom he consulted, was still opposed to Ibn al-Furát, and argued that to appoint him again so soon would be undignified: it would be said that the Caliph had disgraced him only to seize his wealth. To Mu'nis's mind there was but one suitable person. Of all the secretaries of al-Mu'taḍhid's day, who re-

1 See Mas. *murúj*, VIII, 109 (trans.)..."une robe de laine préparée dans la gélatine...".

mained? Of the Banú'l-Furát one was dead, the other in disgrace; al-'Abbás ibn al-Ḥasan had been murdered; Muḥammad ibn Dá'úd and Ibn 'Abdún had been executed. There was left only 'Alí ibn 'Ísà, and he was in Mecca. Mu'nis described him as being "reliable and trustworthy and pious and dutiful and competent"; and suggested that his own chamberlain Yalbaq should be sent forthwith to fetch him.

It is probable that at this time 'Alí was known to Ja'far merely formally, as a distinguished former minister, so that affection or dislike went for nothing in his decision. The only objection that might be urged against his investiture was the part he had taken in the conspiracy of Ibn al-Mu'tazz. But Ibn al-Furát had minimised his guilt, and the calumnies of Sawsan had been silenced. Ja'far, in fine, took Mu'nis's advice: and Yalbaq was ordered to summon him post-haste from Mecca.

Al-Kháqání was told that 'Alí was being recalled to fill some minor office: and he boasted in his assembly that he had written to appoint him assistant to 'Abd Allah. He learnt of his true destiny only when 'Alí was within a day or two of arrival. Then he and his son were aghast: they even thought of having 'Alí assassinated. One of 'Abd Allah's henchmen was heard to say, "'Alí ibn Abí Ṭálib was killed right enough. Who is 'Alí ibn 'Ísà that he should not be killed too?"[1] Such a solution, however, was hardly practical. So al-Kháqání made a desperate effort to recover his position with bribes; and he even fancied that he had won: that instead of being made Vizier 'Alí would be delivered over to him. When therefore on 10th *al-muḥarram* 301 (16th August 913) he learnt that 'Alí had at length arrived, he came as usual with his two sons to the palace, where they sat in an antechamber awaiting the hour of audience.

1 Qudh. fol. 90 a.

Presently Mu'nis came out, and calling to the Chamberlain and officers, bade them wait on the Vizier. Al-Khaqání was thunderstruck: "Who is the Vizier?" he asked faintly.

"Why," answered Mu'nis, pointing to 'Alí as he appeared, "Abú'l Hasan 'Alí ibn 'Ísà."

'Alí had reached the city at daybreak. The Caliph had received him at the hour of Morning Prayer. The Vizierate had been conferred upon him forthwith: and it was on his leaving the Presence that this encounter took place. Al-Khaqání, at once abjectly humble, began to excuse himself, pleading that office had been forced upon him. But 'Alí cut short his protestations; and whilst he himself rode in procession with Mu'nis and the Uncle to his house, the fallen minister with his sons was taken in charge by the guard.[1]

[1] M. [illegible], H. [illegible]–4, 281; 'A. 37, 39, 40, 41.

CHAPTER III

'Alí ibn 'Ísà *in the Vizierate. His appointments and reforms. The* qádhís Abú 'Umar *and* Ibn al-Buhlúl.

'Alí thus first became Vizier at the age of fifty-five. He was invested later in the day with the black robes of office; the Caliph bestowed on him the estates that both Ibn al-Furát and al-Kháqání had enjoyed in turn before him; and his salary was fixed at 60,000 *dínárs* a year, a large sum, but one, so it appears, out of which he had to pay his office staff.[1]

Since, after all, he had been forced into accepting office, he must have looked back with regret at his former refusal of the Vizierate: in the ten years' interval how many sad, how many calamitous events had taken place, and with him in power all might have been avoided! The task before him was arduous—how arduous his absence from Court must have forbidden him to foresee. He took up his abode again at the Báb al-Bustán; but his family were to enjoy very little of his company. His assembly was at the Vizierate, and there business kept him, literally, from morning to night. "Every day he would go there at dawn, and work there until the latest times of the last Evening Prayer. Then he would depart to his house."

'Alí followed the example of his predecessors in this, that he gave the most important offices of State to his friends and relations, although, to be sure, only to those well qualified to hold them. Thus his brother Ibrahím took the War Office, and a fellow-townsman (of Dayr Qunnà) the office in which he himself had graduated, the *díwán al-maghrib*; whilst his cousin Sulaymán (the son of al-Ḥasan ibn Makhlad) con-

1 Von Kremer: *Ueber das Einnahmebudget*, 52, note 3.

trolled the corresponding office, the *díwán al-mashriq.*[1] His brother ʻAbd ar-Raḥmán is not mentioned as holding any official position; but doubtless, now as ever after, he was ʻAlí's general *aide-de-camp.*

Sulaymán ibn al-Ḥasan had been employed before by ʻAlí, in a minor post in one of the *díwáns* he had managed. But he seems to have taken no part either in the war of the secretaries or in the great conspiracy; and when Ibn al-Furát came to power, he had given Sulaymán the same *díwán* in his own right. The temptation to intrigue, however, was too much for Sulaymán. In spite of having received such generous treatment at his hands, he made a bid to replace Ibn al-Furát in the Vizierate; and one day, when he rose to recite the Sunset Prayers, an incriminating letter fell out of his sleeve. He was banished to al-Baṣrah for some months; but later, when in his absence from Baghdád his mother died, Ibn al-Furát pardoned his transgression, and gave him fresh employment.[2] Perhaps it was by way of demonstrating Sulaymán's gratitude for this second favour that ʻAlí now appointed as his cousin's deputy in the *díwán al-mashriq* Ibn al-Furát's nephew al-Fadhl ibn Jaʻfar.[3] He seems indeed to have felt no objection to employing clerks of the Furát faction. Most of the more important were in hiding (and intriguing on their patron's behalf); but one of them, a certain Hishám ibn ʻAbd Allah, was for the time being on good terms with ʻAlí ibn ʻÍsà, who gave him the important appointment of the *díwán ad-dár*, now apparently a kind of central exchange between the other offices.[4]

ʻAlí certainly cannot be accused of using his position

1 ʻA. 42 gives Sulaymán the *díwán ad-dár*; but this seems to be wrong.

2 H. 102.

3 H. 208.

4 H. 79, 279. ʻAlí, the son of Hishám ibn ʻAbd Allah, is Hilál's authority for much of the information retailed in the *kitáb al-wuzará'* about Ibn al-Furát.

to benefit his relations. In the case of his sister Asmá' indeed he did precisely the opposite. During his Vizierate it had come to the ears of Ibn al-Furát that Asmá' (who was married to 'Alí the son of Muḥammad ibn Dá'úd) was in great straits for money, whereupon he released for her use certain of the sequestrated estates formerly belonging to her father-in-law. 'Alí ibn 'Ísà, however, when he came to power, considered the proceeding out of order, and whatever private assistance he may have given his sister, denied her the enjoyment of what was properly the State's.[1]

Among the most important of 'Alí's appointments was that of Abú 'Umar, the *qáḍhí* that had taken part in the conspiracy of Ibn al-Mu'tazz (and escaped with bleached hair), to the jurisdiction of East Baghdád.[2] Abú 'Umar (Muḥammad ibn Yúsuf)[3] was a jurist of the Málikite school, and had acted for some years, during the reign of al-Muktafí, as his father's colleague in the chief judgeship. The opinions expressed by his contemporaries on Abú 'Umar's character are extraordinarily much at variance with what is recorded of his actions. To be sure, one *qáḍhí* attributed the first decline in the status of his profession to Abú 'Umar's influence;[4] but he is described in a later obituary notice (presumably put together from fourth/tenth century materials) as proverbially learned and patient, as a model Traditionist (that had learnt his first Tradition at the early age of four), and as a *qáḍhí* unrivalled for the subtlety, propriety and conciseness of his rulings. He too used to hold meetings for the rehearsal of Traditions with al-Baghawí and Ibn Sá'id.[5] But his resemblance to 'Alí went no further than this. He had early shown himself an all too supple courtier,

---

1 H. 147–8.   2 'A. 42.
3 b. 243 (857–8), d. 320 (932).
4 Tan. *nish.* 118. Honesty in *qáḍhís* came to be exceptional.
5 Dh. *t.* fol. 124 b; Jaw. fol. 171 a.

and one that would stoop to real villainy to please a patron. It was he that had conveyed the fatal false safe-conduct to the General Badr, in the hope of currying favour with the Vizier al-Qásim;[1] and in times to come he was more than once to behave in a manner far from creditable. As I have noted, his part in the plot of Ibn al-Mu'tazz very nearly resulted in Abú 'Umar's execution. His father had obtained his release only by making a payment to the State of 20,000 *dínárs*.[2]

Abú 'Umar had a hated rival in the present Chief *qádhí* (the office went with the jurisdiction of the Round City and Western Baghdád in general), one Ibn al-Buhlúl, who had been appointed by Ibn al-Furát on al-Muqtadir's restoration. Ibn al-Buhlúl[3] was a Ḥanafite, originally from al-Anbár on the Euphrates. Both his father and grandfather had been well-known Traditionists; his father had actually been a younger contemporary of Abú Ḥanífah, and had himself made a compilation of Traditions. Ibn al-Buhlúl had owed his first appointment, which he accepted somewhat reluctantly (it was in his native district), to al-Muwaffaq. He had first come to Baghdád in the reign of al-Muktafí, when he was given an appointment in Persia, which, however, he never took up. Unlike Abú 'Umar's, Ibn al-Buhlúl's reputation accords well with what we know of him. It is recorded that he was able, reliable, generous, chivalrous and cultivated, pious and humane in his judgements, his only fault being that his interests were too literary. He was a grammarian of the Kúfan school, having composed a book on the subject. He wrote verse, and was in general an accomplished writer and an eloquent speaker. What he most prided himself on, however, was his memory (which was truly prodigious) for

1 Ṭab. III, 2212–5. 2 M. I, 14; Ham. *tak*. fol. 7 b.

3 Abú Ja'far Aḥmad ibn Isḥáq, b. 231 (845–6), d. 318 (930).

biographical details and commentators' observations, but above all for poetry, ancient and modern. He delighted to engage in literary discussions before an audience, when he might have an opportunity to display his extraordinary powers of memorisation. On one such occasion, a funeral, he entered into a contest of the sort with aṭ-Ṭabarí without knowing who he was. And their conversation so pleased him that at their next meeting he went out of his way to resume it, and would not rest till he had the historian worsted.[1]

Abú 'Umar was mortally jealous of Ibn al-Buhlúl: he could not forgive him for having supplanted him as Chief *qádhí* (for the office would certainly have fallen to him). An anecdote well illustrates their rivalry. One of the freedmen of al-Mu'tadhid had asked that 'Alí should pray over him at his funeral; but 'Alí, seeing Ibn al-Buhlúl among the crowd of notables attending the ceremony, motioned him forward to perform the duty in his stead. A malicious onlooker (the narrator) hastened to Abú 'Umar, to observe how he took the incident, and found him "black in the face" with mortification. He then hastened in turn to Ibn al-Buhlúl, and delighted him with an account of his rival's fury.[2]

In the case of one of his appointments, 'Alí was met with a blank refusal on the part of a jurist to take the office of *qádhí* at all. This was Abú 'Alí ibn Khayrán,[3] a light of the Sháfi'ite school and the author of a handbook on the law. Such a refusal to engage in worldly affairs was characteristic of the Sháfi'ites. Ibn Khayrán himself reproached a famous fellow-jurist (Ibn Surayj) for accepting a judgeship. When Ibn Khayrán declined his offer 'Alí put him under arrest, and on being

1 Yáq. *ud.* I, 82 *et seqq.*; Dh. *t.* fol. 111 a–b; Tan. *nish.* 126–7.
2 Tan. *nish.* 127.
3 Al-Ḥusayn ibn Ṣáliḥ, d. 310 (922–3).

criticised for this apparently high-handed action, confessed to having given the order as an example for later ages. "My sole intention," he said, "was to have it said of our epoch that there existed in it one who was kept under arrest in his house, in order that he might be constrained to accept the place of kadi." (De Slane's translation.)[1]

One of 'Alí's first duties was the punishment of the fallen faction—for as well as al-Kháqání and his sons their chief supporters had been arrested. The method in use invited corruption: it was to obtain from those in disgrace bonds for vast sums, and then to exact of these only an indeterminate proportion.[2] 'Alí instead imposed quite moderate fines. But he made release dependent on their payment in full. He also forbade such haphazard retribution as the sacking of houses or the violation of harems. Moreover, as the penalty consisted strictly in the fine itself, after having obtained his bond, he detained al-Kháqání not in the prison, but in his own house. Of the whole faction only Ibn Thawábah was put to the question, possibly in return for his torture of Ibn al-Furát.[3]

Al-Kháqání, on the other hand, was more than ready, if occasion arose, to do 'Alí a bad turn; and occasion did arise, soon after his arrest. He had left the *díwáns* in a state of unimaginable chaos. Every day they were besieged by a crowd of courtiers and citizens who presented to the distracted 'Alí a multitude of claims. Some of these were already registered—but many more were not; and as most were attested not by the Vizier but by minor officials (to whom he had delegated the authority as a favour), it was difficult to decide which of them were authentic. Hishám ibn 'Abd Allah counselled a bold discrimination. But 'Alí

1 Khall. I, 417. See too Qaz. I, 213–14; Tagh. II, 249; Ath. (Tornberg), VIII, 183, Jaw. fol. 170 a.

2 Tan. *farj.* I, 122.

3 M. I, 27; H. 281–2; 'A. 41.

himself was afraid of committing an injustice, and after some cogitation resolved to lay the matter before the Caliph. In the meantime, however, the courtiers, many of whom were interested in seeing the claims honoured, had gained the Caliph's ear themselves. They had persuaded him to have the papers sent for confirmation to al-Kháqání.

During his term of office al-Kháqání had striven to maintain his reputation as a devotee, thereby to mask some few of his shortcomings. As before, he was often to be found, especially when urgent business required his attention, in prayer so earnest as to cause a delay. He was in prayer now, when the papers were brought in. Nevertheless when his son 'Abd Allah, seeing his preoccupation, began to sort them himself, al-Kháqání interrupted his devotions to rebuke him. Having completed them, he protested that such a function was for a Vizier alone: and on looking through them pronounced all the papers to be perfectly in order. When the messenger had retired, al-Kháqání explained to 'Abd Allah the motive of his action. By passing all the claims as valid he would earn the thanks of the claimants and at the same time embarrass 'Alí ibn 'Ísà with the expense. The courtiers, for their part, were duly delighted: and the historian suggests that the brevity of al-Kháqání's confinement was due not solely to 'Alí's lenience, but as well to their powerful gratitude.[1]

Nothing could, in fact, aggravate 'Alí's difficulties more acutely than a new call on the Treasury. The state of the finances alarmed him: he saw that unless he could quickly improve it, he would soon be involved in embarrassments such as had led to the dismissal in turn of the two Viziers before him. The cause of the evil was two-fold: the yield of the revenue was too low, and the rate of expenditure was too high: on his comparing estimated income with estimated outgoings he discovered a deficit. The high rate of

1 M. I, 31–2; H. 278–80.

expenditure was due to the extravagance of the two previous Viziers and of al-Muqtadir himself. Al-Kháqání had gone one better even than Ibn al-Furát by granting a general increase of wages to the civil servants, the troops and the palace retinue;[1] al-Muqtadir, as I have mentioned, had greatly increased the latter's numbers. The cause of the shrinkage of revenue was to be sought less recently: here, indeed, Ibn al-Furát must have brought about an improvement, since under his *régime* most of Fárs was once again subdued. It was the civil wars and rebellions of the last hundred years that were chiefly responsible. The shrinkage in some cases was very large: certain districts near Baghdád, for example, appear to have contributed now only slightly more than one thirtieth of what they had contributed a century earlier. The system of farming the taxes was liable to abuse at the best of times, and when, as in the recent years of disorder, the agents were almost entirely free of supervision by the Government, it easily became an instrument of local tyranny. The farmers, from a tax on whose lands the bulk of the revenue was raised, were harassed by the excursions of war. The iniquities of the tax gatherers discouraged them finally. Wide lands, in consequence, fell out of cultivation.

'Alí could hardly hope to do more than restore the yearly balance of income and outgoings. And even in order to achieve this he could not simply reverse the policy of Ibn al-Furát that had done most to upset it. To dismiss all Ja'far's new attendants was clearly out of the question. To abolish altogether the mischievous increases in pay would call down on his head the execrations of the whole palace. Before braving this he determined to regulate the collection of taxes, in the expectation of increasing their yield.

The misrule of the rebels in Fárs had led to a wide-

1 M. I, 29. 'A. 41 states that these increases amounted to more than 1 million *dínárs* a year.

spread emigration of farmers and a consequent fall in the revenue derived from the land. To make up the loss a *takmilah*, or extra tax, had therefore, "according to the ancient Code of Fárs", been levied on those who remained. This tax had borne upon them very heavily. Its incidence, moreover, was unjust: some of the farmers were powerful enough to refuse payment of a part of their dues, so that the others had to make up this deficiency also. On the reconquest of Fárs, in spite of its having been instituted by the rebels, the *takmilah* had continued in force, till, early in his Vizierate, the question was brought to 'Alí's notice. It was suggested to him that a substitute for the *takmilah* was available in an ancient tax on fruit-trees which had been abrogated more than a century before by the Caliph al-Mahdí. A troop of farmers arrived in Baghdád to prove this point. They showered samples of rotten grain and dried fruits, which they produced unexpectedly from their sleeves, upon the floor of 'Alí's assembly in illustration of their argument. In the end a Court heard the case, and ruled in favour of the fruit-tax. The fruit-growers then made a belated objection, that since the tax had been abolished by a Caliph its restoration was illegal. To this 'Alí replied that it was now to be restored by order of al-Muqtadir, and that the order of one Caliph was as good as that of another. As well as the *takmilah* 'Alí removed in turn other burdensome special taxes, to wit, the "*makas*" in force at Mecca, an exhorbitant customs-toll in the ports on the tidal estuary of the Dujayl,[1] and the wine duty in Diyár Rabí'ah.[2] It may have been in connection with his investigation into the finances of Fárs that 'Alí composed (if in fact he did so) the short handbook on the geography of that province attributed to him.[3]

1 The modern Kárún.

2 H. 286, 340–5, quoting two letters written by 'Alí on the subject of the *takmilah*; M. I, 29; Iṣṭ. 158; Ḥaw. 217; Bal. 171.

3 Ḥ. Kh. v, 509–10.

CHAPTER IV

'Alí's *reforms* (*continued*). *His secretarial skill. His economies and consequent unpopularity.*

As a complement to his amendments of the law, 'Alí took great pains to introduce a fresh spirit into the methods of its administration. In his first circular to the provincial governors he set forth his principles in uncompromising language. He dismissed none without a trial; but he warned them that corruption or embezzlement would no longer be tolerated. If they needed it, they had grace for changing their ways; but those who should be found wanting at the end of it must not expect to retain their positions. "Rest assured," he wrote, "that with me there is no indulgence, nor shall I countenance any abatement in the rights of the Commander of the Faithful. I shall not remit a *dirham* of his money, nor overlook in relative or stranger any shortcoming in governmental affairs." And with such as did not mend their ways he was as good as his word. When the term of probation was over he made many changes both in the offices and in the provincial appointments.[1]

Bribery was universal; and it seems generally to have been tolerated by Viziers as long as it was moderate: so that officials might receive as it were tips; and these were even allowed for in the Government accounts.[2] But at the same time it seems always to have remained technically an offence to give or take bribes: rival ministers, for example, would often accuse one another of corrupt practices. 'Alí made his views on the subject perfectly clear. Nevertheless one official at least was bold enough to offer him a bribe

1 M. I, 27–8.

2 H. 168–9.

himself; and another (as I shall shortly have to relate) actually succeeded, albeit under peculiar circumstances, in making him accept one. The former was a defaulting tax-farmer, who, having heard the Vizier express a desire to see the citrons of a particular district, sent him a basketful as a present. He scooped out the insides of several citrons and inserted in each a little velvet bag containing a thousand *dínárs*. 'Alí, however, was proof against any such brutal temptation however ingeniously presented, and was only led to suspect the tax-farmer of still graver peculations. How strict were his opinions on the question is clear from his eunuch's refusal to keep a consideration for his part in the transaction (he had presented the basket). "I dare not accept anything," he said.[1]

In a second circular 'Alí exhorted the governors to enquire diligently into the rights of every appeal against the decisions or action of tax-collectors, assessors or other officials, that the people might recover their faith in the power of justice. When he was assured of the negligence or dishonesty of an official he was moved to fury. A certain crop-assessor was found to be slightly at fault in the measurement of a field, "whereupon", so he relates, "a letter arrived from 'Alí ibn 'Ísà with thunderclaps of indignation ...". The people were quick to take advantage of 'Alí's benevolence. Occasionally, indeed, the governors trembled for their authority. 'Alí allowed the imprisonment and shackling of debtors to the State, but he would not countenance their illtreatment. One agent protested that if his hands were tied in this way all government would be at an end, and that no revenue would be forthcoming. His prophecy was disproved, however. The peasants had begun to believe that a fair profit would be secure to them. "Oppression and injustice," they said, "have been removed." Next

1 H. 318–19.

year the revenue of this very district was enormously increased, and so it was throughout the provinces.[1]

As well as in his financial reforms 'Alí was active in furthering good works. He gave instructions for old mosques and hospitals to be repaired and new built throughout the empire. To build a mosque was of course a delight to him. At least one was erected on his estates. He had made the experiment of setting up four mill-wheels; but when it was found that they took away too much water from the fields, he had the building that housed them converted into a mosque.[2]

The need for hospitals had been felt very acutely in Baghdád the last two years. There had raged an epidemic of plague (of which al-'Iráq is thought to be the home,[3] and from which it has seldom long been free); and large numbers had died.[4] There were already four hospitals in Baghdád; but 'Alí now built another at his own expense at the western limit of the city by the Muḥawwal Gate in the Ḥarbiyyah quarter where the pestilence had carried off whole households, and in the others improved the patients' accommodation and the condition of the attendants.[5]

He entrusted the management of the new hospital to a physician with whom he was very friendly and in whom he had every confidence, Abú 'Uthmán Sa'íd ibn Ya'qúb of Damascus. The name of this personage indicates that he was a Muslim; but if he was, he differed thereby from many of his profession, for the practice of medicine was largely in the hands of unbelievers. Even when doctors were Muslims they were very seldom pure Arabs, and it seems likely that Sa'íd ibn Ya'qúb was a Syrian of Christian extraction,

1 Ham. *tak.* fol. 12 a; M. I, 30–1; S.J. fol. 56 b.
2 H. 287.
3 Von Kremer: *Culturgeschichte*, II, 493, note 1.
4 S.J. fol. 56 a; Ath. (Búláq), VIII, 26, 30; Tagh. II, 188.
5 Dh. *t.* fol. 3 a; S.J. fol. 59 b; M. I, 28; and cf. S.J. fol. 63 b.

since he knew either Syriac or Greek, from which he translated a number of medical treatises into Arabic. The Arabs had always prided themselves on their ignorance of the sciences, which they left with disdain to be cultivated by the conquered peoples. Consequently the many valuable translations of the last century, which placed the ancient wisdom at the disposal of the Arabic world (and by which it was later to be handed on, increased, to a barbaric Europe), had been made almost entirely by converted or unconverted Syrians, Persians or Jews; and it was by students of these races that the chief School of Medicine, at Jundí-Shápúr in Khúzistán (itself a Persian, Sasanian foundation), was for the most part attended. Arabs who set up as physicians had great difficulty in attracting patients; for the people were persuaded that only foreigners, and preferably infidels, were possessed of the necessary gifts.[1] The *magnum opus* of Sa'íd ibn Ya'qúb was a study of Galen on the Pulse. 'Alí put him in control of the older hospitals as well.[2]

Mecca benefited in several ways from his solicitude. He had found the water supply in particular very defective. It was usual to bring water from Jiddah (the Red Sea port) by caravan, and the necessary animals were obtained by a periodical impression. 'Alí now bought outright a troop of camels and donkeys and set aside a fund for their upkeep. At the same time he had a well dug, called after him *al-jarráḥiyyah*, in the Millers' Market. He also caused another abundant spring to be opened and its channel widened.[3]

I suspect, in this connection, that it was 'Alí that persuaded al-Muqtadir and the Lady to build the aqueduct in Mecca, which is mentioned as being completed in 302 (914–15). In the same year also al-Muqtadir improved the additions that his father had

1 Browne: *Arabian Medicine*, 8.
2 U. I, 234; Qif. 409.
3 H. 286–7.

made in the north wall of the great mosque by replacing the wooden columns that carried the roof by columns of stone with teak-wood capitals surmounted by plastered arches. The work was supervised by the *qádhí* Muḥammad (or Aḥmad) ibn Músà,[1] a friend of ʻAlí's; and I have no doubt that it was carried out at his suggestion. Al-Muqtadir made another addition to the enclosure at about this time, and though there is no proof of ʻAlí's having proposed it, it seems likely that all this reconstruction was part of one scheme. He threw into it the small court which still forms a projection in the alignment of the west side. Hitherto there had been two small gates in the part of the wall which was then demolished. Al-Muqtadir now built instead in the outer wall of the new court one larger gate, known ever since as the Báb Ibrahím. Mecca also benefited now from a new foundation of ʻAlí's, the *díwán al-birr*, or Office of Good Works. The function of this office was to administer funds derived from the taxes of Baghdád, partly for the upkeep of the Holy Places at Mecca and Medina and partly for the defence of the frontiers. These two duties were often united—the care of the heart of Islam and the keeping intact of its body.[2]

Some sides of ʻAlí's character—his propensity for saving, his ascetic outlook—must have been most antipathetic to the Caliph. But with his abilities, particularly his secretarial skill, Jaʻfar was profoundly impressed. It was usual for Viziers, when they had occasion to write in the Presence, to hold their pen-case (which included an ink-pot) in one hand with the paper, and write with the other. In consequence a fair

1 It is my conjecture that the Muḥammad ibn Músà of al-Fákihí (*Chroniken der Stadt Mekka*, I, 344) is identical with the Aḥmad ibn Músà of Ray, mentioned by H. 131. They were both *qádhís*, both living in Mecca; and the names Aḥmad and Muḥammad are particularly liable to confusion.

2 Wüstenfeldt: *Chroniken der Stadt Mekka*, *loc. cit.*; H. 286.

copy had almost always to be made. 'Alí, however, was so dexterous that he could write a despatch straight away. (And his writing was evidently not merely legible, it was beautiful: for he is mentioned in the *fihrist* not only as an author but also as a calligraphist.)[1] When the decision about the *takmilah* was arrived at, he wished to send word of it to Fárs without the slightest delay. He wrote the necessary communication, accordingly, still standing before Ja'far, and it was signed and sent off forthwith. Ja'far, who was himself the pupil of another celebrated calligraphist,[2] was so forcibly struck with this extraordinary accomplishment, that he gave orders for the ink-pot in future to be held on such occasions by an attendant.[3]

'Alí's virtuosity as a ready writer had already been remarked by the people. He had earned their admiration on one occasion by immediately answering with his own hand a petition presented to him as he was stepping into his barge. Usage, ordinary Vizierial hauteur, would have suggested that he should put it aside for later perusal. But 'Alí, with his pious humility and his ever-present sense of the uncertainty of the future, preferred to attend to it at once. Still standing, and holding the paper in his hand, he wrote his answer without hesitation on the back.[4]

Being supremely capable himself—it was said, for example, that, unlike almost all his colleagues, he could write every kind of despatch unaided[5]—'Alí was inclined to be exacting with his subordinates. When they were slow or stupid, he could not refrain from baiting them. One of his ministers was a reverend secretary that had once acted as Deputy Vizier to

1 *fih.* 9. 2 *fih. loc. cit.* 3 H. 342.

4 Ḍháf. fol. 140 b; Yáq. *ud.* v, 279.

5 Yáq. *ud.* v, 278. In all he is said to have written during his tenure of office over 30,000 State despatches. Yáq. *ud.* v, 280; Ḍháf. fol. 141 a.

Ismá'íl ibn Bulbul, and enjoyed ever since a very general esteem. In some respects he was a man after 'Alí's own heart, modest, honest and disinterested; but in the execution of business he was neither clear nor quick. 'Alí took to consulting, in his presence, the under-clerks of his *díwán*, and in order to make him look foolish in the eyes of the other officials, only asked his advice when he was sure that the minister would be unable to supply it. The poor man was so galled by continual taunts that at length he sought a private interview with 'Alí. He put forward his claims to a better treatment (he was more efficient at his work, he asserted, than he seemed); and insisted that he should either receive it, or else be allowed to retire. 'Alí was touched at his frankness, and persuaded of the justice of his argument. And the next day his brother Ibrahím was amused to observe that his attitude to the slow-witted minister underwent a remarkable change.[1]

It must be confessed that 'Alí himself was vain of his accomplishment as a secretary. It was this vanity that forced him, in the one instance recorded, into accepting what amounted to a bribe. He had prepared a report, bringing a certain tax-farmer of the Furát faction to task for various defaults; and he felt confident that no holes could be picked in it. The tax-farmer, however, having received permission to consider the report at home, showed it to Ibn al-Furát, who detected in it a couple of technical errors. Then, prompted by Ibn al-Furát, he returned to 'Alí, and in a private meeting gave him the alternatives of dropping the prosecution or having his incompetence as a secretary made public. 'Alí could not bring himself to face the loss of his cherished reputation. He purchased the defaulter's silence with the cancellation of his debts to the State.[2]

1 H. 324–5. 2 H. 128–30.

During his first year of office 'Alí was called to a melancholy duty. Nothing had been heard of Ibn al-Furát for a full twelve months. Now he was reported to have died in prison and his coffin was brought out to receive the last prayers of the Vizier. 'Alí had always admired his former master. On returning to his assembly after the sad ceremony, "Alas," he said, "clerkship this day is dead!" But he was deceived: the coffin held not the body of Ibn al-Furát, but that of a captured rebel. For reasons of policy it had been thought wise to conceal his death. No one could know whether Ibn al-Furát was indeed dead or alive. The deception would therefore be feasible. 'Alí was amazed when he learnt the truth. "No one," he exclaimed, "should relate all that he hears, or believe all that he is told!"[1]

He might well be shocked at finding himself kept in ignorance of such an important secret of State. Here was evidence that Ja'far was taking the advice of others behind his back. By this time 'Alí had begun to carry out the other part of his programme. He had cut down salaries: and the expected storm had arisen. He was accused on all sides of meanness and avarice. He was the negation of all that was traditionally noble. He was execrated alike by the courtiers, the commanders, the men-at-arms, the Harem, the eunuchs and every category of the palace servants. He suspected therefore that this was the first-fruits of an intrigue against him.[2]

'Alí certainly carried his economies to great lengths. And once at least, if we are to believe an unnamed tale-teller, they very much defeated their own ends. He considered that Ibn al-Furát had allowed too much for the repair of dykes; and having cut down the estimate for a particular dyke, went on to contend that since it was situated in land held by a tenant in fief, he must defray the cost himself. The result was that when

1 H. 30, 283.   2 M. I, 29.

the floods came the dyke, never having been touched, gave way: and sums many times greater than that economised by 'Alí had to be spent in reclaiming the area inundated.[1]

The truth is that 'Alí found it now not only a necessity, but a real pleasure, to be frugal. His sojourn in Mecca, the humiliation of his captivity, his enforced solitude, and the holy exercises that he had afterwards so untiringly performed, had developed his taste for the ascetic. The days were gone when the learned had gathered at his house, at all events the learned in matters secular. Aṣ-Ṣúlí asked Ibn Ṭúmár the *naqíb* why those pleasant parties had been abandoned, and Ibn Ṭúmár replied that not only had the Vizier no time for them, he had no money: all that was not spent on his household, for necessaries, was devoted to religious charities.[2] 'Alí indeed was charitable, so it appears, on an amazing scale. He was, to begin with, a rich man: his income when he was out of office amounted, according to aṣ-Ṣafadí,[3] to 80,000 *dínárs* a year; and of this he spent as much as 50,000 in charity, keeping only 30,000 for his own wants and the wants of his household. But now that he was in office, he enjoyed not merely the large salary I have mentioned, but the produce of the Vizierial estates, so that his income was swollen to as much as 700,000. In spite of this great difference, however, he increased his private expenditure only by 10,000 a year. All the remainder was set aside for good works, such as pensions for learned men, whom he supported, at one time and another, to the number of forty-five thousand.[4]

'Alí gave no more parties, but in moments of relaxation he still received at least one visitor in Ibn Mujáhid

1 H. 257. 2 Yáq. *ud.* v, 278; Ḏháf. fol. 139 b.
3 Ṣaf. (B.M. Or. 6587), fol. 132 b; Yáq. *ud.* v, *loc. cit.*
4 Yáq. *ud.* v, 280; Ḏháf. fol. 141 a. Dh. *t.* fol. 225 a; Tagh. II, 312–13; and S.J. fol. 137 b all raise the proportion given away.

the "Reader", who came to him regularly on Fridays, to read the *qur'án*. Sitting before him Ibn Mujáhid would recite the sacred text, and they would discuss grammatical, theological, and moral points arising. Possibly they worked on 'Alí's book on the Significations etc., in which Ibn Mujáhid collaborated. On these occasions 'Alí would instruct his chamberlain to refuse entry to all callers.[1] On Fridays also 'Alí would always attend the public prayers in one of the great congregational mosques. Sometimes he would favour the Mosque of the Round City, sometimes the Mosque of ar-Ruṣáfah.[2]

'Alí was convinced that economy was just as necessary in small matters as in large. He spent a long time, for instance, in examining the food supplied to the royal ducks. He thought that the best barley was too good for them, and insisted on the official in charge feeding them with the barley that was sodden from lying at the bottom of the barges in transport. The official mocked at 'Alí's particularity in private. By working it out he discovered that the Vizier's salary for one hour was more than equal to the sum that could be saved. But 'Alí on hearing of it admonished him for his levity. He assured him that the scale of a transaction affected the principle on which it should be dealt with not in the least.[3] During the short nights of summer, again, 'Alí reduced the supply of oil and candles issued to the palace servants. The official responsible objected that this was an unwonted economy. 'Alí replied that when the servants needed more they asked for it soon enough. When therefore a chance for reduction occurred, it should most decidedly be taken.[4]

One very cold day, when most people were sitting round braziers muffled up to the chin in quilts, 'Alí

1 S.J. fol. 138 a.
2 S.J. fol. 56 b; H. 282.
3 H. 351.
4 H. 353.

had audience of Ja'far. To his surprise he found him bareheaded in a large saloon. He asked whether to keep out the cold the Caliph was in the habit of taking hot drinks or much spiced food. Ja'far said, No: he took musk, for example, only in one particular dish. 'Alí noted the fact, recollecting that the Caliph's monthly bill for musk was quite high. As he was leaving the Presence, Ja'far called him back. He taxed him with intending to reduce the supply. 'Alí had to admit it was true. The Caliph laughed. "I do not wish you to," he said. "The money is probably spent on various occasions, and meets some people's expenses. I should not like you to cut it off."[1]

By the end of his first twelve months in office 'Alí had thus gained an equivocal reputation. His pious ways created no doubt a favourable impression. His professional skill was certainly much admired. By the farmers and peasants who benefited from his reforms he was universally blessed. But his retrenchments ran counter to the interests of many others (and they more powerful), so that in their eyes his virtues were completely eclipsed.

1 H. 352–3.

CHAPTER V

‘Alí’s *negotiations with the* Carmathians. *The foundation of the* Fáṭimid Anti-Caliphate, *and the attack on* Egypt.

During the first year of his Vizierate ‘Alí had also engaged in diplomacy, in the hope of preserving peace. For it was essential to the success of his financial schemes that the forces of the Caliphate should be occupied as little as possible in fighting, war being the swiftest consumer of treasure. The Carmathians were the most likely enemy: his efforts, accordingly, were concentrated on them, and with the happiest results. Unfortunately for his policy, however, hostilities were to break out elsewhere.

About a year before ‘Alí’s return from Mecca, Abú Sa‘íd al-Jannábí had made another demonstration against al-Baṣrah. His Carmathians completely routed the small force that the commandant gathered together and sent out against them. But they then withdrew without attempting to take the city. Nor did they again reappear.[1] When ‘Alí became Vizier, he considered that the relations between the sectaries and the ‘Abbásid Court should be placed on a more satisfactory footing. Hitherto al-Jannábí had done little more than threaten attacks. But even these threats were disturbing. ‘Alí was anxious to obtain some better assurance of peace. He accordingly prepared an embassy to convey a letter to the Carmathian headquarters. His aims were, first, the conventional one of “urging” al-Jannábí “to obedience, and rebuking him for what was said of his people in the matter of their abandoning the prescribed prayers and almsgiving and allowing what was prohibited”, and, secondly, the practical one

1 ‘A. 38.

of obtaining the release of the Orthodox prisoners still in Carmathian hands.

The ambassadors proceeded to al-Baṣrah. But there they were met with the news of al-Jannábí's assassination: he and four of his chief officers had been murdered in his tent by a Russian slave. The ambassadors were uncertain what to do: but 'Alí instructed them to continue their journey in spite of what had occurred. They found on their arrival that al-Jannábí had been succeeded by his eldest son Sa'íd, who was to rule with the help of a council. The embassy was well received. The letter was read, and answered, politely, with the contention that the sectaries had been driven against their wish from out the community of Islam. The prisoners, too, were duly released, and accompanied the envoys on their journey home. Moreover, whether by reason of 'Alí's diplomacy, or of the death of Abú Sa'íd, the Carmathians ceased in fact to menace the Caliphate for a number of years.[1]

The Caliphate was to be attacked from quite another side, but by a force that had, nevertheless, a close connection with the Carmathians. The Ismá'ílí propagandists had had especial success among the Berbers in parts of Ifriqiyyah, and during the final decade of the third century (A.D. 903–913), they led the converted tribes against their Aghlabid rulers (tributaries to the 'Abbásids). They fought in the name of a new *Mahdí*, a certain 'Ubayd Allah ibn Muḥammad, who, like his predecessors, the "Man with the Mole" and the "Man with the She-Camel", claimed to be a descendant of Muḥammad ibn Ismá'íl. The success of the movement was imperilled when, before he had yet announced his Imámate publicly, this 'Ubayd Allah was arrested on suspicion and imprisoned in Sijilmásah[2] by the governor; but in 296 (909) the rebels took Sijilmásah, found him still alive and set him free. By this time the

1 M. I, 33–5; Dh. *t.* fol. 2 a–b. 2 In southern Morocco.

Aghlabid ruler had been finally defeated and had fled to Egypt. Even the nominal ownership of the province, therefore, was now lost to the 'Abbásids. 'Ubayd Allah proceeded in 297 to Raqqádah, where he was proclaimed "Commander of the Faithful". From this event dates the foundation of the great Fáṭimid Anti-Caliphate.[1]

The Anti-Caliphs called themselves *Fáṭimid*, because they traced their lineage back to Fáṭimah the Prophet's daughter. Fáṭimid is thus synonymous with *'Alid* (from 'Alí, Fáṭimah's husband), except that it is not applicable to 'Alí's descendants by his other wife. The legitimacy of the Fáṭimids' claim to the Imámate-Caliphate was never admitted by the 'Abbásids, nor generally by the rest of the Shí'ah, but, for reasons that I have given when describing the beliefs of the Carmathians, the Anti-Caliphs may very well have been impostors from the legitimist point of view, while yet acting honestly from their own. It is significant that very soon after 'Ubayd Allah's accession the missionary that had done everything to win over the tribes and subdue the country for him suddenly declared that he was not the Imám after all. It looks as if he may suddenly have discovered (perhaps on a higher initiation) that the Mahdí's descent was, as the esoteric tenets of the sect allowed, not bodily but merely spiritual.

The Mahdí had both the missionary and his brother assassinated before they were able to do him serious damage. But even so some of the tribes rose against him. The civil war was only quelled after much fighting. Parts of the province moreover still remained to be subdued. For the first two or three years of his reign therefore the Mahdí was fully occupied at home. In 300 (A.D. 912–13), however, after his son had taken Tripoli, he was tempted to extend his empire still farther east, if he could do so, and take in Egypt.[2]

1 See *Encyclopédie*, II, 93 (art. *Fáṭimites*). 2 Maq. *it*. 40–1

It is thought that al-Jannábí made his descent on al-Baṣrah at the Mahdí's behest, and that it was so half-hearted because doubts of the Mahdí's legitimacy, in spite of his precautions, had reached even to al-Baḥrayn. The plan was for the Carmathians to invade al-'Iráq, whilst the Fáṭimids invaded Egypt. Barqah (Cyrenaica-Benghazi) was in fact attacked in 300, but the 'Abbásid governor then defeated the insurgents—he was not even aware, so it appears, that they were the Mahdí's men.[1] It was only two years later, after 'Alí had concluded his agreement with the Carmathians, that the Government at Baghdád felt any reason for alarm. Then a sudden appeal was received from Egypt. Tagín, the governor, was in direst need of help. At the end of 301 (914) an army of more than forty thousand men had been landed on the African coast from a fleet of two hundred ships. Barqah had again been attacked, and this time captured. A month later Alexandria itself had fallen. The Fáṭimids were now advancing upon Fusṭáṭ.

This news was the more shocking to al-Muqtadir and his advisers in that hitherto they had scorned the power of the "*shí'í*" or the "son of the Baṣran", as they called 'Ubayd Allah. They had examined his genealogy and decided that it was false. But now reinforcements were at once sent from Syria, and Mu'nis was ordered to proceed with a force to Egypt as soon as he could equip it. 'Alí, for his part, organised a camel post to bring daily tidings of the war.

Tagín appears to have set out against the enemy as soon as the first fresh troops, presumably those from Syria, arrived. And after several indecisive engagements he won a complete victory. "Thousands were slain on each side". Seven thousand Fáṭimids were either killed or captured. So within six months of its

1 Ṭab. III, 2288.

first fall Alexandria was retaken. The Fáṭimids forthwith abandoned Barqah also, and retired once again to the west.[1]

The months of waiting, although they had been few in fact, had seemed long and anxious to the metropolitans. Opinion among them had grown more and more dejected: when therefore the news of victory at length arrived, their rejoicing was proportionately heart-felt. 'Alí had earliest knowledge of it and hastened to the pleasant duty of informing the Caliph. Al-Muqtadir, in his delight, ordered a prodigal largesse to be distributed among the people. He even desired to make 'Alí a present. But 'Alí with his wonted modesty refused it. Later it was known that he himself had bestowed in alms, "in token of his thankfulness to God", the price of an estate, a considerable sum, that his steward had sold for him.[2]

Almost simultaneously with the first bad news from Egypt other bad news had reached Baghdád, no less shocking and from nearer home. Early in 302 (914) certain Arab tribes of the desert, led by an 'Alíd, had seen fit to imitate the Carmathians and ambush the caravans as they were returning from Mecca to al-'Iráq: they had stolen everything they could, carrying off almost three hundred women into captivity, and leaving the rest to perish of hunger and thirst. As usual there was an outcry in the capital. But the unfortunate 'Alí, with his hands already more than full with the Egyptian campaign, could spare no troops at present to go out and punish the offenders: all he could do was to write a letter to the 'Alíd leader, demanding the return of the loot and prisoners. This, as might be expected, was ineffective. Later, however, 'Alí was able to send out a force under the new Chamberlain,

1 Ṭab. III, 2291–3; Tagh. II, 181–2; Dh. *t.* fol. 2 b; S.J. fol. 57 b.

2 'A. 51–3.

Naṣr al-Qushúrí, which captured the bandit and brought him to Baghdád.[1]

It seems likely that 'Alí imagined this attack on the caravans actually to have been the work of the Carmathians. In 303 (915–16), at any rate, so we are told, "he looked again into the Carmathian business", and came to the conclusion that they must be bought off. Accordingly he sent another embassy to Ḥajar, laden this time with presents of various kinds. In return for their continued good behaviour, also, he offered the sectaries the use of the port of Ṣíráf on the coast of the Persian Gulf opposite their dominions.

The sending of this second embassy aroused, it seems, a good deal of adverse comment in Baghdád. 'Alí's motives were misconstrued: he was thought to cherish Carmathian sympathies himself. His policy, however, proved so successful that later the people saw that their suspicions had been baseless. Nevertheless these suspicions were to be used against him, more than once, with some effect.[2]

1 'A. 54; Tagh. II, 194; Dh. *t.* fol. 3 a, b; S.J. ff. 59 b, 62 b.
2 'A. 59; Dh. *t.* fol. 3 b; S.J. fol. 59 b.

CHAPTER VI

The consequences of the Egyptian *campaign—the revolt of* Ibn Ḥamdán. 'Alí's *growing unpopularity; his misfortunes and fall.*

The financial drawbacks of the war in Egypt were apparent almost at once. Mu'nis arrived with his army only as the last Fáṭimids were vanishing; but the Egyptians soon felt and resented the burden of this multitude of soldiers quartered upon them; the farmer of the taxes complained to Baghdád, and some of the troops were soon transferred to Syria. Nevertheless two hundred camel-loads of silver coin had to be sent by special convoy to Fusṭáṭ;[1] and this, seeing that, far from any such transaction's being normal, Egypt was expected to provide for its provincial garrison and send a large surplus to the capital, was a very grave matter.

The concentration of the armies in Egypt led, moreover, to fighting elsewhere. First al-Ḥusayn ibn Ḥamdán (the same that had deserted Ibn al-Mu'tazz—and had meanwhile been reconciled with al-Muqtadir)[2] rebelled not long after in his native Mosul; and later the Greeks, seeing the pre-occupation of the 'Abbásid forces in these domestic difficulties, made bold to advance into Muslim territory.[3] 'Alí was thus faced with a double embarrassment. He met it by sending out a force under the highest in rank of al-Mu'tadhid's freedmen against al-Ḥusayn; and by recalling Mu'nis from Egypt to "restore the frontiers". The former officer, however, had no success in his campaign. 'Alí was therefore obliged to invite Mu'nis to intervene

1 'A. 53; Tagh. II, 182–3.

2 'A. 30–1; M. I, 15.

3 'A. 55.

here also, and his intervention was so effectual that al-Ḥusayn at once began to temporise. He complained that he had been forced into rebellion by the disfavour of the Vizier. (Perhaps he had been the victim of one of ʻAlí's thunderclaps.) At the same time, however, he retreated northwards, and as he did so his army gradually melted away till he was left almost alone with his family. Mu'nis took him easily, and carried him in chains to the capital.

At Baghdád a triumph was made of the victory. The great archway at the bridge-head was festooned. The prisoners were paraded through the streets on camels in mock finery, al-Ḥusayn on a wooden contrivance that caused him to bow absurdly from side to side. The Caliph set his subjects an example by witnessing the spectacle in person. His eldest son, a boy of five, took part in the procession. He was accompanied by ʻAlí ibn ʻÍsà, Naṣr the Chamberlain, the chief officers, and, not least, the elephant.

The returned troops judged the occasion a good one for demanding a rise in pay; but none of the officers would hear of it, or receive their spokesmen. By way of protest therefore they gathered outside the gateway of ʻAlí's house and set fire to it, after which they slaughtered the horses in his stables. They then proceeded in a body to the oratory outside the walls to the north-east of the city—a place consecrated by custom to the voicing of complaints—and continued their clamour till Mu'nis appeared to soothe them. Mu'nis compounded with them for a very slight increase, whereupon they confessed themselves sorry for what they had done.[1]

The outrage on his property was only a fresh sign of ʻAlí's growing unpopularity. Others had already occurred. One day, for example, about a year before, when the Caliph was riding out to the parade ground,

1 ʻA. 56–8; M. I, 36–8.

'Alí had been thrown from his horse in an attempt to overtake him. The wits had at once seized on this mishap and made it the theme of a rhymed lampoon. —'Alí's fall from his horse portended a fall from office. They were glad of it for a good omen. "East and west" 'Alí had neglected the revenue (a peculiarly unjust accusation, this); so that the Imám (the Caliph) had not benefited by any accumulation.[1]

But by this time 'Alí was well used to criticism in verse. More than once, recently, he had had to bear the abuse of the atrabilious Ibn Bassám. When 'Alí was banished to Mecca, Ibn Bassám had composed mocking lines on the event; and when he had returned as Vizier, the poet published others, in which he declared that he had "all his life desired 'Alí to attain the Vizierate", but complained that, now, when that desire was at last gratified, others "had been advanced before him, who, when he approached them, would hold no converse with him". One day, among the morning's petitions, 'Alí came on a paper with other verses expressing disgust at his elevation, and although they were unsigned he had no difficulty in guessing their authorship. "This is surely Ibn Bassám," he said, "and yet, by God, he has never suffered through any fault of mine!"[2]

Now, again, when he was riding through a lane, a paper was dropped in his way from an upper window. On one side of it were written verses desiring his death. 'Alí read them through and wrote an answer in the same metre on the back. His end was foredoomed: till his time came, "though a lion were to attack him raging, he would prevail against it". He then had the paper laid again where it had first fallen.[3]

1 'A. 51.

2 Yáq. *ud.* v, 319, 324; Qudh. fol. 91 a.

3 H. 354–5. Apparently 'Alí was quoting these verses—they were not his own. At any rate they appear in the *Arabian Nights*,

He could bear such hostility calmly. What really distressed him was the knowledge that the Caliph was being influenced against him, that all his labours, successful as they had been, might suddenly be brought to naught by an intrigue. He had had his first warning of such hidden machinations in the pretended funeral of Ibn al-Furát. And in fact the latter's partisans had been at work almost ever since 'Alí took office. Ibn al-Furát himself remained in prison, with no apparent prospect of release. But his cause was kept continually before al-Muqtadir by a certain Ibn Farjawayh, one of his supporters, who had been lucky enough to escape arrest. Ibn Farjawayh communicated with his patron through one of the Court physicians, and in accordance with his instructions assailed the Caliph, in a series of letters, with constant praise of Ibn al-Furát and constant criticism of the Vizier.

The chief score of criticism was of course 'Alí's parsimony. But he was accused as well of undue clemency to discharged officials: it was said that he failed to exact the customary fines from them—and as such sums would be paid into the Privy Purse,[1] this was a shrewd hit. 'Alí's attitude in such circumstances was unconventional enough. "I will not use treacherously any official that I have trusted," he would say.[2]

This accusation probably had some foundation in fact. Certainly there is recorded an analogous instance, of 'Alí's excusing a defaulting official the payment of his debt to the State. The man cared only for bread baked at home, so he used to take some out with him

in the tale of Nur al-Din Ali and the Damsel Anis al-Jalis. Burton (Library ed.), 1, 365, renders them thus:

Needs must I bear the term of Fate decreed,—And when
that day be dead needs must I die;
If lions dragged me to their forest lair,—Safe should I live
till draw my death-day nigh.

1 See H. 79. 2 M. 1, 43.

to eat with his mid-day meal. When his accounts were being examined, two small rounds of the bread fell by chance out of his sleeve; on which 'Alí, assuming this to be a sign of sad poverty, felt bound to take pity on it.[1]

Yet if anyone had a right to criticise 'Alí on the score of depriving the Caliph of money rightfully his, decidedly it was not Ibn al-Furát. True, it was not his way to excuse the payment of fines:—on the contrary, he preferred to exact them and devote the proceeds to his own uses. This is what he had done with the greater part of the considerable sums wrung from the partisans of Ibn al-Mu'tazz. He had escaped detection by confiding the whole business, not to the officials of the Treasury, but to two Jewish money-changers; and had represented the total in an account to the Treasury as only about one-tenth of what the secretaries computed it really to have been. The money-changers had duly paid up this sum on demand; but 'Alí, when he came to power, resolved to recover what he could of the rest. Under pressure, the two Jews confessed to a large sum as the amount of their profits on the whole transaction. 'Alí, however, did not require them to disgorge this amount in a lump. Instead he made an arrangement, administratively very convenient, whereby at the beginning of each month they were to supply the Vizier with an advance from which he might meet certain recurrent expenses, and to reimburse themselves, though without the usual charge of interest, from part of the revenues of al-Ahwáz and Wásiṭ.[2]

In 302 (914–15) a very wealthy man, formerly in the service of the Ṭúlúnids, had been suddenly arrested and thrown into prison. As much as six million *dínárs'* worth[3] is said to have been seized from him, partly in

1 H. 348–9. 2 H. 79–81.

3 The various authorities give the total seized at various figures, from four to twenty millions.

cash and bonds, partly in jewels, horses and other possessions. There was some justification for his despoilment in the fact that he was known to have kept for himself a part of the dowry of Khumárawayh's daughter, who had been married to al-Mu'tadhid, and whom he had escorted from Egypt to Baghdád. Moreover, the man remained exceedingly well-to-do; but since no formal case was made out against him, the affair had rather the air of an official robbery. 'Alí is not mentioned as having had any hand in his arrest; apparently the eunuch that carried it out (with the assistance of the Chief of Police) acted on al-Muqtadir's orders direct. But if it was in confiscations as high-handed as this that the Caliph was pleased to deal, no wonder if 'Alí's scruples in the infliction of penalties should seem to him wantonly remiss.[1]

Ja'far was quite taken in by the diplomacy of Ibn Farjawayh. So little did he suspect that he was working for Ibn al-Furát that in the end he himself went to Ibn al-Furát for advice on the subject. Ibn al-Furát confirmed the allegations of Ibn Farjawayh. Ja'far consequently began seriously to contemplate dismissing 'Alí even before the outbreak of the Egyptian war. Mu'nis, however, whom he consulted, was set against it, and for the time being 'Alí was safe.[2] But with Mu'nis's departure for the war he was bereft of his most influential supporter. About the same time, moreover, he was unlucky enough to make a new enemy.

The highest officials of State, among them 'Alí, Mu'nis, the Uncle and Naṣr the Chamberlain, were one day gathered solemnly in conclave, deliberating the conduct of the campaign against the Fáṭimids, when into their midst burst Umm Músà the *qahramánah*. Unabashed by their grave demeanour she seated her-

1 M. I, 35; H. 223; 'A. 47–8; Dh. *t*. fol. 3 a; S.J. ff. 59 b, 84 a–b; Tagh. II, 231.
2 M. I, 43–4; H. 30.

self upon the cushions beside 'Alí, and produced for his perusal a list of petty wants from the Lady "for a small increase in the lodging allowance of one of the retinue, and a slight rise in pay for one of the eunuchs". The Vizier was angry at such an interruption of business. He threw the paper aside and resumed the discussion.

Umm Músà was deeply offended. "Is this the way in which the princes' wants are attended to?" she cried.

"O, such a one," replied 'Alí, "we are engaged on affairs of life and death, the preservation of the very foundations of the State, and you distract us with a matter of no importance!"

But Umm Músà was not to be shaken; and when 'Alí even went to the trouble of explaining to her the gravity of the situation, she only wondered that anything so remote could seriously engage their attention. This was too much even for 'Alí. He broke up the assembly in a rage. Umm Músà, on her side, retired feeling that she had been slighted; and from this time on she treasured up in her heart a passionate malevolence against the impertinent minister.[1]

The absence of Mu'nis from the capital made less difference to his prospects than Ibn al-Furát had hoped, since both the Uncle and the Chamberlain—who was somehow connected with the general, sharing his surname *al-Qushúrí*—were on 'Alí's side.[2] Ibn Farjawayh, indeed, gave up hope of convincing the Caliph of 'Alí's misdeeds: instead he began to vaunt the contrasting qualities of Ibn al-Furát. To win over the courtiers he promised that if Ibn al-Furát were restored to the Vizierate he would once more increase their wages. To Ja'far himself he promised 1000 *dínárs* a day, and to his sons and the Lady, 500 between

1 H. 353–4.

2 H. differs from M. here, stating that the Uncle and Naṣr were opposed to 'Alí; but this is evidently wrong.

them.[1] No one appears to have enquired whence all this money was to be produced.[2] Indeed the courtiers were indifferent. As for the Caliph, he was so delighted to find that the future might not after all offer the prospect only of progressive economies, that he began once more to visit Ibn al-Furát in prison.[3]

The difficulties of 'Alí's position were increased by a drought which ruined the harvest of the year 303 (915–16). In the following spring also his brother Dá'úd died, his funeral being attended by all the eminent.[4] This brother is not mentioned in any other passage. It is therefore impossible to say in what degree 'Alí was attached to him. But his death may well have come at a moment to make 'Alí's burden seem intolerable. Soon after, at any rate, in the face of so much opposition and misfortune he began to despair of remaining in office. Indeed he regarded his dismissal as certain, unless he could forestall it by retiring. He would ask therefore to be allowed to retire again to Mecca; but in case this move should only precipitate his fall, he took the precaution of putting his property beyond reach of confiscation by the State. An arrangement was legal by which property made over as a pious foundation was administered by the donor and his heirs. Hence they continued to enjoy what they cared of it, without its being theirs to lose. 'Alí now made over the bulk of his property in this way. He also set free his slaves.[5] He was anxious,

1 Of these 500 *dínárs* a day the Lady in fact received two-thirds, and al-Muqtadir's two sons, the Princes Abú'l-'Abbás (afterwards ar-Rádhí) and Hárún, one-third between them. M. 1, 42.

2 Only these allowances were provided for, uncertainly enough, from prospective fines, and exactions on account of bribes. See M. *loc. cit.* and below, p. 153.

3 M. 1, 44; H. 30–1.

4 'A. 63. S.J. fol. 62 b states also that a son of 'Alí's, by name 'Abd al-Wahháb, died in this year. No other reference, however, is made to any such son.

5 H. 283.

moreover, if he should after all have to suffer the consequences of dismissal, to leave his successor in office as little as possible wherewith to charge him. He accordingly obtained on al-Muqtadir's authorisation an acknowledgement from every recipient of a salary (including the Caliph's family and harem) that he or she had been paid what was due to them in full.

When 'Alí was explaining his case to Ja'far he argued almost too eloquently. He pointed out how in contrast with Ibn al-Furát and al-Kháqání he had drawn nothing from the Privy Purse. As for the future, if, though he did not wish it, he was to continue in office, not only would he still draw nothing from the Privy Purse, he would guarantee at the end of one year to pay a million *dínárs* into it, so well re-established would the finances then be.

Ja'far was momentarily touched. He protested: he was far from even contemplating 'Alí's dismissal. His only sentiments were gratitude for his good management of affairs and confidence in his ability. He would afford him what help he could. The Vizier might count on his co-operation.[1]

'Alí left the palace feeling somewhat reassured. If he was not to have the retirement he desired, at least it seemed that the Caliph would support him. He reinforced his appeal to Ja'far with a letter to the Lady. It seems that she had written to him setting forth the heads of complaints that had been made against him. Evidently she was anxious to be fair to him. Indeed the Lady always had something of a weakness for 'Alí: his piety appealed to hers. In his answer 'Alí began by repeating his argument about his care for the Privy Purse. Only here he stated (the two accounts being at variance) that the expenses of war had forced him to draw from it a sum that he was now on the point of repaying. But "when," he went on, "would not al-

1 H. 349–50; M. I, 40; Tagh. II, 200; S.J. fol. 63 a.

Mu'tadhid bi'llah have spent double the amount on his excursions against his enemies?...Al-Muktafí, though he was in the habit of scrutinising the slightest and most insignificant trifles, would pay out sum after sum...." 'Alí recalled the successes of his reforms—"my good treatment of the people, my restoration of ruined districts, and the removal from them of tyranny and oppression." The people nowadays respected law and order, whereas before they used "to rise up against the officers, and throw stones at them, as I have heard, as they went up and down the Tigris". The complaints of the troops had been utterly unsubstantial. They were simply trying to exact a gratuity. The Lady might have heard of his wish to resign. It was not out of idleness or discontent that he had made the petition. He was ready to bear any reverses of fortune—"even if ashes were heaped upon my head"—in the Caliph's service. What he could hardly support were the continual calumnies of his enemies and their senseless criticism of his actions.[1]

What the Lady thought of the letter, indeed whether or not she ever received it, is not recorded.

It was now only a few days before the Great Feast. The Court, particularly the Harem, was in its annual excitement over the event. 'Alí had all his preparations well in hand. He had called in a proportion of the revenue dues from certain districts in advance, to meet the special expense. He had nothing therefore to fear (as Ibn al-Furát had had) on this score. Nevertheless the Feast was to prove his undoing.

Umm Músà was of course particularly officious on such occasions. Many of the arrangements for the Harem were in her hands. On this account she came once again to visit the Vizier with a list of requirements. But she was told by his chamberlain, to her indignation, that he was asleep and not to be disturbed.

1 H. 283–5.

For some time Umm Músà's dislike of 'Alí ibn 'Ísà had been growing. Last year he had attacked her brother for abusing his privileges to enrich himself; and only with difficulty had she succeeded in saving him from actual prosecution.[1] At this final insult therefore (for so she construed it) her wrath passed all bounds. She went off boiling with rage to pour out the tale of her woes to the Lady.

'Alí woke up just too late. But in the hope of mending matters he sent after the *qahramánah* entreating her to return. She would not be mollified, however, and laid her train against him.

Two days before the Feast, on 8th *dhú'l-ḥijjah* 304 (2nd June 917), and exactly one week after his conversation with the Caliph, 'Alí was arrested on his way to the palace.[2]

1 'A. 58. Umm Músà may have had another reason for bearing 'Alí a grudge. On Ibn Ṭúmár's death in 301 (914) her brother had been appointed *naqíb* in his place; but after he had held the post for a time the Háshimites complained that he was unsatisfactory, and he was replaced by Ibn Ṭúmár's son. Although we are not told that 'Alí had anything to do with his dismissal, it is quite likely that, as Vizier, he had. 'A. 47.

2 H. 285–6; M. 1, 40; 'A. 61.

CHAPTER VII

The second Vizierate of Ibn al-Furát, *and his fall. The elevation of* Ḥámid ibn al-'Abbás, *and the appointment as his Assistant of* 'Alí ibn 'Ísà.

When he took office for the second time Ibn al-Furát found the finances almost as well regulated as they had been nine years before, when he had done so first. He had now regained the Caliph's favour completely. The courtiers rejoiced at his restoration. Nevertheless at the end of thirteen months the cavalry were on the point of rioting for their pay, and the Vizier was in such straits for money with which to furnish it, that he was forced to ask a gift of the Caliph from the Privy Purse. Moreover he had by then so far lost his influence at Court, that soon after, when his enemies accused him of treason, Ja'far was ready to believe them, while no one came forward to defend him. Such was his use of the year that was all 'Alí had asked for the maturing of his schemes.

At the outset funds were comparatively plentiful, thanks to 'Alí's four years' exertions. Besides, not only were 'Alí himself and his subordinates, including his brothers Ibrahím and 'Ubayd Allah,[1] very heavily fined in the customary way, but Ibn al-Furát also devised a new method of raising money from dismissed officials. He assumed that they had accepted bribes, and required that they should refund on this account certain sums, fixed arbitrarily by him, to a specially created Office of Bribes (*díwán al-maráfiq*). He also fined and imprisoned again the unfortunate al-Kháqání, alleging that 'Alí had treated him too leniently.[2]

1 Dh. *t.* fol. 4 a. The statement given here, that 'Alí was shortly released, is evidently incorrect.

2 M. I, 41, 42; H. 31–2, 86.

It was soon clear, however, that the mere fulfilment of his undertakings would involve him in difficulties. The funds at his disposal were simply not large enough to meet the expense of the Caliph's and the Lady's allowances and the general increase of salaries that he had promised. Moreover, extravagance prevailed both in small matters and in great. It was related, for example, that on his taking office the price of ice and candles and paper at once went up, so profuse was his use of them—the ice and candles for the entertainment on hot nights of his guests, the paper (supplied by him) for their petitions.[1] In the very first month of his Vizierate, also, vast sums were spent on the reception of ambassadors from Byzantium, sent by the Emperor (Constantine VII) to arrange a truce for the exchange of prisoners.[2]

Then Ibn al-Furát was faced, very soon after his restoration, with a serious rebellion; and this was not merely expensive, it gave his enemies a chance to attack him. Incidentally, too, it allowed 'Alí ibn 'Ísà, quite by chance, to regain some of the favour he had lost with al-Muqtadir. The rebel was a certain Yúsuf ibn Ráfi' ibn Abí's-Sáj, who for some seventeen years had ruled almost independently in Muslim Armenia and Azarbayján, being obliged only to pay a yearly tribute to the Caliph. He had continued to pay this tribute, more or less regularly, till the disgrace of Ibn al-Furát in 299 (912);[3] but ever since he had withheld the greater part of it, so that much gold had accumulated in his coffers. 'Alí, with whom he had prevaricated, had taken no steps to coerce him. Nor, probably, would Ibn al-Furát have taken any, had not Ibn Abí's-Sáj, feeling himself strong in this wealth, now sought to extend his rule.

1 H. 63; *fakh.* 312.

2 M. I, 53–5; 'Ar. 64–5; Fid. II, 69; Salmon: *Introduction*, 132 (text, 49).

3 Ṭab. III, 2203, 2204–5, 2280, 2284; 'A. 19, 31.

The governor of Ray having lately shown signs of disaffection, Ibn Abí's-Sáj made this a pretext for expelling him; and overran the surrounding country with his army. Upon this the Caliph protested; but Ibn Abí's-Sáj then announced that he had acted on orders from 'Alí ibn 'Ísà, sent to him shortly before the latter's arrest. Ibn al-Furát at once suggested to Ja'far that 'Alí was indeed responsible, that he was actually guilty of having plotted with Ibn Abí's-Sáj. 'Alí, still in prison, was therefore called to answer the charge. He showed conclusively that it was groundless by appealing both to the records and to the officers.[1] For such an order to be authoritative it must have been registered, and must have been conveyed to its recipient by one of the officers; but no evidence of its despatch was forthcoming. Ja'far was delighted with the way in which 'Alí had exonerated himself: he gave orders that he should be treated in prison with special consideration. By attempting to implicate him Ibn al-Furát had only improved 'Alí's position, and, if anything, worsened his own.

On the other hand the Caliph was angry at the attempted deceit of Ibn Abí's-Sáj. A force was immediately sent against him; but it was defeated, and Mu'nis, who (the truce being over) was again engaged with the Greeks, had once more to be summoned and put in command. On his approach Ibn Abí's-Sáj withdrew from the invaded territory, only tarrying to extort a year's taxes from the inhabitants; and at the same time he besought Ibn al-Furát to allow him to retain Armenia and Āẕarbayján as before. Ibn al-Furát himself was inclined to consent; but Naṣr the Cham-

1 So M. According to 'A., however, he produced an authorisation signed by the Caliph, his aim having been to pit the two rebels against each other;—but surely even al-Muqtadir could hardly have forgotten so soon having given his sanction to so important a move.

berlain, who was always ready to oppose him, persuaded Ja'far to refuse. Mu'nis was therefore ordered to pursue the rebel. When they met, however, the ever-victorious general was for once defeated; Ibn Abí's-Sáj completely routed his army, and only forbore out of magnanimity to take Mu'nis himself prisoner.[1]

By this time Ibn al-Furát was in extremely bad odour not only with Ja'far but with many of the courtiers. He had alienated some of the latter by recovering at their expense the whole of his confiscated estates, which al-Muqtadir had distributed among them on his fall; and he had offended others by passing them over for employment in favour of his relations.[2] This hostile party was led by Naṣr the Chamberlain and by a certain Ibn al-Ḥawwárí, who was gradually becoming one of the most influential persons at Court. They seized every chance that came their way of injuring Ibn al-Furát, who retaliated by depriving them, wherever he was able, of their offices. Their satisfaction therefore was great when one of his chief supporters, Ibn Muqlah by name, deserted his patron and came over to them.

This Ibn Muqlah (Muḥammad ibn 'Alí ibn al-Ḥasan) was to become one of the most celebrated calligraphists in the history of Islam[3]—he had much to do with adapting the clumsy and confusing Kúfic lettering to the more flowing style used ever since. But at this time he was a man of no more than thirty-three years of age, that had not yet made his mark. He had first been engaged as a Government clerk at the age of sixteen, on the formation of the *díwán ad-dár*, in which he worked under Muḥammad ibn Dá'úd for the modest remuneration of 6 *dínárs* a month;[4] and he had continued to work under Ibn al-Furát after the separation from the *díwán ad-dár* of the Offices

1 M. I, 45–7; 'A. 56, 67, 70–1.
2 H. 97.
3 *fih.* 9; *fakh.* 318 (etc.).
4 Dh. *t.* fol. 183 b.

of East and West, gradually rising, as time went on, to more and more responsible posts.[1] His ambition was first stirred when Ibn al-Furát, as Vizier, allowed him to profit by a very considerable sum on a sale of Government grain: this had been the foundation of his fortune.[2] By now he was definitely of the Furát faction: on his patron's disgrace he had gone into hiding, and though 'Alí had offered him employment, he had declined it. He had preferred to await Ibn al-Furát's restoration; and when at last it came Ibn Muqlah considered that he was entitled, in return for his self-sacrifice, to a peculiar place in the Vizier's esteem. There were others, however, that had even greater claims on it; and Ibn Muqlah was piqued to find that these were acknowledged. He resolved to avenge himself by revealing a secret that he knew would damage Ibn al-Furát, it might be fatally; he would reveal it to Naṣr the Chamberlain, to whom he had recently been made secretary. The secret was this, that whereas Ibn al-Furát had sworn to the Caliph before being restored to power that he had accounted for every part of his wealth, in reality he had kept large sums concealed on deposit with various citizens, and had now recovered them. Naṣr seized eagerly on this means of damaging the Vizier: he at once told Ja'far, and Ja'far was duly enraged.[3]

Ibn al-Furát would not at first believe that his friend and *protégé* had betrayed him. He even sought a reconciliation; but Ibn Muqlah, really ashamed of what he had done, was only driven thereby the more irrevocably into the arms of his new allies. Ibn al-Furát was advised to recover his favour with the Caliph by bribing him with money obtained from a levy on his followers. But he wisely declined, supposing that this would only seem to confirm the story of his hidden wealth.[4] The discontents of the cavalry, moreover,

1 H. 119. 2 H. 215. 3 M. 1, 52. 4 H. 98.

made any such action futile. Ibn al-Furát could not afford the risk of a riot in the city; there was nothing for him to do but ask Ja'far for help. He did his best to excuse the necessity he was put to: the campaign against Ibn Abí's-Sáj had proved very expensive; moreover, since Ibn Abí's-Sáj had seized the revenues of Ray for himself, the Government was so much the poorer. But Ja'far was firm: the Vizier had undertaken to supply *him* with money; that he should now be asked to supply the Vizier with it was preposterous.[1]

Ja'far hearkened at length to the advice of Naṣr. He agreed that they must find someone to replace Ibn al-Furát. The obvious candidate was 'Alí ibn 'Ísà. But there were grave objections to his restoration: he was exceedingly unpopular at Court; to restore him so soon would seem at least capricious—in view of his having been fined it might seem positively dishonest. 'Alí himself was clearly unsuitable; but since he could be depended upon to be disinterested, his advice on the problem would be invaluable. A list of possible Viziers was accordingly drawn up, and sent to 'Alí in prison.

On Alí's fall, the houses of his brothers and most of their supporters had as usual been sacked.[2] But none of their estates were sequestrated;[3] and 'Alí's own house appears to have been respected, and his women to have come to no harm, since it is one of the remarkable facts recounted of him, that they passed through all the vicissitudes of his career unscathed.[4] He was lodged in the palace itself, in the keeping of a *qahramánah*, Zaydán, who had formerly guarded Ibn al-Furát.[5] It appears that his quarters were not uncomfortable, and that he had no more to suffer than anxiety and boredom.[6]

1 M. I, 56.
2 'A. 61.
3 M. I, 40; S.J. fol. 62 b.
4 Yáq. *ud.* v, 280.
5 'A. 61; H. 286; M. I, 40.
6 H. 347.

The versifiers of the capital, as was their wont, had mocked 'Alí on his fall;[1] and a wit had summed up the change of Viziers by saying, "They have deprived us of a *qur'án*, and given us a guitar". This saying, when it came to the ears of Ja'far, had troubled his conscience: he felt that he owed this "*qur'án*" some recompense for having used it so ill;[2] and this feeling had been stimulated by 'Alí's clever defence of his conduct against the imputations of Ibn al-Furát, until now the Caliph would have been ready, if circumstances had allowed it, to reinstate him.

'Alí found it impossible to recommend wholeheartedly any of the nominees on the list. Most of them indeed he condemned. His own brother, Ibrahím, for example, was "grasping, avaricious and unsuitable". His cousin Sulaymán ibn al-Ḥasan, otherwise suitable, was "too young" (only forty-three). For Ibn al-Ḥawwárí he could find no words but "There is no god but God!" If he favoured any it was Ḥámid ibn al-'Abbás, the tax-farmer of Wásiṭ, who was "very rich", and if "aged" still "virtuous". In the end Ḥámid ibn al-'Abbás was actually appointed. But it is difficult to judge how much 'Alí's remarks may have weighed with Ja'far in making his choice, for there were other circumstances that also favoured it.[3]

This Ḥámid appears to have begun life very humbly, as a date-seller and water-carrier.[4] But somehow he had amassed a large fortune, and had been given important fiscal contracts by the Government. He had long been noted for the pomp with which he surrounded himself. Al-Mu'taḍhid had commended the state he kept up in Fárs as being likely to impress the

1 Quḍh. fol. 91 a. 2 S.J. fol. 63 b.
3 'A. 72–3.
4 Yáq. *ud.* v, 325; Mas. *murúj*, viii, 258–9. See Massignon: *Al-Hallaj*, 211.

people with the majesty of Government.[1] When he moved to Wásiṭ he continued to live in the same sumptuous way, and lately the display of his wealth had attracted the attention of one of Ibn al-Furát's supporters, by name Ibn Jubayr, who was visiting the town. Ḥámid's contract for the collection of the revenue had expired in the last year of 'Alí's Vizierate, and in the hope of securing its renewal he had withheld part of the dues (as a hostage). It now occurred to Ibn Jubayr that if Ḥámid could be forced at least to discharge his debt—and possibly to disgorge some of his riches by way of a fine as well—the money might be exceedingly useful to his patron.

Ibn al-Furát allowed him to write to Ḥámid. But Ibn Jubayr wrote so fiercely (it seems that he had a personal grudge against him) that Ḥámid was both infuriated and alarmed. He replied in violent language, and at the same time he began a counterplot. He cultivated his friendship with the local agent of the Lady: made him fine gifts to exemplify his generosity; hinted at his profound understanding of statecraft; told him what he would do with rascals like Ibn al-Furát and his crew if he were Vizier. The agent was far from loath to be the means of raising a minister to power. He wrote on the subject to his mistress and the Chamberlain.

Such was the situation when news of Mu'nis's defeat reached the capital. So inexplicable an event was at once put down to an occult combination of forces. Rumours had been current before of collusion between Ibn al-Furát and Ibn Abí's-Sáj. Now they seemed to be confirmed. Ibn al-Furát saw that he must make an effort to prove them unfounded. But in order to do so he pitched upon a very bad expedient. He supposed that there was no hope of an inferior general's succeeding where Mu'nis had failed. Why then should

1 H. 83.

not the Caliph release al-Ḥusayn ibn Ḥamdán, who might be regarded at least as Mu'nis's equal, and send him to the rescue? Al-Ḥusayn had often fought in the Caliph's service before. There was no reason why he should not do so again. Such a proposal, however, might well shock al-Muqtadir. Ibn al-Furát hesitated before making it, and consulted his supporters. One of them must have been treacherous or at least indiscreet, for whilst the Vizier was still undecided, Naṣr came to hear of his intention. Naṣr at once informed al-Muqtadir that he had proof of the Vizier's treachery. If, he said, Ibn al-Furát were to propose the release of Ibn Ḥamdán, the Caliph must know that it was his plan for the two rebels to unite against him. As for a Vizier to replace him, Naṣr was persuaded that Ḥámid ibn al-'Abbás was the most suitable aspirant.

Ja'far was quite taken in by this stratagem, and when Ibn al-Furát put forward his proposal he was assured of his guilt. (The history of eight years before repeated itself. In neither case was Ibn al-Furát to blame. Yet the threat of conspiracy was always potent to frighten Ja'far, so that he listened to the denunciations of Naṣr as he had listened to those of al-Kháqání.) He sent word secretly to Ḥámid that he should come forthwith to the capital, and on hearing that he had set out, issued two orders. One was for the arrest of Ibn al-Furát and the chief members of his faction. The other was for the execution of Ibn Ḥamdán.[1]

Ḥámid arrived with an *éclat* substantiating his reputation. He was accompanied by four hundred armed retainers, of whom the chief were accoutred like generals of the Caliph's army. But he had not been in the capital twenty-four hours before it became evident that he was laughably ignorant of both Court etiquette and the proper management of affairs. He made no

1 M. 1, 56–8; H. 32–3; 'A. 72, 73.

move towards taking the administration in hand, preferring rather to sit and jest with visitors. His chamberlain afterwards made a cautious protest. A Vizier, he said, should dress, sit and frown as befits his station. "Do you mean," answered Ḥámid, "that I should dress up, rise to no one, laugh in no one's face, nor talk with him? Verily God has given me a merry face and a pleasant temper: I am not one to frown up my face and sour my temper for the Vizierate!"

Ḥámid had not yet been invested; but reports of his behaviour were at once brought to al-Muqtadir. He was greatly annoyed, since having once appointed Ḥámid, he could not immediately dismiss him; and vented his annoyance on Ibn al-Ḥawwárí, whom he held chiefly responsible for Ḥámid's promotion. Ibn al-Ḥawwárí, however, had still a plan by which he thought the difficulty might be surmounted. It was to appoint 'Alí ibn 'Ísà Ḥámid's Assistant. This proposal was quite likely to please the Caliph, seeing that he had wished actually to restore 'Alí to the Vizierate; for though 'Alí's restoration to that dignity had been deemed injudicious, to this appointment the same objections did not hold good. Ja'far, however—always careful to spare the feelings of his ministers, as long as they were in power—stipulated that Ḥámid should himself ask for 'Alí's release. Ibn al-Ḥawwárí returned accordingly to Ḥámid, and told him plainly that he had created a bad impression, that 'Alí's appointment was in any case certain, and that if he wished to save appearances, his only course was to do as the Caliph suggested. Now Ḥámid had been friendly with 'Alí during the latter's Vizierate;[1] so when he was invested with the robes of office, though he felt the compulsion to be humiliating, he duly requested that he might be given 'Alí ibn 'Ísà as Assistant. On this, however, Ja'far professed to doubt whether 'Alí

1 S.J. fol. 67 a.

would consent: "He will not consent," he said, "to being a follower after being followed." Ḥámid afterwards scoffed at this suggestion—and with justice, as it turned out. "Why should he not consent?" he said, to the amusement of his hearers: "A minister is like nothing so much as a tailor, that sews one garment worth a thousand *dínárs* and another worth ten *dirhams*."[1]

Ja'far determined to visit 'Alí himself; and Zaydán even prepared the prisoner for his arrival. But when it came to the point, the Caliph felt too much ashamed of the way in which he had treated 'Alí to face him. He therefore sent him a message, couched in the most tactful language, by Naṣr[2] and Ibn al-Ḥawwárí. It began: "If we had not known your distaste for the Vizierate, we should never have dismissed you." 'Alí was still unaware that Ibn al-Furát had fallen. He was not therefore surprised when he was again asked to choose a Vizier. The question was broached in this fashion apparently because the Caliph was anxious, before inviting him outright to become Assistant, to dismiss as unsuitable everyone that he should propose, and so make it harder for 'Alí himself to refuse.

'Alí was reluctant to make an unconsidered pronouncement. But since reviewing the list he must have pondered the problem, for when they pressed him, he was ready with fresh advice Two of his candidates were at Court—but neither, as he himself admitted, was particularly promising. Two were "experienced Statesmen" of a "pronounced efficiency" who had long served the Ṭúlúnids—but they were in Egypt. Naṣr and Ibn al-Ḥawwárí could therefore dismiss them all as ineligible, and went on to ask 'Alí's opinion of Ḥámid. 'Alí replied in a sense less favourable to Ḥámid than before—perhaps on con-

1 M. I, 58–9.
2 H. has Mu'nis al-Qushúrí—for Naṣr al-Qushúrí? Mu'nis was away in Persia, and it was Naṣr that had worked the whole intrigue.

sideration he felt that he had exaggerated his good points. Ḥámid was suitable enough as an Inspector, or a Collector of Taxes, he averred, but he had none of the qualities demanded by the Vizierate. On this they informed him bluntly that Ḥámid had been Vizier three days.

'Alí was mystified: if Ḥámid was Vizier, why had they consulted him? Because, they answered, Ḥámid had shown himself utterly inadequate—yet he could not be so soon dismissed. The Caliph wished to bolster up his authority by the appointment of an Assistant, and he was anxious that the Assistant should be 'Alí himself. "Ostensibly you will be his Secretary and Deputy, but actually you will be Vizier." 'Alí reflected that the alternative was an indefinite prolongation of his imprisonment, and he consented.[1]

It only remained to be seen whether Ḥámid would accept with a good grace the position into which he had been forced. The Caliph was anxious to mollify him: so in a letter introducing 'Alí as his Assistant, he was careful to lay stress on the subordinate nature of his office. When 'Alí was ushered into the Vizier's assembly, Ḥámid greeted him with apparent cordiality. He proffered him a seat at his side; but 'Alí was tactful enough to decline it and sit in a lowlier place farther away. This made it clear that he had no wish to oust Ḥámid from his pre-eminence. Their partnership was to begin, at least, on no untenable footing.[2]

1 H. 347–8. Did 'Alí, whilst in prison, pronounce himself once, or twice, on candidates for the Vizierate? Three accounts of such a performance, given in 'A., in the *kitáb al-uyún* (published in 'A.), and in H., all differ from one another; but whereas the first two differ very slightly from each other, the whole arrangement of the last is totally unlike theirs. In the first two 'Alí merely comments on a given list of names. In the last he himself supplies the names (themselves, all but one, different from those given in the other lists). I have therefore supposed that he was *twice* consulted. See too Quḍh. fol. 91 b.

2 'A. 73–4; Mas. *murúj*, VIII, 273; Ath. (Búláq), VIII, 38.

CHAPTER VIII

The Trial of Ibn al-Furát.

The first matter requiring their attention was of course the case of Ibn al-Furát. It was to be heard in the Caliph's presence, before a tribunal of lawyers and courtiers, headed on the one hand by the *qádhís* Ibn al-Buhlúl and Abú 'Umar (who still had jurisdiction over West and East Baghdád respectively), and on the other by Naṣr the Chamberlain and Ibn al-Ḥawwárí.

Ḥámid was still indignant over the way in which he had been treated at Wásiṭ. He was determined to secure the condemnation of Ibn al-Furát for treason. With a discreet use of insinuation and circumstantial evidence he could hardly have failed to make his case. For the Caliph was incensed with the prisoner, and the sentiment of the Court was hostile to him. But Ḥámid would not be content with an interpretation of facts. He preferred the reinforcement of false witness.

He opened the proceedings by summoning a man of Jundí-Shápúr, who declared that he had himself borne messages from Ibn al-Furát to Ibn Abí's-Sáj between Qazvín and Ardabíl and between Iṣfahán and al-Baṣrah. He was a Shí'ite, and for this reason had been chosen by Ibn al-Furát's steward as a go-between, since the plot a-hatching in this correspondence was of a Shí'ite complexion, its object being the setting up as Caliph of an 'Alid of Ṭabaristán. Ibn Abí's-Sáj, who was now all-powerful in north-western Persia, was to have advanced on the capital, whilst Ibn al-Furát was to have prepared the ground for their *coup d'état* at home.

Rumours of this tenor had of course long been current—the Banú'l-Furát were well known to have

Shí'ite sympathies. But the effect on the Court of this explicit statement was profound. (In this and subsequent trials it is to be remarked that the wildest denunciations were often the most effective.) Abú 'Umar, either because he was carried away by the emotion of the moment, or because he believed that to take such a line was politic, gave it as his opinion that such conduct was worthy of the severest punishment. He did, indeed, add something about the production of proofs, but the emphasis of his pronouncement lay entirely on the condemnation. Ibn al-Buhlúl, however, of whom al-Muqtadir next sought a verdict, expressed a more balanced view, being encouraged to a free expression of his opinion, as he confessed afterwards, by the disapproval of the charge evident in the face of 'Alí ibn 'Ísà. He began by citing an admirable precept from the *qur'án* (XLIX, 6), "O you that believe, if a rascal come to you with news, beware lest in ignorance you fall upon a people, and after repent what you have done." On so important a matter, he went on, the evidence of one man could not be accepted without corroboration, especially against anyone like Ibn al-Furát, who by his very position was more than usually exposed to the enmity of all and sundry. In any case an effort should be made to estimate the credibility of the witness. Let him, for example, since his claim to have been there was a salient point in the charge, describe the town of Ardabíl, which was well known to the *qádhí*.

The words of Ibn al-Buhlúl sobered the passions that had been roused by Ḥámid's accusation. Moreover the witness under cross-examination was unable to give a single satisfactory reply, and afterwards, on being beaten, confessed that his tale was untrue. By this time the opinion of both Caliph and Court had completely veered round. Ibn al-Furát was now pitied, and Ḥámid contemned. 'Alí had disapproved of the whole proceeding. He made no attempt to conceal his feelings, and when the witness was non-plussed, had confessed to the Caliph that he had striven in vain to dissuade Ḥámid from using him. Afterwards Ibn al-Buhlúl regretted that his action had been the cause of the man's receiving the severe punishment the Caliph had decreed for him: he felt that he might have acted from mere stupidity or have been irresistibly tempted. He therefore arranged privately with 'Alí (whose duty it was to instruct the Chief of Police) that all but a mild part of it—fifty strokes of the lash—should be remitted.[1]

Ibn al-Furát was thus exculpated on the count of treason; but he was still to be tried for financial misdemeanours. He was to be examined, if not before the same tribunal, at least before one composed also of lawyers and officers. But over this the Caliph no longer presided (although he listened to the proceedings from a hidden point of vantage). Nor, it appears, did the two principal *qáḍhís* attend: Ḥámid, 'Alí, and Ibn al-Ḥawwárí were left in control.

Ibn al-Furát was aware of the Caliph's presence, and he determined to defend himself and damage his adversaries with well-timed oratory. The rose-coloured robes in which he appeared were emblematic of his self-confidence. He took the initiative into his own hands by taunting 'Alí. What had brought him to the low level of second-in-command, he asked. 'Alí was silent. "I was like a fire," he said afterwards, "on which water has been poured."

And Ḥámid fared no better. Ibn al-Furát made the most damaging insinuations about his contract at Wásiṭ, which (against all rules) he had continued to hold since becoming Vizier, so that he too was kept

1 H. 100–2; Yáq. *ud.* 1, 89–91. M. 1, 61 states that the man received the punishment, and after being imprisoned was banished to Egypt.

silent, though with rage. He was only spurred into speech by the prisoner's gentle enquiry: for what were they met? He accused him on three counts—but Ibn al-Furát was able to defend himself on two, and simply to declare that the third was false. Ḥámid was reduced to threatening him with torture. But here again Ibn al-Furát challenged his right to inflict it. Ḥámid must remember, he said solemnly, that he was no longer an obscure tax-collector. "You are not now dividing a barn, or abusing a farmer, plucking out his beard and beating him, or slaughtering an official's horse and hanging its head round his neck—no, this assembly and palace are the assembly and palace of the Caliph, whence justice radiates throughout the world."[1]

Ḥámid was clearly outmatched. At this point therefore 'Alí intervened. He proceeded to a count that had been more carefully prepared than Ḥámid's. Its aim was to convict Ibn al-Furát of having accepted bribes. For this purpose it had been necessary to call in evidence some official that had offered them. 'Alí had chosen a certain Abú Zunbúr al-Mádhará'í, who was one of a family that had served for many years in Egypt first under the Ṭúlúnids, and later, after the restoration of 'Abbásid rule (which Abú Zunbúr himself had done much to bring about), under the governors appointed from Baghdád. When Vizier early in 302 (914) 'Alí had given Abú Zunbúr the management of the Egyptian revenues; and he had evidently been satisfied with him, for when the list of prospective Viziers was sent to him in prison, he had commented favourably on Abú Zunbúr, though declaring that he "did not know him" personally; and later, when asked to name a Vizier, he had again suggested him. It was thought now that, being a stranger, Abú Zunbúr might have remained sufficiently aloof from Court

1 H. 68–9, 90–2; M. 1, 62.

intrigues to be relied upon. Also he was known to be hostile to Ibn al-Furát, because on taking office in the preceding year the latter had persecuted the whole Mádhará'í family.[1]

The summons of Abú Zunbúr to the capital had caused quite a stir. Was he being called to the Vizierate, or only to be "examined"? He had not known himself—and against the latter contingency had hastened on his arrival to offer gifts to Ja'far, to the Lady, and to 'Alí ibn 'Ísà. 'Alí had refused his politely, suggesting that he had better give it to the Caliph as well. For Abú Zunbúr had nothing to fear—he was only required for the trial.[2]

In accordance with his instructions, Abú Zunbúr accused Ibn al-Furát of having accepted, during his first Vizierate, huge bribes both from him (he had been in charge of most of the Syrian revenues) and from the official that had held the corresponding position in Egypt. But Ibn al-Furát was non-plussed for no more than a moment. He quickly improvised an effective, if specious, reply. On the one hand he challenged Abú Zunbúr to produce his receipts for the moneys conveyed; on the other, he asserted that if he had indeed conveyed them, Abú Zunbúr was himself a criminal. Abú Zunbúr had no answer; he had to confess that receipts are not given in such transactions; and he failed to perceive that the question of his own guilt was beside the point. Ibn al-Furát followed up his advantage. Perhaps, he said, as Abú Zunbúr claimed to have made them, these payments were in fact legal. But if so, they must have continued to be legal throughout the Vizierate of 'Alí ibn 'Ísà. In this case, if 'Alí had indeed received them, he called upon *him* to account for them. If not, he called upon Abú Zunbúr.

Now Ḥámid, in his turn, could contain himself no

1 Kin. 251, 269; H. 347–8; 'A. 65, 73; M. 1, 61.
2 'A. 74–5.

longer. He broke in with the most shocking abuse of the prisoner. Abú Zunbúr used this diversion to guarantee the payment of 500,000 *dínárs* to the State if Ibn al-Furát were handed over to him for examination; upon which Ḥámid went one better with an offer of 700,000. Ibn al-Furát jeered at Abú Zunbúr's proposal as a cheap way of escaping his debt to the State (which came to considerably more than a million), and Ḥámid's too was open to the same criticism. Nevertheless, both offers were afterwards laid before Ja'far.

'Alí alone still trusted to argument. But the charge that he next brought against Ibn al-Furát—of employing Christians in the Ministry of War—was bound to collapse, since precedents were easy to cite from the successful and therefore presumably virtuous practice of al-Muwaffaq and al-Mu'taḍhid.[1]

By way of retort Ibn al-Furát could think of nothing more damaging than a reference to the equivocal part played by 'Alí's uncle Muḥammad ibn Dá'úd in the plot against the former Vizier al-'Abbás ibn al-Ḥasan. But as he spoke loud enough to attract Ja'far's attention, his purpose was evidently to remind the Caliph of his deposition and of the conduct at that time respectively of 'Alí and Ibn al-Furát himself. He went on to denounce Ḥámid, and insisted that his words should be recorded and shown to the Commander of the Faithful. First, Ḥámid was not of the class from which Viziers were drawn; secondly, he had intrigued for the Vizierate solely in order to escape the payment of a huge sum, accumulated by withholding dues on his contract at Wásiṭ; and thirdly he was guilty of the most flagrant immorality in omitting to terminate the said contract on his elevation. These contracts were between the Vizier (on behalf of the Caliph) on the one hand, and the farmer of taxes on the other. If one

1 Cf. Macdonald: *Muslim Theology*, 124: "Success can legitimate anything in the Muslim State."

man was at the same time both Vizier and farmer, the Caliph was cheated of his proper control.

Ḥámid listened to this tirade with incredulous ears. Beside himself with rage, feeling that mere abuse was no longer adequate, he commanded the retinue to pluck out the offender's beard. No one, however, dared obey him. So he leapt forward himself, and with a sharp tug raised from Ibn al-Furát a protesting cry.

Ja'far, hidden in his alcove, was scandalised at this barbarity. He hurriedly sent a slave to remove Ibn al-Furát to the security of his prison; and with this fitting climax the proceedings came to an abrupt end.[1]

After the trial much recrimination took place between the authors of the prosecution. Everyone blamed Ḥámid: his conduct had been not only unseemly but embarrassing—"You have ruined us!" cried 'Alí and Naṣr. Ibn Muqlah, too, had been a disappointment to them. At the last moment his courage had failed him—though his scruples did not hinder him from signing a deposition of evidence, he could not face his former patron in court. Then Abú Zunbúr had annoyed 'Alí, Naṣr and Ibn al-Ḥawwárí by electing, suddenly at the end of the trial, to offer Ibn al-Furát the help of 50,000 *dínárs* in paying off any fine that might be inflicted upon him. "You come to accuse," they protested, "and you stay to befriend."

Only one further, somewhat half-hearted, attempt was made to obtain satisfaction from the defaulter; and this was no more successful than those that had been made before. Ḥámid now turned his attention to Ibn al-Furát's son al-Muḥassin and to his steward Músà ibn Khalaf. They had already been taken in hand by a minor official; but Ḥámid considered his methods too gentle, and decided to examine them himself. As a result Ibn Khalaf, who was an aged man

1 H. 92–6; A. 75; M. 1, 61–3.

and crippled with dysentery, died; whilst al-Muḥassin, tortured almost to madness, consented to the payment of a sum much greater than he could hope to raise. 'Alí was naturally horrified at the conduct of his colleague; and having tried in vain to prevent the murder, he did his best to make up for Ḥámid's iniquitous treatment of al-Muḥassin by helping him to pay off his fine.

Ja'far, meanwhile, was wavering over Ḥámid's proposal to "farm" the examination of Ibn al-Furát. On the one hand he was anxious that he should not suffer, but on the other he saw no other way of getting any money out of him. Zaydán observed the Caliph's hesitation, and told Ibn al-Furát of it. Ibn al-Furát was reluctant to part with his riches; but with the example before him of the fate of al-Muḥassin and Ibn Khalaf he could not contemplate with anything but terror the prospect of delivery into the hands of Ḥámid. If payment was inevitable, payment voluntary and direct to the Caliph was not only infinitely preferable, it might even be turned to political advantage. Some pretext for so sudden a *volte-face* must of course be advanced: Ibn al-Furát accordingly hit upon the ingenious, if transparent, expedient of a dream. His brother Aḥmad, he declared, had appeared to him in a dream, urging him to secure his safety by paying up, and recalling a large forgotten sum, which had been set aside for the benefit of his heirs. This ghostly advice was not to be rejected: so Ibn al-Furát was sending the Caliph a draft for 700,000 *dínárs* on a number of deposit holders.

Al-Muqtadir maliciously showed the letter to Ḥámid and 'Alí. Both were thrown into the greatest consternation. Ḥámid was incensed at losing all chance of present revenge, 'Alí was disquieted at the magnitude of the bribe. ("He is aiming," he thought, "not only at escaping ill-treatment, but at a return to office.")

The bribe, however, was not as large as it seemed. For one of the deposit holders demurred, as Ibn al-Furát had intended that he should, from payment. He admitted to having had a deposit; but declared that the late Vizier had already withdrawn it completely and spent most of the money on perfumes for the Caliph at the last New Year. The *qádhís* Ibn al-Buhlúl and Abú 'Umar, however, who were both on the list, were obliged to accede to the demand—Ibn al-Buhlúl because his honesty forbade him to prevaricate, Abú 'Umar because he was terrified at the ferocity of Ḥámid. Abú 'Umar regained the favour of Ibn al-Furát by reimbursing the amount on the minister's return to power; but Ibn al-Buhlúl was too poor to do this—he had to rely on Ibn al-Furát's gratitude for his timely defence.[1]

1 M. I, 63–8; 'A. 74; H. 96, 99; Yáq. *ud.* I, 88.

CHAPTER IX

The rivalry of Ḥámid ibn al-'Abbás *and* 'Alí ibn 'Ísà. Ḥámid's *contract, and its consequences.*

As time went on the assurance given to 'Alí on his release came true: "ostensibly you will be his Secretary and Deputy, but actually you will be Vizier." Ḥámid became a cipher: consequently official power was concentrated more and more in the hands of 'Alí. He no longer made any pretence of referring State business to his superior. He had begun by paying him visits of consultation twice a day; but after two months he payed them only once a week; and by the next year he ceased to pay them altogether. Ḥámid only appeared at State ceremonies—his sole privilege was to wear the sable robes of the Vizierate. A rhyme was circulated *à propos*: "Here's the Vizier, but no black gown; there's the black gown—but no Vizier!"[1]

Ḥámid naturally resented his eclipse. Nevertheless he and his coadjutor kept frigid peace till the advent to Baghdád of the tax-farmer from Egypt, whom 'Alí had sent for in order to examine his accounts. The man hastened to make the Caliph and the Lady presents, upon which they intervened to quash the investigation. He then attached himself to Ḥámid, who was nerved by the sight of his rival's discomfiture into asserting himself further. He devised a plan that he hoped would at once delight the Caliph and discredit 'Alí. It was to undertake a contract for the taxes of the *sawád*, al-Ahwáz and Iṣfahán, in which he would guarantee to exceed by 400,000 *dínárs* a year the sums payable under the contracts fixed by 'Alí ibn 'Ísà. One of his advisers warned him that by so doing he might well find him-

1 *fakh.* 316; M. I, 59; Ath. (Búláq), VIII, 38.

self more than ever in the power of 'Alí ibn 'Ísà, who, being bound to represent the Government, would have him, as tax-farmer, at his mercy. But another encouraged him, judging that the immediate advantage of the Caliph's approbation would outweigh any such remoter drawback.

Ḥámid confronted 'Alí in al-Muqtadir's presence. "You have taken to managing affairs alone," he began. "You do not see fit to consult me in anything. But the Commander of the Faithful must be told the truth: you have let slip 400,000 *dínárs* a year..."—and Ḥámid went on to unfold his plan.

'Alí replied that Ḥámid was unfit to receive such a concession. He was notorious as an oppressor of the defenceless—by ruthless squeezing he might fulfil his obligations for a year or even more, but at the cost of such ruin as it would take years to repair.

And 'Alí was not merely arguing to defeat an opponent, he was expressing his cherished convictions. Ḥámid's scheme would reverse what was his favourite policy—moderate taxation in the hope of promoting prosperity. Al-Muqtadir, however, understood none of his aims. He could never refuse an offer of more money. Moreover he evidently doubted 'Alí's sincerity, since before he closed with Ḥámid, he gave 'Alí, whom he still valued the more highly of the two, the chance of undertaking the contract himself. 'Alí of course declined it—"I am a Secretary of State, not a tax-farmer," he said. "Ḥámid is better suited to the business." But he asked Ja'far to remember that what might make it possible, if anything would, for Ḥámid to carry out his proposal was only his, 'Alí's, care for the people—his having appointed agents that had put an end to injustice. Moreover Ḥámid could not pretend that he would bring more land under cultivation for the year, because the season for cultivation was already passed.

Ḥámid and 'Alí were henceforth at open war. Each was supported by a corps of clerks, for Ḥámid had demanded that a number of the latter should be put at his disposal to unravel the complications of his new business. 'Alí was determined to make his task as hard—as unprofitable—as he could: accordingly he assessed the amounts payable under the contract on the highest returns of the last three years for which they were available. Their subordinates argued each point out between themselves quite amicably, but Ḥámid could never meet 'Alí without breaking into the most unseemly abuse, "vilifying him and his ancestors". The scandal became so notorious that al-Muqtadir was forced to summon them both to his presence, and patch up a peace.

Once the sum of Ḥámid's dues was fixed, 'Alí pressed him so hard for punctual payment, that he was constrained to ask leave of the Caliph to visit al-Ahwáz and see to the matter himself. In his absence the battle went on, but so much to his disadvantage that Ja'far began to lose confidence in his scheme. Ḥámid's agents in Baghdád urged him to take some bold step and recover the ground he had lost. In reply Ḥámid wrote a letter which was delivered sealed into the Caliph's hands. He reminded the Commander of the Faithful that he had proposed the contract in the hope, not of enriching himself, but of demonstrating his own skill in government and finance, and the incapability of 'Alí ibn 'Ísà. He had promised an increase of 400,000 *dínárs* a year, but since coming to al-Ahwáz he saw that he could furnish in addition another 200,000, for which he enclosed his bond.

Ja'far was overjoyed at the receipt of this good news. He perceived that he had misjudged Ḥámid ibn al-'Abbás—he was clearly possessed of unsuspected talents. In future the collection of taxes should be left entirely in his hands. 'Alí ibn 'Ísà should confine himself to the direction of expenditure—"for in this he is more perspicacious than Ḥámid."

For a time 'Alí was really alarmed at the turn events had taken: with Ḥámid in such high favour he felt insecure. But time was his ally, and he had not long to wait for the appearance of those evils in which he had foretold Ḥámid's undertaking would result.[1]

The 'Abbásid Empire, says Ḥamzah of Iṣfahán, from its foundation in the year 132 (749–50) prospered for one hundred and seventy-seven years, such disturbances as broke out in that period being "short of duration and swift of end". But in the thirteenth year of the reign of al-Muqtadir, towards the end of 308 (the beginning of 921), says he, there began an epoch of anarchy that was to end only with the extinction of the 'Abbásid power, though not of the dynasty, and the transference of that power to the hands of a provincial conqueror.[2]

Since the restoration of order by al-Muwaffaq and al-Mu'tadhid, riots in Baghdád had been rare. The defeat of Ibn al-Mu'tazz had been followed by the sacking of the conspirators' houses, but this was not a very serious disturbance. On the first fall of Ibn al-Furát, however, there had ensued a riot that lasted for three days and was only suppressed with difficulty. Under 'Alí's direction security had again been firmly established—Ja'far had confessed as much by venturing to make an appearance in public for the first time in the six years since his deposition.[3] Towards the end of 'Alí's Vizierate, and again under Ibn al-Furát, the soldiers had threatened a mutiny, but they had gone no further and the townspeople had not joined in.

1 M. I, 59–60, 69–70, 71–2; 'A. 78–9.

2 Ḥam. I, 201–2. Paraphrase in S.J. fol. 70 a and Tagh. II, 208.

3 Tagh. II, 190; Dh. *t.* fol. 1 b; S.J. fol. 57 a.

In 306 (918–19), however, two measures were introduced which tended to weaken the authority of the Government.

The first of these, which was nothing less than the appointment, at the Lady's instance, of one of the *qahramánahs*, Thumal by name, as President of the Court of Appeal, may perhaps be dismissed as merely a striking evidence of the influence of the Harem. For although it caused at first the gravest scandal to all respectable Muslims and filled them with shame, it was followed by no very extraordinary effects. Thumal, indeed, was a very masculine person: she had had years of practice at the Dulafite Court with refractory slaves and concubines, and had acquired a reputation for severity and hardness of heart. She sat now to hear appeals on Fridays at a mausoleum newly built by the Lady in ar-Ruṣáfah; and although at her first session no litigants appeared, afterwards she was supported by a *qáḍhí* whose opinion she sought on each case, and between them they discharged their business to the appellants' satisfaction.[1]

The second of these measures was the appointment for each quarter of the city of local jurists, by whose judgements on cases of crime the police were to abide; and whether it was that these jurists were unduly amenable to the influence of their neighbours, or that under a less summary procedure than that which had been observed hitherto means were more readily found of defeating justice, the new system resulted in a sad relaxation of police control. The Chief of Police himself was new to his duties, and was proving himself altogether so inadequate, that the thieves and hooligans of Baghdád congratulated themselves on having nothing to fear from him; and though he was replaced not long afterwards by one more capable,[2] these two

1 'A. 71; S.J. fol. 67 a; Tagh. II, 203, 215; Dh. *t.* fol. 4 b.
2 'A. 109.

circumstances combined to produce an alarming increase of crime.[1]

The disturbances that occurred in 308 (920–1), however, were not in the first place the work of criminals. Nor, unlike those of forty years before, were they the work of the soldiery, acting at the behest of rival generals. These were truly popular riots: the citizens rose now in protest against misgovernment. In order to recoup himself for the payments that he had promised the Caliph, Ḥámid had forced up the price of grain at Baghdád by prohibiting its import from the provinces: consequently the whole community suffered from the high cost of bread. The people first showed their dissatisfaction by looting certain millers' shops; then, as 'Alí rode through the streets, angry voices appealed to him from the crowd. Later a mob gathered in the open space before the palace and refused to disperse unless attention were paid to its wants. It was explained to the Caliph that the tumult was directly due to Ḥámid's economic policy: the Caliph therefore decided to recall Ḥámid from his tour, so that he might settle the matter himself. 'Alí and his colleagues had not forgotten how completely Ḥámid had regained the Caliph's esteem by his latest move: on his coming, accordingly, they hastened to pay him every respect. A notable company conducted him to the Presence, where the Caliph gave him a robe of honour as if he were a general fresh home from a victory. Yet however politely Ḥámid might be treated at Court, the citizens, who knew well enough whom they had to thank for their woes, were determined to make their resentment against him felt.

On the next Friday bricks were thrown at the preachers as they ascended their pulpits in the two chief mosques (those of the Round City and of ar-

1 M. 1, 69; 'A. 71.

Ruṣáfah). The pulpits were next wrecked themselves and the sanctuaries profaned by an inrush of hooligans, who tore the clothes off the backs of innocent citizens and wounded many by flinging bricks. An onslaught was made upon Ḥámid's house, but the rioters, who were armed only with stones, were driven off by his archers. Next day the lodging of the new Chief of Police suffered a like attack. He, however, was less well protected: his horses were slaughtered; and to save himself he escaped to his other house across the river, only to find that undergoing a similar treatment. 'Alí does not appear to have been molested at all, but Naṣr was set upon in the Mosque of the Palace itself, and pelted with stones.

Ḥámid made no attempt to remove the causes of discontent—the only remedy he could apply was force. A troop of his retainers rode into the Mosque of the Round City and fought with the rioters, many of whom they cut down, though a few of their own number were also killed. Peaceful citizens passed the Friday night in terror, lest on the one hand they might be impressed by the rioters, or on the other they might be arrested by the police. They woke up (if they had ever slept) to find that the bridges had been burnt (by a mob estimated at ten thousand) and the prisons opened. Later in the morning al-Muqtadir sent out a company of the palace guards in war boats to contend with the insurgents. Hárún (son of the Uncle, recently deceased) rode with a large body of troops to the Báb aṭ-Ṭáq (the great gate at the bridge head). Having surrounded the mosque there, he arrested everyone, including innocent devotees, that he found inside. He then packed them all off to the Constabulary, where they received various punishments, ranging from beating and the cutting off of hands to death. At the same time the Chief of Police made a vain effort to clear the streets. In the process several persons were killed; but the rioters were in no way cowed, and retaliated by setting fire to the local market.

By the Sunday the fury of anarchy had somewhat abated. Nevertheless Ḥámid was recognised when crossing the Tigris, and stoned. Also, the many bad characters that infested the capital were not so easily restrained, and continued to loot and terrorise, in spite of continued beatings, mutilations and executions.

Meanwhile the body-guard had taken its cue from the populace and murmured in the palace itself of the scarcity and the expense of bread. This at last woke al-Muqtadir to the reality of the famine; so he gave orders for all the grain stores—of which some belonged not to Ḥámid, but to members of the Royal Family—to be thrown open and their contents sold to the public at a reduced rate. This rate was also imposed on private grain-sellers, and Hárún visited every market to ensure its observance.

Grain was now cheap; but it was no more plentiful: supplies were soon exhausted, so that the people were no better off than before. There was nothing for it but to abrogate Ḥámid's contract altogether: the Caliph accordingly sent him a letter to this effect, and at the same time he sent 'Alí another, instructing him to appoint his own revenue officers for the administration of the districts involved. Ḥámid was deeply chagrined at this; but he saw that he had lost the game beyond hope, and even suggested resigning.[1] Yet for some reason, perhaps because he was contemplating, but was not yet ready for, the reinstatement of Ibn al-Furát, or because he was reluctant to forgo the chance of impeaching Ḥámid, al-Muqtadir refused. Ḥámid made the best of a bad situation by retiring to Wásiṭ,

1 S.J. fol. 70 a states that Ḥámid, fearing to be dismissed, presented al-Muqtadir with a garden embellished with furnished bowers, on which he had spent 100,000 *dínárs*; and that al-Muqtadir, in return, went no further in the matter of replacing him.

and there he seems really to have made an effort to undo what he had done before by despatching as quickly as possible all the grain that he could lay hands on to Baghdád. Later, when he returned to the capital, he was thanked by the people as a benefactor. Nevertheless al-Muqtadir had no illusions about the failure of his enterprise. He pinned no more faith to such financial jugglery; and shortly afterwards revenue farming was forbidden to statesmen and officers by decree.[1]

1 'A. 84, 85; M. 1, 72–5; Ḥam. 1, 202–3.

CHAPTER X

Medical questions: Sinán ibn Thábit; ar-Rází. ‘Alí *and* al-Ash‘arí. Aṭ-Ṭabarí *and the* Ḥanbalites. ‘Alí *as a* Ṣúfí: ash-Shiblí; al-Ḥalláj.

As soon as he found himself virtually independent of Ḥámid, before they fell out, ‘Alí had resumed all the points of his former policy. In 306 (918–19) he drew up a budget and attempted to balance revenue and expenditure, as I shall relate below; and in the same year he exercised himself again with medical questions, which another severe outbreak of plague had rendered acute. Sa‘íd ibn Ya‘qúb, in whose charge he had put the metropolitan hospitals, was no longer in this position. His place had been taken by a certain Sinán ibn Thábit, who was now one of the Caliph's two chief physicians, the other being a Christian, Bukht-Yishú‘ ibn Yaḥyà.[1] Sinán was also a non-Muslim—he belonged to the sect of the so-called Sabians of Ḥarrán in north-western Mesopotamia, a sect tolerated by the Muslims because they confused it with that of the true Sabians of al-‘Iráq (followers of John the Baptist), but which actually maintained an antique pagan cult. His father, Thábit ibn Qurrah, had been a notable translator of philosophical and scientific works. Sinán appears to have been appointed by Ibn al-Furát soon after he became Vizier for the second time. He was then also given authority over the hospitals at Mecca, Medina and Tarsus.[2] In effecting his reforms ‘Alí found him an able and zealous ally.

The text of two letters, written by ‘Alí to Sinán on administrative subjects, is fortunately preserved in

1 Qif. 104.

2 S.J. fol. 63 b.

Ibn Abí Uṣaybi'ah's *ṭabaqát al-aṭibbá'*.[1] The first deals with persons confined in State prisons. "I have been thinking over the question of the prisoners," it begins. "Owing to their numbers and the hardships of their situation they cannot fail to be overtaken by diseases, since they are unable to help themselves or consult doctors about their disorders. You must therefore appoint doctors to visit them daily. They should take with them medicines, drinks and such invalid foods as may be necessary."

In his second letter 'Alí instructs Sinán to send out doctors to visit all the villages in the *sawád*, where the people were helpless against the pestilence. These doctors were to take stores of medicines and foods with them and stay at each village as long as they were needed.—In the course of their circuit the doctors came to a village inhabited almost wholly by Jews. Neither they nor Sinán, whom they consulted, knew whether non-Muslims were entitled to their assistance (though Sinán and indeed most of the doctors were non-Muslims themselves), so Sinán applied to 'Alí for a ruling. 'Alí replied that he agreed that it was right to tend both *ahl adh-dhimmah*, that is, the people of tolerated religions—and animals; but that there was an order of eligibility in which they should be ranged. Muslims should be healed before *ahl adh-dhimmah*, and *ahl adh-dhimmah* before the beasts of the field.

The same author quotes another letter of 'Alí's about the administration of the funds of a hospital. This establishment, situated in al-Mukharrim, was known as the Hospital of Badr al-Mu'taḍhidí (the general whose disgrace and death had been brought about by al-Qásim ibn 'Ubayd Allah), and it was kept up on half the funds of a *waqf*, or religious trust, founded by al-Mutawakkil's Turkish mother, the other half being distributed monthly among the Háshimites,

1 U. I, 221, and also in al-Qifṭí's *ta'ríkh al-ḥukamá'*, 193–4.

or members of the Prophet's family. The present administrator of this *waqf* was a certain Abú'ṣ-Ṣuqr al-Kalwádhí. Now Sinán complained to 'Alí that he was favouring the Háshimites at the expense of the hospital: winter was at hand and the patients had less than enough fuel, provisions and blankets. 'Alí at once wrote on the back of Sinán's letter a note to Abú'ṣ-Ṣuqr remonstrating with him. That he should have favoured the powerful Háshimites at the expense of the miserable inmates of the hospital was a particularly unpleasant reflection on his honesty and his charity. He required that Abú'ṣ-Ṣuqr should at once provide the hospital with every necessity, that he should correct the misappropriation of the funds, and that he should furnish a report to show exactly how the money at his disposal was spent.[1]

At some time of his life the famous philosopher and physician, Abú Bakr Muḥammad ibn Zakariyyá ar-Rází (known to the schoolmen of Europe as Rhazes), was in charge of a hospital at Baghdád; but so little is known of his life, which he spent mostly at his native Ray, that it is impossible to say when this may have been. Only as he died not long after, and was blind at the end of his life, it was probably some time before this, perhaps during the reign of al-Mu'taḍhid. Ar-Rází is said to have chosen the site for the great hospital called the 'Adhudí (after the Buvayhid prince, the *'Adhud ad-Dawlah*), doing so by hanging up pieces of raw meat in various quarters of the city and observing where it took longest to go bad. The story cannot be true as it stands, because ar-Rází died before the 'Adhudí Hospital was founded (329/940–1),[2] but it may well be true of some other Baghdád hospital. Very probably ar-Rází was acquainted with 'Alí from his sojourn in the capital. At all events in the list of

1 U. 1, 222.
2 By the Emir Bachkam. See below, p. 365.

his writings given by Ibn Abí Uṣaybi'ah there occurs the mention of a treatise, on the diseases of the exterior of the body, that ar-Rází addressed to him.[1]

It was possibly at about this time that 'Alí was attacked for certain of his religious writings by another famous contemporary, about whose life almost equally little is known. This was Abú'l-Ḥasan al-Ash'arí, the founder of Orthodox Muslim Scholasticism.

Al-Ash'arí came of an ancient and celebrated Baṣran family, purely Arab and rigidly Orthodox. He was brought up in an atmosphere of old-fashioned piety; but his acute mind soon revolted at an enforced subscription to doctrines that appeared to be illogical, and on growing up he joined the Mu'tazilites. As time went on, however, he found their position of compromise more and more unsatisfactory. They obeyed neither pure reason nor what seemed to him the clearly intended sense of the *qur'án* and Tradition. His early training probably prevented him from swinging further to the side of free thought. Instead he determined to reinstate the teaching of the Prophet in all its purity—but, unlike the old-fashioned Orthodox, he would support each tenet with arguments logically developed from the irrefutable data of Revelation.

Al-Ash'arí made his great decision in *ramaḍhán* of the year 300 (April–May 913), and his fame immediately spread till he became one of the most celebrated doctors of the age. He fought innumerable battles with the Mu'tazilites, including his former master; but as the Mu'tazilites were in a comparatively weak position (since their allegiance was divided between faith and reason), he was generally victorious. Though verbally al-Ash'arí was a formidable dialectician, he remained a poor writer. Nevertheless, he composed more than three hundred treatises, tracts and replies to the questions that were showered upon him by both Orthodox

1 U. I, 231.

and Mu'tazilite. One such tract was in refutation of a book by 'Alí ibn 'Ísà. Unhappily, however, the title of the latter is not given in the passage concerned.[1] In this passage, also, the name 'Alí ibn 'Ísà is not qualified by any addition, such as "Ibn al-Jarráḥ" or "the Vizier". Yet I believe it to refer to our 'Alí rather than to ar-Rummání, for example, who, though a definite Mu'tazilite, and so perhaps a more likely adversary for al-Ash'arí, was still a young man (only twenty-eight) when al-Ash'arí died.[2] Another reason, moreover, for thinking that our 'Alí ibn 'Ísà is here referred to, is that his friend Abú Bakr ash-Sháfi'í was also involved in an argument with Abú'l-Ḥasan al-Ash'arí on Moral Theology, in consequence of which he felt impelled at least to modify certain of his views, and corrected the passages in his treatises bearing on them with marginal notes.[3]

On what grounds 'Alí was attacked by al-Ash'arí it is impossible to say. It may have been for his holding Mu'tazilitish views. As I have remarked, it can only be surmised, from slight indications, that 'Alí sympathised with the Mu'tazilites at all. One sentiment, however, he certainly shared with them: a cordial detestation of the fanatical Ḥanbalites. On one occasion certain of this sect built a mosque, which soon became a centre of disturbance, their intolerant views causing them all too easily to clash with those that did not share them. Complaints of their conduct were made to 'Alí; whereupon he declared that a building not founded in the fear of God deserved to be pulled down and all trace of it destroyed.[4] At this time the heads of the party were incensed with the now aged historian

1 Spitta: *Zur Geschichte Abu'l-Ḥasan al-Aš'arî's*, 79: No. 83.

2 *fih.* 63. Yáq. *ud.* v, 281 states that ar-Rummání was born in 276 (889–90) instead of 296 (908–9); but as he died only in 384 (994–5), this would make him live to the age of 108.

3 Sub. *ṭab.* I, ff. 269 b–270 a.

4 H. 335; Tan. *nisḥ.* 174.

aṭ-Ṭabarí. They could not forgive him for having denied their master, Ibn Ḥanbal, the place of an authoritative jurist.[1] ‘Alí wished to bring their discontent to a head, and in 309 (921–2) urged aṭ-Ṭabarí to confront them in his presence. The historian refused, however, partly no doubt because he felt himself too feeble for such an ordeal (he was then eighty-nine years of age), but also perhaps because he knew that his enemies had succeeded in inflaming the opinion of the people against him.[2] That they had done so in fact became clear next year when he died. The people then accused him at least of Shí‘ite sympathies and even of actual heresy. They refused to allow his burial in the day-time, so that his relations were obliged to bury him secretly after dark.[3] ‘Alí commented on the sad event: "By God," he said, "were these people to be questioned as to what is meant by a *ráfidhí* (a Shí‘ite) or a heretic, they would neither know nor be capable of understanding!"[4]

At some time of his life ‘Alí is said to have undergone a sudden conversion. One day, so the story runs, as he was riding in the midst of a great procession of State, some strangers in the crowd asked, "Who is this?"; whereupon a woman from nearby replied, "How long will you ask, Who is this? Who is this? This is a slave fallen from the protection of God, and now God puts him, as you see, to the proof." At this ‘Alí returned immediately to his house, sought permission to retire from the Vizierate, departed to Mecca and there abode.

This tale is quoted by al-Qushayrí[5] (fifth/eleventh

1 *Encyclopédie*, I, 193 (art. *Aḥmed b. Muḥammad b. Ḥanbal*—Goldziher).

2 Tagh. II, 213–14; Dh. *t*. fol. 5 a.

3 M. I, 84.

4 Ath. (Búláq), VIII, 45; quoted in translation in E. G. Browne's *Literary History of Persia*, I, 360–1.

5 Qush. 56; also, in a shortened form, S.J. fol. 138 a.

century), one of the leading authorities on Ṣúfism, as an example of sudden turning to the mystical path; and it is repeated by al-Qazwíní,[1] writing two hundred years later, as the only matter of interest to be recorded of 'Alí ibn 'Ísà as an eminent Baghdádí. As it stands, however, it is impossible to fit it into the framework of 'Alí's life. On several occasions 'Alí besought the Caliph, it is true, to excuse him from the Vizierate; but the Caliph invariably refused him, and after each of his terms of office he was imprisoned. He retired from Baghdád to Mecca twice; but on the first occasion, in 296 (909), he had not yet become Vizier, and on the second he chose it as his place of exile after trial and imprisonment. In detail, therefore, the story cannot be accepted. Its purport, nevertheless, may be true: 'Alí may very well, at some time of his life, have undergone a spiritual regeneration.

Ṣúfism, that is, Muslim mysticism (*Ṣúfí* comes from *ṣúf*, wool, a mark of the ascetic being his white woollen robe), was not yet integrally welded in the faith of Islam, as it afterwards came to be: indeed it was only now beginning to take on its characteristic form. Those that were thus giving it shape, the pioneer mystics, were meeting with a very bitter opposition, but behind them there remained a soberer school (whence they had arisen), that could still live unmolested. The mysticism of its adherents was so discreet as hardly to mark them off from the generality of stricter devotees. 'Alí certainly never compromised his worldly position by a subscription to prohibited doctrines; but he may very well have made his own the views of such as these.

As for the date of this conversion, if it was real at all, I should incline to place it at 'Alí's banishment to Mecca in 296 (909); for this appears to have been a real turning-point in his life. After this, for example, he

1 Qaz. I, 134.

never resumed the habit, innocent but definitely mundane, of giving entertainments at his house; and from now his love of frugality became ever more marked. His incrimination in the conspiracy of Ibn al-Mu'tazz, which so brutally disturbed the hitherto placid course of his life, and the fear of death that was brought home to him so nearly by the executions of his uncle and his cousin, may they not have convinced him of the vanity of worldly achievement? Ever after, at any rate, though he was to play such an important part in affairs, he always shrank from the honours of office, and accepted them only as a burden to be borne in duty. And since the Ṣúfís always claimed a special contact with the Divine power, may not the miracles with which 'Alí was graced at Mecca be taken as evidence that he and his companions, at all events, believed this contact to have been vouchsafed him?

Yet there is no mention of 'Alí's having had dealings with any of the moderate Ṣúfís. The only Ṣúfís with whom there is record of his coming in contact are two of the "pioneers", ash-Shiblí and al-Ḥalláj, both after their deaths to be venerated as saints. The first, Abú Bakr ash-Shiblí,[1] was a friend of his, that used to come to his house; but how far 'Alí sympathised with his religious attitude it is hard to judge, for ash-Shiblí had other attractions for him: he was not only a saintly ascetic, he was also (unlike most of his Ṣúfí brethren) a retired official—of 'Alí's own, the class of *kuttáb*, Government secretaries—and an eloquent poet. Ash-Shiblí used to meet Ibn Mujáhid the Reader at the Báb al-Bustán. On one occasion Ibn Mujáhid promised 'Alí on ash-Shiblí's arrival that he would defeat him in argument. Ash-Shiblí, however, was too clever for him, and even forced him to admit that he was unacquainted with an interpretation given to a certain verse of the *qur'án* (the subject of all others in which

1 Dulaf ibn Jaḥdar, b. 247 (861), d. 334 (945).

Ibn Mujáhid was expert). However, Ibn Mujáhid seems to have borne him no malice: and to the surprise of onlookers he would afterwards rise to ash-Shiblí even when he would remain seated at the entry of 'Alí himself.

When ash-Shiblí turned Ṣúfí, he had renounced secular learning, casting his books into the Tigris. His mystical experiences led him to a position like that of al-Ḥalláj (which I shall shortly describe): al-Ḥalláj suffered martyrdom for his views; and ash-Shiblí escaped a similar fate only by feigning madness. For a time he was interned in a hospital. He used to throw stones at some of those that came, perhaps in malignant curiosity, to visit him; but he received 'Alí with pleasure. 'Alí arranged with al-Muqtadir to send a Court physician, a Christian, to attend ash-Shiblí; with the curious result that the physician turned Muslim. Al-Muqtadir, when he heard of it, made an epigram: "We knew that we had sent a doctor to a patient, but we did not know that we had sent a patient to a doctor."[1]

'Alí's dealings with al-Ḥalláj were merely, as far as we know, official. Early in 301 (913), some two months after his elevation to the Vizierate, al-Ḥalláj had been brought to Baghdád under arrest for heresy; and it had fallen to 'Alí to examine him. A judgement had already been pronounced against him in his absence five years before in 296 (908–9), but he had fled from the capital and remained until his capture in hiding. His crime was a claim to Divinity: for this is what his teaching appeared to signify in the eyes of the jurist, an "Externalist",[2] that condemned him.

1 S.J. fol. 132 a–136 b; Tagh. II, 313–14; Dh. *t.* fol. 227 a; Khall. I, 511.

2 *dhá̤hirí*, that is, one opposed to hidden, or "Internal", interpretations of scripture. The Dhá̤hirite was a distinct school, akin to the Ḥanbalite.

Al-Ḥalláj's doctrine was developed from that of various comparatively innocuous Ṣúfís; but he had pushed it to a dangerous conclusion, and taken a step that placed him in opposition not merely to Orthodox feeling, but even to the feeling of these Ṣúfís themselves. What distinguished the Ṣúfís from the generality of Muslims was of course their conception of the soul's relation to God. Whereas the Orthodox conceived that the whole duty of man was to worship God in fulfilling the rites he had prescribed (and the Shí'ah in an absolute obedience to the decrees of the Imám), the Ṣúfís felt, temperamentally, that real religion consisted in the preparation of the soul to receive the Divine contact. For most of al-Ḥalláj's masters (though each had his own theories) this preparation took the form of a rigorous asceticism and an extreme quietism: they mortified the body in the expectation of receiving heavenly grace. One of them, however, put forward an idea that al-Ḥalláj was to develop: that of the love of the soul for God (an idea at most latent in primitive Islam). Another, also, had raised the Orthodox conception of religious duties to a more truly spiritual plane, teaching that the mystic should reach out, as it were, to meet the Divine touch, and so modifying the current cult of complete passivity. Al-Ḥalláj combined these two innovations. For him in the union with the Divine essence, brought about by spiritual effort based on ascetic practice, the love of God was gratified and perpetually renewed. He was united with God, yet remained himself. He was supernaturally endowed as being the instrument through which God might work his will.

It was these last claims that the moderate Ṣúfís could not stomach. For them the mystical union involved annihilation in the Godhead; and they reprobated, likewise, the spiritual pride of one that could assert, for example, as al-Ḥalláj asserted (consistently with his doctrine), that he could write verses inspired as were those of the *qur'án*. But if the Ṣúfís were scandalised at such claims, how much more were the Orthodox, to whom all mysticism was suspect: to their rigid monotheism such pretensions could seem nothing less than the most blatant blasphemy. Moreover, they were hardly less repugnant to Shí'ah feeling, as compromising the exclusive privileges of the Imám; and this was not without importance, for one of those that initiated the proceedings against al-Ḥalláj was the present head of the Twelvers.

As for 'Alí's dealings with al-Ḥalláj, there is undoubtedly something queer about them, something in which we may see perhaps a secret sympathy between them. In the first place, when al-Ḥalláj was brought before 'Alí in 301 (913) to be examined in the presence of jurists, no mention whatever appears to have been made of the condemnation, with its concomitant sentence of death, that had been pronounced against him before. 'Alí instead pretended to question him on matters of sacred and profane knowledge, and professed to find him as ignorant of the one as of the other. Now al-Ḥalláj was anything but an ignoramus: not only had he spent many years in the study of every branch of religious learning, he had schooled himself as well in philosophy and the "foreign" sciences and was a poet versed in the poetry of others—he, at any rate, must have been playing a part. Moreover, a mass of papers had been discovered in al-Ḥalláj's house at as-Sús and brought to Baghdád, where 'Alí had looked through them; so that he had had opportunity enough to learn that al-Ḥalláj was far from being as simple as he pretended. It looks very much as if 'Alí, seeing the impossibility of exculpating al-Ḥalláj altogether, may have chosen to condemn him, not as a heretic, but as a charlatan. He was thus able to sentence him merely to a punishment of derogation. He caused al-Ḥalláj's beard to be shaven off, and had him beaten with the flat of a sword, after which both he and his servant, arrested with him, were exposed for four days in a pillory and then imprisoned in chains.

Again, what happened subsequently at least does nothing to contradict the supposition that ‘Alí was secretly drawn to al-Ḥalláj. As time went on, al-Ḥalláj was treated with ever-increasing consideration in his confinement, till at length he was permitted to receive callers and have members of his family to live with him. It is true that this improvement in his condition was brought about mainly by other powerful persons interested in him, yet the Vizier's sanction at least must have been required for these changes, and ‘Alí remained in office for the first four years of al-Ḥalláj's incarceration. The most influential of al-Ḥalláj's friends was Naṣr the Chamberlain, who openly revered him and obtained all kinds of graces for him from Ja‘far and the Lady, to whom he is said actually to have presented him. By the time that ‘Alí returned to power in 306 (918) al-Ḥalláj had quite a following at Court. But the favour he now enjoyed stirred up various jealousies, notably that of a secretary and former disciple, who worked zealously to inflame opinion against him. This indeed was no hard task: his teaching needed little misrepresentation to scandalise the conventionally pious. At length it was resolved to try him again. Simultaneously he was deprived of the privileges he had enjoyed. The decision seems to have been taken whilst Ḥámid was still away in Wásiṭ. Al-Ḥalláj, accordingly, came up again before ‘Alí.

This time their position was much more difficult than it had been before. Now that al-Ḥalláj's capacities were so well known, it was no good pretending that he was merely a guileless, illiterate seer. But if the outcome of the process was to be his destruction, ‘Alí was resolved to have nothing more to do with it. He therefore declined to preside at his trial, alleging that at a preliminary interview al-Ḥalláj had threatened him with supernatural vengeance.

The trial was thereupon taken in hand by Ḥámid, now returned, who showed himself balefully desirous, perhaps because it offered him a welcome chance to assert his authority, of obtaining a conviction. It rested, however, with Ibn al-Buhlúl and Abú 'Umar, as jurists, to discover some evidence of heresy; and, each once again true to his nature, whereas Ibn al-Buhlúl honestly declared that he could find none, Abú 'Umar obligingly detected adequate offence in certain teaching of al-Ḥalláj's regarding a mystical substitute for the performance of the Meccan pilgrimage. In spite of this second disagreement between the adjudicating lawyers (for at his first trial there had been a similar discrepancy of opinion upon his guilt), Ḥámid insisted on al-Ḥalláj's condemnation. Naṣr did his best to save him; but the Caliph was finally prevailed upon by Ḥámid, who threatened him with a popular rising, to consent to his execution: and al-Ḥalláj was accordingly put to death, publicly and in a most cruel way.

His followers asserted that he had not really suffered this martyrdom: that at the last moment the body of an enemy had been substituted miraculously for his. It was reported that he had been seen on a road not far distant from the city, riding upon an ass; and they were confident that he would return to them, in glory, after a space of forty days.[1]

Later, when one of the secretaries had occasion to search through certain papers of 'Alí ibn 'Ísà's, among them he found a portfolio of compositions by al-Ḥalláj that had got mixed up with State documents and forgotten. One of these compositions was entitled, *Excellences of the Vizierate*.[2]

1 For the foregoing see Massignon: *Al Hallaj*, particularly chapter VI. The guess at a hidden sympathy between 'Alí ibn 'Ísà and al-Ḥalláj is mine, however.

2 H. 209.

CHAPTER XI

The machinations of the Furát *faction. The disgrace of* Umm Músà. *The embarrassments and fall of* 'Alí ibn 'Ísà.

In the year 310 (922–3) 'Alí fell ill, so that he had to keep to his house. Al-Muqtadir determined to pay him a visit; but as a preliminary sent his son Hárún with Mu'nis and all his "intimates" (the inner circle of courtiers) to enquire how he did. This proved to be the best cure that he could have devised. For 'Alí was so horrified at the Caliph's showing him such a singular honour, that the next day, weak as he was, he got up and went to the palace on business.[1]

For the moment he was once again in full favour. Though the Caliph had rejected Ḥámid's proffered resignation, he desired to replace him: now, therefore, he offered the Black Robe to 'Alí, either with the title of Vizier, or, as a concession to his reluctance, without it; but 'Alí persisted in refusing.[2] He saw clearly that the times were unfavourable to lengthy terms of power. Whether or not he became Vizier, he would soon fall; and if he was in any case to be examined by a hostile successor, in his present position he would at least be able, as mere Assistant, to take refuge from attacks under the superior authority of Ḥámid. Al-Muqtadir was annoyed by his obstinacy; and his annoyance was aggravated by 'Alí's giving him advice that he took—probably with justice—to be no more than half serious. As 'Alí would not be Vizier himself, the Caliph asked him to suggest someone else for the office; and 'Alí suggested, with what al-Muqtadir considered an ill-timed levity, the *qáḍhí* Abú 'Umar. Now the appointment of Abú 'Umar would have been clearly absurd,

1 S.J. fol. 76 a. 2 'A. 85.

not on account of his character—little admirable in some respects though it was—but because the elevation of a *qáḍhí* was unprecedented. Ja'far believed, therefore, that 'Alí was mocking him, and long remembered the incident with resentment. He rejected the proposal, of course, alleging that it would create an undesirable impression abroad. It might be supposed at Constantinople, for instance, that there was a dearth at his Court of competent secretaries of State, or, worse still, that he, the Caliph, was incapable of making a sensible choice.[1]

'Alí continued, therefore, in the Vizier's absence to discharge all his duties, and to prosecute his campaign of economy, which since regaining power he had renewed. He was not to be permitted to work for long in peace, however: at Ḥámid's decline the faction of Ibn al-Furát had taken heart, and was working again for his reinstatement. His son al-Muḥassin, after escaping from Ḥámid's clutches, had but one idea—to get Ḥámid in turn into his, and avenge his sufferings. He found an eager accomplice in Mufliḥ, chief of the negro eunuchs, who cherished a loathing for the Vizier on account of a certain jest that the latter had made at his expense—"I shall buy a hundred black slaves and call each of them Mufliḥ," Ḥámid had announced on one occasion; at which Mufliḥ, cut to the soul, resolved, if the chance came his way, on revenge. And Mufliḥ was by no means powerless: lately, for his able control of the palace eunuchs, he had risen high in the esteem of the Caliph, and had received as marks of favour valuable fiefs and estates. Al-Muḥassin now secured his help in making Ja'far an offer to extract the usual large sums of money from a comprehensive list of victims, including Ḥámid, 'Alí, Naṣr, Ibn al-Ḥawwárí, and Umm Músà: on the condition, of course, of his father's being restored to power.

1 H. 322.

At first Ibn al-Furát himself was reluctant to join them—he professed a disinclination for the cares of authority. Later, however, he was provoked by the hostility of Ibn al-Ḥawwárí into working against him, and from this he was led on to engage once more in politics for his own advantage.[1]

The schemes of the faction were furthered by an indiscretion on the part of Umm Músà, which ended in the ruin of herself and her family. She elected to give her niece in marriage to a great-grandson of al-Mutawakkil, spending vast sums in largesse and entertainments, so that the wedding attracted much attention. Now it happened that this prince (a good-looking young man and well-dressed) was a friend of 'Alí ibn 'Ísà, who, it was whispered, was forming him for the Caliphate. When, therefore, al-Muqtadir fell seriously ill for some days, it was a simple matter, on his recovery, for Umm Músà's enemies—that is, presumably, the Furát faction—to declare that her connection with the prince was treasonable, that she had been preparing to secure her position by setting him up as Caliph. Umm Músà was arrested and confronted by her mistress. She, her brother, her sister and all their family were then handed over to the ferocious Thumal, who tortured them pitilessly to discover every source of their wealth. Their estates were confiscated, and the sums extracted from them were so considerable that 'Alí found it necessary to create a special *díwán* for their reception. 'Alí's connection with the suspect prince no doubt worsened his own position. He does not seem to have been openly accused of complicity, however.[2]

'Alí's relations with Umm Músà had continued to be somewhat strained. During his present term of office as Assistant to the Vizier they had again clashed

1 M. I, 87; H. 69, 243–4.
2 'A. 108–9; M. I, 83–4; S.J. fol. 76 a.

over an attempt that 'Alí had made to bring to book a *protégé* of hers, a Government agent that was in debt to the State. Umm Músà contrived to have the prosecution quashed; whereupon 'Alí, with characteristic lack of proper pride, sought to ease the situation thus created by congratulating the official on his escape from the impersonal grasp of the law. All he received for his pains, however, was a set of satirical verses, in retort.[1] This official was still Government agent at Iṣfahán at the time of Umm Músà's disgrace. Now, therefore, 'Alí was at last enabled to replace him with a nominee of his own.[2]

Ibn al-Ḥawwárí was in some way implicated in the supposed plot, and his favour with the Caliph began to decline. His adversaries did their best to compromise him still further—thus, once on his way to the Harem Ja'far picked up a paper on which were written obscene verses designed to inflame him against the Secretary, in which the latter was referred to as "Cock of the Palace". Ibn al-Furát planned with elaborate care a scene intended to expose Ibn al-Ḥawwárí's peculations and his own scrupulosity. It was indeed no difficult matter to attack Ibn al-Ḥawwárí: Ḥámid had heaped sinecures upon him and his twelve year-old son, so that he drew a huge salary, whilst all the work of his offices was done by deputies. Ibn al-Furát borrowed a sum appropriate to his purpose in *dirhams* from the Caliph and the Lady, declaring that it was for an urgent need and promising to repay it; then he had the *dirhams* changed for new-minted *dínárs*. Ja'far was now in the habit of visiting him on Thursday afternoons when he fasted, and on the next occasion found him seated with the golden pile on the carpet before him. Ja'far enquired what the *dínárs* were for. Ibn al-Furát replied that they represented the daily appropriations of the villain, the criminal, Ibn al-Ḥawwárí,

1 H. 355. 2 M. 1, 84.

—also he wished to repay with them the loan that the Commander of the Faithful had so generously made him. Ja'far was duly impressed with the illustration: he vowed that he would tolerate Ibn al-Ḥawwárí no longer. And he was touched—especially when he recollected how much he, the Caliph, had taken from the unfortunate minister—at the exactitude of Ibn al-Furát.[1]

Meanwhile 'Alí's measures of economy and reform had aroused the hostility that was inevitable. Soon after his assumption of power under Ḥámid in the year 306 (918) he had drawn up another report on the financial situation, similar to that which he had made five years before.[2] Basing his figures for the revenue on the returns for the last complete year, namely 304 (916–17), and those for expenditure on the current scale, he had computed a deficit of more than two million *dínárs*, or about one-seventh of the entire revenue.

And this was for what might be considered a normal year. But as regards expenditure, the first three years of Ḥámid's Vizierate had been very far from normal. To begin with, Ibn Abí's-Sáj was still defiant at the time of Ḥámid's elevation, and large sums had had to be spent in preparations for a renewal of the campaign against him. Then in 307 (919-20) the Fáṭimids had for a second time invaded Egypt, and the cost of opposing them had been so great that the contributions of two years due to Baghdád from the tax-contracts of Egypt and Syria had been swallowed up in defraying it. This money had at least not been spent in vain: Mu'nis had been twice successful—he had defeated and captured Ibn Abí's-Sáj, whom he had brought as a

1 H. 84–5; M. 1, 86–7, 87–8.

2 H. 323; Ḥaw. 128. It is this report that forms the subject of Von Kremer's monograph on 'Alí ibn 'Ísà and his statesmanship: *Ueber das Einnahmebudget des Abbasidenreichs*.

prisoner to Baghdád, and he had again driven out the Fáṭimids.[1] But its expenditure had none the less made all the more necessary a drastic retrenchment.

In order to carry this out 'Alí was obliged again to dock the general increases of pay that Ibn al-Furát had renewed on his return to power.[2] Murmurs of dissatisfaction, consequently, soon began to make themselves heard. The Háshimites in particular, resenting the reduction of their allowances, had soon been up in arms. One day, as early as 306 (918–9), when 'Alí was coming away from a consultation with Ḥámid (for they were still on good terms at the time), a party of Háshimites had set upon him and abused him; they had pulled him off his horse and torn his jacket, and had only been prevented from doing him bodily injury by the intervention of some officers. It was not that they felt any particular grudge against 'Alí as a man—indeed they had every reason for regarding him with gratitude for the many charitable gifts he had made them: their trouble was purely economic, they had pestered Ibn al-Furát in a like way, during his last Vizierate.[3] The Caliph had then extorted an apology from representatives of the family by temporarily excluding them from Court. But now he resorted to sterner measures: the offenders were put in chains, scourged, and sent in a prison ship for a brief exile in al-Baṣrah, where they were paraded in mockery on donkeys.—The truth is that the feeling of reverence for the Prophet's family was very strong, and that sometimes members of it would abuse their privileged position. 'Alí always remembered the tactless behaviour of one such Háshimite, who presented him as Vizier with a petition for some unheard-of favour; and when he wished to leave his assembly, intending

1 M. I, 48–50, 75, 76 (extract from the *kitáb al-'uyún*); 'A. 77, 79, 80, 84, 85, 86; Maq. *it*. 43; S.J. fol. 70 a; Tagh. II, 210. Cf. H. 290.

2 H. 291.

3 'A. 62.

to think how he could most reasonably meet the man's demand, insisted on his signing it straight away.[1] On the occasion of his assailants' banishment to al-Baṣrah, the governor, to whose care they were consigned, felt impelled to treat them with an incongruous deference, giving them money secretly, and when the order came for their release, providing them with a boat and food for the journey. Moreover, on their return to the capital Ḥámid sent them presents, as did likewise Umm Músà, her brother, and 'Alí himself.[2]

In other respects, also, besides his reduction of salaries and allowances, 'Alí pursued the same policy as before. Thus he issued stringent orders forbidding the bribery with which subordinates throughout the administration were wont to propitiate their superiors. Though at the final stage these bribes formed a source of income recognised as legal at any rate by Ibn al-Furát, 'Alí judged that in the long run their suppression would be not only of moral, but also of material benefit to the State: "Bribery," he declared, "leads to the loss of dues, the ruin of the land, and the oppression of the subject." The disadvantage of the reform was, as 'Alí had found to his cost before, that whereas its drawbacks were obvious immediately, its virtues required time to appear.[3]

The malcontents delighted to ridicule the anomalous relationship of Ḥámid and 'Alí. One of the usual rhymes, after assuring 'Alí that he is Vizier indeed—that Ḥámid is merely a screen for him, "just to improve a bad business"—enquires "how many ones make one?";[4] and another speculates over a successor for Ḥámid, and enumerates the most likely candidates. In the latter, the Lady's secretary, al-Khaṣíbí, is suggested for one; or, it is asked, shall "the prisoner of Zaydán" be released, for Ḥámid is "old and feeble",

1 H. 331; Tan. *nish.* 48.
2 'A. 75–6.
3 H. 291.
4 *fakh.* 316.

and 'Alí ibn 'Ísà "stingy, forbidding, and a giver of short weight"?[1] Al-Muqtadir, in fact, was still undecided about a new Vizier. For a time he had in mind another party, a certain Muḥammad ibn al-Ḥasan al-Karkhí, from whom he had received the usual undertaking to extract a fixed sum from Ḥámid and 'Alí; and al-Karkhí might well have been made Vizier, had not Ja'far, with engaging simplicity, enquired the opinion of Ibn al-Furát. As a result of their weekly intercourse Ibn al-Furát's ascendancy over the Caliph was now again absolute; and when, since he was himself aiming at reinstatement, he pronounced himself against al-Karkhí, the Caliph abandoned all thought of him forthwith.[2] Soon after, Ja'far again asked his advice about another similar proposal; and in regard to this the minister might have been expected to be very much less impartial still.

Ḥámid, alarmed for his safety at the trend of events, had cast about for means of extricating himself from the perilous situation in which he would find himself, should Ibn al-Furát, as seemed only too probable, return to office. His proposal, if not subtle, was in the light of the past at least bold—it was simply to have the control of affairs committed again to him. Some monetary inducement is likely to have accompanied it, or it is hard to imagine why al-Muqtadir should have treated it even as considerately as he did. However, he insisted that Ḥámid should give him a written list of proposed appointments (for the *díwáns* were also to be redistributed), as well as a statement of his financial undertakings, in order that he might submit them to the judgement of his favourite counsellor.

Needless to say, the scheme of Ḥámid met with Ibn al-Furát's approval even less than that of al-Karkhí—and with justice. As he truly observed: 'Alí, whom Ḥámid now proposed to displace, was infinitely his

1 'A. 109. 2 H. 81–2.

superior: if then he had failed with 'Alí's co-operation before, why should he be expected to succeed now without it? He went further: if it was a question of money, he said, he would offer five times whatever Ḥámid had offered, if only the Caliph would release him and set him up once more. The Caliph was already prepared by al-Muḥassin's earlier proposal: where interest and inclination marched so harmoniously together, how could he refuse?

Ḥámid recognised in time that his game was up; and prudently sought permission to retire, whither the humiliating neglect of 'Alí had already urged him, to Wásiṭ. His hated deputy had the field to himself for a few days; then, on 20th *rabí' al-ákhir* 311 (7th August 923), whilst he was awaiting the hour of audience as usual in an ante-room of the palace, surrounded by officers and pages in attendance, he was arrested and hurried off to the all too familiar apartments of Zaydán the *qahramánah*. That same day the Caliph summoned Ibn al-Furát from his prison to be Vizier, and presented both him and al-Muḥassin with robes of honour. He then commanded the princes, and all the officers and pages and eunuchs, to accompany them in triumph to their abode in the city.[1]

1 M. I, 85–6, 89; H. 244, 288.

CHAPTER XII

‘Alí *on trial.*

By a coincidence, exceedingly unfortunate for ‘Alí, the Carmathians, who had remained quiet ten whole years,[1] chose almost the very day of his arrest to descend on and sack al-Baṣrah. They were led now, not by al-Jannábí’s immediate successor, his eldest son Sa‘íd, but by a younger brother of the latter, Abú Ṭáhir Sulaymán.[2] If it had not been for the adventurous spirit of this young man, encouraged perhaps by the directors of the secret Ismá‘ílí organisation,[3] his desire to emulate the exploits of the "Man with the Mole" and withal to enrich himself and his followers, it is probable that the Carmathians would never have troubled the Caliphate again. For ‘Alí’s policy of conciliation had shown them the advantages of friendly intercourse; their sectarian enthusiasm had by now almost completely evaporated; and until Abú Ṭáhir attained the age of leadership, the council of elders, headed by Sa‘íd, appears to have been content with a prosperous inactivity.

On the occasion of the earlier attack on al-Baṣrah, al-Jannábí the Elder, Abú Sa‘íd, had ridden away after defeating the defending force and robbing the killed; but now Abú Ṭáhir surprised the watchmen on the walls at night and his men swarmed into the city before the inhabitants could organise any resistance. During

1 S.J. fol. 69 a, followed by Tagh. II, 207 and Ibn Khaldún, IV, 89 (the latter’s authority accepted by De Goeje: *Carmathes*, 78), records an attack by the Carmathians on al-Baṣrah in 307 (919–20). But no such attack is mentioned in any of the earlier histories.—Abú Ṭáhir is said to have taken command in 305 (917–18). See Dh. *t.* fol. 206 a.

2 Cf. Mas. *tan.* 391.

3 See *Encyclopédie*, II, 813 (art. *Ḳarmaṭes*).

ten days he burnt quarter after quarter, retiring nightly to his camp outside the walls. The garrison and the citizens put up the best defence they could, but many, including the governor, were killed, and gradually they were beaten back to the Tigris, into which numbers cast themselves in despair. For seven days more the Carmathians remained to load their camels with plunder and with such women and children as they had captured and wished to keep as slaves. Then they departed once more into the desert.

The attack had begun only four days after 'Alí's arrest, whereas, according to al-Mas'údí, the journey from Ḥajar took the Carmathians six days to accomplish: it is therefore extremely improbable that the two events were really connected. Nevertheless, the commander of the force that Ibn al-Furát had hurried to the relief of the garrison sent back a report (whether or not he was prompted to do so before setting out) in which he announced the discovery of a secret understanding between the fallen minister and the Carmathians. The Carmathians, he wrote, had mystified the townspeople on their arrival with a dark saying: "How foolish of your Princeling to part with that elder!"; and only when the news of the restitution of Ibn al-Furát reached them had they recognised "that elder" to be 'Alí ibn 'Ísà, on which they guessed that the Carmathians had learnt of the event by pigeon-post. In proof of collusion between 'Alí and the Carmathians some of those that had been captured were ready to testify that their rulers had received not only presents and arms from him but a letter urging them to descend on al-Baṣrah. These prisoners would proceed to Baghdád, to appear as witnesses in court.[1]

Meanwhile 'Alí and Ibn al-Furát had again changed

1 M. I, 104–5; 'A. 110–11; Mas. *tan.* 380; Ḥam. I, 203; S.J. fol. 77 a; De Goeje: *Carmathes*, 80, quoting passages from the *kitáb al-'uyún*.

places—'Alí was now back once more with Zaydán in the very apartments just vacated by Ibn al-Furát, and Ibn al-Furát was installed again in the Palace of Viziers, which at great cost he was refurbishing and enlarging, so that his family might live with him there instead of at his private house in the city.[1] His faction were revelling in their return to power; whilst their adversaries, as will appear, were suffering an unprecedented persecution.

Perhaps because the Carmathian witnesses had not yet arrived, Ibn al-Furát first questioned 'Alí on matters of finance. They had been too long in opposition for Ibn al-Furát to account him otherwise than as an enemy; but that opposition had been so almost entirely political that he felt no animosity against him. Yet he was determined to profit again in their present encounter by his own self-assurance and 'Alí's lack of it. From the outset he intimidated his unhappy rival, who appeared in the assembly "as if dead from fear and distress", by keeping him waiting, standing before him, whilst he pretended to be immersed in the business of letter-writing. In the silence broken only by the scraping of the reed on the paper 'Alí's agitation mounted till he could hardly bear it; but at length the Vizier looked up: "God bless you!" he said, "sit down." The relief was too much for 'Alí: if he had ever had any thought of doing battle, he at once abandoned it. He threw himself on the Vizier and covered his hand with kisses, declaring that he was "his slave and servant, his pupil...and the pupil of his brother Aḥmad (on whom God Almighty have mercy!)". Ibn al-Furát acknowledged the tie: he had nothing against him personally...only affairs of State had come between them, he said.[2] On this, 'Alí, somewhat reassured, appealed to the assembly for sympathy: anyone in his position, he complained, with the Caliph hostile

1 H. 178–9. 2 H. 130.

and the Vizier far from well disposed, was fair game for calumny. And afterwards he found courage to defend himself on every point brought up against him, and even to make some damaging criticisms of the Vizier.

Choosing a count not unlike that with which 'Alí had before charged him, Ibn al-Furát began by accusing 'Alí of venal partiality towards the Mádhará'ís. In the first place, after he, Ibn al-Furát, had replaced them by an agent of his own choice, who secured their bond for a large payment on various heads, 'Alí in turn had dismissed him and reinstated the Mádhará'ís, although their debt was less than half discharged—and this without the Caliph's consent. In the second place, though 'Alí had afterwards himself made a contract for a yearly sum to be paid by Abú Zunbúr into the Treasury, he challenged him to prove that the terms of this contract had been in fact fulfilled.

Against the first accusation (of having acted without orders from the Caliph) 'Alí defended himself by reminding Ibn al-Furát that for the first seven months after his release, during which the events referred to had taken place, he had acted on Ḥámid's orders, and that consequently Ḥámid and not he was responsible. As for the second accusation (that he had forgone payments from Abú Zunbúr) he denied that it was true. The first year's contribution had been received in full, while during the second and third the Fáṭimids had invaded Egypt, so that some of the taxes could not be collected, and what surplus there was had been spent on the needs of Mu'nis's army. 'Alí accounted also for the payments of the last two years; but his answer is not recorded. He was in a position to plead, and possibly did so, that after further experience of the methods of Abú Zunbúr he had dismissed him himself.[1]

Ibn al-Furát declined to take seriously 'Alí's plea

1 H. 44.

of the superior authority of Ḥámid. He had crossed Ḥámid on points far more significant than this, and if he had indeed disapproved his action in dismissing the agent that Ibn al-Furát had appointed, he should have complained of it to the Caliph. As for his arrangement with Abú Zunbúr by which the latter's debt was commuted to an annual payment under a new contract, it was utterly unprecedented, as 'Alí, who had spent his whole life in Government offices, must admit.

However, Ibn al-Furát passed next to a criticism of 'Alí's financial dealings in general: by cutting down pay and allowances (including the allowance guaranteed to the Caliph only by Ibn al-Furát himself) 'Alí had saved in his five years of control a large sum, which he must have either embezzled or wasted. But to this also 'Alí had an answer: since he had prohibited bribery and taken nothing from the Privy Purse, both sources, though they had been open to Ibn al-Furát, had been closed to him; and he had therefore drawn on those afforded by his economies instead. 'Alí was now even emboldened to make an accusation against Ibn al-Furát, of having depleted the Privy Purse of almost 17 millions during his first Vizierate. But when the latter challenged him to put the charge in writing, he felt uncertain of his figures, and was obliged somewhat feebly to desist. Ibn al-Furát thereupon denied the truth of this allegation, and declared that, far from depleting the Privy Purse, by subduing Fárs he had done something to replenish it.

At the beginning, in the middle, and now again at the end of the proceedings, 'Alí was adjured to state the amount of money that he was capable of paying as a fine. He persisted in asserting that 3000 *dínárs* (an insignificant sum) was all he could produce. Though 'Ísà his banker had signed a declaration that 'Alí had on deposit with him no less than 17,000, 'Alí absolutely denied that the money was his. He supposed that it belonged either to the *díwán al-birr* (which he had managed for all but a short interval ever since its foundation) or to 'Ísà himself; and in the latter case he attributed the confusion of accounts not to 'Ísà's carelessness, but to his having been terrorised.

Ibn al-Furát had now stated his case against 'Alí as far as administrative matters were concerned; and for the present, so it seems, he carried the examination no further. But there was still the question of 'Alí's dealings with the Carmathians to be raised; it is not clear how soon after his arrest this first interview with Ibn al-Furát took place, but it was only when he had been in prison some two months that he was called to answer the graver charge. This was not the first time that he had been accused of a treasonable sympathy for the sectaries. As long ago as 303 (915–16) his sending an embassy to them had been hotly criticised, and it appears that after his fall in the following year Ibn al-Furát had sought to inflame Ja'far against him by suggesting that in fact he secretly shared their views.[1] But as long as the Carmathians remained quiet in their distant province the accusation aroused no more than a mild disgust. Only now that they were once more on the war path it at once regained all its ancient sting—from now on, it may be noticed, a favourite way of injuring an enemy is to call him a Carmathian.

To judge a religious-moral case such as this the presence of Ibn al-Buhlúl and Abú 'Umar was again required; moreover, since Ibn al-Furát felt himself to be on firm ground, it was suggested to the Caliph that he might with advantage attend again unseen. 'Alí was to be confronted not only with the prisoners from al-Baṣrah, but by a certain Ibn Fulayḥah,[2] whom he had formerly employed on missions to the Carmathians.

1 H. 68.
2 This name is given as Qalíjah or Qulayjah in Yáq. *ud.* 1, 85.

Two counts were preferred: first it was contended that the phraseology of 'Alí's letters, drafts of which were produced in court, betrayed on his part a far from orthodox tenderness; and secondly it was alleged, on the deposition of this Ibn Fulayḥah, that as well as arms 'Alí had sent the Carmathians a certain marvellous unguent, preservative against fire. Ibn al-Furát went on to suggest, also, although he did not follow up the charge, that it was owing to 'Alí's reduction, under the pretext of economy, of the garrison at al-Baṣrah that the Carmathians had found it so easy to enter and destroy the town.

Once again the two *qáḍhís* were opposed in their judgements. Both, however, refused to support the indictment. Abú 'Umar indeed went so far as to state that 'Alí had virtually acquiesced in rebellion—on which 'Alí, who knew that the Caliph was listening, glanced at him indignantly; but he refused to sign a conviction of his guilt, and even when pressed would record it as his opinion only that the letters were actually in 'Alí's handwriting. Ibn al-Buhlúl, as usual, was much more explicit. 'Alí had replied that the object both of his presents and his letters had been to conciliate the Carmathians. The Caliphate was practically powerless against them: its only weapon was diplomacy. As a result of his policy he had to show, not only an agreement by which they had released their Muslim prisoners to the number of three thousand, but a ten years' immunity from their attacks. Nor was this last the effect of chance: for besides an assault on the Pilgrimage, the Carmathians had twice meditated a descent on al-Kúfah and al-Baṣrah;[1] and they had only been deterred by their desire to preserve an intercourse which, owing to 'Alí's efforts, they had seen to be advantageous. Ibn al-Buhlúl assumed the morality of his attitude. That granted, 'Alí could by no means

1 See De Goeje: *Carmathes*, 80, citing the *kitáb al-'uyún*.

be deemed guilty of misconduct in so addressing even those who were admittedly the enemies of the State. It was urged that in his dealings with the infidels, he had no right to make use of terms that might allow it to be thought for a moment that their infidelity escaped him, or met with anything but his most ferocious condemnation. But apart from the consideration that if he had couched the letters in an offensive tone, it would have defeated his object, Ibn al-Buhlúl denied that 'Alí had had in fact any technical reason for assuming that they were infidels at all. They had headed their missives with invocations as orthodox as could be, of God and the Prophet;[1] and if this did not obliterate the iniquity of their rebellion against the Caliph, at least it excused their correspondent from the obligation of tempering his appeal with the anathemas of religion.

Ibn al-Furát was furious enough at this; but when Ibn al-Buhlúl brushed aside as unsupported Ibn Fulayḥah's allegation about the ointment, his rage knew no bounds. He meted out abuse all round, not forgetting to raise his voice so that al-Muqtadir should hear. Abú 'Umar, by his abstention, had imperilled the foundations of government; Ibn al-Buhlúl, rather that that of judge, merited the title of advocate for the defence; as for 'Alí, he was nothing less than a Carmaṭhian himself, an enemy of the Caliph, of the 'Abbásid dynasty, of all Islam.

Ibn Buhlúl was indignant at this denunciation, and retorted that he was now actuated by that very regard for the truth that had caused him before to interpose in the Vizier's favour, when Ḥámid, in a weightier case than this, had supported his impeachment with false witness. 'Alí, on the other hand, was petrified. He could only sit mumbling in his place. On this Naṣr

1 For the truth of this contention see the text of the Carmathian letter quoted in Dh. *t*. fol. 2 a–b.

the Chamberlain and al-Muḥassin intervened, apparently by a preconcerted plan. In the ensuing pause they requested the Vizier to grant them a private interview with the delinquent; and, taking him each by the hand, they raised him to his feet and led him from the room.

They hoped to procure 'Alí's admission that he could after all disburse more than a paltry 3000 *dínárs*; and it needed but little eloquence to work upon his already overstrained nerves. Disregarding the *qádhís'* verdict, they assured him that his conduct was utterly indefensible; his only hope lay in immediate capitulation; otherwise the Caliph would not hesitate to take his life. 'Alí was terror-stricken, and notwithstanding his previous obstinacy, was persuaded without argument to sign a bond for as much as one hundred times the amount. It was agreed that one-third should be an "accelerated" payment—'Alí only stipulated that he must first be released so that he might confer unhindered with friends and financiers. Having attained their object, however, Naṣr and al-Muḥassin retired. They left it to Ibn al-Furát to settle the terms of execution.

Though he had so tamely acquiesced in the main demand, 'Alí now rallied himself to create as favourable an atmosphere in which to beg for facilities as he could. He reminded Ibn al-Furát of their long collaboration, and even suggested that he considered as still binding a compact that they had made before either had been raised to the Vizierate with its hostile ambitions, to further each other's interests, and to refrain from mutual calumny. To be sure it was somewhat late to assert the cogency of such generous principles; yet the recollection of old times seems really to have mollified the Vizier—he resented nothing, so he averred, but imputations against either his efficiency or his loyalty. Setting aside that of his own assessors, he accepted 'Alí's estimate of the amount due to the

State for arrears of taxes on his properties,[1] and he even allowed this to be included in the total of the fine, provided that it did not exceed a certain sum. The strictness of ‘Alí's morality was evidently relaxed on this occasion; for, painful to relate, on subsequent examination it was discovered that the figure he now gave represented less than half the true amount. Also he attempted to trick the Vizier over the wording of his bond with respect to the dates of payment; but this was more easily detected. Ibn al-Furát, however, seemed to consider such a deceit quite in order: he took it in good part, and was charmed with his own sagacity in exposing it. Al-Muqtadir approved the bond; but, pending the fulfilment of certain provisos, ‘Alí was returned to his prison.[2]

1 There is a slight discrepancy on this point between the accounts of H. and M.

2 H. 288–96; M. 1, 104–10; Yáq. *ud.* 1, 85–7.

CHAPTER XIII

The violence of al-Muḥassin *and its results.*

Whilst 'Alí's trial was in progress the Vizier's son al-Muḥassin had begun a vindictive persecution of the fallen faction. The ill-treatment that he had received from Ḥámid seems to have affected his brain: on the one hand he looked upon anyone connected even officially with Ḥámid as an enemy, and on the other he revelled in cruelty for its own sake. 'Alí had helped al-Muḥassin to pay off part of his fine—al-Muḥassin had every reason therefore to feel at least grateful to him. But 'Alí's connection with Ḥámid—even though they had been at daggers drawn—was enough to convert him, in al-Muḥassin's mind, into an arch-enemy: and he besought the Caliph with extravagant persistence to deliver him into his hands.

It was precisely this that 'Alí especially dreaded. He had stipulated in his bond that he should be confined in a safe place—that is, beyond the reach of Ibn al-Furát and his son; but days passed, and there was no sign of his removal. The Lady and Zaydán took his part: they reminded Ja'far of his long service and piety, and insisted that the condition to which he had assented in accepting the bond should be fulfilled; but al-Muḥassin's persuasions were stronger: he convinced the Caliph that 'Alí, in spite of the *qádhís'* verdict, was indeed a Carmathian at heart, and therefore an outlaw.

Ja'far came to hold the view that 'Alí must either pay in the palace at once, or take the consequence—delivery over to al-Muḥassin. But 'Alí, in his interviews with the latter, the Vizier being absent, relied faithfully on the terms of his bond. At the same time he was not obstinate: in order to raise money he sent for the overseer of his estates, Ibn Jání, and his Christian secretary, Ibn Ayyúb, through whom he quickly negotiated the sale of a house and some land in the city. This brought in very little; but al-Muḥassin had been depicting 'Alí to the Caliph as defiant, and it was enough to jeopardise the success of his intrigue. However, he found that Ibn Ayyúb was to be deterred by threats from visiting the prisoner. Ibn Jání, being more pertinacious, had first to be tortured till he fainted and almost expired. Again the days passed and 'Alí was unable to proceed with his business. The impatience and wrath of al-Muqtadir grew in proportion.

At length, more than a fortnight after 'Alí had signed the bond, the Caliph consulted the Vizier. But by this time he was so well primed with the arguments of al-Muḥassin that he interpreted the silence that Ibn al-Furát then judged it best to maintain as a desire to curry favour with the public by a lenient treatment of his rival. Ja'far argued that 'Alí being a Carmathian proved, both his life and his possessions were forfeit. He was willing to spare the one, if he might be sure of the other; but at present he was receiving no satisfaction whatever, and so, after due deliberation, he was handing over the recalcitrant prisoner to his trusty servant the Vizier's son. "Frighten him," he charged al-Muḥassin, "and if he acknowledges his deposits and pays up what he has agreed to, well and good; but if not, shackle him. Then if he gives in, well and good; but if not, put on him...the Woollen Shirt. Then, if he still persists, apply torture to his body, in the presence of some of the officers, in recompense for his rebellion."

The carrying out of these orders was painful to witness. 'Alí was old—he was already in his sixty-fifth year—and he was resigned: as a butt for the insane spite of al-Muḥassin he made a truly pathetic figure; and the onlookers were soon moved to compassion.

Al-Muḥassin gladly convoked a tribunal of officers, headed by Naṣr the Chamberlain and Názúk the new Chief of Police. He began amicably enough by adjuring 'Alí once more to fulfil his bond. 'Alí, however, referred again to the condition of his first being confined elsewhere, upon which al-Muḥassin changed his tone. He sent for a heavy shackle and the fearsome Woollen Shirt; but the smith had only begun to fix the shackle on 'Alí's leg, when Naṣr rose from his seat and prepared to leave the court. Al-Muḥassin was indignant: he complained that when *he* had been tortured Naṣr had sat by without objecting. But Naṣr retorted that if this was to be the result of the Caliph's policy of putting his fallen ministers to the question, his service would become intolerable: if one remained to witness the proceedings one made an enemy of the victim; if one went away one offended the executioner.

When he had gone, in fastening the shackle the smith struck 'Alí's ankle with the hammer. 'Alí, wincing with pain, enquired what the man had against him; to which he replied that 'Alí had reduced his pay by a *dínár* a day. This barbarity in turn scandalised Názúk, who also stood up to depart; and though al-Muḥassin objected that he, as Chief of Police, was bound in duty to remain, he followed the Chamberlain out. "I cannot consent," he said, "to be present at the torture of a man whose hand I have kissed for ten years."

Al-Muḥassin prevailed on the other officers to remain. Two of them did their best to dissuade him from proceeding further; but he insisted that 'Alí's fate lay entirely in his own hands. Yet 'Alí still refused to undertake what he knew he could not fulfil: if he were now to consent he would be prosecuted later for not keeping his word, so that far from there being any real inducement to submit, by doing so he would merely put himself in the wrong. Al-Muḥassin, however, was naturally unmoved by such an argument: he ordered the attendants to put on the Woollen Shirt.

It was evident that nothing short of a countermand would restrain al-Muḥassin from enforcing the extreme measures that had now become for him an end in themselves. But fortunately for 'Alí there was watching the proceedings an unexpected ally, and one powerful enough to effect his will. In the recent intrigues for the Vizierate Mufliḥ the Negro had worked for al-Muḥassin and his father; but he had been prompted to this entirely by his aversion to Ḥámid. For 'Alí he felt no such antipathy, and pitied his present miserable lot. Mufliḥ recognised that al-Muḥassin was bent on proceeding as far as, if not further than, his mandate allowed, and he determined to frustrate his intention. Leaving the meeting place unobserved, he hastened to the Presence, and obtained by his pleading a command for the torture to cease and the minister to be returned to his confinement. 'Alí was rescued by his intercession from the malice of his tormentor, but not before he had had a taste of the brutality in which it might be vented. A cuffing about the head by ten burly retainers was no mean chastisement; but it elicited from him no more than pious ejaculations. Al-Muḥassin thus enjoyed the luxury, though curtailed, of inflicting pain; but he had failed to advance the Caliph's cause, and had come near to seriously compromising himself.

Ibn al-Furát was much perturbed at the possible consequences of al-Muḥassin's barbarity. Though the Caliph had authorised it, he could not always be relied upon to remember or support anything that he had said. Moreover, there was no doubt that public opinion would deprecate the oppression of one whom, though it might dislike his politics, it regarded as a model of piety and wisdom. His secretary, whom he consulted, suggested that he should excuse al-Muḥassin to the

Caliph: by magnifying the gravity of his indiscretion he would encourage al-Muqtadir to belittle it, and also disarm his critics. Nor had Ibn al-Furát to pretend a dismay that he did not feel, his sympathy for 'Alí was genuine—in remonstrating with al-Muḥassin he reminded him that he was actually beholden to 'Alí for financial assistance[1]—and in his letter to the Caliph he exaggerated it in the most affecting terms. He received the reply for which he had hoped: the Caliph would have no reflections cast upon al-Muḥassin, who in acting as he had, was but carrying out his instructions against an obstinate outlaw. Nevertheless, the outlaw had undergone punishment enough for the present: he was at once to be released from his bonds; divested of the Woollen Shirt; and removed from the control of his perhaps too zealous inquisitor.

'Alí had borne his ordeal with fortitude; yet it shook his pertinacity, and he now undertook to pay the "accelerated" part of his fine at once. So that he might arrange the terms of payment, al-Muqtadir decided that he should remove from the palace to the house of Ibn al-Furát: ten days later, accordingly, he was sent to the Vizier with a letter from the Caliph, who now insisted, ingenuously enough, that 'Alí should be considerately treated. The conduct of al-Muḥassin had disgusted the Lady and Zaydán. Yet Zaydán remained friendly to Ibn al-Furát, and now counselled him, in his own interests, instead of keeping 'Alí at his own residence, to hand him on to one of the chief officers, by name Shafí' al-Lu'lu'í. Ibn al-Furát agreed: there was no knowing how much bodily harm 'Alí had sustained from his rough handling; he was an old man; whatever happened he must not die where the Vizier might be suspected of having contrived his death:—he therefore sought and obtained al-Muqtadir's permission to lodge him wherever he pleased. As for 'Alí himself, the move

1 Ath. (Búláq), VIII, 48.

was precisely what he had worked for all along: he would now be able to interview friends and financiers in comparative security, and arrange for the discharge of his debt. Shafí', to be sure, was as reluctant to receive him, and for the same reason, as Ibn al-Furát; but there was no gainsaying the order of the Vizier, and he prepared to take 'Alí in charge.

'Alí had the tact to improve the Vizier's humour, before their interview, by leading the Afternoon Prayer in the arcade outside his assembly, and afterwards by rising at the entrance of al-Muḥassin. So their discussion was conducted in a friendly spirit, although al-Muḥassin did his best to provoke a quarrel by reopening the question of the Mádhará'ís. He was enraged, also, at 'Alí's first request—that the produce of certain of his trusts should be released to furnish money for the payment of his fine—, since before, in a like case, 'Alí had denied just such a relief to his father. Ibn al-Furát himself reproached 'Alí for this ungenerous inconsistency, and showed how he, in contrast, had actually granted this demand before it was made; but he refused to allow him to be involved again in the case of the Mádhará'ís, who were now in Baghdád and could answer for themselves.

On this al-Muḥassin suddenly changed his tone. 'Alí was his *shaykh*, he said: it was not of his own choice that he had acted as he had. No more harsh words were spoken after this; and 'Alí secured the concession of most of his other requests.

Just as he was preparing to take his leave, another son of the Vizier, by his concubine Dawlat, a mere youth, al-Ḥasan by name, came into the assembly. 'Alí immediately rose from his place and kissed his hand; whereupon the Vizier was so flattered that he forthwith called for his treasurer; ordered him to put two thousand *dínárs* at 'Alí's disposal for the payment of his fine; and commanded al-Muḥassin to contribute another thousand. 'Alí, who had thus gained more in the interview than he could have hoped for, expressed his profound gratitude for these attentions, and so far forgot his recent injuries as to lose himself in reverences to al-Muḥassin. All the onlookers except the Secretaries of State rose as he made to depart, and the chamberlains lined up to conduct him to the landing-stage. He stepped with Shafí' into his barge, well content with his diplomacy and not too desperate of his prospects; and, being accorded the place of honour, rowed with him to his house.

Soon after they had gone, the call to Sunset Prayer interrupted the sitting. When his devotions were over, Ibn al-Furát talked with his secretaries; his thoughts were all of the scene that had been enacted in his assembly that afternoon. 'Alí's patience and humility amazed and somewhat disgusted him. "I do not approve his way," he said, "for my heart is like the hearts of the camels, which in adversity cannot but puff up and grow bold."

'Alí's optimism was justified. Not only was he no more hindered in the collection of the money, but the necessary total was the more quickly arrived at, in that many officials of the Court, emulating the generosity of the Vizier, came forward with offers of contribution. Some 'Alí refused, but he accepted the help of such as he considered owed him some recompense for his misfortunes. In short, it was not long before the fine was paid off, upon which his estates were released from sequestration.

The Vizier was now faced with a problem: what was to be done with 'Alí?—for the possibility of his simply being set free seems never even to have been considered. He informed the Caliph, and probably it was true, that 'Alí's continued residence with Shafí' al-Lu'lu'í, in whose charge he was receiving all the consideration due to his rank and his age, was becoming, to an alarming degree, a source of speculation; and that this, by returning him to the palace, would only be encouraged. Al-Muḥassin, despite his late fleeting sympathy, was for killing him out of hand; but his father preferred a less drastic course, and after consulting with the Caliph, decided to banish him. 'Alí was permitted to choose his place of exile, and immediately fixed on Mecca. An agent of the Banú'l-Furát, by name Ibn al-Kúthání,[1] was appointed his guardian; a liberal allowance was made for himself, the agent, and the camel-men; and as soon as the preparations for his departure were complete, he set out joyfully for the blessed goal.[2]

One of the metropolitan poetasters composed an ode of jubilation on 'Alí's banishment.

...He is gone, scorned, driven forth, deprived,—with ruin and disgrace for company.
[But] whilst his kinsfolk are met in an assemblage of mourning,—the people are holding a marriage feast....
He straitened the world upon its people,—it was as if the universe were in duress....
May God destroy him and never bring him back,—for his destruction would be very pleasant to the soul!

1 His name is given in an extract from Ham. *tak.*, M. I, 113.

2 H. 130–1, 296–308; M. I, 110–13; 'A. 113; Dh. *t.* fol. 66 a; Tagh. II, 219.

END OF PART TWO

Part Three

CHAPTER I

The "Year of Perdition"

The year of Ibn al-Furát's third Vizierate was afterwards known as the "Year of Perdition", because of the ruthless violence that he and al-Muḥassin employed at that time against their enemies.[1] Afterwards Ibn al-Furát confessed to a definite policy of terrorism—he had tried benevolence before, so he said, and gentle dealing with his adversaries, but they had availed only to ruin him: this time he would try a drastic severity.[2] Yet it is doubtful whether such was indeed his intention at the time of his restoration. It seems more likely that he was led into such courses by the vindictive madness of al-Muḥassin, which he came to tolerate because al-Muqtadir tolerated it himself. When al-Muḥassin killed his first victim, Ibn al-Furát was terrified at the possible consequences, and attempted to prove that the man would have died in any case. But far from even deprecating the misadventure, al-Muqtadir approved al-Muḥassin's zeal—and next day his singing-girls improvised a song: "Well done, O al-Muḥassin, well done!"[3]

I believe rather that at the beginning Ibn al-Furát simply intended to mulct his adversaries in the usual way. Far from adopting methods of "frightfulness", he treated Ḥámid, for example, and Ibn al-Ḥawwárí, both of whom he had got into his power whilst 'Alí's trial was dragging on, with even more than ordinary consideration.

1 'A. 110. 2 H. 105. 3 M. I, 93.

Before Ibn al-Furát had been reinstated, Ḥámid, in order to protect himself, had persuaded the Caliph to renew his contract in Wásiṭ for the current year. But Ibn al-Furát was not to be cheated so easily—he proceeded to sue him for what he already owed. Ḥámid, however, was so strong in his position at Wásiṭ, being both popular and possessed of a formidable bodyguard, that two companies of regular troops had actually to be sent from Baghdád to enforce his submission. On this, hopeless of further defiance, Ḥámid decided, rather than meet arrest, to return, as if summoned, to the capital, and prove again the power of bribery. In order to keep up the pretence of a royal invitation, he set out with all the pomp he could command; by doing so he sacrificed a secrecy that might have enabled him to reach Baghdád unimpeded, but at the same time he convinced the metropolitans (and even Ibn al-Furát and his satellites themselves) that he was to be restored to office. However, he was not permitted to complete his journey: Názúk was sent out to prevent his approach and came up with his train on the Tigris near Ctesiphon, only to find that Ḥámid had fled into the country. Even so all might have been well with Ḥámid if only he could have obtained a meeting with the Caliph. But, as the historian remarks, "his good fortune was over, and its term expired."

Naṣr, whom he visited in the disguise of a monk, was willing to befriend him; but Mufliḥ, through whom alone he could gain access to al-Muqtadir, took this chance of avenging Ḥámid's unforgiven insult, and contrived instead that he should be handed over to Ibn al-Furát. Face to face with him, Ḥámid could hardly believe that what he had so much dreaded had actually come to pass, and he adopted a tone of bluster till with the departure of the escort that Naṣr had sent with him it became clear that he was to remain. As his assurance diminished, so that of Ibn al-Furát increased, for not till that moment had he been certified that the Caliph was not indeed preparing his supersession. Indeed, how uncertain was the position of the Vizier, and how apprehensive his temper, may be judged from the circumstance that during these days of tension, the only members of the faction that had remained at large were himself and his secretary, Zangí. His relief on discovering that his terrors were ill-founded was very naturally attended by an excellent good humour, and it was now that he gave orders for Ḥámid to be served in his confinement with such uncommon attention.

He set aside a spacious room for him, in which he caused fine rugs to be laid, and provided him with food, drink, scent and clothes befitting his high rank. In treating him generously Ibn al-Furát hoped to show Ḥámid how well worth his while it was to submit to his demands of payment; for he threatened him, if he refused, with delivery over to al Muḥassin. By this method he soon obtained all he required, not only for the State, but for himself.

The lot of Ibn al-Ḥawwárí, upon Ibn al-Furát's resumption of office, was not dissimilar to that of Ḥámid. He, too, for some time enjoyed a false security: but having no retainers to protect him, nor being at a distance sufficient to procure him even an ephemeral immunity, when the time came, he was without difficulty caught and arrested with his supporters. It had been evident ever since the fall of Umm Músà that he was labouring under the displeasure of the Caliph, but on the change of government he had half hoped, by cultivating the society of the new Vizier, to effect a gradual recovery of his position. He was disabused of his hopes only at the very moment of arrest. Then, indeed, he was robbed of his wealth and plundered of his possessions; but by the tactics of good treatment that had achieved their object so admirably in the case of Ḥámid, Ibn al-Furát obtained from him an admission of deposits large enough to satisfy him; whereupon his agent was released to supervise their collection, and he had every reason to expect an early delivery.

At this juncture, however, the hopes of both Ḥámid and Ibn al-Ḥawwárí were suddenly dashed by an unforeseen development. The atmosphere of friendliness in which their case had so far been conducted had long chafed al-Muḥassin; and when it seemed likely that both were to get off without bodily hurt, his indignation was immense. He at once enlisted the help of Mufliḥ, and sent by his hand a proposal to the Caliph, in which he represented that both Ḥámid and Ibn al-Ḥawwárí were concealing a large part of their resources. Let the Caliph but put him in control, and he would see of how much he was being deprived. Al-Muḥassin sought actually to have the whole management of affairs confided to him—he asked that he might be created Deputy-General to the Vizier; and though Ibn al-Furát was furious at being slighted in this manner, the Caliph acceded to his demand. In spite of Ibn al-Furát's remonstrance that he had given an express undertaking to the contrary, both Ḥámid and Ibn al-Ḥawwárí were delivered over to al-Muḥassin.

Al-Muḥassin reserved the worse treatment for Ḥámid. He tortured both him and Ibn al-Ḥawwárí, but he outraged the dignity of Ḥámid's age—for he was old and grey—by forcing him to dance before him in the skin of an ape. However, he wrung no money from either, and when he had sufficiently diverted himself at their expense, they were severally banished. Ḥámid was sent to Wásiṭ; but on the journey down-stream he was served with a poisoned egg, and died on the morrow of his arrival. Ibn al-Ḥawwárí was sent to al-Ahwáz, accompanied by two fellow-victims, Ibn Muqlah and 'Alí's cousin Sulaymán, who had each suffered imprisonment, the one with, and the other without, torture. Their jailer kept his instructions secret, but on reaching the neighbourhood of al-Baṣrah, he suddenly caused Ibn al-Ḥawwárí to be cast headforemost into the river. For two hours the wretched man was dragged along by the heels, after which he was taken out, and being found to be still alive, was forthwith strangled by attendant blackamoors. The feelings of his companions are not described; but they were not in fact to meet a similar fate.[1]

One of Ibn al-Furát's longest-standing enmities was for 'Alí's brother Ibrahím. Whenever he was in power he had pursued Ibrahím with his malice: on first becoming Vizier, when he had banished 'Alí to Mecca, he banished Ibrahím to aṣ-Ṣáfiyah; and on his restoration he had fined Ibrahím 50,000 *dínárs*, of which 30,000 had been paid up. Afterwards, when 'Alí was made Assistant to Ḥámid, Ibrahím had declined a Government post in the express hope of securing himself against further molestation, and had had the rest of his fine remitted by the Caliph. Yet now when Ibn al-Furát became Vizier for the third time, Ibrahím did not venture to pay him the customary visit of congratulation. Ibn al-Furát thereupon invited him to call on him. On his doing so, however, Ibrahím was arrested, and although he was able to refer to the *díwáns* for confirmation of his exemption, Ibn al-Furát insisted on his paying the outstanding remainder of his former fine, and 20,000 *dínárs* in addition. Al-Muḥassin extracted this sum from him by torture, after which Ibrahím was again banished to al-Baṣrah. He died there soon after; and it was generally supposed that he had been poisoned.

'Ubayd Allah ibn 'Ísà was so ill at the time that he had to be carried to al-Muḥassin's assembly on a

1 M. I, 91–3, 94–104, 113; H. 34–40, 174–7, 302; 'A. 111–13; S.J. fol. 78 a–b.

stretcher. Yet even this did not deter the latter from torturing him also, repeatedly. Indeed he desisted only when some friends of the unhappy man undertook to pay on his behalf what al-Muḥassin required. When the money was produced, 'Ubayd Allah was exiled to al-Kúfah.[1]

As for 'Abd ar-Raḥmán, he had held the *díwán as-sawád*, the most important of all the offices, whilst 'Alí had been Assistant:[2] he was therefore fairer game than either of these two brothers. However, he concealed himself so effectually in the house of a fellow-townsman,[3] that although the most rigorous search was made for him, he succeeded in escaping capture.

So the catalogue of atrocities continues, with monotonous regularity. In the end al-Muḥassin's cruelty came to be so much dreaded that the mere threat of being delivered over to him was enough to elicit promises of payment from possible victims.[4] He was now nicknamed *al-khabíth ibn aṭ-ṭayyib*, the Good Man's Miscreant Son; and the title was well-deserved by him, if not by his father. For if al-Muḥassin was responsible for the ferocity of the inquisition, the Vizier was by no means averse to its yield of gold. This was unparalleled: Ḥamzah of Iṣfahán puts the sum extorted from Ḥámid alone at 2,700,000 *dínárs*.[5] Ibn al-Furát was evidently determined that whatever happened he would not fall this time owing to a shortage of funds. But in the event the remedy that he chose proved as fatal as the disease.

In the midst of it all Mu'nis returned, triumphant as usual, from a border raid. He was assailed on all sides with tales of al-Muḥassin's frightfulness. The most was made of the ill-treatment of one of his friends, a certain Ibn Bisṭám, who had the misfortune to be

1 H. 43, 134–5; 'A. 114. Cf. H. 313.
2 H. 313.
3 H. 160.
4 H. 44.
5 Ḥam. 1, 203.

related to Ḥámid.[1] 'Alí ibn 'Ísà, he was told, had been tortured and banished; Ḥámid ibn al-'Abbás, tortured and murdered. It was not long before there was an anti-Vizierial intrigue in full swing, with Mu'nis as pivot. Ibn al-Furát still had Mufliḥ on his side, and through him had been working, not without success, to gain an influence in the affairs of the Lady. But Naṣr was by this time distinctly hostile; and so, it appears, were Shafí' al-Lu'lu'í and another influential officer, his namesake Shafí' al-Muqtadirí.[2]

The Vizier could not afford to be too openly inimical to Mu'nis. He therefore made an effort to conciliate him by rehabilitating the unfortunate Ibn Bisṭám. Nevertheless he aimed at removing him again from Baghdád, and soon found a pretext for advising the Caliph to order his departure to ar-Raqqah on the Euphrates. On the general's arrival a crowd of disbanded cavalrymen had flocked to his camp for rations and pay. With their support, so Ibn al-Furát argued with al-Muqtadir, Mu'nis might become dangerously powerful; at all costs, as the Caliph valued his throne, the soldiery must be prevented from taking the management of affairs again into their own hands. But besides this, the presence of Mu'nis's army at ar-Raqqah would ensure the payment of taxes in the western provinces, where recently they had been withheld. He could thus pay his troops out of them, and so relieve the overburdened Treasury. He would also be put in charge of the Mádhará'ís, and could further, if they were willing, or compel, if they were not, the collection in Syria and Egypt of the vast sums for the payment of which they had compounded with the Vizier.

Mu'nis had no answer to this argument; and he submitted to the Caliph's order, although he was well aware by whom it had been suggested. However, he

1 H. 42. 2 'A. 113.

obtained leave to remain until after the Feast, for it was yet the hungry month of *ramadhán*. The Vizier did his best with hypocritical civility to mitigate the unpleasantness of his departure. But it fell on a day of pouring rain; and Mu'nis set out from the parade ground at ash-Shammásiyyah in an exceedingly bad humour.[1]

1 M. I, 115–16; H. 42–3, 45–6.

CHAPTER II

'Alí ibn 'Ísà *on his travels.*

Al-Muḥassin was not content with removing 'Alí from the capital. He was still bent on destroying him. He instructed Ibn al-Kúthání either to poison him on the way to Mecca or to kill him once they arrived. 'Alí, however, suspected his intention: and by being careful in eating and drinking he accomplished the many stages of the journey in safety—happily for him the track was temporarily free from lurking Carmathians. And once in Mecca he was among friends. The local postmaster, an agent of Shafí' al-Lu'lu'í,[1] had been instructed to succour him, and 'Alí also confided his fears to the *qádhí*, Aḥmad ibn Músà. His fears were justified, for Ibn al-Kúthání in fact attempted his life. He compelled the unfortunate old man to kneel down, and was on the point of cutting his throat, when his assistant seized his arm and prevented him. Whether it was that this assistant acted out of pure compassion and a regard for right, or that he had been engaged by the *qádhí* to keep watch, 'Alí's escape was a signal for his partisans to attack his guardians; and this they did with such a will, that the guardians in turn would have been killed, had not 'Alí himself intervened to rescue them. He showed his gratitude to the man that had saved his life by supporting him and his family for a long time.

What precisely happened next is not clear. One account declares plainly that 'Alí gave Ibn al-Kúthání and his coadjutors the necessary provisions and packed them off to Baghdád; but another indicates hardly less plainly that he still had their company later. It would

1 Shafí' was Postmaster-General. See 'A. 121.

surely have been injudicious for 'Alí to proclaim so flatly his escape from surveillance, and in so far their return seems improbable; but for some reason, and possibly this very one, Ibn al-Furát was uneasy at 'Alí's continued residence in a place as near even as distant Mecca. Perhaps he feared that he was aiming at a recovery of his position: if he remained there in a crisis he might too easily be recalled to Baghdád. In any case, as soon as Mu'nis was safely out of the way—for Mu'nis always took 'Alí's part—the Vizier again seized his estates, and ordered him to a city remoter still, both geographically and spiritually—to Ṣan'á', capital of the Yemen.[1]

Ṣan'á' at this time was in the hands of a local potentate, by name As'ad ibn Ibrahím, of the Banú Ya'fur (whence he was also known as Ibn Ya'fur). This family, who claimed descent from pre-Islamic kings of the Yemen, the Ḥimyarites, had now been in precarious possession of the city and a varying extent of territory for some sixty years; they acknowledged the suzerainty of the 'Abbásids, and their Court, together with the people of Ṣan'á', formed a small Orthodox block in the midst of a population largely Shí'ite.[2] The rule of the present Ibn Ya'fur was wider spread and more firmly settled than that of any of his predecessors; nevertheless it did not by any means extend over the whole province. Of the three parts into which the Yemen is divided naturally, the coastal plains, the mountains, and the table-land that slopes away inland from the mountains (that are really its edge) to the desert, only the latter two were his. The plains were ruled by the family of Ziyád, whose founder had been sent by al-Ma'mún to frustrate the designs of the Shí'ah in the Yemen, but which had now been inde-

1 'A. 113; H. 130–1, 307–8; M. 1, 113, giving an extract from Ham. *tak.*

2 Rus. 113.

pendent of the 'Abbásids for half a century. The town of Ṣa'dah, at some distance to the north of Ṣan'á', was in the hands of a Zaydite Imám.

This present division was the outcome of years of fighting—the Yemen, by reason of its situation at a remote distance from the capital, had long been a favourite place for the launching of sectarian rebellions. The Carmathians, for instance, had overrun the country in the reign of al-Muktafí, and had plunged it into twelve years of chaos, during which Ṣan'á' itself changed hands no less than twenty times. The present Ibn Ya'fur had re-established his rule in 303 (915–16).[1] Ever since the Yemen had enjoyed an unaccustomed tranquillity.

That part of the Yemen for which 'Alí was bound was very different from his native 'Iráq. Here were no mud plains, but fertile hills cut in steps for vines. Baghdád's extremes of heat and cold were here replaced by a temperate warmth that varied little from season to season—the climate of Ṣan'á', its fresh mountain airs and water, were famous throughout Islam. Its rains fell not in winter, but in summer with the monsoons. The houses of Ṣan'á' were built not of brick like the houses of Baghdád, but of stone, and sometimes they had roofs of marble so fine that the shadows of birds gliding far up overhead might be seen on them from beneath. Otherwise the Yemen was also remarkable for its apes, the dark complexion of many of its inhabitants, its peculiar fruits, unknown to Persia or Byzantium, and the precious minerals that were to be extracted from its mountains.[2]

Ibn Ya'fur himself lived in one of a number of mountain strongholds, about forty miles from Ṣan'á'. His palace stood in the midst of a considerable, though

1 Cf. Lane-Poole: *Mohammadan Dynasties*, p. 91.

2 *Encyclopédie*, IV, 150–1 (art. *Ṣan'ā'*); Khald. IV, 212–13; Ham. *jaz.* I, 196; Faq. 34, 37, 124; Ḥaw. 20; Iṣṭ. 24; Muq. 98, 101.

somewhat ruinous town, with a congregational mosque and as many as thirty subsidiary mosques, a market street, and baths. About this stretched cultivated fields with subordinate villages, so that the inhabitants need not rely at all upon communication with the outside world. The outside world was indeed as much cut off as it could be, the only approach to Shibám, as the place was called, being by a narrow path that wound through difficult country and ended in a bridge over a deep chasm.[1]

The order for 'Alí's transference was sent to the governor of Mecca. It was soon known in Ṣan'á' that he was coming, and Ibn Ya'fur sent out a party to meet him. 'Aríb gives us to understand that Ibn al-Kúthání and his companions were still with him and that it was only by 'Alí's intervention that the Yemenites were prevented from murdering them; but perhaps this is merely another version of the attack made upon them, according to Hilál, in Mecca. In any case the party proceeded on its way, and when near its goal was met by a brother of the chieftain himself.[2]

A Vizier of the Caliphs was no doubt a great personage. Moreover, 'Alí's reputation for godliness can only have been enhanced by his coming straight from the holy city. He was welcomed with becoming deference. A large house was set apart for his accommodation and another for his now functionless guardians. Whether 'Alí was admitted to the seclusion of Shibám we are not told. Probably he was, for Ibn Ya'fur was wont, in imitation of his royal forefathers, to hold himself aloof from the common gaze and seldom appeared in Ṣan'á'.[3]

Later, 'Alí wished to make a return for his kind reception, and his benevolence took the same form as it had taken before in Mecca. Ṣan'á' lies at the foot of

1 Rus. 113; Ham. *jaz.* I, 86. 2 'A. 113.
3 Mas. *murúj*, II, 55; Ḥaw. 20.

a hill, the Jabal Nuqum, on a slope of which stood the ruins of Castle Ghumdán, a famous stronghold of the Ḥimyarite kings. In its prime Ghumdán had risen many storeys high, and its walls had been encased outside with various coloured marbles; but it had often been damaged and restored, till in the wars that followed the rise of Islam it had been finally ruined. Ibn Ya'fur prided himself on his ancestors, and wished to repair this monument of their greatness. He was deterred from this undertaking, however, by a local soothsayer.—'Alí did not offer to pursue the experiment. Instead he caused a well to be dug out in the debris, and built an aqueduct to the town.[1]

1 Niebuhr, I, 332; Ham. *jaz.* I, 195; Faq. 35; Mas. *murúj*, IV, 50; Nicholson: *Literary History of the Arabs*, 24. An aqueduct still brings drinking water to Ṣan'á' from the Jabal Nuqum; see *Encyclopédie*, IV, 149.

CHAPTER III

The end of Ibn al-Furát.

Having got rid of Mu'nis for the time being, Ibn al-Furát now set about getting rid of Naṣr al-Qushúrí the Chamberlain. Naṣr had been perfectly well-disposed to him on his return to office; but al-Muḥassin, in his insane lust for blood, had planned to have the Chamberlain assassinated: Naṣr had discovered his intention, and was consequently antagonised.[1] Ibn al-Furát tempted Ja'far to arrest him and seize his riches, which he asserted to be vast. Naṣr, however, engaged the Lady to defend him, and she turned the tables deftly on the Vizier by alleging that he was seeking for a nefarious end to deprive the Caliph in Mu'nis and Naṣr of his staunchest supporters.

Naṣr was safe for the moment; but Ibn al-Furát soon returned to the charge. It happened at about this time that Ibn Abí's-Sáj (who had been released and reinstated the year before)[2] defeated a rebel in Persia. Now Naṣr was on exceedingly bad terms with Ibn Abí's-Sáj: the news of the victory was consequently distasteful to him. Ibn al-Furát, to give his dejection a suspicious air, suggested that Naṣr had in fact been in league with the rebel, with whom, fearful of his own future at Court, he had planned to capture Baghdád and dethrone the Caliph. An incident supported the allegation. A mysterious individual was discovered lurking in the most secluded part of the palace. He insisted on seeing "the master of the house", and since he refused to explain himself further, was beaten to death. His body was then soaked in naphtha and burnt, thus making his identification impossible. During his

1 'A. 113.   2 M. I, 82.

flogging the man had cried again and again, in Persian, "I don't understand!", as though in bewildered innocence; and Ibn al-Furát was suspected of having contrived the whole scene. Nevertheless he convinced the Caliph that Naṣr was to blame: the safety of the palace was in the Chamberlain's care—if strange people were found wandering about, he must account for them. The man was a Persian; probably he was an emissary of the defeated rebel; very likely he was an assassin suborned by the conspirators to murder the Commander of the Faithful. The Commander of the Faithful was horrified: for the second time he sanctioned the Chamberlain's arrest.[1]

Naṣr gave himself up for lost. But the Lady spoke for him again, and while Ja'far was still undecided, the occurrence of a catastrophe put Ibn al-Furát in turn on the defensive. The caravans of the *ḥajj*, returning from Mecca to Baghdád, were attacked by Abú Ṭáhir and his Carmathians, who slew such as resisted. The officer in charge of the road and the safety of the pilgrims, a brother of al-Ḥusayn ibn Ḥamdán, known as Abú'l-Hayjá', was taken prisoner, as were also the Lady's uncle and many officers, notables, and women and eunuchs of the Harem. The Carmathians carried off such men, women and children as they judged fit for slavery and with them every camel, horse, and object of value. The remainder were left behind with the dead in the midst of the desert, without means of transport or food, even without clothes.[2]

Ibn al-Furát was in no way to blame. He had even made a special provision for the safety of the pilgrims this year. Moreover, he had actually sent Abú'l-Hayjá' warning, which the travellers had refused to heed, of the Carmathian ambush; and now he quickly despatched a convoy to the scene of disaster with every

1 M. I, 117–19; H. 47–9.
2 M. I, 120–1; 'A. 118–19; Mas. *tan.* 380; Tagh. II, 223–4.

variety of garment—shirts, drawers, turbans, cloaks and dresses—as well as animals to carry the victims home.[1] But the event stirred the people to vent their disgust at his barbarous rule. That very night the pulpits in the mosques were broken and the niches defiled. Next day the sufferers' wives formed a procession, which met another composed of the wives of al-Muḥassin's victims—the women ran shrieking barefoot about the streets, tearing their hair and blackening their faces. Ibn al-Furát and al-Muḥassin were in constant danger: whenever their barges were recognised they were stoned. The tumult soon became general, and to check it the Chief of Police had to ride into the mosques with his men-at-arms.

Then the first survivors came in, and it was Ibn al-Furát's painful duty to explain matters to the Caliph. As he went to the interview his heart misgave him, and not without cause. For al-Muqtadir's first action was to call Naṣr in consultation; and Naṣr very adroitly used the occasion to avenge his recent wrongs. It was now his turn to accuse Ibn al-Furát of plotting —to depose the Caliph in revenge for the injuries he had suffered at his hands, and set up in his stead Abú Ṭáhir al-Jannábí. In proof he pointed to the virtual banishment of Mu'nis; the Vizier's attempt to ruin him, Naṣr, himself; the episode of the mysterious Persian; and Ibn al-Furát's well-known schismatic leanings. He urged that Mu'nis should be sent for, since without Mu'nis to defend it the city was in danger.

Al-Muqtadir, though he followed his advice, seems to have attached no more weight to Naṣr's story than it deserved. But he was now quite prepared to believe him as innocent as the Vizier; and he endeavoured to bring about a reconciliation between them. Ibn al-Furát could not take the situation so lightly. The summons of Mu'nis especially perturbed him. He and

1 H. 210.

al-Muḥassin saw little hope of mending matters, and each acted characteristically. With one of the eunuchs as intermediary Ibn al-Furát began recalling past services, and offering bribes, to the Caliph. Al-Muḥassin had a few remaining enemies murdered. Their families and supporters prepared for the worst by going into hiding.

Mu'nis on his arrival was greeted with such enthusiasm as positively embarrassed him. It began to be rumoured that Ibn al-Furát was at once to be dismissed; and speculation over his successor became so general that the Caliph was compelled to issue a denial. A section of the palace retainers tried to force his hand by threatening revolt if Ibn al-Furát were not at once arrested. Naṣr approved their action, and even detained the Vizier and his son as they left the Presence. Mufliḥ, however, whether from statesmanship, or a lingering loyalty to Ibn al-Furát, advised al-Muqtadir to agree to their demand in principle, yet by procrastination to preserve his majesty from the reproach of seeming to yield to threats. Ibn al-Furát and al-Muḥassin were accordingly allowed to row home; but they no longer looked forward even to a respite. Al-Muḥassin, after a secret consultation with his father, vanished. The Vizier proceeded with his duties, inwardly perturbed, but with such apparent calm that his staff were convinced that the danger was past.

Next day he dismissed his assembly early. As the clerks were dispersing, one of them, remembering something he had left undone, returned to his place and sat on writing. Presently, hearing the tramp of men-at-arms, he looked up, to see Názúk and Yalbaq enter at their head, each with a naked sword and dagger. Finding the assembly deserted, they made for the private apartments:—he knew that his master must be taken.[1]

1 M. I, 121–6; H. 49–52; 'A. 119–20; S.J. fol. 79 b.

Ibn al-Furát was not confined in the palace, because the officers refused to allow it. They guessed how soon the Caliph's secret visits would begin again; he was safely in disgrace, and they were determined at least to keep him so. Hence he found himself climbing the landing-stage to the house of Shafí' al-Lu'lu'í. The steps were steep and slimy, but no one would give him a hand. He complained that he was being treated worse than others. "Others," Shafí' answered sententiously, referring to 'Alí, his late charge, "others have been more God-fearing than you."

Nevertheless he was provided with a comfortable lodging and excellent food. He had the width of the river between himself and the Caliph, yet he by no means despaired of rehabilitating himself. Who was to be Vizier was what interested him most; and when he heard that it was to be al-Kháqání's son, 'Abd Allah, Ibn al-Furát could hardly believe it. "It is not I," he laughed, "but the State that has fallen!" In truth the choice was amazing: in all the history of the Vizierate no one had brought such ridicule on himself, or such chaos into affairs, as al-Kháqání; and 'Abd Allah his son had helped to make things worse. However, 'Aríb assures us that the young man had sobered down and was now a model of propriety and statesmanship. His cause had been taken up with zest by Naṣr and Thumal the *qahramánah*, and since al-Muḥassin had been careful to get rid of everyone more suitable, Mu'nis also had urged 'Abd Allah's appointment.[1]

Ibn al-Furát was anxious at all costs to escape being handed over to the Vizier and the hostile officers. To this end he sent a message to Ja'far through Shafí', offering, if he would guarantee his safety and that of al-Muḥassin, to give him large sums of money, jewels and valuables, but threatening, if he would not, to withhold everything. Shafí', however, bore him a

1 M. I, 127, 129; H. 53, 123; 'A. 120.

grudge for some past difference; he never delivered the message, and Ibn al-Furát was committed to the mercies of the Vizier.[1]

Even so he pursued the same tactics: his riches were so famous that he could not hope to pretend successfully that he had nothing to yield. He was determined to save himself by their very fame: he would yield them gradually, tantalisingly, but only in response to gentle dealing—he would acknowledge some of his deposits on being asked politely to do so, but at the least hint of force he would show himself adamant, and admit not a *dirham*. The plan worked admirably: he was in fact put to the question by his examiner, Ibn Ba'ud Sharr, but he was rescued by the intervention of the Caliph's cousin Hárún (son of the Uncle) in whose charge he had been placed; and whereas Ibn Ba'ud Sharr obtained nothing from him by violence, Hárún in return for his kindness received his bond for two million *dínárs*. Ibn al-Furát made certain stipulations regarding the payment of this sum, but Hárún considered them perfectly reasonable: and the proposal was laid before the Caliph.

Meanwhile the hue and cry was up against al-Muḥassin. A proclamation threatened the direst penalties against anyone who should harbour him; yet he could nowhere be found. It was not until some time afterwards that one night a loud clamour disturbed the sleeping city. Lights flaring, drums beating, shouts: the townsfolk jumped up in alarm, thinking that the Carmathians were upon them; but it was only that al-Muḥassin had been discovered. He had been betrayed by a stroke of singular misfortune. He had been hiding with his mother-in-law, who had skilfully disguised him as a woman; and they were returning from the Quraysh cemetery, to which, as

1 H. 70. M. I, 129 states that Shafí' *did* deliver the message, but that the Caliph rejected the proposal.

pious females, they made daily pilgrimage, when they found themselves benighted and still far from home. They feared to be stopped and questioned by the police if they were found wandering about, so they sought shelter for the night, on the recommendation of a friend, with a woman of the quarter through which they were passing. Unluckily, al-Muḥassin was detected to be a man by a young and inquisitive negress, who promptly told her mistress. Now the woman happened to be a widow of a certain official, an agent of 'Alí ibn 'Ísà's, who had been arrested at al-Muḥassin's orders, and had died of distress at the mere sight of the tortures inflicted on his fellows. She at once recognised al-Muḥassin, despite his shaven and painted cheeks, and hastened to denounce him. He was taken to the palace just as he was; and a curious crowd gathered to look at him.

Ibn Ba'ud Sharr set about torturing al-Muḥassin at once; and forced him to sign a bond for no less than three million *dínárs*. Al-Muḥassin, however, had no intention of paying, as soon became evident. Force proving of no avail, Hárún tried persuasion, and arranged an alternative payment of one million in seven days. But before signing this second bond, al-Muḥassin demanded the first; and as soon as he obtained possession of it, swallowed it. After this, the most exquisite torments were powerless to move him. If, as Hárún suggested, he was to die in any case, what should induce him to pay?

As for his father, still in comfortable confinement, he was disappointed to receive no reply to his proposal; and when he was called again to be examined before the Vizier, he perceived that his enemies were determined on his ruin. In arguing with his opponents he made a false step in putting the blame for Mu'nis's banishment on the Caliph. For when Mu'nis called for proofs, Ibn al-Furát caused a basket to be brought into the court containing letters which bore out his contention, but in which the Caliph referred to the general in terms far from complimentary. Mu'nis at once confronted Ja'far with the offensive documents, whereupon Ja'far flew into a rage at being put in such an awkward position. He ordered the guard to set Ibn al-Furát in a pillory and flog him. After five strokes he promised to disclose 20,000 *dínárs*, but still maintained that he possessed no more.

In continuing the examination of the two prisoners Hárún soon perceived that they were desperate men, prepared for death and impervious to violence. He therefore retired from the contest, which was taken up by Názúk. But even the martial methods of Názúk were of no avail: the palm-rod, however fiercely wielded, could coax no more gold from Ibn al-Furát; the wounds with which al-Muḥassin's body was torn began to suppurate, he was often delirious, but in his lucid moments he remained as unshaken as ever.

In this predicament the Caliph was anxious to try a return to methods of persuasion, to give the prisoners hope and lodge them in the palace. But the Vizier 'Abd Allah, though he appeared to agree with him in public, pointed out in private to Mu'nis and Naṣr that such a course might still lead to what they were all interested in preventing, a complete reconcilation between Ibn al-Furát and the Caliph. There was one method, however, which appeared to be infallible, of forcing the Caliph to do whatever they required: the soldiery must once again be persuaded to threaten mutiny.

'Abd Allah's advice was acted upon; but it produced consequences that he had not foreseen, and were very little to his taste. Not only did the troops prevent the return of Ibn al-Furát and al-Muḥassin to the palace, they insisted on their immediate decapitation. 'Abd Allah considered this execution of ministers a most dangerous precedent. But Ja'far, although he also was of course more than loath to sanction it, was thoroughly intimidated—he dared not risk his throne.

On Sunday, 12th *rabí' al-ákhir* (18th July 924), Ibn al-Furát dreamed a dream: his brother Aḥmad appeared to him saying, "To-morrow you shall break your fast with us." An astrologer, too, had predicted the morrow as being a critical day in his life, and so he awaited it with anxiety. Názúk, as Chief of Police, would be charged with his execution: his movements, therefore, were closely watched. In the morning Názúk was called to the palace, and Ibn al-Furát took hope—but in reality Názúk had gone to receive instructions from the Caliph himself, as he declined to act on an order at second hand. Later he returned and sat with the prisoner. Presently his servant came in and laid something at his feet—it was the head of al-Muḥassin.

The horror of death seized on Ibn al-Furát. He besought Názúk to listen. He would give the Caliph anything. Would he not carry a message? But Názúk dared not, even if he would. He signalled to two black executioners, who immediately entered and struck off the prisoner's head.

The two heads were shown to al-Muqtadir. Afterwards they were placed together in a sack weighted with sand, and cast, by his command, into the Euphrates.[1]

1 So M. and H. According to 'A. and S.J., into the Tigris. M. I, 129–38; H. 53–62; 'A. 120–1; S.J. fol. 79 b–80 a.

CHAPTER IV

A comparison. The Vizierate *ill-filled.* 'Alí *given a new post, and later recalled to* Baghdád.

In the assembly of al-Kháqání, one evening, the conversation turned on the comparative merits of 'Alí ibn 'Ísà and Ibn al-Furát. It had long been the fashion to extol Ibn al-Furát as a brilliant man of affairs: when he and his brother had worked together, it was said that they surpassed all their predecessors in ability;[1] and if Aḥmad had been incomparably the abler of the two, after his death his brother inherited all the good repute that they had won together. Now al-Kháqání himself and Ibn al-Furát's secretary, the so-long-indispensable Zangí, both expressed their views. They allowed 'Alí an unchallengeable superiority in the actual writing of despatches, and al-Kháqání described him as "very religious, exceedingly discreet, and scrupulous in money matters". Ibn al-Furát, on the other hand, was the more energetic, so he said, in handling the revenue and in his political dealings; and Zangí put in a plea for him as a despatch writer, sending to his house for examples of his letters to show how excellently he would compose them. It was only, he said, that his hand would "betray him".[2] Indeed the difficulty he experienced in writing adequately had always been a real drawback in the career of Ibn al-Furát. It had once given the hostile Vizier, al-Qásim ibn 'Ubayd Allah, an opportunity of humiliating him. In Zangí's absence Ibn al-Furát had been unable to send off an urgent despatch, so that al-Qásim had given it instead to his rival, Muḥammad ibn Dá'úd.[3]

Once Ibn al-Furát had asked his adherent Ibn Jubayr

1 H. 142. 2 H. 85–6. 3 H. 128.

which of the two, himself or 'Alí ibn 'Ísà, was the better secretary. Ibn Jubayr had at first flattered the Vizier, but the latter, guessing his judgement to be insincere, had pressed him to tell the truth. On this Ibn Jubayr admitted that 'Alí ibn 'Ísà had a gift that he lacked: he could write a despatch off in the Caliph's presence, enclose it in an envelope, seal it, and place it in a courier's bag, without anyone else's reading a syllable of its contents. Ibn al-Furát, in contrast, had always to send for Zangí (who himself had an assistant), so that State secrets, in his hands, were never perfectly safe.[1]

'Alí's repeated reversals of Ibn al-Furát's enactments indicate well enough what he thought of him as a statesman. For the rest, he had always kept for him the respect he had felt for his *ustádh* of the *díwán ad-dár*. And for his part, Ibn al-Furát, after they had long been placed in mutual opposition, was always ready to acknowledge 'Alí's ability. For example, certain orders were laid before him as having been signed by 'Alí ibn 'Ísà, about which he at once declared that 'Alí, whose care and competence were so well known, would never have passed them.[2] On the other hand, after examining a couple of agents that 'Alí had employed and finding their accounts to be in disorder, Ibn al-Furát had been moved to reproach him for what al-Qudhá'í states to be the only shortcoming that 'Alí's enemies could find to charge him with.[3] "O 'Alí ibn 'Ísà," he apostrophised him, "you busied yourself with the morals of the realm (an allusion, presumably, to 'Alí's attempts to suppress corruption), with looking into the ducks' food and docking people's pay, and with other such poor slight matters...." With his attention concentrated on trifles, he had no eye, thought Ibn al-Furát, for the broad issues of statesmanship.[4]

1 H. 63.
2 H. 68.
3 Qudh. fol. 89 b.
4 H. 260.

In Ibn al-Furát there was certainly a vigour that his rival wanted, a power that selfish ambition had turned to evil ways. When his malignant influence was no more to be dreaded, its absence was felt, not only as a relief, but as a void. The chroniclers make this very clearly felt. There is a lassitude in their recital of subsequent events that suggests that they form but an epilogue to the stirring act just closed. The dearth of secretarial talent formed indeed a very real void. Ibn al-Furát was gone; and who was left?—A crowd of incompetent clerks, whom al-Muḥassin had not even considered it worth while getting rid of. ʻAbd Allah was as incompetent as any, and his inability was soon intensified by a serious illness, of which he was in the end to die. His position was anyhow weak in the extreme, but he made it even weaker by embarking on a foolish intrigue against Naṣr, which damaged the Chamberlain, but only enough to ensure his hatred. Seeing his decline, al-Khaṣíbí, the Lady's secretary, set about working to replace him; and succeeded, by wringing a large sum out of al-Muḥassin's widow, in winning the Caliph's approbation so far, that in *ramadhán* of the next year he was appointed in ʻAbd Allah's stead. Al-Khaṣíbí had the support of Naṣr and Thumal, who, with the recent death of Shafíʻ al-Lu'lu'í,[1] were now, after Mu'nis, the most influential people at Court. His high favour with the Lady, moreover, lent him importance; but there his qualifications for the Vizierate ended. If ʻAbd Allah had been incapable, al-Khaṣíbí was wantonly neglectful of his duties. Nightly drunk, next day he was seldom enough recovered to work. Business got fantastically behindhand; and if it had not been for the energy of al-Kalwádhí[2] (who

1 Ath. (Búláq), VIII, 53.

2 His name is also given as Kalwadhání. They are alternative adjectives formed from the name of the town near Baghdád, Kalwádhá.

here emerges as a promising Secretary of State), the machinery of government might well have broken down. Al-Khaṣíbí lasted hardly as long as his predecessor. With slender pretext, or with none at all, he would fine the rich, and so gratify al-Muqtadir with contributions to the Privy Purse. But his power waned with the exhaustion of this resource, and having no other he fell.

The truth is that al-Kháqání and al-Khaṣíbí were styled Vizier, but the title no longer connoted the grand office of past days. With the decay of order, force had come into its own: the military again dominated the civil power. Mu'nis already made and unmade Viziers: he was soon to be tempted to try his hand at making and unmaking Caliphs. On his return from driving Fáṭimids out of Egypt, he had been officially entitled *al-mudhaffar*, Victor;[1] later he had been made a Boon-Companion. Yet al-Muqtadir had not so long ago sent him to ar-Raqqah when he was not wanted; but that had been whilst Ibn al-Furát was still alive. Ibn al-Furát was gone now; there was no one to pit against Mu'nis now. Mu'nis the Victor could do what he pleased.

More than once the soldiers had been stirred up artificially to revolt; and this method of coercing the Caliph was so obviously effective that it was not long before they began to use it on their own account. Naṣr discovered a conspiracy, to which some of the chief officers were party, to set upon the Caliph and seize his person. Yet he feared to make enemies of such giants as they were grown by revealing the scheme. Instead he worked in secret to frustrate it, by augmenting the body-guard, and sending the ringleaders on distant missions. It was as the result of another demonstration that al-Kháqání was dismissed. Through his incapacity prices in Baghdád had risen to prodigious

1 M. I, 76. Cf. 'A. 125.

heights, and in conjunction with this he had been unable to find funds for the soldiers' pay. Al-Khaṣíbí, in his turn, was warned of their temper on his very first day of office. He was greeted by a shower of arrows as he rowed past an island on his way up to the palace, and only escaped with difficulty to the bank.

To confound this confusion yet worse, at the next season of Pilgrimage the Carmathians again attacked the caravans, after which they descended on the city of al-Kúfah and sacked it for six days. Al-Kúfah, to be sure, was less important a city than al-Baṣrah, which had already twice suffered in this way; but it was older, it enshrined more touching memories, and above all it was but half the distance from Baghdád. The capital was in a panic. The quarters on the west bank of the Tigris were vacated by their inhabitants. An expedition was fitted out at unexampled expense and hurried under Mu'nis to the martyred town. But it arrived too late. By that time, the Carmathians, as usual, had disappeared. That was their secret; they came and went with such suddenness and rapidity; with a few hundreds they routed armies of thousands. Al-Kúfah was sacked in 313 (926); and though in fact nothing definite was heard of them for the next two years, the shadow of their terror lay dark upon the land. For fear of them the pilgrims would not venture next year to Mecca. Rumours of their approach were so rife that the Meccans themselves removed their women for greater safety to aṭ-Ṭá'if. So great was the state of alarm in which they continued to keep the Government that it was resolved to maintain a special force in readiness to withstand them.

Such was the situation of imminent anarchy and defeat to which the 'Abbásid Caliphate was reduced towards the end of 314 (beginning of 927). It was generally agreed that a new Vizier must be found; and Mu'nis now urged, as he had urged on the fall of al-Kháqání, that al-Muqtadir should recall 'Alí ibn 'Ísà. A year before al-Muqtadir had scouted the idea, but then al-Khaṣíbí had been at hand with promises of gold. Now there seemed to be no alternative; he was more favourably inclined; and 'Alí was sent for.[1]

'Alí was no longer in Ṣan'á'. Two years before, on the fall of Ibn al-Furát, Mu'nis—his consistent champion—had at once suggested to al-Kháqání that 'Alí should be allowed to return to his beloved Mecca, and al-Kháqání had acquiesced. Agreeable as Ṣan'á' was, 'Alí had longed to leave it; and when at last the order came, in giving thanks to God for this relief, he made a vow, never, should he return to power, to pursue with vengeance any that had wronged him.[2] He seems to have remained in the Yemen until midwinter, to travel with the pilgrims. Then he parted on the best of terms with Ibn Ya'fur,[3] who made him a farewell present of clothes and perfumes worth fifty thousand *dínárs*.

On arriving in Mecca 'Alí wrote to al-Kháqání congratulating him on his advancement to the Vizierate, and condoling with him on the recent death of his father. He besought him also to protect his wife and children, and to assist them by securing the good management of his estates and properties. Al-Kháqání assured him in reply that he had already done so; and looked upon it as a duty for which he expected no thanks. Indeed he was in some sort under an obligation for the manner in which 'Alí had treated his

1 M. I, 141–7; 'A. 122–8; Ḥam. I, 204; Mas. *tan.* 381; S.J. fol. 81 b; Tagh. II, 227. 'A. definitely, and M. more vaguely, place the Carmathian attack on al-Kúfah in the year 312, but this is clearly wrong.

2 H. 311; M. I, 151.

3 The "Abú Ja'far" of M. is surely a copyist's transformation of an unusual into a common name (of a "surname"—Ibn Ya'fur—into an unidentifiable *kunyah*).

father and himself on their former fall from power, which, though just, had been inordinately lenient. This private letter was followed soon after by an official despatch containing a most unexpected command: al-Kháqání, again at the instigation of Mu'nis, had persuaded an exceedingly reluctant al-Muqtadir to appoint 'Alí as Inspector-General of Syria and Egypt, at a salary of 2000 *dínárs* a month. 'Alí accordingly completed his devotions, and proceeded to Egypt in company with the returning pilgrims.[1]

'Alí remained in his new position throughout the Vizierate of al-Kháqání; and was duly confirmed in it by al-Khaṣíbí. It was probably congenial, since the necessary journeys from Fusṭáṭ to Damascus permitted him, positively invited him, to a yearly Pilgrimage. He began by looking into the affairs of Egypt; then, after three months, he proceeded to ar-Ramlah,[2] at that time the capital of Palestine, a walled city of Muslim foundation, notable for its exquisite mosque (which had been planned by the 'Umayyad Sulaymán to eclipse the Dome of the Rock), its marbles, its figs, and its delightful situation.[3] In 313 (926) he performed the Pilgrimage with the Egyptians, and probably went up afterwards into Syria. That he fulfilled his duties with his customary efficiency witness the bonds for 147,000 *dínárs* that his chamberlain Salámah took on with him from Mecca on this occasion, and was charged to hand over to the Treasury at Baghdád.[4] 'Alí visited Syria twice in all, and took the opportunity, when in Damascus, of hearing Traditions from its celebrated *shaykhs*.[5]

The affairs of Egypt were in a sorry state. The two Fáṭimid invasions had unsettled the people. After the first the governor had discovered that some of the

1 M. I, 141; H. 309, 322; 'A. 124.
2 Tagh. II, 226.
3 Le Strange: *Palestine*, 303–308.
4 M. I, 146.
5 S.J. fol. 139 b.

notables were actually corresponding with the Mahdí; whilst others of the Egyptians appear to have become so much impressed with Fáṭimid doctrine that their opposition to the teaching of the Orthodox *shaykhs* produced a formidable commotion. After the repulse of the second invasion, there was a general rising in the province, which for some time was cut off from all communication with the capital. There were many changes in the governorship; but quiet was in no way restored till Tagín (who had been governor at the time of the first invasion) was re-appointed for the fourth time in 311 (924). Tagín alone appears to have been capable of controlling the Egyptians—many of these difficulties might have been avoided if he had never been dismissed. But for some reason Mu'nis disliked him, and on each of his visits to Egypt he had replaced him by a favourite of his own. On his final appointment Tagín was faced with a plot against his life, but by banishing the ringleaders he contrived to avoid a civil war. The country was but half recovered at the time of 'Alí's inspection.[1]

We catch a glimpse of 'Alí's first arrival at Fusṭáṭ.[2] The fame of his austerity had gone before him; and the secretaries, who would have to account to him for their stewardship, were somewhat alarmed at the prospect of so unaccommodating an overseer. When it was known that he was approaching, Tagín rode out to meet him. He was confronted with an equipage that had little of the pomp he might have expected: 'Alí entered the city mounted on nothing more magnificent than a donkey, with his head and shoulders muffled up in a doctor's hood. Yet Tagín felt that it was by no

1 Tagh. II, 183, 195–6, 205–7, 209–10, 211–12, 222–3.

2 He arrived from Mecca on 1st *rajab* 313 (22nd September 925), according to Eut. II, 517; but I think that this is more likely, in reality, to be the date of his return to Egypt after visiting ar-Ramlah.

means incongruous that he should have to dismount to him. And a nearer view of ‘Alí did nothing to diminish the awe of the secretaries.

For he lived up to his reputation. A few days later he rode in from his first tour of inspection in a rage, exclaiming: "Thieves, thieves!" so that the secretaries eyed one another self-consciously. It transpired that ‘Alí had crossed a culvert that had recently received its yearly repair. He saw that its upkeep could require but little expenditure; yet immense sums had been allocated for the purpose. Now the official responsible was none other than Abú Zunbúr al-Mádhará'í, who was by now once more installed as Collector of Taxes. ‘Alí, in his fury, roundly accused him of swindling. Abú Zunbúr made no defence for the moment, and left the assembly; but later they had a private conversation, in which he convinced ‘Alí that the expenses incurred by his official position—presents for the Caliph and the many important functionaries at Court, the maintenance of a proper state, the entertainment of distinguished visitors—outran by hundreds his allotted pay, and that, painful as it had been to him, he had been forced to adopt this expedient in order to bridge over the discrepancy. ‘Alí showed that despite the strictness of his principles he was not impervious to argument, and excused him.[1]

He had reason to be grateful to Abú Zunbúr. On Ḥámid's fall Abú Zunbúr had been arrested and brought from Damascus to Baghdád. In return for the remission of part of the fine that had been imposed on him, Ibn al-Furát had required him to bring false witness against ‘Alí—to swear that ‘Alí had taken bribes from him—but Abú Zunbúr had refused. Ibn al-Furát was genuinely surprised at this refusal, since before, when he, Ibn al-Furát, had been on trial before ‘Alí and Ḥámid, Abú Zunbúr had consented to give

1 H. 319–21.

evidence against him. But Abú Zunbúr pointed out that not only had the evidence been truthful in his case; whereas he was bound to 'Alí by long ties of friendship and gratitude, all that he had to thank Ibn al-Furát for was the persecution (during his second Vizierate) of himself and his family. However, Abú Zunbúr had succeeded in coming to an amicable settlement of his own affairs with the late Vizier; whilst his nephew, Muḥammad ibn 'Alí, who had also been arrested, bought his life and freedom from al-Muḥassin with costly presents. The Mádhará'ís had left Baghdád with Mu'nis; and Abú Zunbúr had come by way of Syria to Egypt.[1]

On one of 'Alí's journeys to Mecca the Mádhará'ís, uncle and nephew, set out with him, though bound, apparently, for another destination. This was probably in 313 (926),[2] the year of the Carmathian attack on al-Kúfah, when 'Alí travelled from Fusṭáṭ, as I have mentioned, with the Egyptian caravans. He invited them both to perform the Pilgrimage with him; but the nephew demurred, saying that he could not stand the heat of the holy city. Abú Zunbúr, however, consented; and later he accompanied 'Alí on his second journey to Damascus.

His inspectorship gave 'Alí the right to appoint and

1 H. 44–5; M. I, 114–15.

2 This passage—S.J. fol. 138 a—suggests, though it does not actually state, that it was from Baghdád, and consequently at some other time, that Abú Zunbúr accompanied 'Alí to Mecca; but this cannot, I think, be so. He had never met Abú Zunbúr before the latter came to Court in 306 (918–19), see 'A. 73; and the only occasion on which he travelled from Baghdád to Mecca after this date was on his banishment in 311 (923), when Abú Zunbúr was undergoing examination by Ibn al-Furát (leaving the capital later with Mu'nis). After this, again, 'Alí performed the Pilgrimage only in 312 and 313 (925 and 926), and then for the last time in his life. In 312 he came from the Yemen with the pilgrims. There remains, therefore, only 313, when he and the Mádhará'ís were, in fact, all employed in Egypt and Syria together.

dismiss. Accordingly he dismissed in 313 (925–6) the then Chief *qáḍhí* of Egypt, a certain Ibn Mukram, who, though he had held the appointment two years, preferred to live in Baghdád and perform the functions of his office through a deputy. Ibn Mukram had been appointed by Ibn al-Furát on his final return to the Vizierate, as the result of singular intrigue. His predecessor had sent a friend to 'Alí, before the latter's arrest, requesting permission to retire; but 'Alí had refused it. He believed the *qáḍhí's* reluctance to remain in office to arise from his dislike of the then recently installed governor, a young and irreverent relation of the Caliph's; and was prepared rather to recall the latter. The messenger, however, saw how, nevertheless, he might obtain the *qáḍhí's* relief: 'Alí's fall was expected daily; he would simply wait for Ibn al-Furát's restoration, when the *qáḍhí's* dismissal would follow as a matter of course. For Ibn al-Furát bore him a long-standing grudge, and would be only too pleased to turn him out. It happened exactly as he had foreseen: the *qáḍhí* was duly dismissed, and Ibn Mukram replaced him.[1]

In the course of his attempts to improve the yield of the Egyptian revenues, 'Alí got himself very heartily disliked by the "Copts", as we learn from a Christian chronicle. He wished to impose the poll-tax usually exacted from the "people of Scripture" on "all the monks and the poor and the feeble, and all the monasteries in the lower valley of the Nile, and the bishops and monks that were in the monastery at Míná"; so he rounded up some of the said bishops and monks for the purpose. These ecclesiastics, so it appears, had enjoyed hitherto an exemption from this tax—possibly by an arrangement come to at the conquest. On 'Alí's attempt to levy it, therefore, they at once sent a

---

1 Kin. 531–2; Dh. *t*. fol. 68 a; Tagh. II, 226.

delegation to Baghdád to protest; and were answered with a confirmation of the privilege.[1]

'Alí was joined in Egypt by the faithful 'Abd ar-Raḥmán,[2] who left Baghdád on the fall of 'Abd Allah al-Kháqání. Moreover, his cousin Sulaymán (who had escaped from surveillance on the execution of Ibn al-Furát)[3] was appointed, presumably by Alí's contrivance, as Tax-Collector of Syria.[4] Abú Sahl al-Qaṭṭán, too, had joined 'Alí once more; and on one of their excursions into Syria a lucky accident permitted him to found a modest fortune. A chieftain that they were visiting wished to present 'Alí with a perfume-case, in the shape of a silver fish encrusted with jewels; and when he, as usual, declined it, their host pressed it on Abú Sahl. Abú Sahl dared not accept it without 'Alí's permission; but 'Alí, to his joy, allowed him to keep it.[5]

When the message came recalling 'Alí to the Vizierate, the cousins, as well as Abú Zunbúr, were all in Damascus. They all set out together, but seem to have been slow in doing so—unless it was that 'Alí looked into the affairs of each place on their route—for they did not arrive in Baghdád for some ten weeks after al-Khaṣíbí's arrest. They struck the Euphrates at the bridge of Minbaj, and thence travelled down the river by boat. So joyful were the people at 'Alí's return that numbers of them went out as far as ar-Raḥbah to welcome him. At Hít and al-Anbár the crowds increased. He entered the capital on 5th *ṣafar* 315 (11th April 927) in a veritable triumph.[6]

1 Eut. II, 517.
2 Cf. H. 138, where Tagín reminisces to 'Abd ar-Raḥmán in Egypt.
3 M. I, 140. 4 H. 310. 5 Yáq. *ud.* VI, 307.
6 H. 309–10; 'A. 129; M. I, 149–50.

CHAPTER V

The second Vizierate

'Alí had not the smallest wish for office. On the contrary, his one desire was to escape it—perhaps, after all, it was merely reluctance that had kept him so long upon the road. Almost his first action on arriving at Baghdád was to implore the Caliph to excuse him. But loath as al-Muqtadir had been to recall him, antipathetic as they were to each other in every way, for the time being he was convinced that 'Alí was indispensable. He received him with every mark of honour, sending him, on the day of his arrival, before his investiture, which took place next morning, valuable presents—20,000 *dínárs* in gold, and a number of gorgeous robes, carpets, and animals for his stable. But 'Alí was no more impressed with the Caliph's affability than with the fickle acclamations of the Baghdádís. He even composed some lines on this latter theme:

The people are all for the world and its master; but if, one day, it turn against him, they will turn too....[1]

The task with which 'Alí was confronted was desperate indeed. And in order to cope with it, once he saw that there was nothing for it but to acquiesce, he adopted desperate measures. All-night sittings were now the rule in the Government offices. The financial reports were to be rendered weekly instead of monthly; accounts were daily to be balanced. Every pension or salary was drastically reduced, and any for the receipt of which a very good reason could not be cited were docked altogether. The secretaries found themselves

1 S.J. fol. 81 b; Tagh. II, 230; Dh. *t.* fol. 68 b; Qudh. fol. 91 a.

doing much more work for much less pay. The eunuchs, the minstrels, the jesters, the cooks, the crowd of hangers-on of every description with which the palace swarmed, found that their fat days had come to an end. 'Alí soon became, as usual, extremely unpopular. He was abused by the eunuchs in public. He was lampooned by a Court poet whom he had dismissed. But 'Alí did not care, and in this was his strength—the sooner he was deprived of the hateful and arduous office the better pleased he would be.

What he did resent were reflections on his competence. And on this account his already none too harmonious relations with al-Muqtadir were nowise improved by an incident that occurred at the outset of his Vizierate. Al-Muqtadir sent him an order that al-Kalwádhí and Abú 'Umar the *qáḍhí* were to be retained in their positions. 'Alí had had no intention of dismissing either, but their retention or dismissal was entirely his province, and he was profoundly irritated at this interference on the part of the Caliph. Al-Kalwádhí indeed was his right-hand man. It was he that had preserved a semblance of order amid the late secretarial chaos. It had been generally expected that 'Alí would give the plum of office, the *díwán as-sawád*, to 'Abd ar-Raḥmán; so al-Kalwádhí was duly flattered when it fell to him—deputising generally for 'Alí in the control of the *díwáns* (as he would otherwise have had to do) was both hard work and dull, because 'Alí was in the habit of reading all the reports himself "day and night". By this time Ibn Muqlah was also back from the exile at Shíráz into which he and Sulaymán had been sent together; after Sulaymán's escape Ibn Muqlah had obtained leave to move to al-Ahwáz, and later to return to Baghdád. 'Alí now gave him the management of the Office of Private and New-made Estates. Sulaymán shared the Financial Secretaryship with 'Abd ar-Raḥmán; another of 'Alí's brothers,

Muḥammad, took the *díwán* of the Harem; Abú Zunbúr received the *díwán* of Estates Confiscated from Ibn al-Furát; and Ibn al-Furát's own nephew, al-Faḍhl ibn Ja'far, whom 'Alí had employed during his first Vizierate, represented the former faction in the *díwán al-mashriq*. No less than five of these ministers were future Viziers. 'Alí had clearly assembled in his service all the available talent.[1]

With 'Alí's unworldliness went a certain blindness to the claims of his friends; the pressure of work too made him irritable. It was the duty of his faithful adherent Abú Bakr ash-Sháfi'í to show him daily the petitions of the people, and one morning Abú Bakr presented among them a petition of his own, asking a recompense for the ills that he had suffered at the hands of al-Muḥassin (imprisonment, torture and a fine) simply because he was 'Alí's friend. 'Alí was so used to halving and quartering such claims that he was inclined at first to halve or quarter the indemnity of Abú Bakr. But Abú Bakr protested. If his lot in the days of the Vizier's disgrace was to be blows, and in the days of the Vizier's prosperity a refusal of his requests, where was his advantage? 'Alí was much amused at his so plainly putting a price on their friendship. He allowed his claim in full, and nevermore denied him anything.[2]

'Alí had not the heart to blame al-Khaṣíbí for the confusion into which he had allowed things to slide. He was so childishly incapable. He had kept no satisfactory record even of his fines; and if he was found wanting in this, the department where if anywhere he shone, inadequate indeed must have been his control of the rest. It was rumoured that his predecessor, al-Kháqání, had died of poison, and that the crime was

1 M. I, 140, 151–2; 'A. 130–2; H. 312–14; Ath. (Búláq), VIII, 55–6.

2 Tan. *nish.* 47–8; H. 330–1.

to be attributed to al-Khaṣíbí; but of this there was no proof, and 'Alí did not press the accusation. On the other hand there was no doubt that in the course of his exactions he had exposed honourable ladies, such as al-Muḥassin's widow, to shameful indignities; but on the whole 'Alí blamed those who had appointed him more than al-Khaṣíbí himself. He bluntly told the Caliph as much, and illustrated his theme with Sasanian example. The old Persians knew that if a man was unable to manage his own affairs, he was all the more unable to manage affairs of State....The modern Muslims, it seemed, had this to learn.[1]

At the sight of 'Alí's assiduity al-Muqtadir seems to have had one of those momentary revulsions of feeling that did something to redeem his general worthlessness. And while the mood was on him he ordered 'Alí's confiscated riches to be restored to him. 'Alí promptly bought estates with the money, and added them to the pious foundation that he had devoted to the people of Mecca and Medina.[2] He had no need of it himself; indeed he protested that the income from the Vizierial estates and the monthly salary amounted to much more than he required. But al-Muqtadir insisted on his taking the usual dues.—Perhaps he was nervous lest the Vizier's frugality should expose the more luridly his own extravagance.[3]

It was al-Muqtadir's extravagance, doubtless, that was in the main responsible for the depletion of the Privy Purse. But 'Alí was able to prove that robbery had contributed. One day he enquired where a certain celebrated rosary was kept, and was assured, in the Jewel Treasury. The Jewel Treasury was ransacked from top to bottom, but it could nowhere be found; whereupon 'Alí produced it from his sleeve—he had seen it for sale in the market at Fusṭáṭ, and recognising

1 M. I, 153, 154–6; Ath. (Búláq), VIII, 55–6.
2 'A. 131; Quḍh. fol. 90 b.   3 M. I, 159.

it, had bought it himself. Its loss was a grave matter—if the Jewel Treasury was not secure, what was? Zaydán had had access to it, and was consequently suspected. But it was the principle that was so alarming: it was a symptom of the general disease.[1]

Chaos had been everywhere triumphant, but nowhere did it reign more completely than in the army finances. 'Alí's attention was called to their unsatisfactory state hardly a month after his arrival by a riot of the cavalrymen, which continued for almost a week. Untold damage was done in the course of this insurrection. The Palace of the Pleiades—one of the glories of al-Mu'tadhid's reign—was gutted; the buildings in the Táj Palace known as the Citron, the Planet and the Dome of the Ass[2] were sacked; and the celebrated menagerie that played so decorative a part on State occasions was either destroyed or dispersed. The rioters were only appeased in the end by Mu'nis's promises of satisfaction. For 'Alí discovered that the paymaster had indeed kept them in arrears of their allowances, and had appropriated large sums to himself. He fined the paymaster heavily, dismissing him and his staff; and found means with comparative ease to fulfil Mu'nis's promises, allowing him to choose the districts on whose revenues he might draw. But the incident led him to examine the whole question of military pay, and he found it all highly perturbing.[3]

What disquieted him most were the fantastic arrangements made by al-Khaṣíbí for the levying and support of the Carmathian defence force. Al-Khaṣíbí had rightly wished to retain Mu'nis and his troops at home: his plan had been to commit the raising and command

1 'A. 130; Jaw. fol. 82 b.

2 This appears to have been a tower like the Malwiyyah minaret at Sámarrá, with a spiral ramp outside, up which a small donkey might be ridden. See Herzfeld: *Samarra*, 36.

3 M. I, 157, 159–60; Ḥam. I, 204–5; Ath. (Búláq), VIII, 61.

of an army to Ibn Abí's-Sáj; Ibn Abí's-Sáj was to proceed with the army to Wásiṭ, and there he was to establish a base from which he could cover at need the cities of al-Baṣrah and al-Kúfah, and even carry the war into the Carmathian country. This was initially foolish. The men thus impressed would be mountain-bred, used to a well-watered and temperate land; they would be at a hopeless disadvantage in the arid and parching deserts into which he proposed to send them. (Many years before, in the days of al-Mu'taḍhid, al-Jannábí himself had explained this point to a captured 'Abbásid general. His chief protection, he said, against attack by the Caliph's forces was the inclement climate of al-Baḥrayn.)[1] But that was not all. In order to provide funds for the maintenance of this force al-Khaṣíbí had allotted the whole revenue of the eastern provinces, with the exception of Iṣfahán, a sum calculated at no less than three million *dínárs* a year. Worse still, he had consented to the stipulation that no Government paymaster should accompany the expedition. Consequently it would be impossible to tell what was raised, or how it was spent.

'Alí had an alternative scheme. He would employ five thousand of the Banú Asad and five thousand of the Banú Shaybán, bedouin Arabs well suited to desert warfare, whose needs could be met with a third of the sum required for the Persian force. He accordingly obtained al-Muqtadir's permission to stop Ibn Abí's-Sáj proceeding further, and prepared to put his own plan into execution. Now Ibn Abí's-Sáj had been very reluctant to leave his station in Persia; but once having raised an army and set it in motion, he resented what he regarded as a caprice on the part of the Government. He therefore ignored 'Alí's command; marched southwards to Ḥulwán as if making for Baghdád; and was only deflected to Wásiṭ by a peremptory order from

1 Tan. *farj.* I, 110–11; Jaw. fol. 27 a.

Mu'nis. Once there his troops behaved in the most truculent way, terrorising the unfortunate townsfolk, and ravaging the countryside. Complaints were made to the general, but he took no notice. The citizens of Wásiṭ began to think that they would as soon have the Carmathians for company as those that had been sent to keep them away.

Installed at Wásiṭ, Ibn Abí's-Sáj remained inactive. He shortly discovered, to his complete distraction from military affairs, that his chief counsellor, or Vizier, as he liked to style him, was busily intriguing with Naṣr against him, with the ultimate intention of himself replacing 'Alí in the real Vizierate—an-Nayramání (for that was his name) had asserted that Ibn Abí's-Sáj was secretly a Carmathian himself, and as Carmathians were detected everywhere these days, he was half believed.[1] However, 'Alí himself is unlikely to have wished to press the war against al-Jannábí—we know what he thought of Ibn Abí's-Sáj's soldiers. Besides, war would bring in its train further expense—as before, if the finances were to have a chance of righting themselves, peace was essential. Unlucky 'Alí! His schemes were fated to fail: the greater part of his short Vizierate was to be disturbed by war.

For more than a year the Greeks had been showing themselves uncommonly aggressive on the northern frontiers. Having recently defeated the Bulgarians after a long conflict, they had now turned their arms with unembarrassed vigour against the enfeebled Caliphate. They had repulsed the summer raiders, and later they had taken and sacked Samosata, where they had defiled the mosques with the celebration of Christian rites.[2]

It was decided to send Mu'nis against them. Every-

1 M. I, 147–8, 153–4, 166–72; 'A. 128, 130–1, 132; Ath. (Búláq), VIII, 55.

2 M. I, 146–7, 159; Ḥam. I, 205; Ath. (Búláq), VIII, 56, 57.

thing was prepared; the general had even been invested with a robe of honour; when on the day fixed for his departure he suddenly refused to go into the palace and take leave of the Caliph. A confidant had warned him that a plot was afoot there to assassinate him. A pit, so ran the rumour, had been dug in one of the saloons, on the principle of an elephant trap: Mu'nis, left alone with the Caliph, was to be lured by him into treading on its yielding cover, whereupon the eunuchs were to set on him and strangle him; and it was to be given out that he had stumbled into a cellar and broken his neck. Another version attributed the scheme to the Lady; but in any case Mu'nis was not going to risk his life in the palace. On the other hand decorum would not permit him to depart without seeing al-Muqtadir, so he was forced to wait on events. It soon became evident that the episode was viewed with concern. Mu'nis found himself joined by the entire army. Abú'l-Hayjá' and his brothers insisted in the most embarrassing way on swearing that they would fight with him, as they said, "until his beard grew". The Caliph found the palace deserted, and himself defenceless. Whether or not he had indeed planned Mu'nis's murder, he now saw that at all costs he must be placated, and immediately wrote a note in his own hand denying the truth of the hateful allegation. Mu'nis replied with suitable humility; dismissed to their stations the troops that had gathered about him; and protested that he was not to be held responsible for their behaviour. Harmony was thus outwardly established. Mu'nis shortly set out up the Tigris. But of that discord between the general and the Caliph, which was eventually to prove so fatal to both of them, the first note had been struck.

Mu'nis, as I shall relate, never reached the frontier. But the Muslim arms were generally victorious, and the summer raid from Tarsus was again successful, in the months that followed. Indeed so hard pressed were the Greeks, that before the end of the year we find a courier from the Emperor proposing another armistice. But in the meantime, graver hostilities had broken out in the south.[1]

1 M. I, 159–60, 161; 'A. 133.

CHAPTER VI

The alarum of the Carmathians. 'Alí's *despair and his disgrace*

Ibn Abí's-Sáj was after all unprepared; an-Nayramání's case was still unsettled; no money was as yet forthcoming from Persia; when in *ramadhán* 315 October–November 927) the Carmathians, without waiting to be attacked, made a sudden move. The governor of al-Baṣrah reported a force to be advancing across the western desert in the direction of al-Kúfah. As soon as he received the news, 'Alí took every possible measure of defence. He recalled Mu'nis, who had reached Ṭakrít, to Baghdád; ordered Ibn Abí's-Sáj to forestall the Carmathians at al-Kúfah; and caused to be prepared there in advance an abundance of provisions for man and beast and the material for a camp. Unhappily, however, these plans went wrong. Ibn Abí's-Sáj dared not or could not move without paying his men. He had to wait for a letter to reach the capital; for 'Alí to appeal to the Caliph for funds on loan from the Privy Purse; for the money to be conveyed to Wásiṭ. And by that time the Carmathians had obtained a start of one day. Consequently they reached al-Kúfah before him; and themselves took possession of the camp and supplies that 'Alí had intended for him. Yet even so Yúsuf had no doubt that he could defeat them. He proposed a battle for the day after to-morrow, unless al-Jannábí should immediately acknowledge al-Muqtadir; and sat down to compose a letter announcing his victory. Al-Jannábí, however, chose to fight next day; and whether it was that Yúsuf's calculations were thereby upset, or that the scale was turned against him by the unexpected deprivation of his men and the refreshment of his opponents, his army was completely routed, and he was himself taken prisoner.[1]

When news of the defeat arrived, followed by fugitives naked and afoot, the citizens of Baghdád were again terrified for their safety. Before telling the Caliph, 'Alí debated with Mu'nis and Naṣr what had best be done. The Carmathians were known to have struck north from al-Kúfah by 'Ayn at-Tamar towards al-Anbár. The main thing was to prevent them crossing the Euphrates. To effect this it was resolved to man a river fleet consisting of five hundred light boats, which 'Alí hired for the purpose, as well as a number of barges, and send it from the Tigris along the communicating canals. There was no provision, however, in 'Alí's precarious budget for such expense; so, notwithstanding his instinct for economy, he appealed passionately to the Caliph to devote the Privy Purse in its entirety for the defence of the State. The predecessors of al-Muqtadir, he cried, al-Mu'tadhid and al-Muktafí, had amassed the treasure against an emergency: and the emergency had arrived. Never since the death of the Prophet had there befallen the Muslims anything more grievous than this. If the Caliph had nothing to give, there remained for him no refuge but the farthest limits of Khurásán. Al-Muqtadir was so frightened that he consented: 'Alí received the half million of *dínárs* that remained. Moreover the Lady was prevailed upon to produce an equal sum; and by sending round inspectors to secure the immediate payment of revenue owing, 'Alí was able to meet the demand.

In addition to the boats and barges a force was sent by land to al-Anbár, and it arrived in time to sight the approach of the Carmathian horsemen. Al-Anbár lay on the east bank of the Euphrates, and so, by way of

1 M. I, 165, 172–4; Ath. (Búláq), VIII, 57–8; 'A. 132; Ḥam. I, 205.

protection, the officers in command destroyed the only bridge. Al-Jannábí, however, managed to land a hundred men by boat; made a surprise descent on the town; defeated the occupying force; and sent the inhabitants fleeing for their lives to Baghdád. He next restored the bridge, and led his army across, leaving his baggage, and with it the unfortunate Ibn Abí's-Sáj, behind.[1]

No natural barrier now remained between the Carmathians and the capital. Nobody could doubt any longer that they intended attacking it forthwith. The alarm occasioned by the defeat of Ibn Abí's-Sáj had by now developed into a veritable panic. The narrow lanes of the city were choked with would-be fugitives and their belongings. Those rich enough to do so were frantically hiring or buying barges or pack-animals, to transport their families and possessions to Wásiṭ and al-Ahwáz by river, or by caravan to a remoter refuge in Persia. Thieves, taking advantage of the general turmoil, began to range the city for loot. It was only by measures of the utmost severity that Názúk succeeded in preserving order. With 'Alí's approval, anyone, innocent or guilty, who was found loitering in the streets after dark, he forthwith decapitated.

Názúk was also entrusted with the defence of the city. Since it was from that direction that an attack was expected, he had the three northernmost gates on the west bank closed. The moat that ran outside them would thus form an obstacle to the advance of the enemy, should they indeed approach so near; and so that they might find nothing at hand with which to fill it in, he also commanded the reed-workers, who had their station outside the next most southerly, the Anbár Gate, to remove their stores within the walls.[2]

1 M. I, 175–6, 180–1; Ḥam. I, 206; S.J. fol. 85 b.
2 Ḥam. I, 206; M. I, 175, 179; Ath. (Búláq), VIII, 58.

Similar measures of defence were taken by Mu'nis at a distance of seven miles from Baghdád on a branch of the 'Ísà Canal.[1] The army of the Commander-in-Chief had been reinforced by the *Ḥujarí* guards and the *Maṣáffí* infantry under the leadership of Naṣr, as well as by the contingents of Abú'l-Hayjá' and his brothers, until the forces totalled forty thousand men. The Carmathians numbered but fifteen hundred, or by a more generous computation, two thousand seven hundred. In either case the disproportion was thus enormous. Yet for some reason, no attempt was made by the 'Abbásid forces to sally forth against them as they approached. It was resolved merely to cut the culvert spanning the canal, and await the attack with the uncertain protection of flowing water. The whole conduct of the defence in the encounter was indeed peculiar. De Goeje[2] even suspects Abú'l-Hayjá' of Carmathian sympathies, and supposes there to have been an understanding between him and al-Jannábí. To be sure it was he that urged the cutting of the culvert and the inactivity which, as he was careful, afterwards, to point out, proved so masterly. But this does not explain why Mu'nis and Naṣr, whose word carried very much more weight, should have acquiesced. As the Carmathians drew near, many of the Caliph's troops turned tail and fled for fright. Mu'nis cannot but have been aware of their temper: he was perhaps content to stay in what seemed a secure position, rather than risk an advance with supporters so undependable. He met the assault with a hail of arrows, under which the Carmathians searched in vain for a ford. They then attempted to make a detour, only to discover that Mu'nis and Naṣr had flooded the country so that it was quite impassable. Finding the approaches to Baghdád thus barred to them, they turned back

1 Near the Babylonian ruin of 'Aqarqúf.
2 *Carmathes*, 98.

towards the Euphrates, picking their way along the banks of dry land that remained.

It was a day of tension in Baghdád. No one doubted for an instant that the Carmathians would take the city. The well-to-do kept their boats moored at the landing-stages ready to row off down stream at a moment's notice. At 'Alí's order Názúk and his men remained alert at the Ḥarb Gate the day long, nor did they dismount from their horses until far into the night. Robbers and any who should appear about with arms were threatened with summary execution. Nevertheless the markets on the west bank were empty: the shopkeepers had removed the stock to their houses. Every hour came a despatch from the camp by the pigeon-post that 'Alí had inaugurated. And at length the good news arrived and was spread abroad from the palace: the Carmathians had retreated, the city was safe. Al-Muqtadir, to signalise his gratitude to God, distributed a largesse of 100,000 *dirhams*. 'Alí followed his example with another of half the amount.

In the meantime the bargemen, who had arrived too late to prevent al-Jannábí from crossing the river, had succeeded in again destroying the bridge at al-Anbár, so that the Carmathian army was thus cut off from its base. Intelligence of this manœuvre had reached Naṣr, and on the discomfiture of the Carmathians, he was struck with the possibility of turning it to advantage. His plan was to land a force by means of the barges on the west bank of the Euphrates, attack the baggage camp, and rescue Ibn Abí's-Sáj. Naṣr himself had a fit of fever before he could carry it out, but Mu'nis approved it, and instead sent Yalbaq with six thousand men. Al-Jannábí was in fact prevented by the cutting of the bridge from transporting his army back across the river; but he succeeded in bribing a local fisherman—it is said with a thousand *dínárs*—to row him over alone. His presence was enough to hearten the men whom he had left in charge of the camp; and they met Yalbaq's attack with such fortitude that he was beaten off. Yalbaq and his men thereupon fled back to Mu'nis; while the Carmathians, finding their passage no longer impeded, recrossed the river as soon as they could find the means to do so, and reassembled on the farther bank. The defeat was perhaps of little consequence to the 'Abbásids, but it was fatal to Ibn Abí's-Sáj. For al-Jannábí recognised that the main object of the attack had been his rescue; and to prevent its recurrence straightway beheaded him.[1]

Mu'nis appears to have followed the Carmathians to al-Anbár; but by the time he arrived, they had moved from their camp into the desert. Once out of danger, the troops took it upon themselves to riot for a rise in pay. They claimed it as the reward of victory, although they had done nothing to withstand the enemy, indeed many had run away at the first threat of battle. Seeing no need to remain, Mu'nis thereupon returned to Baghdád, where the men continued their clamour, with the result that al-Muqtadir gave way to it, and granted them an increase of a *dínár* apiece.

By this time 'Alí was in any case in despair over the finances. The most drastic measures seemed unavailing to redeem the three years' neglect that had preceded his term of office. Hard as he had tried, beyond a certain figure, and one that he still thought much too high, it had proved impossible to cut down the allowances to the Lady, the Harem, and the household. In addition to this, Naṣr had lately been showing signs of disaffection. He was jealous of 'Alí's regard for Mu'nis, and felt himself slighted. When therefore 'Alí heard of this new burden on the exchequer, it was more than he could bear. He wrote to the Caliph begging to be

1 Mas. *tan.* 383; Ḥam. I, 206–7; M. I, 176–80; 'A. 132–3; Ath. (Búláq), VIII, 58; S.J. fol. 82 b–83 a; Dh. *t.* fol. 69 b; Tagh. II, 229–30.

allowed to resign. He was too old, he said, too old to cope with affairs. Al-Muqtadir must excuse him.

Al-Muqtadir, however, would not hear of it. He protested that he looked on 'Alí as a father, and it was only when 'Alí persisted in his demand as he had never persisted before, that the Caliph sought Mu'nis's advice upon the subject. In doing so he disclosed to the general that there were three candidates for the Vizierate. The first was al-Fadhl ibn Ja'far; the second, Ibn Muqlah; and the third was no less a personage than an-Nayramání, the minister of Ibn Abí's-Sáj. But Mu'nis rejected them all. Al-Fadhl was too nearly related to Ibn al-Furát: his appointment would cause a scandal. Ibn Muqlah was too young. An-Nayramání was incompetent. No, he quite agreed that 'Alí must remain. He spoke to 'Alí himself about it, but 'Alí was adamant. If he could be assured of Mu'nis's continual presence at Court, it would be different. With Mu'nis's authority behind him he might succeed in carrying out the necessary reforms however unpalatable they might be. But Mu'nis was always being called away on expeditions, and as soon as his back was turned, government became impossible.

Naṣr, whom the Caliph next consulted, was by no means so impartial. He dismissed al-Fadhl on the same grounds as Mu'nis, and declared that nobody feared or respected Ibn Muqlah. His favourite was an-Nayramání. For some time Naṣr and an-Nayramání had been, as we have seen, in communication—an-Nayramání's arrest by Ibn Abí's-Sáj had interrupted their intrigue; but when Ibn Abí's-Sáj was taken prisoner, an-Nayramání had escaped to Baghdád. It was an-Nayramání's specious financial schemes that tempted al-Muqtadir to appoint him; and it is probable that he would now have been made Vizier, had it not been for the opposition of Mu'nis and Hárún, which continued irreconcilable. But Naṣr was eager both to be rid of

'Alí and to have the new Vizier, whoever he might be, beholden to him. He therefore abandoned his first choice, and now inclined to Ibn Muqlah. Mu'nis had no such rooted objection to him, and with the Caliph Ibn Muqlah was in high favour for a piece of astuteness in which he had been aided by Naṣr himself. He had improved upon 'Alí by establishing a private bird-post at al-Anbár before the Carmathians attacked it: the governor had written daily despatches to 'Alí, but Ibn Muqlah had received hourly news of the latest developments. These had been conveyed through Naṣr to the Caliph, who was delighted to have this unofficial intelligence and forestall the Vizier. Naṣr therefore pressed the claims of his new *protégé*, and in due course he was appointed.

'Alí knew al-Muqtadir too well to trust his word. He knew that the refusal of his request for resignation meant nothing, and prepared, as if he were the most stiff-necked clinger to office, for arrest and imprisonment. He sent his wife and children with his clerks and followers into hiding, and remained alone in his house with 'Abd ar-Raḥmán.[1] His misgivings and these precautions were justified all too soon.

Very likely al-Muqtadir had been sincere in his protestations; but with much drinking his temper had grown so inconstant that the least stimulus would change its direction. And so now his passing regard for 'Alí (if it may be taken for genuine) was suddenly changed into a determination, not merely to accept his resignation, but to disgrace and punish him; the stimulus, in this case, being supplied, not by any action on the part of either Naṣr or Ibn Muqlah, but by the independent machinations of a certain Ibn Zabr,[2] a

1 M. I, 166–72, 182, 184–5; H. 314–16; 'A. 131; Ath. (Búláq), VIII, 59, 62.

2 'Abd Allah ibn Aḥmad, b. 256 (870), d. 329 (940–1). Notice in Dh. *t*. fol. 190 a.

jurist, who also had reason to wish for 'Alí's fall. 'Alí had contracted this new enmity quite recently. On one of his visits to Damascus he had been met by a large concourse of the inhabitants, at the head of whom was this Ibn Zabr, then *qáḍhí* of the city. They had greeted 'Alí with a loud clamour, the meaning of which he could not guess. He had therefore enquired it of Ibn Zabr, who assured him that they were complaining of high prices and lack of trade and beseeching his help. Afterwards, however, 'Alí discovered that they had really been crying out against Ibn Zabr himself, accusing him of "corruption and tyranny and other immoralities"; and on looking into Ibn Zabr's administration of justice he found these charges to be perfectly well founded. On returning to the Vizierate, accordingly, he had dismissed Ibn Zabr; and the latter could do nothing to regain his favour. He coveted the chief judgeship of Egypt; but could see no prospect of obtaining it except on 'Alí's fall, when Mufliḥ the Negro, who was ready to abet him, would urge his suit with the Caliph. Ibn Zabr determined, therefore, to hasten this event: to do so he would play on the Caliph's notorious superstition. He wrote, accordingly, a letter, in which he stated that a man of Khurásán, a copyist of Traditions, visiting Baghdád on his way to perform the Pilgrimage, had dreamt three nights running of al-'Abbás the Prophet's uncle (the eponymous ancestor of the 'Abbásids). Al-'Abbás, in his vision, was building a house in the midst of the city, when, just as he finished, a man came and knocked it down. This happened again and again, whereupon he enquired, "O Uncle of the Apostle of God, who is it at whose hands you suffer thus?" To which al-'Abbás replied, "This is 'Alí ibn 'Ísà. Whatever I build up for my children he destroys."—Ibn Zabr bribed a man, whom he dressed up for the purpose as the said copyist of Khurásán, to place this letter in a pile of petitions to be shown to the Caliph. His scheme worked perfectly. Al-Muqtadir, credulous as ever, believed the dream to be a sure sign from Heaven. He at once decided on 'Alí's dismissal; and that same evening Ibn Zabr received the brevet of his new appointment.[1]

'Alí was arrested at noon on 15th *rabí' al-awwal* 316 (8th May 928), but little more than a year since his triumphal return. The Caliph entrusted the arrest to his cousin Hárún; but Hárún was so ashamed of his commission that on setting out for the Báb al-Bustán he besought an unemployed official that was with him to go on before and give warning. 'Alí, however, needed no warning; he was sitting in the courtyard, waiting: he had been expecting them, he said. He was even dressed for departure: he had his boots on ready and a turban and his doctor's hood, and in his pocket were a *qur'án* and a pair of scissors. The men made a clatter in the silent house, as they ran about it seeking who might be there. But they found only 'Abd ar-Raḥmán looking out of a window, and he came peaceably with them. The small *cortège* returned to the palace without commotion. 'Abd ar-Raḥmán was lodged with the Chamberlain, 'Alí with his old acquaintance, Zaydán.[2]

1 Kin. 540–1. This story is not dated. But Ibn Zabr received his appointment to Egypt in 316 (Kin. 539), so that presumably it was to *this* dismissal of 'Alí ibn 'Ísà rather than to an earlier one that his intrigue led. If so, however, there are some inaccuracies in the narrative: Ḥámid and Umm Músà, for example, are both mentioned. But Ḥámid and Umm Músà cannot have been present *together* at Court either in 304 or in 311 when 'Alí was dismissed before, because in 304 Ḥámid was not yet in Baghdád, whilst in 311 Umm Músà was already disgraced. There is no reason on this account, therefore, to suppose that the story refers to an earlier date than 316.

2 H. 316; M. 1, 185; 'A. 134.

CHAPTER VII

Further tribulations of 'Alí ibn 'Ísà. *The second deposition of* al-Muqtadir.

'Alí had always been both economical and religious. But if in early life contact with the extravagant had forced his instinctive parsimony to the fore, with age and experience of the world, whether or not his religion had a tinge or even a deeper colouring of Ṣúfism, he became more and more addicted to piety, till it was said of him that he held among Viziers the place occupied among Caliphs by the single saintly 'Umayyad, the fanatical 'Umar ibn 'Abd al-'Azíz (a comparison that 'Alí will have thought more flattering than we can think it).[1] Asceticism became with him almost a passion; he came to feel that there was something horrible about luxury. He had been shocked when Abú 'Umar paid him a visit in a brocaded shirt; and reproved him by comparing what they each had spent on the clothes they were wearing. Abú 'Umar took the reproof in good part and twisted his reply to a compliment. Whereas mere judges, he said, need every adjunct of finery to impress the inferiors with whom they are bound to deal, the Vizier moves among intimates who know his rank, and moreover lends splendour to any garment he may don.[2] Nevertheless, at a hint of obligation 'Alí could be positively profuse. On one occasion both he and a certain perfume-seller of al-Karkh, embarrassed over a debt, dreamed in one night that the Prophet commanded 'Alí to relieve him. Not only did 'Alí pay up the wanted sum (exceeding

1 Ibn Qáḏhí Shuhbah: *muntaqà'l-'ibar* (B.M. Or. 3006), fol. 114 b. Cf. Ḏháf. fol. 140 b, and Yáq. *ud.* v, 279.

2 H. 327; Tan. *nish*, 29–30; S.J. fol. 137 b.

by many times the cost of Abú 'Umar's shirt), he offered to double it and more, as a gift. Yet what moved him to tears of joy was the man's refusal of this boon. Such exactitude was uncommon enough.[1]

His fall had been hinted at in certain admonitory verses addressed to him by one of the masters with whom his son 'Ísà, now in his fifteenth year, was studying. This was a certain Ibn Durayd,[2] an aged doctor, addicted, even after the age of ninety, to drink and music, but much sought after for his vast erudition in the Arabic language.[3] "O 'Alí ibn 'Ísà," he had written, "the good of your two days (the day of fair, and the day of evil, fortune) is that you should see your excellence hoped for and your promise fulfilled. And yet I fear that after this you shall see a barrier between yourself and what you desire."[4]

Yet 'Alí felt now rather that a barrier had been removed. A friend, visiting him in prison to discover what were his wants, remarked his tranquil demeanour. "Now is my religion complete for me," he said. "Now I am free to say my prayers and fulfil the duties of supererogation." He had been looking forward eagerly to dismissal. Indeed he had braced himself to the tasks of the Vizierate only by comparing himself to a holy warrior. And now his conscience bade him ignore the confining walls: so that every Friday, at the time when the ranks were forming in the mosques for public prayer, he would go through the form of ablution, and make for the door as if to set out too. Only when stopped by the locks, or the jailer's restraining hand,

1 H. 334–5; Tan. *nish.* 225–6; Tan. *farj.* I, 172–3; S.J. fol. 139 a–b.

2 Abú Bakr Muḥammad ibn al-Ḥasan, b. 223 (838), d. 320 (932).

3 Dh. *t.* (B.M. Or. 48), fol. 227 a.

4 Yáq. *ud.* VI, 483 *et seqq.* (verses p. 491); Fid. II, 79; Dh. *t.* ff. 149 b–150 b; Tagh. II, 256, etc. I take it that these verses were composed during 'Alí's second Vizierate, since Ibn Durayd only came to Baghdád in 308 (920–1)—see *Encyclopédie*, II, 397 *s.v.*

did he feel God would be satisfied that it was not his negligence, but the malice of men, that prevented him from taking part.[1]

It was no surprise to him to hear that Ibn Muqlah had been made Vizier. He had learnt that it was to be so some days before his arrest—to his intense vexation. For during the previous year he and Ibn Muqlah had fallen out, and it was entirely 'Alí's fault that they had done so. Ibn Muqlah had been approached by an eminent grammarian, known as al-Akhfash the Little,[2] who, having come upon evil days, was reduced almost to penury. At his request Ibn Muqlah asked 'Alí to place al-Akhfash on the roll of pensioners; whereupon 'Alí, instead of considering the case calmly, flew into a rage—ridden as he was perpetually with the nightmare of an intractable deficit, perhaps it was hard to be calm at any demand. He turned on Ibn Muqlah and, in an assembly crowded with people, gave him a "gross answer". At this discourtesy "the world turned black" in Ibn Muqlah's eyes; he retired to his house, cursing himself for ever having made the request, and vowing to work for 'Alí's overthrow. As for al-Akhfash, so great were his disappointment and despair, that he forthwith took poison and died.[3]

Partly because he felt that he had only himself to blame for Ibn Muqlah's rivalry, partly because his pride was hurt by the choice to replace him of one whom he considered very definitely his inferior, whilst he was yet in office 'Alí had rather imprudently vented his irritation by showing up before his colleagues the gross incompetence of his successor to be. As a fact Ibn Muqlah had one secretarial accomplishment in which he actually surpassed 'Alí—his calligraphy—

1 H. 282, 359; Yáq. *ud.* v, 279; Quḍh. fol. 90 a.

2 'Alí ibn Sulaymán, *al-akhfash aṣ-ṣaghír*.

3 Yáq. *ud.* v, 224–5 (notice p. 220 *et seqq.*); S.J. fol. 85 b; Tagh. II, 231; Dh. *t.* fol. 98 a; mentioned Mas. *murúj*, VIII, 233, and *fih.* 83.

but this, of course, only aggravated his offence. Now 'Alí could only lament the sad plight into which government would fall. Ibn Muqlah was young, comparatively; he was ambitious; he was improvident. "O Abú 'Amr, should not the control of the Caliphate fall to people according to the capacity of their brains? Do they suppose that Ibn Muqlah can succeed where I have failed, or carry on where I have given up?"

Abú 'Amr consoled him: "They wanted someone that would take the people's money and give it to them, someone that would permit them what you forbade!"[1]

Ibn Muqlah was only a rival; but 'Alí had in Naṣr an enemy that was unwilling to allow him even the calm of his prison. Whether it was that he was merely jealous of, or really feared, the partnership of Mu'nis and 'Alí, the Chamberlain, since he was now unable safely to attack the general (who was indeed absent from the capital), determined to remove the fallen Vizier.

Of all the charges that had been brought against 'Alí before, none had so convinced or disgusted al-Muqtadir as that which accused him of favouring the Carmathians. Moreover his hatred of the heretics had recently been inflamed, when a man was denounced and arrested, who openly confessed, and though beaten and starved to death had refused to recant, his belief in their mission and the Imámate of the Fáṭimid pretender.[2] Naṣr accordingly enlisted the help of the still-smarting Ibn Muqlah, and announced to the Caliph that he had discovered in a certain al-Jawharí a Carmathian envoy that had repeatedly borne letters from Abú Ṭáhir to 'Alí ibn 'Ísà and back. Al-Muqtadir was no less alarmed and infuriated than he had expected. He ordered the Vizier to convene a court before which

1 H. 326, 359–60; Tan. *nish.* 28.
2 M. 1, 181–2; S.J. fol. 84 a.

the traitor should be flogged; and it was only through the intervention of the Lady, who induced her son to see reason in time, that 'Alí was saved. But saved he was; and as if by a dispensation of fate, his enemy was soon after requited.[1]

Abú Ṭáhir al-Jannábí, his attempt against Baghdád having failed, had set off up the Euphrates; and after being driven off from Hít by the townspeople,[2] reinforced with troops, had established himself, by the beginning of 316 (928), at Raḥbat Ibn Málik, from which as a base he raided at pleasure the surrounding country. He was even contemplating a descent on ar-Ramlah, or Damascus, when, in *sha'bán* (September–October 928), the approach of Mu'nis, who had been sent out to pursue him, but more particularly domestic troubles in al-Baḥrayn, forced him to retreat. A second attempt on Hít warned the Government of this movement; and accordingly in the next month another force, led by Naṣr and Hárún, set out to harass the Carmathians on their homeward journey. An imprudent assault on Qaṣr Ibn Hubayrah, to reach which the marauders were forced again to cross the Euphrates, cost them dear in the destruction of a part of their cavalry. Without risking another encounter they vanished into the western desert, and were sighted passing al-Baṣrah at the beginning of the following year. Soon after the successful encounter Naṣr was again attacked with fever, and perforce gave up his command. He at once set off in his litter for Baghdád; but the journey exhausted his strength and he died on the way.[3]

1 H. 316–17; M. I, 186–7.

2 The historian al-Mas'údí was an eye-witness of this attack on Hít. He was caught there on his way from Syria to Baghdád. See Mas. *tan.* 383.

3 Mas. *tan.* 383–5; M. I, 180, 182–3; 'A. 134, 136; Ath. (Búláq), VIII, 59, 61–2.

Whilst 'Alí was still languishing in prison, two events, unimportant in themselves, combined to produce momentous consequences—and incidentally to bring about his release. The passage of the Carmathians had served to kindle into rebellion the enthusiasm of their co-religionists who still inhabited the country about al-Kúfah. The commander that first came against them was defeated; but Hárún, who succeeded him, suppressed the revolt with ease. On setting out he was allotted the revenues of the Jibál on which to support his army, and empowered to dismiss and appoint the agents in that province. Hárún availed himself of this power, and amongst other changes dismissed Abú'l-Hayjá' (the Ḥamdánid) from Dínavar. Abú'l-Hayjá' was furious, and came to Baghdád vowing vengeance against the Caliph's cousin.[1]

Then, no sooner had Hárún himself returned from his victory than he was involved in a quarrel with Názúk. Their respective grooms fell out over a beautiful youth: they came to blows and raised such a commotion that Názúk's policemen intervened and arrested some of Hárún's servants. They marched them off and were preparing to beat them, when their fellows attacked the station and rescued them. Such a defiance of his authority annoyed Názúk, and he complained to the Caliph; but so little satisfied was he with al-Muqtadir's attitude to the episode that the next day he attacked Hárún's house, and although he did not succeed in breaking in, killed some of his men. The Vizier and Mufliḥ contrived to re-establish outward peace; but the two officers, though they went through a formal reconciliation, continued to avoid each other's company.[2]

Their common grievance against Hárún became now a bond of alliance between Abú'l-Hayjá' and Názúk:

1 'A. 137, 138; Mas. *tan.* 391.
2 Ath. (Búláq), VIII, 63–4; M. I, 187–8.

they were eager to discover some means of injuring him. His victory against the Carmathians of the *sawád* had been acclaimed by the people of Baghdád, who clamoured for him to be made Commander-in-Chief; and in this they saw an opening. Mu'nis was still at ar-Raqqah, where he had remained after the retreat of Abú Ṭáhir; but if he were warned that Hárún was working to supplant him, they might be sure that he would hasten home. They went out to meet him, and filled his ears so full with spite that when they came to the city, instead of first visiting the Caliph (as etiquette required) he turned off to his own house. Al-Muqtadir sent up his son the Prince Abú'l-'Abbás with Ibn Muqlah to greet him: and Mu'nis felt sufficiently ashamed of his behaviour to excuse it with a plea of sickness. In fact nothing more might have been heard of the incident had not the *Maṣáffí* infantry a few days later attacked his house. Very probably this outrage had been engineered by Názúk, but Mu'nis laid it at the Caliph's door, and went out in a rage to encamp at the Shammásiyyah parade ground. He was joined there by the malcontents, with whom he proceeded to the oratory, and between them they composed a letter to al-Muqtadir in which they complained that he was dominated by his relatives to the detriment of the State, and asked that he would remove the Lady, her sister, and all the women from the palace, and at the same time reduce the extravagance and luxury of the Court.

Al-Muqtadir replied meekly, agreeing to remedy the abuses they mentioned. But wishing perhaps to apprise Mu'nis of the real cause of his companions' anger, he expressed astonishment that Názúk held himself ill-used, since he, the Caliph, had maintained a perfect neutrality in his dispute with Hárún. As for Abú'l-Hayjá', if Dínavar really meant so much to him, why, he would re-appoint him if he wished, or even improve his position. To withstand words so conciliatory was impossible; nevertheless it was determined to go to the palace and hear them uttered by al-Muqtadir himself. At the Caliph's order the doors were thrown open and the guard under the offending Hárún dismissed. Al-Muqtadir awaited the coming of his detractors seated on his throne, with his sons about him, reading the *qur'án*, in unprotected majesty. Názúk and Abú'l-Hayjá' could no longer persist: they contented themselves for the moment with requiring that Hárún should be banished to the Syrian frontier. Next day the camp broke up; and Mu'nis returned to his house.

Through the scenes that followed it was afterwards suspected that Mu'nis had played but a half-hearted part: that Názúk and Abú'l-Hayjá' were bent on carrying out a plan; and that he judged it best to seem to be with them so that they might not know he was against them. Názúk, if not Abú'l-Hayjá', was now set on deposing al-Muqtadir; and without giving him time to carry out the conditions to which he had agreed—although Hárún, indeed, had already left the city—renewed the agitation after two days. Mu'nis allowed himself to be persuaded into returning to the oratory; the troops encamped there for the night; and next morning, the morning of 14th *al-muḥarram* 317 (27th February 929), they came to the palace in force. Finding the doors locked, they raised a great shout, which penetrated to the chamber where al-Muqtadir was sitting. Immediately he retired with his family into the innermost recesses of the vast building and remained there in safety till at evening, presumably by preconcerted arrangement, they were removed by water to Mu'nis's house. On hearing the clamour of the soldiers, the Vizier, the chamberlains, the eunuchs and the retinue fled headlong for their lives. Názúk forced his way in; and his eager followers set about stripping the rooms of their ornaments and pillaging everything of value on which they could lay hands. Under cover of the confusion Mu'nis hastened to where 'Alí was confined, and set him free. Such a delivery was, of course, highly irregular, but none the less 'Alí made his escape with great alacrity. Still bewildered by its suddenness, he threaded his way thankfully through the thronged lanes to his house at the Garden Gate, where his unexpected appearance produced, no doubt, a considerable ado.

Al-Muqtadir's half-brother Muḥammad had been chosen to succeed him. He was brought that same evening to the looted palace, and proclaimed Caliph under the title *al-qáhir bi'llah* (Prevailing through God). After appointing Názúk Chamberlain as well as Chief of Police, and confirming Ibn Muqlah as Vizier, Mu'nis set a guard about the palace, and retired with Abú'l-Hayjá' for the night. Outside, the city was in a turmoil: the prisons had been opened: rebels and thieves had escaped. In the morning, however, Názúk strove to re-assert his authority, and by the third day quiet was restored. The new *régime* was established. The plot seemed to have taken.

But it was just at this point that everything, with or without the connivance of Mu'nis, began to go wrong. Mistrusting the loyalty of the *Maṣáffí* troops, Názúk had been compelled to replace them in the palace with men of his own. The *Maṣáffís* were consequently offended, and in order to embarrass him, after concerting with the *Ḥujarís* and the cavalry, turned upon him and demanded as accession money a sum far exceeding anything he could pay. Názúk offered them what he could, and hoped to avoid a conflict by commanding his men to humour them. But on the third morning of al-Qáhir's reign, when the populace, exhausted with rioting, had settled down to rejoice over the accession, the truculent soldiers flocked into the very courtyard of the palace where under the arcade al-Qáhir was sitting, and demanded with one voice a year's pay. The Caliph sent forward Názúk to face them; but he had been drunk overnight and was now suffering a reaction. The sight of so many angry faces horrified him, and without attempting to parley he ran back into the palace hoping to make his escape by a side door. In his haste, however, he forgot that by way of fortification many of the minor entrances had been walled up. He reached the hoped-for exit only to find that by his own orders it had been barricaded. He thus lost his momentary start; and before he could turn back to search again, he was overtaken and cut down by a party of the men-at-arms, who by this time were overrunning the palace. At the first alarm the Vizier and all the functionaries of the Court had fled. Al-Qáhir was left alone with Abú'l-Hayjá'. They climbed up on to a roof of the palace, from which they could see the long banks of the river lined with troops and the dense crowds seething about the walls. From there they went down into the gardens and reached the building called the Citron, where Abú'l-Hayjá' borrowed a retainer's cloak and went out to spy how they might make their escape. As he returned one of the attendants by whom they had been followed ordered the eunuchs to attack them. Al-Qáhir ran out and hid again among the trees; but Abú'l-Hayjá' made a stand and fought. He beat back his assailants with such vigour that some of them fell into an ornamental pool; but he was provoked into issuing again from a pavilion in which he had sought a respite, set upon by some of the chief *Ḥujarí* officers, stabbed and beheaded.

The troops had meanwhile surrounded Mu'nis's house and were crying out for al-Muqtadir. Mu'nis urged him to go with them; but he was so reluctant, fearing a trick, that they had to carry him on their shoulders to the barge that was waiting to convey him to the palace. His first care was to issue an amnesty for Abú'l-Hayjá', whom he knew to have been led into the conspiracy by Názúk; but the messenger arrived too late, and returned with news of his death. His next was to hold an audience in which he was formally restored to the Caliphate. He received the renewed allegiance of his subjects, and promised to satisfy the troops.

Al-Muqtadir treated Al-Qáhir magnanimously upon his restoration: "It would have been more suitable," he said, "if they had called you the Prevailed Upon rather than the Prevailing." He put him in charge of the Lady, who lodged him magnificently and exerted herself to make his confinement pleasant.[1]

Perhaps it was Abú 'Umar that was responsible for the Caliph's good humour. During his eclipse al-Muqtadir had actually signed a form of abdication: his gratitude therefore was profound when the *qáḍhí* now returned it to him with the assurance that no one had seen it. Ibn al-Buhlúl had lately resigned his office as Chief *qáḍhí*; he had grown too old to discharge his duties properly: "I should like there to be a gap," he had said, "between dismissal and the grave." Now, accordingly, the Caliph conferred on Abú 'Umar, as soon as he was able, the post he had so long coveted.[2]

As for Ibn Muqlah, although he had continued in office under al-Qáhir, al-Muqtadir was beholden to

1 'A. 139–44; M. I, 188–99; Ḥam. I, 208–9; Ath. (Búláq), VIII, 64, 68–71.

A distant repercussion of al-Muqtadir's deposition was felt in Spain, where in this year the 'Umayyad of Cordova, 'Abd ar-Raḥmán, who had hitherto contented himself with the style of Emir, adopted that of Caliph. Ham. *tak.*, extract in M. I, 366.

2 M. I, 194; 'A. 139; Yáq. *ud.* I, 82, 92; Dh. *t.* ff. 111 a, 124 b. The gap, in the event, was brief enough. Ibn al-Buhlúl died in this very year, 317 (929).

him for having made no such changes in Court procedure as would have been warranted by a new accession, and accordingly maintained him as Vizier.[1] The Caliph (perhaps under pressure from Mu'nis) must also have sanctioned 'Alí's irregular release; for from this time he performed—as he had done before during his terms of office—the important functions of President of the Court of Appeal.[2]

1 M. 1, 199; 'A. 144.

2 'A. 150.

CHAPTER VIII

The destruction of the Maṣáffís. *The breach between* al-Muqtadir *and* Mu'nis. Al-Muqtadir's *manœuvres.*

This second experience of deposition had impressed one fact at any rate on al-Muqtadir:—that the troops were not to be trifled with; and he set to in earnest to raise the money necessary to meet their demands. Clothes, carpets, jewels were put up for sale, likewise many of the royal estates. Grants of fiefs were recalled, that money too might be raised on them; and a special *díwán* was formed to deal with the business. The details of allotment occupied Ibn Muqlah from morning to night. 'Alí visiting him one day found him distributing the produce of the sales to the impatient recipients. Since 'Alí was again in a position of eminence, Ibn Muqlah chose to be polite to him. He even interrupted the sitting to rise and welcome him. 'Alí sat down at his right hand; but observing the pressure of work, felt that he was in the way and begged him to proceed with it. He was greatly shocked to observe the decline in the value of land—through these enforced transactions it had become a drug in the market.[1]

Once they discovered that they had but to ask in order to receive, the troops became quite reckless in their conduct. The *Maṣáffís* constituted themselves sole guardians of the Caliph, and encamped in the courtyard of the palace. They welcomed recruits until their numbers were greatly increased; they entered their wives and children and even their acquaintances on the pay-list; they insisted on the release of trusts for their benefit, and defeated justice both by permitting

1 M. I, 199–201; 'A. 144, 145; Tan. *nish.* 138; Ath. (Búláq), VIII, 70.

crimes and delaying judgement. Finally their officers demanded instant access whenever they desired it both to the Vizier and to the Caliph. In a word they dominated the State. Riots in *sha'bán* and *ramadḥán* (September–November 929) culminated in an attack on the Vizier's house, from which Ibn Muqlah was rescued with no little difficulty. The soldiery defied the Government: it was clear that unless something were done to check their growing insolence, anarchy would ensue. The only remedy, it seemed, was to play off one section against another: accordingly plans were laid for provoking the cavalry into attacking the infantry, and chasing them from the town.[1]

The dissatisfaction with the present state of affairs was brought to a head at the end of 317 (beginning of 930) by news of what good Muslims could only account as the most dreadful catastrophe that had occurred since the beginnings of Islam. With what seemed to them an almost incredible temerity, Abú Ṭáhir had entered Mecca at the time of Pilgrimage, forced his way into the mosque, cut down in thousands the defenceless worshippers, and—most hideous blasphemy of all—removed and carried off the Black Stone itself, the blessed corner-stone of the Ka'bah. How the sanctuary had been despoiled of its most precious relics and ornaments; how the well Zamzam had been filled to the brink with corpses; how seven hundred virgins had been carried off into captivity; each detail more horrible than the last, this tale of woe was received throughout the Caliphate and the countries of Islam with a bewildered consternation. Its effect upon the pious 'Alí must have been dreadful to contemplate. But his feelings on the occasion are not recorded.[2]

It was while sentiment was still at this extreme of tension that the cavalrymen, coming to demand their

1 M. I, 202; 'A. 148; Ḥam. I, 209; Ath. (Búláq), VIII, 73–4.
2 'A. 136–7; M. I, 201; Ḥam. I, 209–10; Mas. *tan.* 385–6.

pay, were informed by the Vizier that the infantry had emptied the Treasury of its last coin.[1] Their rage of disappointment might well have been turned wholly against the Government—Ibn Muqlah's house was in fact set on fire and looted—but by good fortune in a preliminary clash with the foot-soldiers one of the latter was killed; and on his companions fleeing, the cavalry determined to attack them in earnest. The *Ḥujarí* corps, which had long felt aggrieved at the favour shown to its rival, the *Maṣáffí*, now made common cause with the horsemen. At a given signal they drove the *Maṣáffís* from their station in the palace into the arms of their expectant allies, whereupon there ensued a desperate fight in which the citizens joined warmly against the hated tyrants. Orders had been issued that none should be allowed to cross the river alive; and many were drowned in the attempt, so that the waters of the Tigris were polluted with their floating bodies. So few escaped that to all intents the corps existed no more: a number of Blacks that pleaded for mercy were spared; but of the Whites none was permitted to re-enter the city, and the houses of their chief officers and their families were burnt to the ground.[2]

It was now a year since al-Muqtadir had been restored to the throne, and a sad year he had found it. Necessity had forced him to curtail the luxury to which he had been accustomed. At every demonstration of the troops he had feared another insurrection. But it was not in this only that he found his position to have changed for the worse: it was in his relations with

1 A part of the cavalry was called *an-Naṣriyyah*, presumably after Naṣr the Chamberlain, Ḥam. I, 110. Cf. the *Sájí* infantry, called after Ibn Abí's-Sáj.

2 M. I, 202–3; 'A. 148–50; Ḥam. I, 210–11; Ath. (Búláq), VIII, 74.

Mu'nis. Mu'nis, because he had preserved al-Muqtadir's position, if not his life, now expected to be consulted in everything. Even the necessity of gratitude for his services had been humiliating enough to the Caliph, but this supervision was infinitely more so. In these circumstances it was inevitable that Ja'far should cast about for somebody to support him against the general; and it was not long before he perceived that in Yáqút, who had recently arrived from Persia to take up the post of Chamberlain, and in his son Muḥammad, he could command, if he chose to do so, the very allies of whom he felt himself to be so direly in need. This Yáqút had been throughout his reign one of the principal officers at Court—(in the list of modes of address given by Hilál he is bracketed with Názúk);[1] on occasion he had acted as deputy to Mu'nis; and he had been appointed governor of Fárs two years before.[2] Hitherto, however, his sons (for he had two) had taken no prominent part in affairs.

Ja'far gained his first tactical success in securing the appointment of Muḥammad ibn Yáqút to be Chief of Police in place of the two sons of Rá'iq (one of al-Mu'tadhid's freedmen), who had filled the position jointly since the assassination of Názúk, and were Mu'nis's nominees.[3] And having won this advantage, he determined to aim higher: he would dismiss Ibn Muqlah, who was now wholly under the influence of the general, and procure a Vizier subservient to his own interests. Already, shortly after his restoration, Ja'far had wished to promote an-Nayramání, and had even gone so far as once to refuse Ibn Muqlah audience;[4] but Mu'nis appears to have put his foot down, and no more was heard of the scheme. Now, however, the Caliph favoured an aspirant that he considered very much more promising—a certain al-Ḥusayn, a son of

1 H. 154.
2 'A. 133; M. I, 146, 157.
3 'A. 145, 147; M. I, 202.
4 M. I, 185–6.

al-Qásim ibn 'Ubayd Allah. He had been brought to the Caliph's notice by a very ingenious device. He was in league with an impostor, known, on account of his forging prophetical books that he attributed to the Prophet Daniel, as ad-Danyálí. Ad-Danyálí had first won the favour of the Negro Mufliḥ, by proving his descent from a cousin of the Prophet. He had then used Mufliḥ's agency in laying before al-Muqtadir a counterfeit prediction, which stated that all would go well with the Caliphate as soon as the Vizierate was filled by a person in the description of whom certain peculiarities—unusual tallness, pock-marks, a deformity of the upper lip preventing the proper growth of moustaches—precluded its application to any but al-Ḥusayn. Al-Muqtadir was persuaded of the truth of this prophecy. He was determined, from that time forth, to make al-Ḥusayn Vizier.[1]

Towards the middle of *jumádà'l-úlà* (June 930) Mu'nis went on a visit up the Tigris to 'Ukbará; and as soon as he was safely out of the way the Caliph had Ibn Muqlah arrested. He then invited al-Ḥusayn to come to the palace, and promised to install him next day. Unhappily for his schemes, however, Mu'nis was warned of what had happened, and at once hastened back to Baghdád. He was indignant that al-Muqtadir should have deceived him, yet he felt that he could not, for the sake of appearances, protest in person. He therefore confided the mission to 'Alí, whom he instructed to confront the Caliph and insist on the restoration of Ibn Muqlah.

Al-Muqtadir recognised at once that he was not in a position to defy Mu'nis; so he asked 'Alí's advice. 'Alí could only counsel him to placate the general by restoring the Vizier; but this the Caliph considered too frank a humiliation. Let them rather find some compromise: he would be delighted for example if

1 M. I, 215–17; Khald. *Pro.* II, 234–5.

'Alí himself would resume office, or if that were impossible, perhaps he could suggest someone else? 'Alí of course declined the honour for himself, but he thought that his cousin Sulaymán ibn al-Ḥasan might do, or even his brother 'Abd ar-Raḥmán. The Caliph considered: there were two points in favour of Sulaymán: he was own uncle to his favourite al-Ḥusayn;[1] and he disliked Ibn Muqlah almost as heartily as al-Muqtadir himself.

It was therefore decided to appoint Sulaymán; and he was forthwith brought to the palace and invested. But the Caliph made one condition: he stipulated that 'Alí should supervise the *díwáns* himself, and act in general as adviser to the Vizier. 'Alí would thus form as it were a bulwark between the Caliph and Mu'nis. For whereas Mu'nis would not work against 'Alí, at the same time 'Alí was not his tool; moreover 'Alí had this great virtue in the Caliph's eyes: he would make no attempt to usurp an unwarranted authority. On the other hand the arrangement was so far disagreeable to 'Alí that it would inevitably embroil him once more in affairs. Yet it would spare him the title and pomp of the Vizierate, which he particularly abhorred, and to some extent its responsibilities. In any case he consented; and the Caliph was pleased. Al-Muqtadir had had to abandon his cherished plan, it was true. Nevertheless he had certainly improved his position.

The workings of the new *régime* were well exemplified in the treatment of Ibn Muqlah. 'Alí fined him in

1 See Ham. *tak.* fol. 89 a. Al-Ḥusayn's mother, Maryam, was Sulaymán's sister. Later when al-Ḥusayn was raised to the Vizierate, it was said of her that she was the daughter, the wife, the sister, the daughter-in-law, and the mother of a Vizier. She was the daughter of al-Ḥasan ibn Makhlad, the wife of al-Qásim ibn 'Ubayd Allah, the sister of Sulaymán ibn al-Ḥasan, the daughter-in-law of 'Ubayd Allah ibn Sulaymán, and the mother of al-Ḥusayn ibn al-Qásim.

deference to al-Muqtadir's wishes; and at the tribunal before which he was summoned, he even allowed Sulaymán to chide him for having stirred up trouble between the Caliph and his officers. But then in deference to the wishes of Mu'nis, he remitted the fine, and confined the prisoner where his patron had suggested. It was perhaps an undignified rôle for 'Alí to play, but by playing it he at least staved off for a time the inevitable clash.[1]

1 M. I, 203–5; 'A. 150; Ath. (Búláq), VIII, 74; S.J. fol. 96 b.

CHAPTER IX

The Vizierate of Sulaymán. Al-Muqtadir *triumphant.*

It was generally agreed that Sulaymán himself was not especially able. But long ago al-Qásim ibn 'Ubayd Allah had dreamt that he would become Vizier; and so it was felt that sooner or later the dream was bound to come true. Now at last Fate, allied with perseverance, had raised him to this height. And with his eminent cousin to guide him at every turn he easily passed muster.[1]

Nowadays, however, the right conduct of affairs was by no means the straightforward matter it had been when 'Alí was first made Vizier. Rioting in the army had become fatally common. The fate of the *Maṣáffís* might have been expected to deter as an example; but they had been destroyed only with the help of the cavalry, and it was rather this aspect of the affair that the cavalry remembered. 'Alí soon had cause to regret that he was again a public servant, when, hardly a month after Sulaymán's elevation, his house was suddenly surrounded by a band of horsemen. Before help could be summoned they broke into his stables, removed the animals, and made off; whilst the son of his chamberlain Salámah, who attempted to remonstrate with them, was stabbed for his pains and died. About the same time the Negroes that had been spared before began rioting for pay. However, they were promptly driven from the city by archers, and fled to Wásiṭ. There they joined in league with remnants of the Whites; set up a leader; and forced the local governor to give them pay. The insurrection

1 *fakh.* 321–2.

became so threatening that in the end Mu'nis was sent out against them. He sought at first to persuade them into capitulation; but finding them obstinate, surrounded their camp and destroyed them with ease.[1]

After this all was quiet for some months; but about the New Year Sulaymán was twice attacked by cavalry in his house.[2] The first time, when the men marched into his assembly and removed his ink-pot, he jumped into his barge and rowed out into mid-stream; the second time his servants drove the assailants off by flinging brick-bats from the roof. Even in the palace he was not safe: on one occasion some malcontents set fire to the gate, and only desisted from their clamour when they discovered that the Vizier had fled. (He had made his escape through a side entrance, and gone by river to seek refuge with 'Alí.) Ḥamzah of Iṣfahán seeks to give these incidents a portentous meaning by connecting them with certain red lights that were observed at this time in the night sky. But even without this interpretation they were distressing enough. They culminated in *ṣafar* of 319 (February–March 931) in an organised attack on the palace; and it was now that for the first time to their demands for pay the soldiery added a request for the removal of Yáqút and his son from their positions of eminence. The duty of suppressing the disturbances that had occurred must of course have fallen to Muḥammad ibn Yáqút, as Chief of Police. Possibly it was his severe treatment of such offenders as had been caught that had made him unpopular. But this would hardly account for the dislike of his father; and it seems more probable that Mu'nis and his supporters were at the back of the agitation. Muḥammad ibn Yáqút had recently been given the post of *muḥtasib*, or Censor, in addition to his control of

1 'A. 151; M. I, 203; Ath. (Búláq), VIII, 74.

2 It was at the Báb al-Muḥawwal, the extreme limit of the city westward. S.J. fol. 98 b.

the police; and this, as well as augmenting the jealousy of his opponents and arousing their alarm (for the censorship carried with it the command of a considerable body of infantry), gave them a legitimate ground of complaint, in that the duties of the two offices rendered it improper for them to be held by one and the same person, while those of the censorship might be discharged only by a judge or jurist. The rioters made breaches in the palace walls, and again set fire to one of the gates. But on al-Muqtadir's giving them a hearing and promising to attend to their grievances, they dispersed. Two days later, however, they began again; the citizens joined in; the prisons were again opened; and for ten days anarchy reigned. Eventually Ibn Yáqút was reduced to massacring in the markets the offending and the innocent alike; and by these extreme measures order was restored.[1]

In spite of these demonstrations, or perhaps because he thought that he had succeeded in suppressing them, al-Muqtadir took no steps to fulfil his pledge in the matter of dismissing Yáqút and his son. More than two months elapsed without the occurrence of any incident; but at the beginning of *jumádà'l-ákhirah* 319 (June–July 931) the cavalry again revolted; and for almost a fortnight the citizens of Baghdád were subjected to open robbery, and their houses to arson Mu'nis protested to the Caliph that such disorders could not be allowed, and made their continuance a reason for insisting upon the dismissal of Ibn Yáqút from his offices. Al-Muqtadir dared not refuse, but in his heart he was bitterly wrathful. And when a fortnight later Mu'nis, who had been informed that the Chamberlain and his son were now planning his assassination, went on to require that both should be banished from the capital, he gathered courage to oppose him, and even to suggest that if he found their

1 M. 1, 209; 'A. 156–8; Ḥam. 1, 211–13.

company so little to his taste, Mu'nis himself should rather depart.

This was a signal for an open breach: Mu'nis at once proceeded to encamp at ash-Shammásiyyah. He was joined there by many of Ibn Yáqút's men who had demanded their pay in vain, so that his force was swollen to above eleven thousand; moreover presents of money reached him from all sides, and these sums he distributed in his army. On the other side Yáqút attempted to handicap him by decreeing that the armourers should sell to none but the Caliph's supporters; but Mu'nis contrived to defeat this move with counter-threats. At this point al-Muqtadir's momentary courage deserted him, and in an attempt to prevent the situation from worsening, he sent up Abú 'Umar with an impressive gathering of Háshimite nobles to beg the general to return to his house. This step had been decided on in consultation with 'Alí and Sulaymán, and the news of its outcome was anxiously awaited. Members of the delegation reappeared in the afternoon very crest-fallen, telling how Mu'nis indeed had received them courteously by proxy of his secretary, but how, as they were leaving, his men had fallen upon them as they sat in the barge, so that it had almost been sunk. 'Alí then decided to go himself, being sure that Mu'nis would see him, and set out for ash-Shammásiyyah accompanied by Sulaymán, Shafí' al-Muqtadirí, Mufliḥ, and a number of the confidential eunuchs. Great therefore was his dismay when, as they approached the camp, they were stopped by a group of men-at-arms, who beat their horses about the head and spoke menacingly of murdering their riders. They were unable even so much as to approach the general; nor could they discover whether or not he was aware of the way in which they had been received. At sunset they decided that to remain was fruitless and made to depart—only to find that in this too they were to be thwarted: they were prisoners, and resigned themselves to detention for the night.

Al-Muqtadir saw that there was nothing for it but to give in and send his favourites away. However, if they were to leave, it should be in all comfort. A little fleet of eight barges and boats was hastily assembled, into which a guard of forty with money, arms and accoutrements was packed. By sunrise Yáqút and his sons (for his second son, al-Mudhaffar, went with them) were well beyond the limits of the city, on their way to Ctesiphon for the south.

As soon as he was sure of their departure, Mu'nis released his captives and they returned home. He took absolute charge of affairs, and proceeded to replace the exiled officials with nominees of his own. He now divided the office of Chamberlain between Muḥammad and Ibrahím, the two sons of Rá'iq, and restored the censorship to the legal profession. Partisans of the Yáqút family were forbidden to appear at Court, and as if to raze every trace of them from the city, their houses were destroyed by fire.[1]

The rage of the Caliph at this disappointment was vented on the Vizier; and in order to show that he was not yet a cipher, he resolved to dismiss him and appoint in his stead al-Ḥusayn ibn al-Qásim, whom he was all the more eager to promote, as he had been baffled in this purpose before. The joint administration of 'Alí and Sulaymán had had small chance of success. As far as finance was concerned—the department in which 'Alí had always shone—the sales of royal property had still occupied most of their attention; but these had proved totally inadequate to meet the drain on the otherwise ill-furnished Treasury, and they were by this time again in such straits for money, that a number of aspirants to the Vizierate had been encouraged to make offers of supplying the needed funds, in exchange

1 'A. 157, 159–60; M. I, 209–11; Ath. (Búláq), VIII, 76.

for their elevation to office. The condition on which a sound rehabilitation of the finances depended—the better organisation of the territory under the Caliph's rule (itself now considerably reduced)—continual invasions and rebellions had rendered unattainable.

Peaceful intervention could effect little in these days, although 'Alí did what he could when the chance offered. When, for instance, a dispute arose between rival sections of the population in al-Baṣrah, he composed an exhortation, Against Sectarianism, which was a model, not only of diplomacy, but of art. For if its sense impressed the Baṣrans, its literary merit delighted aṣ-Ṣúlí. He compared it in terms of admiration with other productions of the kind.[1]

With al-Muqtadir 'Alí got on no better than usual. Once at least he irritated him by his lack of foresight. The Caliph was supposed never to ask for advice in public: his ministers had always to prime him beforehand with all the information on which he might be called to draw. But on this occasion the conversation took an unexpected turn, so that the Caliph was embarrassed; and it was only when 'Alí assured him that his interlocutor was a person of discretion that he was in any way mollified.[2]

Sulaymán was even unluckier in his dealings with the Caliph. Nothing would accustom him to the solemnities of Court conversation; he had an inveterate passion for punning and the fabrication of proverbs. He was also fond of recalling the misdeeds of the Banú'l-Furát—a subject that was particularly distasteful to Ja'far. The Caliph only silenced him by quoting a couplet that warned him "either to cease blaming them or else to fill their place".[3] It was largely his lack of tact and good manners that decided al-Muqtadir in the end to dismiss him. Sulaymán was arrested on

1 'A. 152–3. 2 Tan. *nish.* 138–9.
3 H. 65.

Friday, 24th *rajab* 319 (13th August 931), and confined in his house.[1]

Al-Muqtadir hoped to ensure the appointment of al-Ḥusayn ibn al-Qásim by arresting at the same time 'Ubayd Allah al-Kalwádhí, who had continued to direct the *díwán as-sawád*, and whom he feared as a possible rival to his favourite. As it proved, his fears were well founded, but his precautions were unavailing; for Mu'nis insisted on al-Kalwádhí's release, and his immediate promotion to the Vizierate.

It was decided that 'Alí should continue as general supervisor; but in addition to this, instead of sharing it as he had done with Sulaymán, he was again given independent jurisdiction in the Court of Appeal. The *díwán as-sawád* was also removed from the control of the new Vizier, and with it certain anomalous but valuable sources of income; moreover various debtors, from whom dues to the State might have been exacted, were protected from prosecution by Mu'nis; with the result that al-Kalwádhí soon found himself in a position no better, if not actually worse, than that which had embarrassed Sulaymán.[2] He calculated the total expenses for which he required funds at 700,000 *dínárs*, and came to al-Muqtadir for help. The Caliph was, of course, indignant enough at the demand; but when al-Ḥusayn came forward with a provocative offer not only to supply this amount but to pay an extra million into the Privy Purse, he was beside himself with fury at his impotence. On the other hand, al-Kalwádhí was by no means dismayed at the suggestion, and expressed himself perfectly ready to resign: al-Ḥusayn evidently had sources at his command from which he himself was debarred. But al-Muqtadir knew that while Mu'nis objected he could do nothing. The only course was to win him over. And so, in the face of all that had passed

1 'A. 161.
2 M. I, 211–13; Ath. (Búláq), VIII, 76–7.

between them, al-Ḥusayn set out to conquer the general.

In the course of his machinations (for he had long intrigued with all and sundry) al-Ḥusayn had taken great pains to secure the support of the Christian clerks. He would tell them how his grandfather used always to wear a cross beneath his robes; and how his ancestors, further back, had been Christians themselves. The clerks had been won over, but unhappily these blandishments had had also a reflex effect. Al-Ḥusayn had come to be suspected of heterodoxy, and this was now a serious obstacle to his advancement. However, the combination of charm and bribery seems to have been too strong even for so stout a bigot as Mu'nis's chamberlain Yalbaq—and to have won Yalbaq was to have won Mu'nis himself. Mu'nis supposed that he had misjudged al-Ḥusayn ibn al-Qásim. He informed the Caliph that he no longer saw any objection to his being promoted to the Vizierate.[1]

The unfortunate al-Kalwádhí was now anxious, as he had before been willing, to resign his office. Troubles had crowded upon him. The Carmathians had once again made a descent on al-Kúfah; the fugitives as usual had caused a panic in the capital; the markets had been closed for a week; and food had been almost unprocurable.[2] He himself had been attacked in the palace by a party of indignant horsemen, and when he fled in his barge was stoned by no less truculent foot. He could not pay them, for no revenue arrived from the provinces. His hands were tied: he was powerless. He shut himself up in his house swearing never again to be tempted into taking office. His resignation was accepted on 30th *ramaḍhán* 319 (17th October 931), and a squad of police was sent to protect his house.[3]

1 M. 1, 217–18; 'A. 164. 2 'A. 162; Ḥam. 1, 213.

3 'A. 164; *fakh.* 322; M. 1, 219 gives date of al-Kalwádhí's dismissal as two days earlier.

It is remarkable enough that Mu'nis should, after all, have capitulated so tamely. But what is even stranger is that he should have agreed also to the removal of one of the most powerful checks on the conduct of the Vizier—the supervision of 'Alí ibn 'Ísà. And al-Ḥusayn not only carried this stipulation, he insisted at the same time that 'Alí should relinquish his position as President of the Court of Appeal. So much he allowed to appear before his advancement; but once he was established, it became evident that even this would not satisfy him. 'Alí visited him on the night of his investiture, when he was receiving the congratulations of the Court; and whether or not he then caught an impression of the malignity with which al-Ḥusayn regarded him, he had not long to wait before being fully enlightened. Al-Ḥusayn, it appears, could not endure so serious a threat to his independence as was constituted by 'Alí's presence: he had urged al-Muqtadir to banish him to Syria or Egypt with 'Abd ar-Raḥmán. Mu'nis had intervened to prevent this; but all even his influence could do had been to procure a mitigation of the sentence of exile. It had been decided instead to send 'Alí to Dayr Qunnà, where he could live in retirement on his estate.[1]

The commotion in the house at the Garden Gate can well be imagined. This thunderbolt had fallen into what all had supposed a settled life. 'Alí's four and seventy years could ill brook such an upheaval: he had thought for peace in his declining age; but now all his cherished habits must be disturbed.

However, there was nothing to be done but obey the Caliph's command. He must remember for comfort the motto on his signet: "God has a hidden purpose in every fearful thing."[2] Though all seemed calm on his

1 M. I, 219, 220–1.

2 Ṣaf. (B.M. Or. 6587) fol. 133 a; Ḍháf. fol. 141 a; Yáq. *ud.* V, 280.

departure, storm was in the air: perhaps it was God's hidden purpose that he should be absent when it broke. He left the city on 22nd *shawwál* (7th November 931), travelling by river to aṣ-Ṣáfiyah.[1]

1 'A. 165; M. I, 221.

END OF PART THREE

Part Four

CHAPTER I

The conversion of Daylam *and its first results. The final estrangement of* Mu'nis. *A new champion for* 'Alí ibn 'Ísà.

It will be remembered that when, in 315, 'Alí was summoned from Syria to resume the Vizierate, he discovered that al-Khaṣíbí had ordered Ibn Abí's-Sáj from his station in Aẕarbayján to march southwards and fight the Carmathians; that 'Alí had for various reasons considered this a mistaken policy; and that he had done his best to reverse it. He had failed; and the policy had proved itself as mistaken as he had predicted, inasmuch as the army of Ibn Abí's-Sáj had been defeated by the Carmathians at the first encounter. But the move had had another consequence, which 'Alí had not foreseen, and which in the end was to prove far more disastrous to the Caliphate. Ibn Abí's-Sáj had solemnly warned al-Muqtadir of what would happen, when he had first received orders from al-Khaṣíbí; but the warning had been disregarded at Baghdád, because it was thought to have been prompted by self-seeking. Ibn Abí's-Sáj had written as follows: "I am on a frontier greater than the frontier against the Greeks, and opposite a barrier stronger than the barrier of Gog and Magog.[1] If I abandon it, there shall come out from it a thing more grievous than the Carmathian thing. Peradventure it shall cause the destruction of the empire in every region."

1 Allusion to *qur'án*, XVIII, 93–7: "They said, 'O Dhú'l-Qarnayn! Verily Gog and Magog (Yájúj and Májúj) do evil in the land. Shall we then pay thee tribute, so thou set a barrier betwixt us and them?'...And they could neither scale it nor dig through it."

The Greeks had always threatened in Asia Minor; year by year expeditions had gone out against them, and the fortunes of war were by no means always with the Muslims. The Carmathians had slain their thousands and loomed large in the south, whence they spread terror throughout the land. What enemy comparable to these had Ibn Abí's-Sáj to oppose? None, they said, but the wild Daylamites, "husbandmen". At Baghdád, in 314 (926–7), the Daylamites were looked upon with the scorn of ignorance; but Ibn Abí's-Sáj had lived for years in the neighbourhood of their country, and observed with anxiety the effect on the tribes of their recent conversion to Islam.[1]

Up to just before the beginning of the third century the inhabitants of Gílán and Daylam (the provinces to the south-west of the Caspian Sea) had remained either heathen or Zoroastrian. But then many of them had been converted by an Imám of the Zaydite branch of the Shí'ah, al-Ḥasan ibn 'Alí, known as *al-uṭrúsh* (The Deaf), who had sought an asylum among them after failing in 290 (902–3) to seize Ṭabaristán from the Sámánids. More than thirty years again before this another Zaydite pretender had actually conquered the province,[2] and though he, and after him his brother, had held it precariously by fighting continually with their neighbours, the brother had finally been driven out soon after the accession of al-Mu'tadhid. In spite of this first defeat, feeling for the Shí'ah remained very strong among the people in Ṭabaristán. When, for example, aṭ-Ṭabarí went home about 290, he so provoked their resentment by defending the "Orthodox" Caliphs that he had to flee for his life.[3]—Al-Uṭrúsh aimed at restoring the Zaydite rule in Ṭabaristán: by converting the Daylamites, he hoped to enlist

1 Tan. *nish.* 156.
2 This is the rebellion referred to in the Introduction.
3 Yáq. *ud.* VI, 456.

them to fight in his cause. By the year 300 (912–13) he was ready, and as the Sámánids were now engaged in Sístán with the Ṣaffárids, and on their eastern borders with the heathen Turks, he judged the moment to be propitious for his enterprise. He was victorious and entered Ámul, the capital, in *jumádà'l-úlà* 301 (December 913–January 914)—just after 'Alí ibn 'Ísà first became Vizier. In the next year the 'Abbásid governor of Ray tried to dislodge him; but al-Uṭrúsh won again, and for the rest of his life continued to rule the province.[1]

The conversion of the Daylamites made them free of Islam; the new enthusiasm of the Faith stirred their wild spirits and urged them to adventure. In fighting to found and maintain al-Uṭrúsh's principality, they had come in contact with both Sámánid and 'Abbásid troops as enemies; and in the intricate civil wars that followed his death, they were sometimes called upon by the several pretenders to his succession, in whose armies they fought, to welcome them as allies. In this manner, though the Daylamites remained devoted Shí'ites, leaders of all parties came to depend on the support of such tribesmen as by their ability in war had won their way to command; and by the year in which Ibn Abí's-Sáj received the order he was so loath to carry out, several such commanders had risen to an eminence that rendered them hardly, if at all, inferior either to the Zaydite leaders themselves or to the generals of Baghdád and Bukhárá. Of these were Mákán ibn Kákúy[2] and Asfár ibn Shíravayh, both of whom, by fighting now on one side now on another, had made themselves practically independent. The internecine rivalries with which Ṭabaristán had now been for years distracted had, in the first place, been

1 Ṭab. III, 2292; Mas. *murúj*, IX, 4 *et seqq.*; Isfan. 195–201; Ath. (Búláq), VIII, 24, 28, 29, 30; 'A. 43, 47; M. I, 36.

2 This appears to be the correct spelling of this name. See Browne's trans. of the *Chahár Maqála*, p. 16. M. has Kákí, and Ath. (Búláq), Kálí.

provoked by the dying testament of al-Uṭrúsh—he died in 304 (917)—in which he preferred as successor over his own sons his son-in-law al-Ḥasan ibn al-Qásim, known as *ad-dá'i ilá'l-ḥaqq* (Summoner to the Truth). The slighted heirs had not been content to obey this behest, and with varying fortunes had opposed the Dá'í and quarrelled among themselves. Both Mákán and Asfár had originally been among the adversaries of the Dá'í; but at the time of which I am writing the murder of his brother by one of al-Uṭrúsh's grandsons, had thrown Mákán on the Dá'í's side. After a succession of reverses they had set themselves up together in Ámul, and had but just driven out Asfár from the subsidiary town of Sárí, where he had proclaimed himself king.[1]

On the departure from Aẕarbayján of Ibn Abí's-Sáj at the invitation of the Caliph, the Sámánids, after making a fruitless attempt to subdue Ṭabaristán, had occupied Ray, and left there a governor. The latter remained there for two years; but towards the end of 316 (beginning of 929), feeling that he was about to die, he evacuated the town and departed for Khurásán, sending at the same time an invitation to Mákán and the Dá'í to replace him. Mákán and the Dá'í accordingly came south and took possession; but by doing so they brought down on themselves a double attack. For their absence from Ṭabaristán tempted Asfár again to try his fortune against them, while their occupation of Ray provoked the Caliph's advisers into sending a force to vindicate his authority. Asfár, being the nearer, struck first, and was so entirely successful in his campaign, that when the force from Baghdád arrived on the scene, he was in possession of the disputed city, and master of Ṭabaristán. The Dá'í had been killed defending Ámul; Mákán had been driven out of Ray with ease, and was now treating for peace.

1 Isfan. 204–13.

The Caliph's army was under the command of Hárún ibn Gharíb, for whom this employment had been found after the deposition of al-Muqtadir, when his enemies had insisted on his banishment from the capital. But even so experienced an officer was no match for the wily Daylamite. He was utterly routed, and was pursued by the victor to the very borders of al-'Iráq. Asfár returned to Ray, and proceeded to extend his power into the surrounding province.

His triumph, however, was short-lived. He was no ruler; and before long the manner in which he oppressed his new subjects, but especially the people of Qazvín, aroused a general dissatisfaction. An ambitious follower, who had distinguished himself in the recent wars, by name Mardávíj ibn Ziyár, soon led a revolt; and working in conjunction with Mákán, expelled Asfár from Ray, pursued him to Ṭáliqán, defeated and killed him. The allies then divided the territory held by Asfár between them, Mákán taking Ṭabaristán and Gurgán, Mardávíj Ray and the northern Jibál. For a time they continued in amity; but so unstable a relation could not endure. Eventually Mardávíj made an attack on Mákán, and after many ups and downs drove him from Ṭabaristán. This victory was all the more signal in that Mákán had engaged the support of the Sámánids, so that in defeating one Mardávíj in fact defeated both. With his capital at Ray Mardávíj was now master of northern Persia, proved in war against his eastern neighbours, and ready to extend his dominion west and south. Such an extension was indeed imperative: for his success and profusion had attracted numbers of fresh tribesmen to his army, and in order to furnish money for their pay he must have the revenue of wide territories at his disposal. One of the earliest of the expeditions that the conquest of such territories required was sent against the ancient and important city of Hamadán. The Caliph's general, however, drove it off, and in the battle a nephew of Mardávíj was slain. This accident so enraged the potentate that he vowed to come against the place in person. At his approach the 'Abbásid forces abandoned the city; but the people declined to submit without a siege. Fierce fighting took place before the city gave in; but it could not hold out against the impetuous Daylamites, and on its capitulation it was sacked.[1]

The indifference that the Caliph and his advisers had displayed to the warning of Ibn Abí's-Sáj had hardly been dissipated by the first movements of the Daylamites. But the significance of their activity was better understood in Persia. One day, in 316 (928), after Mákán ibn Kákúy had taken the city of Qum, 'Alí's Mu'tazilite friend, Muḥammad ibn Baḥr, was visiting his brother in their native Iṣfahán. He found him reading certain very famous verses that had been addressed to the last 'Umayyad Caliph by his governor of Khurásán, warning him of an upheaval impending.[2] Muḥammad at once wrote below them new verses of his own. The 'Abbásids were as heedless now as the 'Umayyads had been then, he wrote, of "the fire that is kindling in every valley".[3]

But when news reached Baghdád of the westward advance of Mardávíj, al-Muqtadir at last was really

1 M. I, 149, 161–2; Isfan. 214–16; Ath. (Búláq), VIII, 56, 64–7, 77; 'A. 137, 154; Khald. IV, 340–1; Tan. *nish.* 156.

2 "I see amidst the embers the glow of fire, and it wants but little to burst into a blaze,
And if the wise ones of the people quench it not, its fuel will be corpses and skulls.
Verily fire is kindled by two sticks, and verily words are the beginning of warfare.
And I cry in amazement, 'Would that I knew whether the House of Umayya were awake or asleep!'"
(Translated by E. G. Browne: *Literary History*, I, 241.)

Compare with these verses others composed at the time of the Zinj rebellion. See S.J. (B.M. Or. 4618), fol. 252 a.

3 Yáq. *ud.* VI, 421–2.

frightened. He therefore commissioned Hárún to advance again into Persia. Hárún's army was considerably strengthened with reinforcements, so that he met Mardávíj in the neighbourhood of the plundered city hopeful of success. But fortune was again with the Daylamites and Hárún was defeated. He did not however despair, but applied to the Caliph for money with which to pay his men and engage others; and it was only when he was outwitted by a treacherous Persian, who had formerly deserted to him from the army of Asfár, that he abandoned as hopeless the attempt to check the onward progress of Mardávíj. He made his way from the mountains down the Diyálá to the Tigris, and encamped with his retainers in the neighbourhood of aṣ-Ṣáfiyah. It thus came about that he was at hand to be of assistance to 'Alí at a moment when that assistance was very badly required. But in order to understand how even in exile 'Alí was not safe from the malice of the new Vizier, we must return to the capital and follow the course of events from the time of his departure.[1]

Mu'nis had all too soon cause to lament his weakness in allowing himself to be persuaded over the appointment of al-Ḥusayn ibn al-Qásim to the Vizierate. From the beginning al-Ḥusayn flaunted his new-won dignity, and would appear for Friday Prayer gorgeously dressed, and girt with a jewel-encrusted sword, to the admiration of the crowd. With his elevation the accession of power to the faction of the Caliph was so marked that time-servers such as Muḥammad ibn Rá'iq and his brother Ibrahím were very easily persuaded to change sides. The intimacy of the Chamberlainship had given the brothers great influence with al-Muqtadir, and despite the fact that they owed their advancement entirely to Mu'nis's good graces, it was enough for

1 Ath. (Búláq), VIII, 77; M. I, 213, 221–2; Ḥam. I, 213.

them to be told that he was contemplating their dismissal and the appointment of Yalbaq in their stead, to convert the attitude of subservience to the general that they had hitherto maintained to one of unashamed hostility. They threw themselves with zest into the intrigue that al-Ḥusayn was preparing against Mu'nis; began corresponding with all his most notorious enemies, such as Yáqút and Hárún; and stirred up the ever-dissatisfied infantry to agitate for the dismissal from their command of Yalbaq, who was deputising for Mu'nis while the latter was sick of the gout. Al-Ḥusayn, while plotting against the general, was aware that his designs were known to him; and went in such terror of retaliation that he took to sleeping nightly in a different place so that his capture might not be prepared. Mu'nis complained of his hostility to the Caliph, and obtained a promise that al-Ḥusayn should be dismissed; but he overreached himself in demanding as well his banishment to 'Umán, for to this al-Muqtadir declined to accede. This opposition, added to the dismissal of Yalbaq, which was carried, warned him that his ascendancy was in peril; so he decided early in the New Year once more to exert the threat of force and encamp at ash-Shammásiyyah. At his command the house of the Vizier was set on fire; but this, instead of cowing his adversaries as he had hoped, only encouraged al-Muqtadir to set a guard about the palace and declare his defiance. Mu'nis then discovered that the Vizier had won the support of the infantry by making up their arrears of pay. Consequently he could not be sure of success in a resort to arms. Finally, a messenger that he sent with conciliatory overtures to the palace was beaten and detained. He therefore determined to leave the city, and proceeded with his supporters up-stream to al-Baradán.[1]

1 'A. 165–7; M. 1, 221–2; Ḥam. 1, 214.

The departure of Mu'nis was a real triumph for al-Ḥusayn. He and al-Muqtadir rejoiced over it together. New honours were pressed on the Vizier: he was created *'amíd ad-dawlah* (Support of the Dynasty); his title was stamped with that of the Caliph on the coinage; he was officially addressed by al-Muqtadir as an intimate; he was made a Boon-Companion.[1] Moreover, he was now free to attack those whom Mu'nis had hitherto protected, and proceeded to wreak his pent-up wrath on 'Alí and Ibn Muqlah. Ibn Muqlah was still in confinement at Baghdád. It was therefore a simple matter to mulct him of 20,000 *dínárs*. Nor should there have been any difficulty in subjecting 'Alí to a similar process; but that when the Vizier's messenger arrived at aṣ-Ṣáfiyah to fetch him, he found Hárún in the neighbourhood. There seems to have been no particular reason why Hárún should have taken 'Alí's part. During 'Alí's last Vizierate they had actually come in conflict over an accusation that Hárún had lodged against his secretary, which 'Alí proved to be groundless.[2] In the interval they can have had few chances of meeting: up to the time of al-Muqtadir's deposition 'Alí had been in prison; whilst ever since Hárún had been absent from Baghdád on his unfortunate campaigns in Persia. Possibly Hárún already hoped to dominate the Caliph himself, and took this opportunity of thwarting a design of the Vizier's, with the object of lessening his influence. But for whatever cause, he now constituted himself 'Alí's protector. He assured him that he might safely remain at Dayr Qunnà; and promised to speak on his behalf to the Caliph, as soon as he should arrive in the capital.[3]

1 'A. 165; M. I, 223. It will be remembered that the first of these titles, *walí ad-dawlah*, had been given to his father, al-Qásim. See above, p. 59.

2 M. I, 163–5.

3 M. I, 225.

CHAPTER II

The end of al-Muqtadir.

When Mu'nis left Baghdád in *al-muḥarram* of 320 (January–February 932), it seemed as if the end for which al-Muqtadir had been working ever since his deposition, that is, for as much as three years, had at last been attained: he was at last free of the general's dominance, which he had found so galling; the Vizierate was at last filled by the favourite for whom he had sustained so many rebuffs. Yet hardly four months were to pass before that favourite was to be disgraced and arrested, hardly ten before the Caliph himself was to lose his life at the hands of the general's supporters.

It was over the finances that, as so many of his predecessors had done, al-Ḥusayn ibn al-Qásim came to grief. After their initial payment the troops soon discovered that there was little more to be expected. They accordingly plagued the Vizier for money and rioted; the very servants of the palace insulted him; and the Caliph, who shared in his unpopularity, soon found that his enthusiasm for the new minister was on the wane. Al-Muqtadir was therefore prepared to listen when al-Ḥusayn was charged with wanton extravagance, if not venality, in defining the terms of a contract; and later, when his attention was drawn to the fact that the Vizier was pledging the income of the following year to meet the expenses of this, he went so far as to allow the appointment of al-Khaṣíbí to the control of the *díwáns*. The fall of al-Ḥusayn was finally brought about by the discovery that his budget was balanced only by the inclusion in his calculations of revenue that was no longer recoverable. He was arrested in *rabí' al-ákhir* (April–May 932); and al-Fadḥl ibn Ja'far (the nephew of Ibn al-Furát), who had been largely instrumental in showing him up, was made Vizier in his place.[1]

But, as well as to his native incapacity, al-Ḥusayn had owed his fall in great measure to the hostility of Hárún. From the moment of the latter's return, the Vizier had lost ground with the Caliph. One of Hárún's first concerns had been to plead 'Alí's cause with al-Muqtadir, and he had had no difficulty in obtaining a reversal of al-Ḥusayn's command. An even shrewder blow to the ascendancy of the Vizier had been marked when Hárún persuaded the Caliph to remit half the fine he had imposed on Ibn Muqlah; and from then until his disgrace, Hárún had approved and seconded every criticism directed against him. Nor did his ambition stop there. For when al-Muqtadir had suggested restoring Ibn Muqlah to office, Hárún had prevented it on account of his attachment to Mu'nis, and had had him sent, by way of precaution, to Shíráz. On the other hand, it was through his influence that al-Faḍhl had been appointed. Hárún was now in fact all-powerful; and as his interests, on account of their relationship, were bound up with those of the Caliph, the latter for a time deferred to him in every case.[2]

At the time of his departure from Baghdád, the power of Mu'nis had seemed on the decline; but in the meantime, by a combination of good fortune with good generalship, he had succeeded to a great extent in rehabilitating himself. He had soon left al-Baradán, and continued his journey up the Tigris, stopping at Sámarrá, to Takrít. But on the way he learned that the Vizier had instructed the governors of those provinces through which he might be expected to pass, to oppose and, if possible, arrest him. Moreover, many of his followers, with or without his permission, had by this time deserted him. His next move, therefore,

1 'A. 173; M. I, 226–8. 2 M. I, 225, 228, 229.

required a nice consideration. Owing to his long attachment to the Ḥamdánids, Mu'nis decided to seek an asylum with them; but to his amazement he learnt that, far from preparing to welcome him, they were arming against him, anxious, by defeating an enemy of the Caliph, to atone for former rebellions, and especially the last indiscretion of Abú'l-Hayjá'. Nevertheless, he was urged by Yalbaq to continue on his way to Mosul, partly because to seem to shrink from meeting them would injure his prestige, and partly because of all adversaries they were the least formidable. The Ḥamdánids, on their side, did their best to persuade him to go elsewhere, but their prevarication only determined him the more firmly to attack them. His advance guard drove their outposts from the pass giving access to the city, and next day the armies met. Though their force was larger than his own, Mu'nis had skill enough to defeat them. The tribesmen that made up their army dispersed into the hills; Mu'nis's men looted their camp; and on 4th *ṣafar* 320 (15th February 932) he entered Mosul and took possession.

With this success, the tide of desertion, which in Mu'nis's decline had flowed from him to the Caliph, now began to flow back. He was soon joined by a number of those that had left him in his adversity; and from this time, through the following spring and summer, his strength steadily grew. A party of Ḥamdánids rallied under al-Ḥusayn, the son of Abú'l-Hayjá'; but Yalbaq, who was sent out against them, scattered them with ease, and before long their leader made overtures of peace and came in to Mosul. Then, when a Greek army was discovered to be descending on Malatia, Mu'nis persuaded its renegade commander to come over and join him. A detachment arrived from Aleppo; then another from Erzinjan; more and more troops deserted from the Caliph; and the capture of a Government caravan yielded a very opportune treasure, with which Mu'nis satisfied the mercenaries that had already joined him, and encouraged others to follow their example.[1]

At Baghdád, meanwhile, al-Fadhl had been finding his task by no means an easy one. In Persia the aggression of Mardávíj, and on the Mesopotamian border the Greek raids, continued unchecked. Twice already the agitations of fugitives from these parts had resulted in riots: once the Vizier was assaulted in his house, and a second time his house was looted, whilst he himself only escaped rough handling by leaping into his barge and rowing away. Then from one side Mu'nis, and from the other the Carmathians, prevented supplies of food from reaching the capital; and the resultant famine had led to a disastrous outbreak of plague.[2] The Caliph was openly censured for neglecting the interests of his subjects; in so far his authority was repudiated; yet neither he nor Hárún seems to have exerted himself to improve the position. It seems that they were rather engaged in private intrigues, and that only al-Fadhl maintained a detached outlook. At any rate he alone appreciated the fact that Mu'nis was now again to be reckoned with. He therefore invited him to return to the capital, hoping thus to convert one who would be a dangerous enemy into a useful ally. Mu'nis received his overtures with alacrity; and as soon as the cooler days of autumn allowed of easy travel, he set out for Baghdád. It now appeared, however, that al-Fadhl had made this advance on his own authority, for as soon as the Caliph was informed of Mu'nis's approach, he sent out a force to oppose it. Nevertheless, as if by a strange compromise, the force in question, though it appeared to be barring his way, never, in fact, contested Mu'nis's advance, but retreated

1 'A. 168–72; M. I, 223, 233–4.

2 Ḥam. I, 214, 215; 'A. 173–4; Dh. *t.* ff. 74 b, 75 a; Tagh. II, 242, 243, 246.

before him to the very gates of Baghdád, till the two armies were encamped opposite one another at ash-Shammásiyyah.

Opinion at Court was, indeed, divided over the return of Mu'nis. Despite his former rivalry with the general, Hárún, because he feared the outcome of a conflict, supported the Vizier in his policy of reconciliation. But Muḥammad ibn Yáqút, who had returned in Mu'nis's absence, and the two sons of Rá'iq, obstinate in their ingratitude, were resolutely opposed to it, and continually urged the Caliph to fight. The miserable Ja'far wavered between these warring counsels, and was followed in his vacillations by the obsequious Mufliḥ. His inclination was to defy the general; yet, as Hárún pointed out, the troops were utterly unreliable, and unless he fulfilled a promise he had made of paying them, would probably mutiny. On the other hand, so Ibn Yáqút would argue, if only he did pay them, Mu'nis's men would desert in a body. Al-Muqtadir would very willingly have paid them; but he had no money, and the Lady, to whom he appealed, swore that she had spent all but her last *dirham* in defending the city against the Carmathians. At one time the Caliph despaired, and was for retiring to Wásiṭ and rallying his loyal subjects in the south. Then, when Mu'nis wrote suggesting that it would be to their mutual advantage to compose their differences, he was momentarily convinced that this was the best course. But in the end inclination triumphed; and though not without misgivings, he gave the word for war.

Next morning, 26th *shawwál* 320 (30th October 932), he said his prayers in the Hall of Public Audience, and afterwards took leave of his mother. He then set out in solemn state for the Shammásiyyah parade ground, where the defending army was drawn up. Al-Muqtadir was wrapped in the Prophet's Cloak and carried his

Sword; the black banner of the 'Abbásids was borne before him, and as he rode, Readers intoned verses from the *qur'án*, copies of which were exposed aloft on spears. In their awe at such a spectacle the people forgot their grievances, and as the procession wound through the crowded streets, blessings were called down upon his enterprise.

When the Caliph reached the parade ground he found that the fighting had already begun. So he retired to an eminence, from which he could observe its course. His men were heartened to the attack with the promise of rewards for killing and taking captive; and to begin with the battle went in the Caliph's favour. But as the day wore on, a message came imploring him to encourage his soldiers with his presence. He therefore left his safe vantage-point and proceeded to the field. He came up, however, to find them already routed. Yalbaq had turned the flank of his army and made an attack from the rear. Many of those who were with al-Muqtadir now fled for their lives. The Vizier, who had hitherto accompanied him, made for the river and safety. Al-Muqtadir was left alone with a few men-at-arms; but he did not lose heart, and urged them to fight on, invoking God's blessing, and brandishing a *qur'án*. As he was thus exhorting them, a cavalcade rode past, headed by 'Alí, the son of Yalbaq. Seeing the Caliph, he dismounted and kissed his hands. But before he could prevent it, one of his Berber horsemen rode out and struck al-Muqtadir with his scimitar upon the shoulder, so that his harness was cut through and gave way. Others followed suit; the Cloak was torn from his back, the Sword and Signet from his hands. "Beware!" he cried, "I am the Caliph!" "It is you we seek!" answered one grimly. The whole troop then surrounded him: another blow cleft his forehead; a third, which he made to ward off with his hand, severed his left thumb. As he fell to the ground, one of the men stabbed him in the throat; a minute later his head was raised upon a spear; and the triumphant Berbers galloped off with their trophy to assure Mu'nis of his victory.

As night drew in over the plain, a man with a load of thorns drove his donkey across the field of battle, and saw lying among the killed a headless body stripped of every garment. In pity for its nakedness, and that it might not be devoured by jackals or birds of prey, he threw over it some of the thorns he had gathered, and went on into the hospitable city to tell of what he had seen.

Such was the miserable end of al-Muqtadir. But the people afterwards remembered the Caliph, and forgot the man. On the place where he lay that night under his shroud of thorns they set up a shrine, whither for many a day pious citizens would come out as on a pilgrimage, and say their prayers.[1]

1 'A. 174–80, 184; M. I, 234–7; *fakh.* 311; Jaw. fol. 169 a–b; Dh. *t.* fol. 75 b; Mas. *murúj*, VIII, 274; Mas. *tan.* 378.

CHAPTER III

The accession of al-Qáhir. *The last of the* Lady. *The fate of* Mu'nis.

The tidings and the dreadful gift with which the savage Berbers had thought so to delight Mu'nis, filled him with horror. He had a presentiment that they too, who had had a part in opposing al-Muqtadir, should come, all of them, to a violent end.[1] Before, when al-Muqtadir had been deposed a second time, Mu'nis had seen that however much they might quarrel, his own power was bound up inseparably with the Caliph's; and so he had seen to it that the plot failed.[2] But now what he had dreaded then had come to pass.

Meanwhile, however, he was master of the situation; for, as the fight went against them, al-Muqtadir's supporters had fled from the city. It was his duty both to preserve order in the capital, and to apply himself to the choice of a new Caliph. He accordingly sent down Yalbaq and his son to guard the palace, and summoned the Doorkeeper of the House of Ṭáhir to tell over the princes in his charge. Mu'nis was truly solicitous to advance one that by his character and in his circumstances would be worthy of his high position, and beneficent to his subjects. He himself favoured the succession of al-Muqtadir's son Abú'l-'Abbás; for to a general good sense and piety he added an attachment to Mu'nis himself that could not but make for stability. Yet Mu'nis was not seeking his own interest; and when it was observed that to promote this prince would in fact be to perpetuate the existing *régime*, he

1 M. I, 241; 'A. 180; Jaw. fol. 168b.
2 Dh. *t.* fol. 74a; Tagh. II, 240.

yielded to argument and turned his choice elsewhere. What his advisers were above all desirous of avoiding was a government in which women should meddle. They had suffered too long the interference of the Lady, and suspected that a grandmother would be fully as apt to intervene as a mother, if indeed she were not even more so. In the end two candidates came to interview Mu'nis: Muḥammad, a son of al-Muktafí, and the unlucky ex-Caliph, al-Qáhir. On the way up the river, however, al-Qáhir contrived to secure from his nephew a promise to defer to him; so that actually there was no choice to be made. And in any case the younger prince was not as free as he might have been of female relatives. In short, al-Qáhir re-ascended the throne, being now thirty-five years of age.[1]

Mu'nis nevertheless had misgivings over the decision; for al-Qáhir had, to begin with, the great disadvantage of being extremely poor. Not only was he unable, through sheer need, to agree to Mu'nis's conditions about the gratuity that by established custom was distributed at an accession among the troops, but his clothes were so shabby that he had to borrow a garment from one of the officers in which to receive the homage of his electors.[2] And in addition to this, al-Qáhir had certain characteristics that would assuredly have caused Mu'nis, had he fully recognised them, to think twice before promoting him. In almost every respect, except perhaps a propensity for drinking, he was the opposite of al-Muqtadir: for where his brother had been generous to a fault, he was no less avaricious; where al-Muqtadir had been malleable, al-Qáhir was determined; he was vindictive, he was cruel, and he was false.[3] He now found an

1 M. I, 237, 241–2; 'A. 180–1, 182; Ath. (Búláq), VIII, 83; Fid. II, 76.

2 'A. 182.

3 Mas. *murúj*, VIII, 287–8; *fakh.* 323; 'A. 183; Mas. *tan.* 388; S.J. fol. 106 b; Dh. *t.* fol. 135 b.

exquisite pleasure in assembling al-Muqtadir's children and alarming them with threats, and sometimes with demonstrations, of violence. In his desire for money he forgot the many benefits he had received from the Lady,[1] and tortured her so mercilessly in his efforts to extract her riches, that she survived her sufferings only a few weeks.[2]

Our last sight of the Lady is a pathetic one. The death of her son and the frenzy of anguish into which it had thrown her had combined with the disease from which she was already suffering to waste her away. Then had come the inhuman treatment to which al-Qáhir subjected her. She had yielded all she possessed; now she was to appoint an agent for the sale of her effects. Two notaries were sent to witness the transaction; and the procedure required that they should see her. As they made the request, they heard the sound of weeping from behind a curtained archway. The curtain was lifted, and they beheld an aged woman, thin and worn with illness and suffering. "Are you Shaghab," asked the notaries, "the *umm walad* of al-Mu'tadhid and the mother of al-Muqtadir?" She wept for a space at the remembrance of her glory; then she said, "Yes." The curtain fell, and the notaries went away very thoughtful and sad, pondering "the revolutions of time, and the course of events".[3]

Having set up a Caliph, Mu'nis had next to choose a Vizier. As so often in the past, he suggested 'Alí, describing to al-Qáhir in affectionate terms "his integrity, his probity, his orthodoxy and his piety". Yalbaq, however, was of an opinion that 'Alí's virtues were not suitable to the occasion. His frugality would

1 See M. I, 226.

2 'A. 183–4, 186; Ath. (Búláq), VIII, 83–4; M. I, 243, 244–5; Jaw. fol. 174 a–b; S.J. fol. 106 a; *fakh.* 324; Fid. II, 77.

3 Jaw. ff. 174 b–175 a; S.J. fol. 106 b. The Lady died very soon after, on 6th *jumádà'l-ákhirah* 321 (3rd June 933); M. I, 260; Dh. *t.* fol. 133 b; 'A. 186.

be fatal in their situation: they must have somebody that would not stand upon points in paying the troops. Let them rather send to Fárs for Ibn Muqlah, who was equally devoted to Mu'nis, and very much more adaptable. Ibn Muqlah was accordingly sent for; but Mu'nis was all the same desirous of having 'Alí once more at hand. So a royal invitation was despatched to aṣ-Ṣáfiyah; and in the course of a few days the old man arrived at Mu'nis's house in Baghdád. Mu'nis and he then rowed together to the palace, where 'Alí was presented to the new Caliph. On nearer acquaintance 'Alí was to form a far from favourable estimate of al-Qáhir's character; but his first impression may have been more agreeable: al-Qáhir had yet to manifest his true nature.[1]

Ibn Muqlah arrived from Fárs, some two months after al-Qáhir's accession, in an aggressive mood. He had a double ambition, in the way of which he would allow nothing to stand: the maintenance of his position by the furnishing of funds to those arbiters of power, the troops; and when that was secured, the direct aggrandisement of himself. Its attainment necessitated a policy of confiscation; and accordingly we read of wholesale arrests. He would fine officials often with little, once at least with no justification, and on more than one occasion he was rash enough to incur what he could ill afford, the displeasure of Mu'nis.[2]

'Alí went to visit him on the night of his investiture, and was at once unmistakeably warned of his hostility. For at his entrance Ibn Muqlah ostentatiously remained seated, whereas manners prescribed that he should rise

1 M. I, 242, 243. In Yáq. *ud.* III, 106, 'Alí is said to have been present at a gathering of notables in Baghdád in 320 (932), during the Vizierate of Ibn al-Furát. "Ibn al-Furát" here might refer to al-Fadhl ibn Ja'far, but more likely the date is wrong. I think it improbable that 'Alí made any excursions to the capital during his exile.

2 'A. 185; M. I, 245–53.

to one of 'Alí's standing.[1] Indeed, the slight was so obvious that the onlookers were considerably intrigued. 'Alí, however, seems to have ignored the offence, for one morning not long after he again attended the Vizier in his assembly. He was dealing with the petition of a certain noble, and 'Alí, struck with the amplitude of the Vizier's provision, commended it. Ibn Muqlah turned to him and said maliciously, "Why then did you not do likewise, O Abú'l-Ḥasan, in your Vizierate?" This reflection on his generosity was not to be borne. 'Alí at once got up and went away.[2]

Yet it was not a mere wish to be rude that dictated Ibn Muqlah's behaviour to 'Alí. He seems still to have feared him as a rival, for at the first opportunity he attempted to remove him from the capital. Tagín, so long governor of Egypt, died about this time; whereupon Ibn Muqlah advised al-Qáhir to send 'Alí, again as Inspector-General, to replace him. On al-Muqtadir's murder there had been further disturbances in Egypt,[3] so that the appointment of a competent official to look into the government of the province was really desirable. With what dismay 'Alí received the order may be imagined; but as it was not to be disregarded, he began, with the utmost reluctance, to make his arrangements for the journey. The further the preparations advanced, however, the more they disheartened him: how could he, so old, so feeble, undertake a long and tiresome voyage? He could not. He had been grossly insulted by Ibn Muqlah, but he would swallow his pride and pray to be excused. He arrived at the Vizier's assembly in a state of trembling agitation; but he pleaded his case so vehemently, he depicted his old age and

1 So M. I, 245. Yet according to a passage in Tan. *farj.*, I, 100 (for which 'Alí himself is one of the authorities cited), it was the custom for the head of a *díwán* never to rise to anyone when engaged in business. But cf. p. 288 above. On this occasion, also, Ibn Muqlah was holding a *levée* specially for visits.

2 H. 326–7; Tan. *nish.* 29.

3 'A. 186.

infirmity in terms so affecting, he behaved with such deference and humility, that Ibn Muqlah was reassured in his fears. He permitted himself to acknowledge 'Alí's deserts, and relented. On his return to the Báb al-Bustán 'Alí had the satisfaction of countermanding all the orders for departure; and retired again into the obscurity of private life.[1]

Whilst he was in this imperious frame of mind, it was not likely that Ibn Muqlah would support without protest the appearance of any rival. But it so happened that about this time the last of al-Muqtadir's partisans to be reconciled to the new *régime*, returned to the capital. Their flight had been made in alarm, but it implied defiance. One by one, however, they had treated for amnesty: Hárún had compounded against the payment of a fine for the return of his estates and his appointment to a governorship in the southern Jibál; Muḥammad ibn Rá'iq and his brother were enticed away from their companions by the offer of al-Baṣrah; Mufliḥ and al-Muqtadir's son, the Prince 'Abd al-Wáḥid, threw themselves on the Caliph's mercy; and in the end Muḥammad ibn Yáqút, of all the most obstinate in his recalcitrance, submitted to Yalbaq, who had pursued the rebels into Khúzistán, and came to Baghdád.[2]

Ibn Yáqút seems to have aimed for a time at setting himself up as an independent ruler, and though this hope was now disappointed, once he was back at Court it did not take him long to discover what promised to be an opening hardly less inviting. He remarked that al-Qáhir was chafing under the restraints put upon him by Mu'nis and his satellites, and set himself to earn the place of especial confidant. He succeeded only too well: for Ibn Muqlah took alarm for his own supremacy. He denounced their intimacy to

1 M. I, 258.
2 Ath. (Búláq), VIII, 84–5; M. I, 253–8.

Mu'nis, and alleged that the Caliph and his new favourite were plotting against him. Mu'nis immediately arrested 'Ísà the Court Physician, who was supposed also to be a party to the conspiracy, and banished him to Mosul. Ibn Yáqút himself, however, escaped and hid, before they could lay hands on him. The Caliph was kept a close prisoner; a guard was set about the palace to prevent the inmates' communicating with the outside world; and so keen a watch was instituted, that even dishes of food were scrutinised by the sentinels before being allowed to pass in.

Now whether or not al-Qáhir had indeed intrigued against Mu'nis already, in these circumstances it was inevitable that he should do so. Nor was he at a loss where to turn for help in his distress. For since the death of al-Muqtadir Mu'nis had favoured above all his officers Yalbaq and his son 'Alí; and by their advancement had alienated two of his staunchest adherents, Ṭaríf as-Subkarí and Bushrà the Eunuch, who felt themselves slighted. Moreover, the *Sájí* troops (so named after Ibn Abí's-Sáj, by whom they had been raised)[1] were disaffected towards the general, because he had failed to keep a promise of increasing their pay. The palace was so closely watched that the difficulties of correspondence were considerable; but they were overcome by ingenuity, and the plot was set afoot.

The first move, however, was made by the Caliph's opponents. For Ibn Muqlah discovered, and was duly enraged at the discovery, that al-Qáhir had undertaken to replace him in the Vizierate by Muḥammad ibn al-Qásim, a brother of al-Muqtadir's whilom favourite, al-Ḥusayn. He urged his companions to depose al-Qáhir outright, and elect in his stead that son of al-Muktafí that they had before rejected. Yalbaq and his son needed little persuasion, and even

1 Khall. (trans.), I, 290, note.

swore fealty in secret to the prospective Caliph. But Mu'nis was reluctant; he mistrusted al-Qáhir's apparent patience; and feared that unless they were wary he would worst them. In the end, however, he was gained over, and the following plan of action was devised. It was decided to obtain a midnight audience with the Caliph for 'Alí ibn Yalbaq, on the plea of a sudden descent of the Carmathians on al-Kúfah: he would attend ostensibly to receive his commission, but in reality he would use the opportunity to seize al-Qáhir's person.

The night arrived, and Ibn Muqlah wrote craving the audience. But having done so he went to sleep: when the answer came it was not delivered to him, and so, on waking, he wrote again. Now al-Qáhir had duly granted his request. On its repetition, therefore, he was perplexed at the evident anxiety of the Vizier. His suspicions were shortly confirmed by Ṭaríf, who came to the palace in disguise and informed the Caliph of his opponents' intentions. Al-Qáhir thereupon summoned the *Sájís* secretly; and when Ibn Yalbaq arrived at the appointed hour, declined to see him. Ibn Yalbaq was considerably elated with both drink and the prospect of success, so that he had thought fit to come with but a few men-at-arms. Yet, though the *Sájís* did their best to capture him, he contrived, with the help of his followers, to escape from them, and crossed the river in a boat. It was not until some days later that his hiding-place was discovered. He was then brought back, beaten, fined and imprisoned.

Yalbaq, meanwhile, as soon as he heard of his son's treatment, came to the palace to expostulate with the Caliph, whom he still supposed powerless. But he too was refused an audience, and as he made to depart was arrested. Ibn Muqlah judged the situation more accurately: without more ado he and his secretaries sought refuge in concealment. As for Mu'nis, al-Qáhir sent for him feigning to desire his advice and saying that "he looked upon him as a father". Mu'nis prevaricated, putting forward as excuses his gout and the difficulty that he experienced in moving; but the persuasions of Ṭaríf, who was sent to fetch him, were so cogent that in the end he yielded. No sooner, however, had he set foot in the palace than he too was seized. Al-Qáhir could hardly believe his ears when he heard of his coming. His triumph was complete.[1]

For some weeks, except the capture of 'Alí ibn Yalbaq, nothing further of importance occurred. Hitherto the army in general—apart from the *Sájís*, who were actively in favour of al-Qáhir—had been kept neutral by the Caliph's promises of payment. But Mu'nis's own men had from the first deplored the imprisonment of their commander; and they worked among their fellows with such zeal that in *sha'bán* 321 (August 933) they began to agitate for his release. Their activity, however, had an effect opposite to that for which they had hoped: al-Qáhir was not to be intimidated. He foresaw that he would have no peace whilst it was still possible to satisfy their demand. He would therefore remove the possibility—he would kill the prisoners.

The executions took place in the prison itself; and in order to wring the utmost delight from his triumph, al-Qáhir attended them in person. On the other hand, in order to procure as much pain as possible to the victims, he arranged the proceedings in the following way. 'Alí ibn Yalbaq was first beheaded. His head was taken in and shown to his father. Yalbaq next suffered likewise; and the two heads were presented to Mu'nis. Yalbaq had wept at the sight of his slain son; but the spectacle of his two friends moved Mu'nis to rage. He cursed their murderer with all his might,

1 M. I, 259–64, 266; 'A. 185; Ath. (Búláq), VIII, 85–9.

and still crying out, was dragged by the feet to the gutter of the court. There "like a sheep's" his throat was cut, as all the time al-Qáhir stood by. The three heads were exhibited in basins to the troops on the parade ground; then, after that of ‘Alí ibn Yalbaq had been paraded about the city, they were committed to a peculiar hoard—the Treasury of Skulls, where in grim proximity the heads of notable rebels mouldered together.[1]

Students of Destiny remarked that with the death of Mu'nis the last of those who had participated in the disgrace and execution of Ibn al-Furát came to a violent end. Naṣr had died in feverish delirium; Názúk, by the daggers of slaves; al-Muqtadir, on the field of battle. With Mu'nis the wheel had come full circle. Ibn al-Furát was avenged.[2]

1 M. I, 267–8; Ath. (Búláq), VIII, 89. 2 H. 62.

PLATE III

THE TRIUMPH OF AL-QÁHIR

dirham (silver) minted at Mosul in A.H. 322 (A.D. 934), showing the style assumed by al-Qáhir on his defeat of Mu'nis

Legends:

OBVERSE

Unchanged from the coins of al-Muqtadir
Even the "*Abú'l-'Abbás son of The Commander of the Faithful*" remains (prophetically enough)

REVERSE

To God
Muḥammad is the Apostle of God
Al-Qáhir bi'llah
He that takes Vengeance on the Enemies Of God for God's Religion

Photographed from the cast of a coin in the British Museum

CHAPTER IV

The triumph and fall of al-Qáhir. *The accession of* ar-Rádhí. *Employments for* 'Alí.

Al-Qáhir had been careful to assert his independence, as soon as he had Mu'nis and his adjutants under lock and key. In proportion as before he had been controlled, so now he would show himself unmistakeably absolute. He would reward those that had suffered on his behalf; he would punish those that had sided against him. On the one hand, accordingly, he gave Muḥammad ibn al-Qásim the Vizierate, and reinstated 'Ísà the Physician; on the other he caused the unfortunate Ibn al-Muktafí to be barbarously destroyed either, according to one account, by being walled up alive, or, according to another, by being crushed to death in a carpet.[1] It was not, however, until after the execution of the chief conspirators that al-Qáhir felt his victory to be sealed. He then adopted a new title—*al-muntaqim min a'dá' dín allah* (He that takes Vengeance upon the Enemies of God's Religion). By paying the army as he had promised he secured a term of real power; and by decreeing that a certain type of barge should be used only by himself, the Vizier, the Chamberlain and the Physician, he hedged himself with an awe that was soothing to his wounded pride.[2]

His success in defeating his enemies, however, appears to have blinded him to the dangers that still threatened him—also, in his new-gained freedom, he behaved in ways that could not but offend his subjects. In the first place Ibn Muqlah was still at large: sooner

1 M. I, 264–5, 266; Ath. (Búláq), VIII, 89, 90.
2 Dh. *t.* fol. 132 a, passage published in M. I, 268.

or later he was certain to plot. Then in the recent distribution of rewards Ṭaríf had not only been ignored, but he was at first ostentatiously slighted by al-Qáhir and later actually imprisoned. The Caliph's attitude in this case is perfectly intelligible. His one thought was now his personal supremacy. But Ṭaríf had not only won this very condition for him, he had saved his life. If then his full deserts were to be recognised, al-Qáhir would be bound to raise him to such a position that he might soon find himself with another monitor, a Mu'nis revived. Similar considerations seem to have swayed the Caliph in his relations with the *Sájí* troops, with the help of whom alone his success had been achieved. For he went out of his way to be offensive to their officers, fearing presumably that otherwise they might also claim an inconvenient modicum of recognition.[1] Then he made a very false step when, in *dhú'l-qa'dah* 321 (October–November 933), 'Ísà the Physician persuaded him to dismiss Muḥammad ibn al-Qásim, and promote his own *protégé*, al-Khaṣíbí. For whilst it was yet uncertain who was to be made Vizier, al-Qáhir summoned in turn three prominent officials (of whom one was Sulaymán) as if to invest them; and as soon as they arrived at the palace, arrested them. His design was to impose fines on them, and secure payment by making their release dependent on it—in other words, to hold them up to ransom. Abuses of the fining system were common enough, but such barefaced brigandry shocked even the opinion of Baghdád.[2] For a time a very pleasing impression was produced by the austerity with which al-Qáhir seemed to conduct his life; moreover, the provisions of a decree that he caused to be circulated, for the prohibition of wines and the banishment of singing-girls, were generally recognised to be perfectly

1 Ath. (Búláq), VIII, 90, 97.
2 M. I, 270, 272; Ath. (Búláq), VIII, 90.

laudable, although they were excessively irksome. But the revulsion of feeling was commensurate, when it was discovered that al-Qáhir was in secret an habitual drinker; that he had gone so far as to murder two eminent persons that had once outbidden him for a couple of fair slaves he coveted; and that the famous decree had in reality no other object than to reduce the price of the very commodities with which it dealt, and of which he was an abandoned *amateur*.[1]

From the moment of his fall Ibn Muqlah had of course been bent on revenge; and now he saw a way of effecting it by instigating the already offended *Sájís* to rise against the Caliph. By chance it came to his knowledge that al-Qáhir had had constructed in the palace a series of underground chambers, which might or might not have been, as the Caliph explained, intended for the use of the women as a bath. It suited Ibn Muqlah to assert that they were meant as *oubliettes*, into which al-Qáhir was hoping to cast certain suspected officers; and colour was lent to his assertion by the fact that these rooms were actually employed as a prison to guard a number of Carmathians, who had been captured in a raid on the sea-coast of Fárs.[2] For Ibn Muqlah had previously engaged a soothsayer to persuade one of the chief *Sájí* commanders, a certain Símá, that the Caliph was contemplating his arrest, so that the rumour of the *oubliettes* formed a convenient corroboration. The *Ḥujarí* guards, generally ready to oppose their rivals the *Sájís* in any way, were by this time so disgusted with al-Qáhir's behaviour that they were ready to make common cause; their respective officers entered into negotiations; the occasion of a marriage festival was used as the pretext for a council of action; and on 6th *jumádà'l-úlà* 322 (24th April 934), Símá suddenly surrounded the palace with his men.

1 M. I, 269, 284–5; 'A. 183, 185; Ath. (Búláq), VIII, 94, 102.
2 Ath. (Búláq), VIII, 102; M. I, 284.

The Vizier and the Chamberlain hastened to warn the Caliph, but they found him overcome with wine. It was not until the soldiery had broken in that he could be roused sufficiently to appreciate his danger. He then fled to what he hoped would prove a safe refuge, the domed roof of the women's baths; and in fact he was so well hidden there, that for a time it was supposed that he had escaped. In the end, however, a young eunuch was prevailed upon to disclose his hiding-place, and led a body of archers to the courtyard below. Al-Qáhir at first declined to leave his retreat, but when one of the men menaced him with an arrow he saw that there was nothing for it but to come down. He was seized as he did so and locked in the very room that for many months had housed the ill-used Ṭaríf.[1]

Thus for a second time al-Qáhir was deposed from the throne of the 'Abbásids, which he had now proved himself so eminently unfitted to grace. He is described by al-Mas'údí as "failing to consider the consequences of his actions"; and to this unfortunate characteristic may be chiefly attributed the transience of his might.[2]

'Alí had succeeded in obtaining a reversal of the decision to send him as Inspector to Egypt; yet the Caliphate of al-Qáhir was not to pass without his being ordered from the capital on another mission, though happily not one that necessitated so long and trying a journey. For when in *dhú'l-qa'dah* 321 (October–November 933) the Caliph dismissed Muḥammad ibn al-Qásim, at the same time he arrested the revenue-farmer of Wásiṭ and the territory known as the Euphrates Irrigation; and on al-Khaṣíbí's becoming Vizier, declared him to have no jurisdiction in those districts, but insisted that 'Alí should take in hand their

1 Ath. (Búláq), VIII, 96–7; M. I, 286–7, 288–9.
2 Mas. *tan.* 388.

revenues and policing direct from him (the Caliph) himself.[1] This time 'Alí seems not to have demurred; but as usual on the occasions of his leaving Baghdád, we now hear lamentably little of his doings. This much we learn, however, that the people of al-Kúfah appealed to him with success against the tyranny of their tax-collector, who had sought to increase his profits by seizing their fruit-crop and including its price in the land-tax dues, whereas they preferred to pay, according to another system, a fixed proportion of its yield in kind.[2] Also, we are informed that in general he brought the district "to prosperity". But how long he stayed there, and what exactly were the terms on which he gave up the position, remain uncertain. All we are told is that some time early in 322, before, but probably very little before, his deposition, al-Qáhir gave a contract for the taxes of Wásiṭ, for thirteen million *dirhams*, to an official named Abú 'Abd Allah al-Barídí (who was shortly afterwards to become notorious). 'Alí witnessed the signing of the contract, but whether or not having done so he then left Wásiṭ is also unrecorded. He was certainly back in Baghdád at the time of the Caliph's deposition, for in the events that immediately followed he played a prominent part. But elsewhere[3] it is stated that only then did he officially give up the Wásiṭ revenue-farm; so perhaps he continued, even after the transaction with al-Barídí, to fulfil some duties in connection with it.[4]

Al-Muqtadir's eldest son,[5] the Prince Abú'l 'Abbás, was now called to the throne—apparently without any dissension. Both he and his mother had up to this

1 M. I, 271. 2 H. 359.

3 Ham. *tak.* fol. 56 a.

4 M. I, 274.

5 Dh. *t.* fol. 144 b, makes his brother and successor, Ibrahím al-Muttaqí, his elder by two years, giving his age as thirty-four in 329 (940–1). But al-Muttaqí was really six years younger than ar-Ráḍhí: see Mas. *tan.* 388 and 397.

time been languishing in confinement; but as soon as al-Qáhir was taken they were brought to the palace, and he was proclaimed Caliph the same day under the title *ar-rádhí bi'llah* (Content with God). Ar-Rádhí was twenty-five years of age at the time of his accession. He was short but slender, "brown-eyed, high-coloured and smooth-cheeked".[1]

His very first action was to send for 'Alí and ask him to become Vizier. 'Alí, as he had done so often before, refused, on the now all too real grounds of old age and weakness. But he suggested that if his brother 'Abd ar-Raḥmán might act as Vizier, he himself would direct him, as he had directed Sulaymán for al-Muqtadir. Ar-Rádhí accepted the compromise, and in the proclamation announcing the succession 'Abd ar-Raḥmán was named as Vizier.

The brothers began that same day to attend to business. Ar-Rádhí had first to receive at their hands the Standard and Signet of his sovereignty. The Signet was in the charge of an official, but the ring-seal that he had used as Caliph had to be recovered from al-Qáhir; and this led to the question of his signing a form of abdication. Abú 'Umar's son, Abú'l-Ḥusayn, now Chief *qádhí*, was sent with three notaries to witness it; but on coming to his prison they were greatly perturbed to find that al-Qáhir obstinately refused to abdicate at all. Abú'l-Ḥusayn returned and reported his objection to 'Alí. To his astonishment 'Alí seemed to consider that al-Qáhir's immorality was enough in itself to unfit him legally for the throne—"there is no need for concern about him," he decided, "his deeds are notorious." But Abú'l-Ḥusayn did not agree with him: he had been made to look ridiculous; he complained most indignantly that al-Qáhir's acquiescence should have been secured beforehand: he and his colleagues were there not to bring about political

1 Mas. *tan*. 388.

changes, but to legalise them. However, the altercation was cut short by the call to Evening Prayer; and 'Alí spent all night taking oaths of allegiance to the new Caliph, so that he had little time to trouble himself about al-Qáhir. What was then his horror to be informed next morning that al-Qáhir had been blinded during the night. The lack or loss of any of the senses rendered a prince ineligible for the Caliphate; but this barbarous expedient for excluding from it one who had already sat upon the throne had never been resorted to before. The suggestion had come from Símá, the *Sájí* commander, and ar-Rádhí had purposely refrained from informing 'Alí of their intention, knowing that he would oppose it.

But from Símá also came another proposal, which 'Alí, when he heard of it, welcomed almost as much as he reprobated the savage treatment of al-Qáhir—a proposal to restore Ibn Muqlah to the Vizierate. Ibn Muqlah had of course remained in close touch with the *Sájís* during the conspiracy against al-Qáhir, and as soon as ar-Rádhí succeeded, had written to Símá, bribing him to secure his appointment, and by way of bait to ar-Rádhí himself, promising to contribute towards the accession money a sum of 500,000 *dínárs*. Símá began by urging, just as Yalbaq had urged at the accession of al-Qáhir, that 'Alí was too parsimonious for their present situation; but ar-Rádhí, having chosen the brothers, was not at once prepared to dismiss them. He therefore showed 'Alí Ibn Muqlah's letter, where upon 'Alí at once advised his appointment. He and 'Abd ar-Rahmán were already repenting their decision to accept office, because of the difficulty of raising money. It was clearly then both to their own advantage and to the advantage of the State, that they should make way for one who had at his command extraneous resources. Ibn Muqlah was accordingly summoned from his seclusion the same day, and invested as

Vizier. 'Alí and 'Abd ar-Raḥmán concluded their task of receiving oaths, and then retired to their houses, sincerely relieved at having escaped so easily from a difficult position.[1]

1 M. I, 290–3 (with extract from the *awráq* of aṣ-Ṣúlí); Ath. (Búláq), VIII, 97–8; Dh. *t.* fol. 135 b.

CHAPTER V

The Buvayhids *and the* Barídís.

I must now describe the rise to power of another Daylamite, 'Alí the son of Buvayh, and of his brothers al-Ḥasan and Aḥmad, who from complete obscurity rose in a few years to be masters of a large part of Islam. Afterwards, when the family had become famous, authorities on lineage discovered that it was descended from the Sasanian Royal House, and it was even found possible to trace its genealogy back to Abraham (and so to Adam himself). Hence the gratifying conclusion was arrived at that the Buvayhids (as they are called) were not really Daylamite at all, but had acquired a Daylamitish character from long residence in Daylam. But whatever his antecedents may have been, Buvayh himself began life as a simple Caspian fisherman, and Aḥmad at any rate, among the three brothers, hewed wood in his childhood.[1]

The eldest, 'Alí, attached himself to Mákán ibn Kákúy, and by his military talent gradually rose to a position of importance. But when Mákán was finally defeated by Mardávij, it became clear that with his diminished resources he could not support a large following. A number of officers, therefore, obtained his leave to seek their fortunes in the armies of the rival he was no longer prepared to oppose; and so it came about that 'Alí ibn Buvayh, among them, entered the service of Mardávíj ibn Ziyár. Mardávíj himself was still absent in Ṭabaristán when 'Alí ibn Buvayh came to Ray, but his brother Vashmgír was acting there as his viceroy. By his engaging manners Ibn Buvayh soon won the favour of Vashmgír's Vizier, and he was

1 *fakh.* 325; Ath. (Búláq), VIII, 91.

very shortly posted to the city of Karach in the central Jibál with instructions to collect the taxes, which had been withheld. His relations with the citizens of Karach and the local governors became so happy that they thanked Mardávíj for having appointed him. Moreover, he wrested some castles in the locality from their heretical occupants and distributed the treasures that they had hoarded as presents among his followers, so that their number soon began to increase. Mardávíj, who from the beginning had had misgivings about his advancement, now sought to embarrass him by quartering a number of officers on his district. But 'Alí ibn Buvayh treated them so handsomely that they soon became his devoted adherents; and when Mardávíj sent to recall them, he easily persuaded them to remain with him. Nevertheless he was not prepared actually to defy his overlord; and thought it more prudent, before Mardávíj should coerce him, to call in the year's taxes and make southwards for Iṣfahán.[1]

It was his design to enter the service of the Caliph, for Iṣfahán was still in the control of al-Qáhir, the governor being none other than Yáqút's second son al-Mudhaffar. (Yáqút, on his exile three years before, had been given Fárs by al-Muqtadir, and at the same time al-Mudhaffar had been given Iṣfahán.) Ibn Buvayh's overtures, however, were ignored, and when he had advanced to within a short distance of the city, he found that al-Mudhaffar had resolved on opposing him. The defending force was more than twenty times as large as his own; but it included a contingent of Daylamites, who, when they found themselves face to face with compatriots, deserted in a body. The remainder were no match for 'Alí ibn Buvayh: he routed them with ease, and entered Iṣfahán.

His victory over a force so much stronger than his own greatly impressed the Caliph; but to an equal

1 M. I, 276–9, 295–6; Ath. (Búláq), VIII, 91–3.

extent it enraged Mardávíj. In order to put Ibn Buvayh off his guard, he wrote him a letter of congratulation; but at the same time he sent his brother Vashmgír with an army intended, not to support him, but to drive him out. 'Alí ibn Buvayh, however, was not deceived by this ruse. Yet he could not face, with his still small force, the army of Vashmgír. But he had learnt that Yáqút in Fárs was now so weak, that he feared less to encounter him. He therefore marched south, and, meeting with no opposition, entered Arraján on the border of the province in the last days of 321 (933). At first he made overtures to Yáqút to join him; but Yáqút did not reply, and eventually they met in battle near Iṣṭakhr, when Ibn Buvayh was again victorious. Yáqút withdrew into Khúzistán, and 'Alí ibn Buvayh took possession of Fárs for himself.[1]

This second success vexed Mardávíj still further: he determined to pursue and vanquish the upstart. With the object of attacking him from two sides, he sent an army into Khúzistán. This again defeated Yáqút and drove him from this province as well; but before Mardávíj could come against 'Alí ibn Buvayh, the latter approached him with an embassy. He offered to acknowledge his suzerainty, and to send his own brother al-Ḥasan as a hostage. Presents made the proposal the more acceptable, and Mardávíj at once agreed to it.

Having occupied Khúzistán with so little difficulty, Mardávíj next contemplated a still bolder advance—he would take Baghdád itself, destroy the 'Abbásid Caliphate, and found a new kingdom on the Sasanian model at a rebuilt Ctesiphon. He even sent two officials to prepare for his arrival in Wásiṭ, where he would reside while Ctesiphon was being restored;—but his visions of glory were abruptly blotted out. By favouring the Daylamites of his army, Mardávíj had

1 Ath. (Búláq), VIII, 93–5; M. I, 280–4, 296–8.

offended the Turks. At the Persian Festival of Fire he flew into a rage with certain of the latter who had disturbed his rest; and next day, a winter's morning, whilst he was in his bath, a number of them, exasperated at the treatment to which he had subjected them, forced their way in and murdered him. Vashmgír succeeded his brother, and for many years struggled to maintain his independence in central Persia. But the grandiose schemes of Mardávíj were never realised, from this time the Ziyárid power declined.[1]

So much for 'Alí ibn Buvayh and the affairs of Persia proper. I must now relate how Abú 'Abd Allah al-Barídí established his power in Khúzistán.

On his second defeat Yáqút had fled to Wásiṭ; but on receiving news of Mardávíj's murder he returned to al-Ahwáz and determined once more to try his fortune against 'Alí ibn Buvayh. He was joined there by Abú 'Abd Allah al-Barídí, who was attached to him as tax-farmer for the province.

Abú 'Abd Allah was an accomplished villain. He had a significant motto: "My drum has a sound that shall be heard one of these days!"[2] He was the eldest of three brothers, the other two being named Abú Yúsuf and Abú'l-Ḥusayn. Their father had been Post-master in al-Baṣrah (whence their surname: *baríd* = post).[3] All three worked for their common advancement, but Abú 'Abd Allah always took the lead. Yet he was of a timid disposition, and had it not been for the incitements of Abú Yúsuf, he would never have accomplished what he did. It was his suppleness and subtlety of mind that distinguished him. He was frugal and chaste in private life—an intellectual rogue.[4]

We first hear of the Barídís in 315 (927–8), during the last Vizierate of 'Alí ibn 'Ísà. At this time all

1 Ath. (Búláq), VIII, 98–9, 103–5; M. I, 300–2, 310–15.
2 M. I, 158.
3 Dh. *t.* fol. 142 a.
4 M. I, 348 (with extract from Ham. *tak.*).

three already held subordinate posts as tax-farmers in Khúzistán;[1] but even then they had earned a bad reputation, and 'Alí, when making fresh appointments, passed them over for promotion. Nevertheless throughout the remainder of al-Muqtadir's Caliphate and that of al-Qáhir they had continued, though with frequent intervals of disgrace and sometimes of imprisonment, to serve the State. Their chief sponsor was Ibn Muqlah: consequently their periods of prosperity corresponded roughly with his terms of office. Khúzistán remained the theatre of their activities, although one of the brothers generally watched their interests at Court.[2] Abú 'Abd Allah's first master-stroke was delivered soon after the accession of al-Qáhir, when he financed the expedition that was sent out to subdue the supporters of al-Muqtadir. On this occasion the revenues of the entire province were put at his disposal, and by a ruthless oppression of the inhabitants he wrung out of them a considerable fortune for himself.[3] To be sure, the family soon after fell once more into disgrace, and he was forced to part with huge sums in bribes;[4] but the experiment once having been successfully carried through, Abú 'Abd Allah was prepared to repeat it whenever he had the chance.

When ar-Rádhí made Ibn Muqlah once more Vizier, the Barídís were restored to their positions in Khúzistán. Abú 'Abd Allah's return to al-Ahwáz thus coincided with the flight to that city of Yáqút after his first defeat, by 'Alí ibn Buvayh. When Mardávíj's army forced Yáqút to retreat to Wásiṭ, Abú 'Abd Allah went with him. Now they came back together.

Al-Barídí saw that he might turn their association to his own advantage. The revenue was in his hands:

1 M. I, 152.
2 M. I, 158–9, 186, 205–8, 223, 246–50; 'A. 138; Ath. (Búláq), VIII, 74–5.
3 M. I, 254–7.
4 M. I, 270, 273–4.

by a judicious use of it he would attract Yáqút's troops to himself, and leave the commander without an army. Yáqút was defeated a second time by 'Alí ibn Buvayh; but this only improved Abú 'Abd Allah's chances. If Yáqút had turned upon him during the weeks that followed, Abú 'Abd Allah would certainly have been worsted; yet, though he was warned against him, Yáqút believed in him wholeheartedly, till it was too late. At length, having misgivings, he advanced with a much diminished force against 'Askar Mukram, where his colleague was encamped, only to be surprised in an ambush by Abú 'Abd Allah's now superior army. Yáqút himself was killed by some Berber men-at-arms as he sat disconsolate by a deserted guard-house. With the commander's death his forces were no longer of any account. As 'Alí ibn Buvayh was independent in Fárs, so Abú 'Abd Allah al-Barídí was independent in Khúzistán.[1]

1 Ath. (Búláq), VIII, 99, 106, 109–12; M. I, 301–3, 319, 320–1, 339–48. Ham. *tak*. fol. 56 a.

CHAPTER VI

The manœuvres of Ibn Muqlah. 'Alí ibn 'Ísà *in trouble. The administration of* 'Abd ar-Raḥmán. *The* "Emir of Emirs", *and the ruin of the* Vizierate.

To go back to the accession of ar-Rádhí. Muḥammad ibn Rá'iq, on his reconciliation with al-Qáhir, had been given al-Baṣrah; then on Yáqút's first defeat by 'Alí ibn Buvayh, he had seized al-Ahwáz for a time as well. Clearly, he was likely to become dangerously powerful unless something were done to check him. Ibn Muqlah, therefore, when he was restored to the Vizierate by ar-Rádhí, decided to summon him to become Chamberlain, and so attach him to the Caliph.

Símá of the *Sájís*, however, having brought about the appointment of the Vizier himself, now wished to have a hand in the distribution of all the offices. Muḥammad ibn Yáqút himself was in Persia, where he had joined his father, but his secretary bribed Símá to favour his recall also to be Chamberlain; and Símá prevailed on the Caliph to appoint him. To compensate Ibn Rá'iq for his disappointment, ar-Rádhí bestowed on him the command of the troops and police at Wásiṭ; thereby adding to the territory under his control, and so achieving the exact opposite of what Ibn Muqlah had intended. But Ibn Rá'iq appeared to be satisfied with this arrangement, and accordingly Ibn Yáqút became Chamberlain.[1]

Shortly after his arrival Ibn Yáqút was sent out to oppose the approach of Hárún. On his reconciliation with al-Qáhir, Hárún had retired to his Persian government, where he had remained ever since; but on the accession of ar-Rádhí, he reckoned that his relationship entitled him once more to a place at Court. Ar-Rádhí,

1 Ath. (Búláq), VIII, 98; M. I, 294 (extract from Ham. *tak*.).

however, had borne a grudge against the Lady his grandmother that embraced her relations as well; also he knew that of al-Muqtadir's sons it was not himself but his brother al-'Abbás with whom Hárún was most friendly. He was anxious therefore to keep him at a distance. Hárún, who had advanced to within twelve miles of the city, refused a parley, and, as Ibn Yáqút was evidently reluctant to face him, pressed a fight. Ibn Yáqút at once retreated, and Hárún was so sure of defeating him that he pursued him almost unattended. By a mischance, however, he was thrown from his horse, and before he could pick himself up one of his own retainers fell upon him and cut off his head. His supporters immediately scattered in all directions; his camp was pillaged; and Ibn Yáqút returned to Baghdád taking to himself the credit of victory.[1]

In his elation he determined, as he was now in his own eyes the most important person at Court, to make himself actually the most powerful. Ibn Muqlah had not forgiven him for the supersession of Ibn Rá'iq. Peace therefore was impossible between them: and in the contest it seemed at first as if Ibn Yáqút would win. He issued instructions that no decrees, appointments or dismissals were to pass as valid without his signature; and ousted the Vizier so successfully from his preeminence that he would only appear in public at ceremonies, and indeed went out of his way to neglect his duties. It was Ibn Yáqút's policy to pose as a bulwark against the encroachments of Mardávíj. But in doing so he discovered that he had best confine himself to words. For when, on his father's eviction from Khúzistán, he proposed to lead an expedition against the invader, he had quickly to abandon the project, on finding the soldiery apter to fight at home than abroad. He was able indeed to appropriate some credit for Mardávíj's assassination, which he declared had been

1 Ath. (Búláq), VIII, 99–100; M. I, 306–9.

brought about by his agents; but by this time he was generally so heartily disliked that the story, even when it was believed, served him but little. At length Ibn Muqlah persuaded the Caliph to dismiss and imprison both him and his brother al-Mudhaffar. Ibn Muqlah celebrated his rehabilitation by appointing his son Abú'l-Ḥusayn to assist him in office and share the title of Vizier.[1]

Since the accession of ar-Rádhí 'Alí ibn 'Ísà had made no attempt to meddle in the business of government. Yet Ibn Muqlah seems still to have regarded him with a jealous eye; and now when he was restored to the full measure of his authority, he took the first opportunity of doing 'Alí a bad turn.

What really happened in this case can only be guessed at. Grave charges were brought against 'Alí ibn 'Ísà; but it is most improbable that they were well founded: 'Alí was given no chance to defend himself, and aṣ-Ṣúlí, at any rate, who was well placed to judge, maintained, even to the point of offending the Caliph and still more the Vizier, that he was innocent. The episode began with the secret appointment of Sa'íd ibn Ḥamdán, a brother of the late Abú'l-Hayjá', to the province of Diyár Rabí'ah. On Abú'l-Hayjá''s death, the chieftainship of the Ḥamdánid family had passed to his son al-Hasan. It was he that before the death of al-Muqtadir had at first opposed and afterwards allied himself with Mu'nis. Ever since he had held the revenue contract for Mosul and the province, and by now wielded in the district all the influence of a hereditary ruler. His uncle Sa'íd, having received the appointment to supersede him, set out from Baghdád to take it up: but the next news that reached the city announced his assassination in the house of his nephew. Ar-Rádhí was scandalised at the crime; and at once

1 Ath. (Búláq), VIII, 99, 102, 106; M. I, 305–6, 310, 318–20, 321.

ordered Ibn Muqlah to lead a punitive expedition against its perpetrator.

It was at this point that 'Alí became implicated. For whilst opinion was still set firmly against al-Ḥasan, the latter's secretary supplied Ibn Muqlah with a letter that he had received from 'Alí ibn 'Ísà, containing what appeared to be proposals of a treasonable kind. The letter purported to be written at the Caliph's instance. It excused al-Ḥasan from the obligations of his contract, and actually instructed him to prevent supplies from being sent to the capital.

As soon as it fell into his hands Ibn Muqlah had the document authenticated by two notaries, and hastened to lay it before ar-Rádhí. As a result 'Alí was next day arrested and imprisoned in the Vizier's house. After much discussion he was prevailed upon to pay a fine of 50,000 *dínárs*, but even with this Ibn Muqlah was not satisfied, and insisted, first that he should swear never again to calumniate him (Ibn Muqlah) or intrigue for the Vizierate either on his own behalf or on anyone else's, and secondly that he should retire once more to aṣ-Ṣáfiyah. It was now that aṣ-Ṣúlí interceded for 'Alí with the Caliph; but ar-Rádhí professed to be convinced that 'Alí had aimed in this case at enriching himself by intercepting, as a go-between, money intended for him, the Caliph, himself. Aṣ-Ṣúlí argued that 'Alí's character, his whole record, forbade the supposition; but he argued in vain. 'Alí perforce departed again for aṣ-Ṣáfiyah—as the poet exclaimed, "there departed, by God, the Beauty of Baghdád and the like of whom men never saw."

The explanation of the affair appears to be this. Ar-Rádhí required some money, and set about obtaining it in a dishonest but by no means a novel way. Obviously a bribe might best be solicited by offering something that might be given in exchange for it. Hence ar-Rádhí's appointment of al-Ḥasan's uncle

Sa'íd; hence his rage at Sa'íd's assassination; and hence his attribution to 'Alí of the covetous motives that had in reality stirred himself. Ar-Rádhí had aimed at causing al-Ḥasan to fear for his position by the prospect of being supplanted by Sa'íd: for in order to ensure a revocation of Sa'íd's appointment al-Ḥasan might very well be expected to pay over a large sum. On the other hand, in case his plan worked, ar-Rádhí must avoid the appearance of inconsequence in first appointing Sa'íd and then at once dismissing him: therefore his commission must be given in secret, and the order for his dismissal likewise.

'Alí had been brought in on account of his transparent honesty. Al-Ḥasan would never suspect him of double-dealing, and if he received notice of dismissal at his hands would take it seriously. Restored to their context the clauses that seemed so incriminating were no doubt innocent enough; but in any case 'Alí had been approached by a third party, so that ar-Rádhí could safely disclaim all knowledge of their existence, and even, as he did, throw all the blame on their unfortunate author. Such was the design of the plot; but the murder of Sa'íd upset it, and left the Caliph not only penniless but suspect.

Ibn Muqlah's campaign against the Ḥamdánids was short and inconclusive. Al-Ḥasan retreated before him from Mosul (to which, after chasing him north, Ibn Muqlah returned); but at the same time he instituted an intrigue with the Vizier's son, who had been left in charge at Baghdád, with the result that two months later, in exchange for a considerable sum of money, the latter wrote to his father requiring his immediate return. Ibn Muqlah left a force behind him in Mosul, but it was no match for the Ḥamdánids. Al-Ḥasan was indeed defeated in his first essay to retake the city; but soon after he won a decisive success, and was able to secure from the Caliph a reinstatement in his government.

'Alí was far from seeking to avenge his injuries, even to the extent of humiliating the Vizier. Very shortly, nevertheless, Ibn Muqlah was obliged to pocket his pride and ask 'Alí's assistance; for when it came to negotiating the accommodation with the Ḥamdánids, al-Ḥasan refused to trust his word, and insisted on dealing with 'Alí and nobody else. Ibn Muqlah was constrained, therefore, to instruct his son to write courteously to 'Alí, giving him the choice of remaining at aṣ-Ṣáfiyah or returning to Baghdád. It is not stated what 'Alí elected to do; but he is hardly likely to have stayed longer than he needed at aṣ-Ṣáfiyah, and a few months later he was certainly back at the capital.[1]

Soon after his return from Mosul at the end of 323 (935) Ibn Muqlah was attacked in his house, from which he and his son had to flee in haste. He suspected that the authors of this outrage were partisans of the Yáqút family—he had already, six months earlier, been molested in this way: altogether he was finding that his triumph over them was costing him dear. In the interval Muḥammad ibn Yáqút had died in prison; and although a number of notaries declared on oath that they could discover on his body no sign of violence, it was generally supposed that the Vizier had had a hand in his taking off. This present discontent was connected also with his name. The Carmathians had just made another attack on the Pilgrimage, and though the caravans had escaped more lightly than sometimes, the journey to Mecca had had to be abandoned. Now it happened that Muḥammad ibn Yáqút, during his first brief period of power, had come to an understanding with al-Jannábí: for so long the Carmathians had lain low: now therefore their renewed activity was

1 M. I, 323–7 (with extract from the *awráq*), 329; Ham. *tak*. fol. 61 a; Ath. (Búláq), VIII, 107.

attributed to his supersession by Ibn Muqlah. From this it came to be murmured that Ibn Muqlah had in general treated the Yáqút family with great injustice; and so, in order to counteract this opinion, and still more to allay the suspicion that Muḥammad ibn Yáqút had met with foul play, Ibn Muqlah, soon after this episode, released his brother al-Mudhaffar from prison. He made, to be sure, a stipulation that al-Mudhaffar should refrain from plotting against him; but al-Mudhaffar was convinced more positively than anyone of his guilt, and deemed himself in no way bound to observe it. He at once set to work intriguing with the *Ḥujarí* Guard, who, before Muḥammad's death, had agitated for his release; and found them disposed to join him.

Then Ibn Muqlah was beset not only with political embarrassments, but also with financial. Even at the beginning of ar-Rádhí's reign the state of the finances had been none too promising; and now a combination of bad luck with ill-conceived policy had rendered it desperate. He had tried the expedient of obtaining advance payments on the year's crops; but when the merchants were disappointed over their delivery, he was compelled to refund the money. His campaign against the Ḥamdánids had as usual been costly; but worst of all, ever since his retirement to Wásiṭ, Ibn Rá'iq had withheld the revenue dues of both Wásiṭ and al-Baṣrah—two of the richest provinces of the Caliphate partly in revenge for his recent rejection as Chamberlain, partly in the express hope of bringing about the fall of the Vizier and stepping into his place.

Ibn Muqlah sent him a message requiring him to pay up these arrears. Ibn Rá'iq, too cunning to refuse openly, returned him a soft answer; but at the same time he despatched a secret communication to ar-Rádhí offering, if he were himself raised to the Vizierate, to pay all expenses and supply the Caliph with an ample allowance. Ar-Rádhí sent him no reply immediately. But on receiving Ibn Rá’iq’s official answer Ibn Muqlah guessed at once that he was meditating defiance, and decided to send his son with an expedition against him. To cloak their real design he advertised his intention of making for al-Ahwáz: it only remained to obtain the Caliph’s commission. For this purpose on 16th *jumádà’l-úlà* 324 (11th April 936) he went to the palace; but as he crossed the great court, he was seized by al-Mudhaffar and surrounded by his companions. Ar-Rádhí, when informed of their action, declared his approval; and in return he gave the soldiery the choice of a new Vizier. The soldiery, after a short deliberation, elected ‘Alí ibn ‘Ísà. “There is no one like him,” they said.[1]

‘Alí was accordingly summoned to the palace. But on no account would he consent to take office. Despite their recent grave difference, the Caliph strove to persuade him; he argued, the *Ḥujarí* officers argued with him: but to no purpose. Only after a lengthy discussion did ‘Alí yield at all. Let them return to the arrangement that had been made at the Caliph’s accession: he would act as adviser, if ‘Abd ar-Raḥmán were Vizier. The compromise was seized upon; ‘Abd ar-Raḥmán was promptly brought from his house by al-Mudhaffar; the Caliph immediately invested him; and the brothers found themselves, almost before they could realise it, rowing back to the Garden Gate, with all the pomp and the responsibilities of State upon their shoulders.

The responsibilities weighed upon them indeed. From the beginning their task was in reality hopeless, and for the next nine months they and their successors —for even ‘Alí’s talents were unequal to this problem

1 M. I, 320, 329–31, 332–6, 337 (with extract from the *awráq*); Ath. (Búláq), VIII, 108–9.

—struggled in vain to meet the demands of ordinary expenditure. The jurisdiction of the Caliph, which had once extended over so wide an empire, was now confined to the immediate neighbourhood of Baghdád. But with this shrinkage of territory the expenses which the revenues of that former empire had gone to defray had in no wise diminished; for the Court had always subsisted on the surplus sent from the various provinces, by contract, after local needs had been satisfied. If the equilibrium of the budget had been precarious even nine years before, when 'Alí was last Vizier, now its list to ruin was clearly beyond all righting.

The Vizierate of 'Abd ar-Raḥmán was notable for no occurrence except the vengeance taken on Ibn Muqlah by al-Khaṣíbí, to whom his examination was delegated.—Al-Khaṣíbí, as the last Vizier to al-Qáhir, had been banished by Ibn Muqlah, on his return to office at the accession of ar-Rádhí, in company with Sulaymán ibn al-Ḥasan, to 'Umán. In the course of their voyage down the Gulf, a storm caught their vessel, and shipwreck seemed imminent. In the horror of death Sulaymán vowed that if he were spared he would forgive the wrongs his enemies had done him. Al-Khaṣíbí pledged himself likewise, but made a remarkable reservation—even in this extremity he could not bring himself to renounce the hope of avenging himself on Ibn Muqlah. Al-Khaṣíbí afterwards escaped from 'Umán, and came secretly to Baghdád. Ibn Muqlah sought for him high and low, but could find him nowhere. So al-Khaṣíbí nursed his rancour, till with Ibn Muqlah's fall its gratification became possible. Then after being beaten at the hands of 'Abd ar-Raḥmán and fined by him a million *dínárs*, Ibn Muqlah was handed over to his enemy, who maltreated him ruthlessly in fulfilment of his oath and mulcted him of another fifty thousand.[1]

1 M. I, 323, 326–7 (with extract from Ham. *tak.*).

The crisis came for the Banú'l-Jarráḥ in *rajab* 324 (June 936),[1] when 'Abd ar-Raḥmán was forced to ask the Caliph for a loan of 10,000 *dínárs*; and ar-Rádḥí then showed that he had other cause of complaint against the brothers. As usual they were dismissed and imprisoned; but so hot was the Caliph this time against them, that they were even in fear of their lives. Ar-Rádḥí accused 'Abd ar-Raḥmán of having appropriated large sums of money to his own use; set his fine at 200,000 *dínárs*, and swore that he would not forgo a *dirham*. 'Abd ar-Raḥmán rather foolishly inflamed his wrath by tricking the envoy that was sent to obtain his bond. He persuaded him to write: "Ja'far ibn Warqá', Agent of the Commander of the Faithful, guarantees 100,000 *dínárs* on behalf of 'Abd ar-Raḥmán ibn 'Ísà".

'Alí feared that in his anger ar-Rádḥí might go to extremes. He therefore obtained the help of Ibn Rá'iq's secretary aṣ-Ṣilḥí (already a person of the first importance) in interceding for him with the Caliph. Aṣ-Ṣilḥí argued that however angry the Caliph might be with one brother, he had no reason to vent his annoyance on the other. But ar-Rádḥí maintained that he had every reason: 'Abd ar-Raḥmán had been absolutely guided by 'Alí in every other action, so there was no cause to suppose that he had moved independently in this. Yet the misdeeds of 'Abd ar-Raḥmán were not grave enough to account for the Caliph's obvious hatred of 'Alí: there was clearly something else behind it, and by a tactful interrogatory aṣ-Ṣilḥí eventually discovered what it was. It was 'Alí's unpolished address that had offended him: "He can never speak to me without beginning, 'O You,'" he complained—an insufferable familiarity. This was in fact a habit of 'Alí's, which had formerly been contrasted with Ibn al-Furát's polite "God bless you". Aṣ-Ṣilḥí

1 Ṣaf. (Paris Arabe 2066), fol. 157 a.

reminded the Caliph that it was a well-known peculiarity, and could not be taken to imply disrespect to him personally. But ar-Rádhí supposed that the talents that aṣ-Ṣilḥí had enumerated might well have taught 'Alí manners. "We meet seldom enough," he said, "surely he might restrain himself." He was persuaded that 'Alí looked upon him as a child—perhaps he remembered that 'Alí, as Vizier, had ridden beside him on his first public appearance as a little boy, long ago in 301 (913–14)[1]—and it required all aṣ-Ṣilḥí's tact to mollify him. In the end, however, he obtained his consent to the brothers' removing to the house of the new Vizier: in due time they paid off their fines; and returned once more to the seclusion of their homes.[2]

Al-Karkhí, their successor, is remarkable only for his extreme shortness, which required that the throne should be cut down four inches that he might converse with the Caliph at ease. But even with this facility he could not discover any way out of the financial *impasse*; indeed he seems even not to have made the most of his means, for on his dismissal many uncashed cheques were found among his papers. He was dismissed after holding office for three months, and now his stature served him well. For he contrived to escape arrest by being carried out of his house in a water-pot, and so avoided a fine.[3]

Ar-Rádhí chose in his place—despite his close connection with 'Alí—Sulaymán ibn al-Ḥasan. But he was soon forced by growing difficulties to recognise that with the loss of all the provinces the present system of government had become unworkable. He sent therefore a belated answer to Ibn Rá'iq, accepting his proposal of providing for the general expenditure

1 'A. 43.

2 M. I, 336–8; H. 332–4; *fakh.* 329; Dh. *t.* fol. 141 a; Tagh. II, 298.

3 M. I, 338, 350; *fakh.* 329–30.

and paying the army. But he was not to be Vizier—as if aware that the old order had passed, the Caliph invented a new title. Ibn Rá'iq was to be styled Emir of Emirs,[1] and his jurisdiction was to extend directly to the taxation and policing of every province, as well as over the administration of the central government: moreover his name was to be mentioned with that of the Caliph in the Friday Prayers. The Secretaries of State set out for Wásiṭ to meet their new master; and at ar-Ráḍhí's order the *Sájís* accompanied them to form his body-guard.

Ibn Rá'iq was amazed at this realisation of his schemes; but he did not allow elation to obscure his foresight. When the *Sájís* arrived he promptly arrested them one and all. He pretended that his object was to devote their share of pay to their rivals the *Ḥujarís*; but in reality he aimed at destroying a force that might prove hostile to his supremacy. The *Ḥujarís* indeed suspected his motives, and encamped by way of protest in the palace grounds; but on Ibn Rá'iq's coming to Baghdád, he insisted on their departure, and in the first flush of his success, carried his wish.

With the year 324 (935–6), therefore, vanished the system of government that had come into being with the 'Abbásid dynasty. Its titles and some of its forms indeed remained; but its reality was dissolved. The glory of the Vizierate had passed away.[2]

1 Arabic, *amír al-umará'*.
2 M. I, 350–2; Ath. (Búláq), VIII, 112; *fakh.* 330.

CHAPTER VII

Bachkam. *The fate of* Ibn Muqlah. *The death of* ar-Rádhí.

The history of the Caliphate during the next decade turns on the conflict of various competitors for the mastery of Baghdád; for all those that had made themselves independent in the nearer provinces of the empire were now in turn to aim at possessing themselves of the capital, and by dominating the Caliph at ruling his realm.

Neither the Fáṭimids nor the Carmathians took part in the struggle. The Mahdí had died in 322 (934), and though his son and successor *al-qá'im* (the Lieutenant) was both warlike and capable, and in fact made another attempt, soon after his accession, to conquer Egypt, he found there his match in a vigorous Turk, by name Muḥammad ibn Ṭughj, known as the *ikhshíd*, whom ar-Rádhí had appointed commandant in 324 (936).[1] The Ikhshíd not only restored the province to order from the fearful anarchy into which it had fallen after the death of Tagín, he was also ready and competent to defend it from outside attack. Al-Qá'im, moreover, was soon too fully engaged with rebellions in his own dominions to have any hope of adding to them.[2] Whilst the rest of the 'Abbásid Caliphate was being hurried to its doom, therefore, Egypt enjoyed a beneficial calm.—At first the Carmathians threatened further trouble. In 325 (937) they again entered al-Kúfah, and when Ibn Rá'iq came against them, Abú Ṭáhir demanded the payment of a heavy tribute from the Caliph.[3] An arrangement was eventually come to

1 M. I, 332. 2 Maq. *it.* 44, 45; Ath. (Búláq), VIII, 98.
3 M. I, 367; Ath. (Búláq), VIII, 117; Tagh. II, 281.

by which each pilgrim of the *ḥajj* was to pay a fixed toll in return for Abú Ṭáhir's undertaking not to molest the caravans.[1] But by now (327/939) the Carmathians were involved in a domestic crisis—the appearance, acclamation and eventual exposure of a bogus *Imám*; and this so drained their strength, that little by little they ceased to inspire their adversaries with any alarm.[2]

The strife within the Caliphate began almost immediately after Ibn Rá'iq's establishment as Emir, when he was prompted to attack al-Barídí in Khúzistán in the hope both of enlarging the area under his control and of weakening a rival. In this, after some set-backs, he was temporarily successful, but his success cost him dear in two ways. In the first place his commander, Bachkam, to whom it was almost entirely due, now began to have designs on the Emirate himself. In the second, Abú 'Abd Allah was provoked into seeking in person the assistance of 'Alí ibn Buvayh.

This Bachkam, a Turk by birth, had begun his career as a page to the Vizier of Mákán ibn Kákúy. The Vizier had later presented him to his master; and Bachkam had remained with Mákán till his defeat by Mardávíj, when with 'Alí ibn Buvayh and others of Mákán's officers he entered Mardávíj's service. He rose to be a leader of the Turks in Mardávíj's army, suffered with them the potentate's insults, and eventually took a hand in his assassination. On it he had fled with a troop from Iṣfahán and found his way to Wásiṭ, where he had attached himself to the ascendant power of Ibn Rá'iq.[3]

'Alí ibn Buvayh was by no means averse from extending the dominion of his family, and welcomed al-Barídí's appeal so far as, early in 326 (end of 937), to

1 S.J. fol. 117 a; Dh. *t.* ff. 144 a, 205 b.

2 M. II, 55–6; Ath. (Búláq), VIII, 123–4; Fid. II, 86; Dh. *t.* fol. 206 a *et seqq.*

3 M. I, 383; Ath. (Búláq), VIII, 122; Fid. II, 86.

send his younger brother Ahmad to join forces with him against Bachkam in Khúzistán. These allies were at first successful; but they soon quarrelled: so that Abú 'Abd Allah fled to al-Baṣrah, of which in the interval his family had obtained control; whilst Bachkam was able to win back a great part of what he had lost. Bachkam now openly disclosed his contempt for Ibn Rá'iq, and began collecting the provincial revenues for himself. Ibn Rá'iq made an effort to obtain the co-operation against him of al-Barídí, but before this could become effective, Bachkam himself attacked al-Barídí and defeated him. He used his defeat, however, by treating the vanquished with especial clemency, to found himself an alliance with Abú 'Abd Allah. For in the meantime his ambitions had been encouraged by the receipt of a communication from Ibn Muqlah, which invited him to advance on the capital and displace Ibn Rá'iq. In *dhú'l-qa'dah* 326 (September 938) Bachkam accordingly set out.[1]

This invitation was the undoing of Ibn Muqlah. After his disgrace for a time he had kept out of sight; but recently the departure for Egypt of al-Faḍhl ibn Ja'far, who had filled for a few months the now shrunken office of Vizier,[2] had encouraged him to demand of Ibn Rá'iq the release of his sequestrated estates. This Ibn Rá'iq had refused: and the refusal so enraged Ibn Muqlah that he at once set about intriguing against him. He would bring another conqueror to Baghdád, and profit by his triumph: he wrote to Vashmgír; he wrote, as I have mentioned, to Bachkam. Rashly, however, he advised ar-Rádhí too soon to arrest Ibn Rá'iq; for ar-Rádhí suspected him himself of favouring a rival for the throne, and betrayed him. As the cruellest punishment that might be inflicted on so

1 M. I, 356–7, 358–9, 368–74, 377–86; Ath. (Búláq), VIII, 114, 115–18, 119–21.

2 M. I, 368, 383–4; Ath. (Búláq), VIII, 114, 120.

skilful a calligraphist, Ibn Rá'iq had his right hand cut off; but Ibn Muqlah defiantly overcame this disadvantage, and in a little while could write again as fairly with his poor stump or with his left hand. With the return of his old proficiency, however, there returned as well his old ambition—injudiciously he predicted his revenge with Bachkam's coming. Ibn Rá'iq cut out his tongue; and left him unattended in a solitary prison, where for two years the wretched man lingered on, till in the end he perished of dysentery and neglect. Ibn Muqlah had sung to his right hand a lament, in which he expressed a hope that was thus soon dreadfully fulfilled:

Without the right hand there is no joy in life,
O Life, since my right hand is gone, go too.[1]

But whilst he lay in his dungeon his schemes matured: Vashmgír, indeed, was too much occupied in withstanding the encroachments of al-Ḥasan ibn Buvayh to pay heed to his suggestion; but Bachkam obliterated from his standards the epithet ar-Rá'iqí, which had indicated his subservience to the Emir, and proceeded up-stream as far as the junction of the Tigris and the Diyálá, where he found Ibn Rá'iq encamped on the west bank. Bachkam's men, however, plunged into the river to swim across, whereupon Ibn Rá'iq's army broke up and fled. Bachkam accordingly entered Baghdád on 12th or 13th *dhú'l-qa'dah* (10th or 11th September 938), and was invested that same day by ar-Rádhí as Emir of Emirs.[2]

The Caliph of course had taken little part in this *coup d'état*; but we learn from a discussion that he held later with certain courtiers, that Bachkam proved a very much pleasanter companion than Ibn Rá'iq. Ar-Rádhí reviewed his reign: some people accused him,

1 M. I, 386–93; Ath. (Búláq), VIII, 121; *fakh.* 320–1; S.J. ff. 114 b–115 a.

2 M. I, 394–6; Ath. (Búláq), VIII, 122.

he said, of having of his own free will yielded up his sovereignty to the Emirs, but in truth he had been forced into it. During the first two years he had been nominally independent; but in reality the *Sájí* and the *Ḥujarí* officers had been so many masters, who all severally desired him to act as they wished. Ibn Rá'iq had delivered him from this particular tyranny; but ar-Rádhí had found Ibn Rá'iq even more despotic and grasping than the soldiers. He permitted every kind of injustice in the collection of money; the Caliph's orders were absolutely ignored; the Emir's followers might rob him to their heart's content, and if he should so much as protest, they banded together to abuse him. On the other hand, with Bachkam ar-Rádhí found himself in a position of assurance such as he had not known before. Of course he had no choice but to put up with him; but Bachkam treated him himself, and insisted on his followers, treating him, with all the deference he could desire. On the occasions when he was obliged to ask the Caliph for money he did so reasonably. Moreover he was a sure defence: he was ready at any time to stand up to enemies or rebels.[1]

The history of the next two years goes to prove that ar-Rádhí rated the services of Bachkam by no means too high. At the outset al-Ḥasan the Ḥamdánid refused to pay his dues, whereupon Bachkam, in company with the Caliph, immediately led an army against him. No sooner had they departed from Baghdád than Ibn Rá'iq reappeared from the hiding in which he had sought safety; but Bachkam was so successful in his campaign, that Ibn Rá'iq was glad to negotiate with ar-Rádhí for certain governments on the western Euphrates, and leave before he should return.[2]

Soon after the successful conclusion of this campaign,

1 M. I, 419 (extract from the *awráq*).
2 M. I, 404–9; Ath. (Búláq), VIII, 124–5.

Abú 'Abd Allah reminded Bachkam of their pact; and received as well as a confirmation in his governorship of al-Baṣrah, the honorary title of Vizier.[1] Once before, during a temporary accommodation with Ibn Rá'iq, he had been similarly honoured. A satirical poem was composed for the occasion, beginning:

O sky, to fall, O Earth, to quake, prepare:
Ibn al-Barídí has become Vizier.[2]

Nor was the present agreement much better viewed. Nevertheless, its fruit was remarkable enough—peace almost unbroken for over a year. Bachkam had once said that Abú 'Abd Allah's turban covered the head not of a man but of a devil:[3] yet this did not now prevent him from marrying his daughter Sárah.[4] Their amity, however, was but outward; and Abú 'Abd Allah soon elaborated a scheme for improving his position at his new son-in-law's expense.

By attacking the Buvayhid outposts at as-Sús (Susa) Abú 'Abd Allah provoked al-Ḥasan ibn Buvayh (who had just been worsted by Vashmgír at Iṣfahán)[5] into descending on Wásiṭ, the eastern quarters of which he occupied. Bachkam easily drove him away; but he determined, on Abú 'Abd Allah's prompting, to retaliate with a campaign in the Jibál. Abú 'Abd Allah undertook to attack the Buvayhids at the same time in the south—but he really hoped instead to take Baghdád himself in Bachkam's absence. Bachkam was only warned of this treacherous design when he had already entered the Persian hills; nevertheless he promptly abandoned his campaign and turned his arms against Abú 'Abd Allah. On reaching Wásiṭ he found that the Barídís had fled to al-Baṣrah;[6] and he was about to

1 Al-Faḍhl having died recently in Palestine.

2 *fakh.* 334. These verses were by Abú'l-Faraj of Iṣfahán, the compiler of the *kitáb al-aghání.*

3 M. I, 385. 4 M. I, 410. 5 Ath. (Búláq), VIII, 125.

6 Ath. (Búláq), VIII, 126–8; M. I, 410–14.

pursue them when a courier overtook him with news of ar-Rádhí's death. For some time dropsical symptoms had warned the Caliph that he was suffering from an intestinal disease; it was supposed that systematic dissipation had undermined his constitution.[1] He died on 15th *rabí' al-awwal* 329 (18th December 940).[2]

It was afterwards calculated that, just as, with the advent of the Emirs, the grandeur of the Vizierate had come to an end, so, with the decease of ar-Rádhí, the glory of the Caliphate was eclipsed. Ar-Rádhí was the last of the Caliphs to control affairs of State; the last of the Caliphs to pronounce regularly in public the *khuṭbah*, or exhortation, at the Friday Prayers; the last whose poetry was current—and the currency of royal poetry had perhaps a political, rather than an artistic, significance; the last to entertain jesters and boon-companions; finally the last whose establishment was on the scale adopted by his forefathers. Ar-Rádhí had cultivated the society of the superior and the learned, he had maintained the Court as a centre of wit and fashion. Under his successor all this was to be changed, chiefly owing to the turbulent times ahead, but in a minor degree because of the new Caliph's tastes, which were ascetic.[3]

1 Dh. *t.* fol. 144 b; Tagh. II, 292.
2 The date is given variously, but this appears to be correct.
3 M. I, 416–17; Ath. (Búláq), VIII, 129.

CHAPTER VIII

The accession of al-Muttaqí. *The* Barídís *in* Baghdád. *The last employment of* 'Alí ibn 'Ísà.

Bachkam lost no time in sending his secretary to Baghdád to supervise the election. A college was quickly assembled, under the presidency of Sulaymán ibn al-Ḥasan (now again in the sinecure of office), consisting of all who had ever held the Vizierate, or managed *díwáns*, 'Abbásid and 'Alid nobles, *qáḍhís* and notaries. So that they might choose the more freely, these personages gave their votes two by two. But as all were assured that Bachkam had already made his mind up over the choice, they all chose the same candidate, ar-Ráḍhí's half-brother Ibrahím, who was acclaimed, less than a week later, under the title *al-muttaqí li'llah* (God-fearing).[1]

The new Caliph was twenty-six years of age. His appearance was remarkable, inasmuch as he had a very pale clear complexion, red hair and blue eyes. His tastes, as I have mentioned, were ascetic. He was given to much fasting, and he took delight neither in love nor in wine:—"I desire no boon-companion," he would declare, "save the *qur'án*."[2]

Al-Muttaqí confirmed Sulaymán as his Vizier; but to preside in the Court of Appeal (usually a Vizierial duty) he engaged 'Alí ibn 'Ísà. 'Alí had never regained ar-Ráḍhí's favour—he and his brother had remained in retirement ever since their dismissal; but the new Caliph was peculiarly touched, no doubt, by his venerable piety. His jurisdiction, however, was restricted to suits between persons unconnected with the

1 M. II, 2, 3; Ath. (Búláq), VIII, 129–30.
2 Dh. *t*. ff. 144 b–145 a; Mas. *tan*. 397; Ath. (Búláq), VIII, 149.

Government. Cases, for example, in which officials or soldiers were involved, came up, not before him, as representative of the Caliph, but before the secretary of the Emir.[1]

During the short interregnum Bachkam had taken the opportunity of playing Caliph himself: he summoned the Jesters and Boon-Companions, to enjoy their wit and gambols. But, alas, their Arabic *finesse* was largely lost upon his Turkish understanding:—he regretted that "he had learnt from them nothing profitable". Yet Bachkam was by no means stupid—indeed he could be witty himself on occasion. But his knowledge of Arabic was far from perfect: he always gave orders through an interpreter, for fear of making unbecoming mistakes in speech. On the other hand, his consultation with the famous physician Sinán ibn Thábit about a cure for his bad temper was exceedingly profitable. Sinán advised him to sleep on his decisions: and this *régime* proved so efficacious that not only did many more heads remain on shoulders than before, but Bachkam grew positively philanthropical. In the months that followed, Wásiṭ received a guest-house, and Baghdád a hospital.[2]

But the months that remained to Bachkam were sadly few. He was to be untimely cut off in mid-career. As soon as the new Caliph was comfortably enthroned, he resumed his campaign against the Barídís. His general, Túzún, having been worsted in an encounter with Abú 'Abd Allah, appealed to him for help. Bachkam thereupon hastened to join him; but before he came up with him, news reached him that Túzún in a second encounter had routed the enemy, who were in full flight for al-Baṣrah. He thus had leisure for a

1 H. 317; Dh. *t.* 145 a.

2 S.J. fol. 123 b; Dh. *t.* fol. 145 a; Ath. (Búláq), VIII, 129; M. I, 417–20. This hospital was the one called later the 'Aḏhudí. See above p. 185.

hunting expedition, for the marshy country of those parts abounded in game. But in the course of this excursion Bachkam and his retainers came upon a Kurdish encampment, out of which, his native love of rapine getting the better for a moment of his schooled restraint, he was prompted to drive the unoffending inhabitants. As they fled before him, he twice shot an arrow at one of them, and missed; whereat a young man from among them was emboldened to retort. He hid in the reeds until Bachkam rode past; then he flung a javelin, which struck the Emir in the shoulder from behind and killed him.

The death of Bachkam left the Caliph and al-Barídí to face each other. And it so befell that his resources were almost equally apportioned between the two. For his army, like the army of Mardávíj, was composed partly of Turks and partly of Daylamites; and on his death each contingent rallied to a commander of its own. The Turks, however, killed the Daylamite leader, whereupon the Daylamites quitted Wásiṭ in a body and joined Abú ‘Abd Allah in al-Baṣrah. The Turks, on the other hand, made for Baghdád, where they put themselves at the service of the Caliph. Moreover, the fear of defeat, which had been so great that he was even contemplating a flight from al-Baṣrah itself, was at once removed from Abú ‘Abd Allah; whilst a very considerable treasure, which Bachkam had amassed, fell into the clutches of al-Muttaqí.

Al-Muttaqí had thus both treasure and arms at his command; but by bad management he squandered the one, and lost the use of the other. The capital was thrown into a panic at the news of Abú ‘Abd Allah’s approach, so fearsome was his name; and the Caliph gave ear to foolish counsels, which bade him buy the aggressor off. In return for 150,000 *dínárs* al-Barídí undertook to advance no further; but he had no intention of observing his undertaking for longer than the money took to reach him. On the other hand, Bachkam's Turks, on whom alone the Caliph might rely for the defence of the city, were emboldened by this evidence of weakness also to demand a gift, and so further depleted the precious hoard. Moreover, although they made a martial show, and went out to the Diyálá, at Abú 'Abd Allah's approach they at once gave way, some openly deserting, and the rest marching off to Mosul.[1]

The advent of al-Barídí was the last of a series of misfortunes to befall Baghdád. Lately the all-important dykes of the rivers and canals had been neglected. With the spring floods of the previous year the Euphrates had burst its banks: the waters, carried along a communicating canal, had entered the western quarters of the city; houses and bridges had collapsed; many lives had been lost and much property destroyed.[2] This year the dykes of another canal had likewise given way before the floods, so that the whole rich district lying to the south-west of Baghdád was devastated,[3] and almost at the same time, as if to symbolise the declension of the dynasty, during a night of storm the great green dome of the Palace of the Round City collapsed, the "Crown of Baghdád" as it is called by al-Khaṭíb, the masterpiece of its founder al-Manṣúr.[4] Then, throughout the year before the markets had been short of grain, and though the cultivators had been grievously oppressed to obtain supplies, they had been unable to furnish nearly enough.[5] Next winter, again, there had been unusually little rain: with the hot weather, consequently, the people were faced with absolute famine. In the train of famine had followed plague—

1 M. II, 9–11, 13–14; Ath. (Búláq), VIII, 130–1; Fid. II, 88–9.
2 S.J. fol. 120 a; Dh. *t.* fol. 144 a; Tagh. II, 287.
3 M. II, 9.
4 S.J. fol. 123 a; Dh. *t.* fol. 145 a; Tagh. II, 292; M. II, 9 (extract from Ham. *tak.*).
5 M. I, 410.

for in the dearth of proper food many unfortunates were reduced to eating grass. The plague was now raging so furiously, so great was the mortality, that decent burial of the dead had become impracticable.[1]

In these trying circumstances a small number of citizens had conducted themselves with becoming charity—for the majority cared only for their own safety, and were bent rather on benefiting themselves, if that were possible, at the expense of their neighbours; and, as we might expect, a leader of the beneficent was 'Alí ibn 'Ísà. It was his custom to distribute alms to the needy at the door of his house, being assisted in this good work by a certain an-Niffarí, who had for some years acted as deputy for absentee Viziers (including al-Barídí himself).[2] 'Alí also supplied burial, during the fury of the pestilence, for innumerable persons among the poor and strangers, and was even put to the necessity of borrowing large sums to meet this expenditure.[3]

The plight of the townsfolk was thus unhappy enough already. But in addition, *ramadhán* was at hand: and that the Fast should fall at midsummer was in itself an aggravation. At such a juncture, therefore, the invasion of so ruthless a tyrant as al-Barídí was reputed to be could hardly fail to terrify the most resigned. Even to the Garden Gate there penetrated the infection of excitement.

We find a little court assembled: 'Alí reclining; with his brother 'Abd ar-Raḥmán, his two sons, Ibrahím and 'Ísà, and an adherent, by name al-Anmáṭi (who tells the story), standing before him. All the latter were exclaiming at the enormities of Abú 'Abd Allah's conduct, his frowardness, the injustice of his

1 M. II, 8; Ath. (Búláq), VIII, 133; S.J. fol. 123 b; Tagh. II, 293.
2 M. I, 368, 409.
3 M. II, 8 (extract from Ham. *tak.*); Yáq. *ud.* V, 280; Ḍháf. fol. 140 b.

rule, and the cruelty of his exactions. It was related how, to spread abroad a terror of disobedience, he would shoe men with horse-irons. Dignity and old age meant nothing to him: no one was safe from his villainy. They urged that 'Alí should leave the city before his arrival, and seek an asylum at Mosul with al-Ḥasan ibn Ḥamdán.

'Alí had not the happiest memories, in any case, of Abú 'Abd Allah. On one occasion, years before, in cross-examining him, 'Alí had invited a rebuff by reproaching him for concealing the true amount of his income: for Abú 'Abd Allah had been able to retort with, alas, only too much truth that in so acting he was but imitating the conduct of 'Alí himself, when he had concealed the true amount of his income from Ibn al-Furát.[1] Of late years, however, they had had little to do with each other, and unless Abú 'Abd Allah bore malice for his first dismissal, 'Alí might at least hope to come off no worse from a present encounter than anybody else. Nevertheless, the least that was to be expected from Abú 'Abd Allah was described as so dreadful, that in the end 'Alí gave way. He instructed al-Anmáṭí to hire a number of boats, into which the household might pack themselves and their belongings, and handed him 200 *dínárs* for his expenses.

Al-Anmáṭí was hardly awake next morning, however, before a message summoned him to attend on 'Alí. On being admitted, he began an apology for not having yet carried out last night's instructions; but 'Alí cut him short, saying that he had thought the matter over, and had changed his mind. For one Created Being to flee from another was, he had decided, contrary to Religion and Morals. He would remain in Baghdád. As for the money, it should be devoted to pious uses.

But 'Alí was resolved, not only on staying, but on going out of his way, as the others considered it, to

1 M. I, 110.

court danger. When al-Barídí entered the city, he insisted on rowing down in his barge to meet him. And his temerity was justified, for Abú 'Abd Allah, in despite of his horrid reputation, greeted him with all the deference due to his rank, with all the honours, in fact, to which a Created Being might aspire. When 'Alí made as if to rise from his barge, Abú 'Abd Allah would have none of it; but himself moved into 'Alí's. Their conversation abounded in conventional expressions of mutual esteem; but 'Alí was particularly gratified at Abú 'Abd Allah's reference to his good works.[1]

The fears of 'Alí's advisers were thus belied; and so, in general, as it turned out, were those of the populace. But as the sojourn of al-Barídí in Baghdád lasted but four and twenty days, he had little opportunity of putting his intentions, whatever they may have been, into practice. In this short time, it is true, he succeeded in destituting the Vizier of the day, and in wringing another 500,000 *dínárs* from the Caliph. But these measures in no way affected the generality and were actually his undoing. In order to coerce al-Muttaqí, he had stirred up the army to importune him for money. But when al-Muttaqí handed him over the said sum, their agitation became directed instead against Abú 'Abd Allah himself. In a body they attacked the house of his brother Abú'l-Ḥusayn, who had accompanied him, and burnt down the gateway. The citizens then joined eagerly in the fray, and declared their intention of seizing his treasure. Abú 'Abd Allah had encamped on the west bank: when he learnt of the attack, therefore, he at once cut the bridge. A fierce fight took place between his men and the Caliph's in mid-stream; and under cover of the contest the Barídís made off to Wásiṭ.

The revolt had been led by two generals, Kúrankíj

1 H. 358–9; M. II, 14; Ḍháf. fol. 140 b; Yáq. *ud.* v, 280.

of the Daylamites, and Tagínak of the Turks. Kúrankíj was the more powerful: al-Muttaqí therefore now created him Emir in the room of Bachkam; and as at the same time it was necessary to replace al-Barídí in the Vizierate, the Caliph appealed to his admired 'Alí ibn 'Ísà, aged as he was, to take up the task again. 'Alí however appears to have demurred, at any rate until a compromise was arrived at: for in the end he was not embarrassed with the title of Vizier, which he so hated, and it was also arranged that 'Abd ar-Raḥmán should share the burden with him. 'Alí was to wait on the Caliph, laying cases before him, giving him counsel and taking his orders; 'Abd ar-Raḥmán was to manage the *díwáns*. But in any case their ministry lasted but little over a week. For Kúrankíj soon pressed them for money: and 'Alí had none to give him. At an evening meeting, attended by himself, his brother, the Emir, and his secretary, 'Alí protested that for the moment there was no source of revenue on which he could draw. As a result, next morning the Banú'l-Jarráḥ received their dismissal. Another official had offered to furnish the necessary funds, and had been accepted by the Caliph in their stead.[1]

This was the last occasion on which 'Alí ibn 'Ísà was to hold even the shadow of office. He was now grown feeble in his extreme old age, and even the effort of attending at conclaves was beginning to tire him unduly. For some time now he had been forced to use a device against fatigue. He would sit, in public, before a curtained alcove, seemingly upright, as manners required, but in reality supported by hidden cushions. He had always valued deportment, and was reputed never to have been seen sitting negligently, or improperly dressed, in his assembly. Even at home he treated his family with unusual ceremony. One of his sons used afterwards to relate, how once, in these

1 M. II, 15–19; Ath. (Búláq), VIII, 131–2; H. 317; *fakh.* 333.

latter days, he had surprised his father lying at full length; yet as soon as he saw him, 'Alí had raised himself into a more seemly pose, in spite of his eighty years.[1]

But however much 'Alí's bodily strength was impaired, his mind continued to work with its accustomed vigour. Only the year before he had coined an aphorism of religious import. He was condoling with the sons of Abú'l-Ḥusayn the Chief *qáḍhí* on their father's death.[2] "A misfortune that deserves a recompense," he remarked as he left, "is better than a favour that arouses no gratitude."[3]

With the death of Abú'l-Ḥusayn, 'Alí must have felt himself aged indeed. Abú 'Umar had been his contemporary, and now his son was dead, and his grandchildren full of responsible years. Henceforward 'Alí retired quite out of public life; but he still occupied a position of especial prestige, and was yet more than once to be called upon for opinion and assistance. Though Baghdád was on several occasions again to fall into the hands of insurgents, he contemplated flight no more; but, fortified in the consciousness of virtue, remained at home, or went out, as he had done for Abú 'Abd Allah, to pay his respects.

1 H. 325; Tan. *nish.* 27.
2 He died in *sha'bán* 328 (May–June 940): Dh. *t.* fol. 144 b.
3 H. 323; Yáq. *ud.* v, 280.

CHAPTER IX

Further vicissitudes of the Emirate.

Further political changes followed hard on the retirement of the Banú'l-Jarráḥ. Kúrankíj had enjoyed the Emirate scarcely two months when his position was menaced by the approach from Syria of Ibn Rá'iq, whom Bachkam's death had tempted to return.

As Ibn Rá'iq neared Baghdád towards the end of the year 329 (late summer, 941), Kúrankíj went out to oppose him, and in the fight obtained a definite advantage. Ibn Rá'iq was even resigned to a retreat, but in a last attempt sent some of his men to cross the Tigris and surprise the Daylamites from behind. The stratagem succeeded: at the first shot the Daylamites fancied themselves entrapped: their camp broke up in confusion, and they fled for their lives. Ibn Rá'iq followed up his advantage. With the applause of the citizens, who had suffered with detestation their insolence and tyranny, he slew pitilessly every Daylamite that fell into his hands, even such as surrendered in the promise of quarter. He caught and imprisoned Kúrankíj. Al-Muttaqí was obliged, in consequence, to restore him to the Emirate.

As soon as he learnt of Ibn Rá'iq's success, al-Barídí at once sent his brothers to turn Kúrankíj's forces out of Wásiṭ; and acclaimed the new Emir in the Friday Prayers. But this promise of harmony between the two was soon dispelled. Two months later al-Barídí withheld his dues; whereupon Ibn Rá'iq set out to compel him. But Túzún (Bachkam's general) and his Turks chose this moment to mutiny: and the Emir was forced to compound with Abú 'Abd Allah, on whom he conferred the Vizierate (for the fourth time) in exchange for his obedience. Before long, however, al-Barídí announced his intention of coming in person to the capital; at which Ibn Rá'iq, infuriated, dismissed him from office. Al-Barídí, in reply, sent his two brothers, Abú'l-Ḥusayn and Abú Yúsuf, to take Baghdád by force.

The armies met near the Diyálá on 15th *jumádà'l-ákhirah* 330 (7th March 942). The Baghdádís rallied to the support of Ibn Rá'iq; but the Barídís defeated him, and entered the capital four days later. Al-Muttaqí and his son, the Prince Abú Manṣúr, immediately fled from the palace. At the Shammásiyyah Gate they were joined by Ibn Rá'iq and the remains of his army. And from there they set forth in the direction of Mosul, hoping to find a refuge with the Ḥamdánids.

The fears of the citizens at the occupation of Baghdád by Abú 'Abd Allah had been exaggerated; but the tyranny of Abú'l-Ḥusayn his brother now surpassed their most dreadful expectations. His *régime* endured less than four months: yet it was computed that in this time about ten thousand persons lost their lives, so rife were lawlessness and oppression. The collections of the land-tax from the Muslims, and the poll-tax from the Christians and Jews, were carried out with frightful severity, and at a season, viz. the spring, when payment would be most onerous. House to house searches for horses were instituted, and under this pretext al-Barídí's men looted the dwellings of the wealthy to their heart's content.

Abú'l-Ḥusayn's advent to the palace had been followed by a massacre of the retinue, the violation of the Harem, and finally the sack of the building itself; and afterwards a like treatment was accorded to the mansions of many eminent persons. The various contingents of the army fought among themselves, Carmathians (for there were by now a number of these sectaries employed as mercenaries) against Turks, each against Daylamites, all against the people. Throughout half the city, and for a considerable time, civil war prevailed. Al-Ḥusayn, installed in the palace that had belonged to Mu'nis, made an attempt to quell it, and took hostages, against the misconduct of officers, of their wives and children. But to this pandemonium the peasants were reluctant to bring supplies. The price of grain therefore again rose to fantastic heights. Famine set in once more: and, as before, it was accompanied by an outbreak of plague. In *shawwál* (June–July 942) Abú'l-Ḥusayn intensified his oppressive measures, and conditions became so intolerable for the generality, but especially for former Government officials, that many of them took up their abode outside the walls. Reduced almost to destitution, they gathered what they could for food, and awaited in resignation the advent of happier times.[1]

Meanwhile the Caliph and the Emir had been received with enthusiasm by the Ḥamdánids. Al-Ḥasan had not himself ventured to meet them, but he had sent his brother 'Alí, who had escorted them from Takrít to Mosul. At their coming, indeed, al-Ḥasan moved up-stream, but a correspondence assured him of their peaceable intentions, and he soon returned to encamp on the opposite bank. The Prince Abú Manṣúr, accompanied by Ibn Rá'iq, crossed over to greet him, and they were received in a shower of gold and silver coins. The meeting passed off to the satisfaction of either side, and the Prince rose to leave and mounted his horse. As Ibn Rá'iq made to do likewise, however, his bridle was seized, whereupon his horse reared and threw him. Al-Ḥasan then ordered his retainers to set upon the Emir and kill him. This they immediately did: and the body of the unfortunate adventurer was without more ado cast into the Tigris. Al-Ḥasan next

1 M. II, 20–6; Ath. (Búláq), VIII, 132–5; Mas. *tan.* 398; S.J. ff. 123 b, 126 a; Dh. *t.* fol. 146 a; Tagh. II, 296–7.

hastened to assure al-Muttaqí that, notwithstanding this violence, his sentiments were all of loyalty. It was merely that he had known that Ibn Rá'iq was negotiating treachery, and had taken the execution of justice into his own hands. The Caliph accepted these advances, perforce, with a good grace. He commanded his attendance: and a week later, on 1st *sha'bán* (21st April), al-Ḥasan crossed over into the city. He was created in turn Emir of Emirs, and in addition received the laudatory title *náṣir ad-dawlah* (Defender of the Dynasty).[1] To cement their attachment he gave his daughter in marriage to the Caliph's son.[2]

The murder of Ibn Rá'iq was a signal for the discontent at Baghdád to crystallise into a plot against Abú'l-Ḥusayn. A party of the Turks indeed made their way forthwith to the Caliph, but the others, led by Túzún, determined to arrest the tyrant. Their plans, however, were betrayed, whereupon they too proceeded to Mosul; and their arrival so encouraged al-Muttaqí, that he determined once more to try his fortune at the capital. He arrived there, towards the end of *shawwál* (June–July 942), in company with the Náṣir ad-Dawlah, but to find that the Barídís, mistrusting the issue of a fight, had fled to Abú 'Abd Allah in Wásiṭ. Their presence, unvanquished, within so short a distance of Baghdád continued, however, to disquiet him. The Náṣir accordingly set out, in the course of the next fortnight, with his brother 'Alí, to drive them further away. Their fears were justified: for on the descent of this army, Abú 'Abd Allah sent out a force to oppose it. The Náṣir remained in Ctesiphon, but his brother advanced to encounter them downstream. The fight lasted for several days, and though in the beginning it went against him, he was finally victorious. His men, however, were too exhausted to

1 M. II, 27–8; Ath. (Búláq), VIII, 135.
2 S.J. fol. 128 b; Tagh. II, 301.

pursue the enemy: it was not until almost a week later that they reached Wásiṭ; and by that time there was nothing to be seen of the Barídís, who had made good their retreat to al-Baṣrah.[1]

This was by no means the first notable exploit of 'Alí ibn 'Abd Allah ibn Ḥamdán. Six years before, at the age of twenty-one, he had led the first of those expeditions against the Greeks that were afterwards to make him famous, and he had led others since. Already the Greeks knew him as a redoubtable commander.[2] But it was for this present defence of his interests that al-Muttaqí now conferred on him the title by which he is best known, *sayf ad-dawlah* (Sword of the Dynasty). Later the Sayf ad-Dawlah was to be the centre of a brilliant court at Aleppo, of which the chief ornament was the poet—accounted the greatest of all the Arab poets—al-Mutanabbí. Al-Mutanabbí sang his praises in splendid odes and so helped to spread his fame; but his fame had a real foundation in his adventurous leadership of many triumphant expeditions.

His present victory, however, had no very lasting effects, and before long he was involved in difficulties with his subordinate officers. It had been his wish to pursue the Barídís to al-Baṣrah, and he had applied to the Náṣir for funds to carry on the campaign. But whether from jealousy or negligence the Náṣir delayed in sending it, and in the interval, Túzún and another Turkish general, by name Khajkhaj, began to show signs of insubordination. When the treasure actually arrived, their attitude became so threatening that the Sayf was compelled to improvise an expedition, and commanded them to collect for their own benefit the revenue of a neighbouring district. This, however, was but a temporary expedient; the Sayf soon saw that with

1 M. II, 26, 29–30; Ath. (Búláq), VIII, 135–6.

2 Ḍháf. fol. 2 a *et seqq.*; Dh. *t.* ff. 141 a, 144 a; Tagh. II, 278, 287; S.J. fol. 120 a.

such turbulent and ambitious officers he could expect nothing but recurrent mutiny. Sacrificing his camp, therefore, to the rapacity of the soldiery, he made his escape secretly to Baghdád.

In the meantime the Náṣir's messenger had returned in consternation, and so alarmed his master that he too decided to withdraw at once to Mosul. Rather than jeopardise his real principality in those parts he would forgo the equivocal delights of the Emirate. Al-Muttaqí implored him to remain; but he persisted. Taking every precaution against the Turks, he decamped towards the end of *ramadhán* 331 (June 943), and was joined by his brother on the way.[1]

In connection with the poet al-Mutanabbí, I may mention here a curious passage in a work written about the end of the fourth/tenth century,[2] in which he is confronted with ‘Alí ibn ‘Ísà. Al-Mutanabbí began his career by believing himself inspired, and preached a new revelation to certain tribes of the lower Euphrates (hence his name: *al-mutanabbí* = he that claims to be a prophet). For this blasphemy he was seized and thrown into prison. And there he remained till after some years he confessed that his pretensions were empty. Ibn al-Qáriḥ, the author of the above-mentioned work, quotes another history to state that al-Mutanabbí, having been imprisoned in Baghdád, was brought before ‘Alí ibn ‘Ísà for examination. As a sign of his mission he exposed a wart on his belly; ‘Alí, however, refused to accept it, and had him beaten and returned to his prison.

It is not absolutely impossible that the story should be true; but it is most improbable, and the author himself admits that it was rejected as false by the

1 M. II, 39–41; Ath. (Búláq), VIII, 140.

2 The *risálah* of Ibn al-Qáriḥ, published in a compilation entitled *rasá'il al-bulaghá'* (Cairo, 1331/1913), p. 197.

people of Baghdád and Cairo. Al-Mutanabbí was born only in 303 (915–16), and is said to have declared himself some time after 320 (932).[1] He might, therefore, have appeared before 'Alí during one of the latter's short terms of office under ar-Rádhí or al-Muttaqí. But it is stated in other accounts that he was arrested, not in al-'Iráq, but in Syria, and imprisoned, not in Baghdád, but in Emessa.[2] In fine, as M. Massignon has pointed out,[3] another pretender of the same kind was in fact brought before 'Alí ibn 'Ísà during his first Vizierate in 302 (914–15),[4] who also showed a wart (on his back) to prove his claim. This cannot have been al-Mutanabbí himself, for he was not yet born; but the anecdote is possibly the foundation of that quoted by Ibn al-Qáriḥ.

1 Khall. (trans.), I, 106, 109, note.
2 *Ibid.* I, 104; S.J. fol. 157 a.
3 Massignon: *Al-Hallaj*, 209, note 3.
4 See 'A. 48–9.

CHAPTER X

The Image *of* Edessa. Túzún. *The second flight and the fate of* al-Muttaqí. Al-Mustakfí.

It was at about this time that 'Alí ibn 'Ísà was called upon to give his opinion on a question of religious right. After a period of quiescence, dating from one of the periodical but inconclusive pacts between the Muslims and the Greeks, which had been negotiated during the reign of ar-Rádhí, war had again broken out between the rival States. The Greeks had profited by the pre-occupation of the Ḥamdánids in al-'Iráq: during the preceding year under the leadership of an able general, the Domestic John Curcuas, they had penetrated even as far as Aleppo, plundering the country, and taking captive some fifteen hundred persons. At the same time, they had suffered certain reverses at sea; but now they carried the war into northern Mesopotamia, sacking Ra's al-'Ayn and laying siege to Edessa.[1] Edessa was a place of peculiar interest to the Christians, for enshrined in its cathedral was a very famous relic, a miraculous portrait of Christ, supposed to have been sent by him with a letter to the contemporary King of Osrhoene, of which State Edessa had been the capital. Although they seemed likely to take the city in any case, the Greeks promised the inhabitants that if they would yield up the image, they on their side would raise the siege and also release a great number of Muslim prisoners. The governor, however, did not dare to agree without consulting the Caliph. He therefore sent a messenger to Baghdád to ask his permission.

1 Vasílief: *Vizantíya i Araby*, I, 244–50; Ath. (Búláq), VIII, 124, 139; Khald. III, 409, 417; S.J. fol. 115 a; Tagh. II, 283; Dh. *t.* fol. 143 b.

Al-Muttaqí at once convened a college of *qádhís* and jurists to consider the proposal. Some were for accepting it; but others were for rejecting it because, although as an object of Christian veneration the image had no intrinsic value, yet it had been in Muslim hands so long, no Emperor ever having presumed to demand it, that to relinquish it now would constitute a notable humiliation. 'Alí was one of the company assembled; and when his turn came to speak, he gave it as his opinion that the fate of Muslims should outweigh considerations of policy. The council was persuaded by the good sense of his ruling; and in the end resolved unanimously to adopt it.[1]

It was not the first time that 'Alí had had to concern himself with the fate of Muslim captives in Greek hands. Once, years before, during one of his Vizierates, a colleague had found him plunged in gloom, and enquired its cause. 'Alí, it seemed, had learnt that the Greeks had recently changed their policy, and were now ill-treating their prisoners. His interlocutor suggested that in order to influence the Emperors (Romanus and Constantine) pressure might be exerted on the Patriarch of Antioch and the Catholicos of Jerusalem, living as they did in Muslim territory; 'Alí was delighted with his advice, and determined to act on it. Some months later a messenger returned with good news. He had actually accompanied the prelates' envoy on his journey to Constantinople, and with his own ears had heard how from one day to another the prisoners had been relieved from misery to comparative ease. They had asked him how this change had been brought about, through whose influence; and he had told them how 'Alí, having become Vizier, had concerned himself with their welfare. At this a woman from among them had cried out, "O 'Alí ibn 'Ísà, may

1 Vasílief, *op. cit.* I, 250–3; Ath. (Búláq), VIII, 143; Khald. III, 417; Tagh. II, 301; S.J. fol. 129 a, etc.

God never forget this deed!", and all the prisoners had blessed him. On hearing this 'Alí wept with emotion, and gave thanks to God. His adviser then took the opportunity of pointing out that the burdens of office, against which 'Alí was always exclaiming, had thus their compensations. "Perhaps," he added, "God makes you powerful and puts these things into your hands, so that you may benefit thereby in the world to come, like as in this world you are distinguished by the honour of the Vizierate."[1]

Perhaps it was the memory of this former benefaction that guided 'Alí in his present decision. In any case al-Muttaqí acted on the resolution of the council. The Christian inhabitants of Edessa were exceedingly reluctant to part with their blessed image: they tried in vain to foist off a copy on the bishop sent to receive it, and only yielded in the end to the threats of the Muslim commandant. But at length it was removed with elaborate ceremony to Constantinople, performing on the way a series of miracles.[2]

To return to our narrative: on the departure of the Sayf from Wásiṭ, Túzún and Khajkhaj were left to quarrel for the Emirate. It was at first settled that Túzún should adopt the title, whilst Khajkhaj commanded the army; but Túzún soon found reason to suspect and blind his colleague, proceeded to Baghdád, and was confirmed by the helpless Caliph in his self-arrogated rank. No sooner, however, had Túzún in turn betaken himself from Wásiṭ, than Abú 'Abd Allah, against whom he had made a demonstration, took the opportunity to reoccupy the city. But Abú 'Abd Allah was himself shortly afterwards beleaguered in al-Baṣrah by the ruler of 'Umán, who ascended the estuary in his fleet: so that the Barídís were delivered from final disaster only when the 'Umánite ships were fired by a crafty mariner. And by now Túzún, having settled himself firmly in

1 H. 327–9; Tan. *nish.* 30–2. 2 Vasílief, *op. cit.* I, 253–4.

Baghdád, was ready again to attack them. Yet Túzún was more desirous of peace than of war, and a pact between them was soon sealed by the marriage of his daughter to Abú 'Abd Allah. In the meantime, however, al-Muttaqí had been scared into quitting Baghdád by the arrival of a certain Ibn Shírzád, who had fled from the Barídís in al-Baṣrah at the time of the siege, had met Túzún on his journey down the Tigris, and had been appointed as his deputy in the capital. The alliance had been represented to the Caliph as a threat to his sovereignty. He had consequently appealed once more to the Ḥamdánids. His appeal had been answered by the appearance of the Sayf ad-Dawlah at the Ḥarb Gate. In short, the Court was now safely removed to Mosul.

On hearing of the Caliph's flight, Túzún was deeply chagrined. He at once returned to Baghdád; and there ensued in the neighbourhood a series of battles between himself and the Sayf, in which the latter was finally defeated. But the Náṣir and al-Muttaqí had by this time withdrawn to ar-Raqqah, and from this sure retreat the Caliph shortly reopened negotiations with the Emir.[1]

Meanwhile the Barídís were reaping the reward of their deceitful ways; they had begun to quarrel with one another. In consequence of a dispute about money Abú Yúsuf was assassinated at the instance of Abú 'Abd Allah; then, eight months later, Abú 'Abd Allah died a natural death himself. Next year the third brother Abú'l-Ḥusayn became embroiled with his nephew Abú'l-Qásim, and came to the capital to secure the assistance of the Emir in driving him from al-Baṣrah. When his suit was neglected, however, he could not resist the temptation of intriguing against Ibn Shírzád, to whom he attributed its failure. As a result, an old condemnation, dating from his notorious

1 M. II, 41–2, 44–9; Ath. (Búláq), VIII, 140–2, 144.

occupation of Baghdád, was produced against Abú'l-Ḥusayn: he was beheaded, and his body, as that of a malefactor, was exposed. Abú'l-Qásim continued to rule al-Baṣrah as a provincial governor, and did so in an exemplary way. But this was, in fact, the end of the family as a force, and with its disappearance, the political situation was greatly clarified.[1]

Whilst he was at ar-Raqqah al-Muttaqí was visited by the governor of Egypt, Muḥammad ibn Ṭughj the Ikhshíd, who offered him his protection and even invited him to come with him to Egypt. He implored the Caliph at least to remain in the safety of ar-Raqqah rather than venture his fortunes again in the capital; but al-Muttaqí was finding the Ḥamdánids by no means docile supporters; moreover he had already begun to treat with the Emir. He had obtained his oath and likewise the oath of Ibn Shírzád, sworn most solemnly before a concourse of notables and judges, to respect his sovereignty should he return. The Ikhshíd's offer, therefore, came too late; and he departed to Egypt. Al-Muttaqí, after obtaining a confirmation of Túzún's pledge, began his journey down the Euphrates in the New Year, 333, and was met by the Emir in the neighbourhood of al-Anbár on 19th *ṣafar* (11th October 944).[2]

As they came face to face Túzún bent down and kissed the ground before the Caliph. But having done so, he declared that the obligations of his oath were fulfilled. The unfortunate al-Muttaqí was seized by his henchmen, borne off to his tent, and there blinded. His cries and the wailing of his women were drowned in a beating of drums. A spectator of the outrage was his successor, who being a son of al-Muktafí, by name

1 M. II, 51–4, 58–61, 78–80; Ath. (Búláq), VIII, 145–6, 158; Dh. *t.* ff. 204 b, 205 b, 208 b.

2 So Mas. *tan.* 397. M. II, 71, has 28th *ṣafar*, but Ath. (Búláq), VIII, 150 states that al-Mustakfí appointed his Vizier on 23rd *ṣafar*.

'Abd Allah, was also his first cousin. This prince was at once proclaimed Caliph under the title of *al-mustakfí bi'llah* (Desirous of Being Satisfied with God Alone).

Túzún is excused by the historians for his treachery towards al-Muttaqí on the ground that he was young and susceptible. Indeed, even as late as a week before, partisans of al-Muttaqí had been satisfied that his intentions were honourable. He was persuaded, however, that if he did not break his oath, al-Muttaqí would break his; and had acted on this assumption. But as if in expiation, he himself succumbed, less than a year later, to the epilepsy from which he had for some time been suffering. His death occurred in *al-muḥarram* 334 (August–September 945); and it opened the political field to a clash of forces that his presence had hitherto restrained.[1]

Three years before, Aḥmad ibn Buvayh had all but taken al-Baṣrah from the Barídís, and had remained for some time encamped in the neighbourhood.[2] The next year, encouraged with false promises of co-operation by Abú 'Abd Allah—who hoped by pitting him against Túzún to weaken both—he had advanced on Baghdád. Túzún had entrapped his army in an ambush on the Diyálá and scattered it[3]. Yet Aḥmad had again come to Wásiṭ, though indeed he had retired on Túzún's approach, six months before the latter's death.[4] To counteract this Buvayhid menace Ibn Shírzád, Túzún's secretary, was now anxious to confer the Emirate once more on the Náṣir ad-Dawlah. But the soldiery clamoured so insistently for him to assume it himself, that he was at length forced to do so.

At the time of Túzún's death Ibn Shírzád was at

1 M. II, 61–2, 67–72 (with extract from the *kitáb al-'uyún*), 81; Ath. (Búláq), VIII, 146, 148–9, 160; Mas. *tan.* 397.

2 Ath. (Búláq), VIII, 143; M. II, 59.

3 Ath. (Búláq), VIII, 144–5; M. II, 50–1, 77.

4 Ath. (Búláq), VIII, 159; M. II, 82 (extract from Ham. *tak.*).

Hít on the Euphrates, engaged in arranging a contract; but he immediately posted to Baghdád. He wished to obtain advances on the security of this contract from various rich citizens in the capital; and he applied to 'Alí among them. His agent prevailed upon 'Ísà, 'Alí's son, to sign a bond on this account in his father's name for 1000 *dínárs*; but 'Alí, when 'Ísà told him of what he had done, was greatly perturbed. In these troublous times, such a security was far from safe: he protested that he could not guarantee more than 500, and went round to explain in person to Ibn Shírzád. Ibn Shírzád, however, was so ashamed of the method he had employed, that he declined to see 'Alí, although he sent out his secretary and one of his colleagues to interview him. The old man went away disconsolate; but it was not so much the question of money that distressed him: it was the spectacle of a great officer of State so demeaning himself.

The efforts of Ibn Shírzád to govern as Emir were even less admirable. He was soon reduced to using the most barefaced oppression in the raising of funds. His power, however, was to last but a short while; for his political measures were equally ill-conceived, and soon brought disaster upon him. The governor he sent to the Jibál was quickly evicted by the Sámánids. His governor of Takrít entered into relations with the Náṣir ad-Dawlah, now once again hostile, so that this district as well was lost to him. But the direct cause of his downfall was the action of yet a third governor, that of Wásiṭ. For the latter, doubting the capacity of Ibn Shírzád to maintain his position, invited one to advance on the capital in whom he had more faith—Aḥmad ibn Buvayh.

The commander acted on his suggestion without delay. When they learnt that a Buvayhid army was approaching, the soldiery at Baghdád were dismayed—without a Túzún, without a Bachkam to lead them, the Turks felt themselves at a loss; and instead of proceeding to defend the city at the Diyálá, they sought the oratory, as if to protest at a decree of Heaven. As the Buvayhids drew nearer, the Caliph and Ibn Shírzád both went into hiding; but when the Turks forthwith abandoned the city and marched north to join the Náṣir ad-Dawlah, they ventured to reappear. By this time the invaders had approached to within a short distance of the city, and before long one of Ibn Buvayh's chief advisers[1] appeared at the gates and requested an interview with al-Mustakfí. The Caliph explained in the course of their conversation that he was delighted at the approach of the Buvayhid general. It was true that he had gone into hiding; but only in order to rid himself of the Turks and obviate unnecessary bloodshed.[2]

1 Al-Muhallabí, probably already deputy to the Vizier aṣ-Ṣaymarí. See Yáq. *ud.* III, 180.

2 M. II, 82 (extract from Ham. *tak.*)–85; Ath. (Búláq), VIII, 160–1; Dh. *t.* fol. 209 a; Tagh. II, 308.

CHAPTER XI

The Mu'izz ad-Dawlah.

Aḥmad ibn Buvayh entered Baghdád on Saturday 11th *jumádà'l-ákhirah* 334 (18th January 946), and encamped by the Shammásiyyah Gate. Next day he had audience of al-Mustakfí and swore allegiance, giving as well an undertaking to respect the rights of Ibn Shírzád. In return he himself was granted the Emirate, that of Ibn Shírzád having automatically lapsed. Moreover he now received a title of somewhat ironical sound, to wit, *mu'izz ad-dawlah* (Magnifier of the Dynasty), whilst his absent elder brothers 'Alí and al-Ḥasan were at the same time created *'imád ad-dawlah* (Prop of the Dynasty) and *rukn ad-dawlah* (Pillar of the Dynasty) respectively.[1]

The whole city was in a ferment at his coming, and many of the notables felt it to be their duty to go up and call on him. 'Ísà and Ibrahím urged 'Alí to do so, and in spite of the fact that movement was now by no means so easy to him as once it had been, he agreed. One winter's morning, accordingly, he might have been seen standing with Ibrahím on the embankment before his house, waiting for his bargemen to pull in. As they looked out, another barge passed by,[2] sitting in which was a man of important mien with two or three companions. The important one, after enquiring

1 M. II, 85; Ath. (Búláq), VIII, 161.

2 In this passage, published in H. p. 6 of introduction, note, and M. II, 104, note, from Ham. *tak.* fol. 99 a, the word *mujtáz* (passing) has been wrongly copied from the MS. as *muḥtáj* (in need), making nonsense. I think also that in the preceding phrase —"*wa'ttafaqa annahu nazila ilà dárihi*", the *ilà* (to), though correctly transcribed, should read *min* (from), to form the sentence:—"Now it happened that he was coming down from his house...".

and being told who 'Alí might be, sent one of the party to land and invite the old man to join them. 'Alí, for whom every action had now to be precisely thought out before it was determined upon, was disconcerted by this sudden derangement of his plans; but after some discussion he was at length persuaded to accede. The whole company then rowed up-stream to opposite the Shammásiyyah Gate, where the barge was moored at the landing-stage, and the important one made as if to disembark.

"Sit, my lord," he said to 'Alí, "sit in your place, till I warn the Emir of your coming."

At this 'Alí was astonished.

"May God prolong your continuance!" he exclaimed, "then you are on terms of friendship, and have influence with the Emir?"

'Alí had not recognised his host. But no sooner had he gone up, than Ibrahím told him who it was. It was none other than aṣ-Ṣaymarí, Ibn Buvayh's Vizier; but he had forbidden his companions to disclose his name. 'Alí was very much perturbed to hear this, and began to have doubts about his other fellow-passengers in the barge, lest they too should turn out to be persons of distinction. However, it was established to his satisfaction that they were not; and he vented his disapproval of the trick that had been played upon him in remarks that for him were almost caustic.

Before long aṣ-Ṣaymarí reappeared, but with the disappointing news that the Emir could not for the moment see them. However, he promised that an interview should be arranged for the next day, and that a barge should be waiting in the morning at 'Alí's steps. 'Alí now took the opportunity of treating aṣ-Ṣaymarí with the deference so great a man deserved, and apologised for having omitted, because he had not known who he was, to do so before. The minister was mildly disappointed that his secret had been given away; but 'Alí went off satisfied, and he returned to his master.

The Mu'izz ad-Dawlah had been unable to receive them for the simple reason that he was drunk. However, he had now recovered enough to understand what was said to him. Aṣ-Ṣaymarí told him that 'Alí ibn 'Ísà had been to call, but that he had had to put him off till the next day.

"Who is 'Alí ibn 'Ísà?" asked the Mu'izz.

"The Vizier of al-Muqtadir," answered aṣ-Ṣaymarí.

"That great one!" exclaimed the Mu'izz, in a tone of awe.

This was the true perspective of the matter. In spite of his deference to the mere minister of this chieftain, 'Alí himself was in truth vastly the more deserving of honour and veneration. The Mu'izz was now but one and thirty years of age, so that 'Alí had known greatness before he was born. The reign even of al-Muqtadir had by now grown almost legendary, a veritable Golden Age.[1] And one who had governed the whole Caliphate during those times of its prosperity must in the eyes of this wild Persian have been a "great one" indeed.

Before the meeting, the Mu'izz ad-Dawlah was in great trepidation lest his manners should fail of pleasing. But he was carefully coached by aṣ-Ṣaymarí, and acquitted himself perfectly well, exceeding indeed his instructions. Their conversation, which was largely concerned with politics, could not, unhappily, be as intimate as he and 'Alí could have wished, for the Mu'izz spoke with ease only his native Persian, whilst 'Alí, however well he was acquainted with that language (and whether he was or not nowhere appears), would not for the world so have defied etiquette as to use it on an occasion of ceremony. At one moment disaster impended, when the Emir took the

1 Cf. Ḏháf. fol. 138 a.

silence of aṣ-Ṣaymarí, who was acting as interpreter, to mean that ʿAlí had said something offensive, whereas he was in reality complimenting aṣ-Ṣaymarí himself. A confusion also occurred when ʿAlí introduced, for the support of a Tradition, the chain of authorities by name. But these difficulties were surmounted, and in general the interview was brought to a satisfactory conclusion. Before ʿAlí took leave, the Muʿizz ad-Dawlah begged to have the honour of gratifying some wish of his visitor. At some pressure ʿAlí was brought to request his protection for his household. It included, he said, "a great number of boys and girls, and old women and kinsfolk, and relatives and followers and friends". The Emir protested that so much was the least he could do. And on this they parted.

The retainers lined up from the doorway to the river-steps. The chamberlain moved forward. ʿAlí ibn ʿÍsà walked in his wake slowly and painfully to his barge. Thus honoured by the new master of Baghdád, a ghost almost of the old *régime*, he walks out into the sunlight on the quay, down to the green Tigris—and so out of this history.[1]

The Muʿizz ad-Dawlah was definitely to remain master of Baghdád, although his mastery was not to go unchallenged. He began his reign, for to such did his rule amount, with a gesture that, though it was dictated by political necessity, was symbolic: mistrusting al-Mustakfí (who had also brought the Caliphate into contempt by a most shameless profligacy) he deposed and blinded him—this unhappy prince went to join in darkness his predecessors al-Qáhir and al-Muttaqí, who were both still living, al-Qáhir in such destitution that he was forced to beg in the streets.[2]

1 Ham. *tak.* ff. 99 a–101 a, published M. II, 104–7 and H. p. 6 of introduction *et seqq.*

2 M. II, 25 (extract from Ham. *tak.*), 80–1; Ath. (Búláq), VIII, 158; *fakh.* 324.

—If he had followed his own inclinations the Mu'izz ad-Dawlah would now have put an end to the 'Abbásid Caliphate altogether, and would either have acknowledged the Fáṭimid, or have raised another prince of the Shí'ah to the throne. He had even singled out one or two suitable persons, but he was dissuaded from carrying out any such plan by aṣ-Ṣaymarí, who pointed out its dangers. If trouble were to arise between himself and an 'Alid Caliph, his Daylamite followers, all devoted adherents of the Shí'ah, would side against him. In the case of an 'Abbásid they would side with him. Policy outweighed religion, and the Mu'izz proclaimed another son of al-Muqtadir, al-Fadhl by name, to have succeeded his cousin. The new Caliph adopted the style *al-muṭí' li'llah* (Obedient to God).

Ever since the deposition of al-Muttaqí, this prince had had designs on the throne. Al-Mustakfí had been apprised of them, and had set on foot a rigorous but vain search for the pretender; but al-Fadhl had eluded his spies, and al-Mustakfí had had to content himself with destroying his house. When he heard of it, 'Alí ibn 'Ísà had predicted al-Fadhl's succession: "This day," he observed, "he has been acknowledged Heir to the Throne." On the arrival of the Mu'izz, al-Fadhl had appealed to him: with the present result that 'Alí's prophecy had come true.[1]

The accession of al-Muṭí' marks a definite, almost a final, stage in the decline of the Caliphate. Hitherto the Caliphs had continued to be served by a Vizier, whilst the Emirs had been content with a secretary: henceforward this rule was to be reversed. Again, already with al-Mustakfí, the Mu'izz had instituted the custom of making the Caliph an allowance of money. But for al-Muṭí' he cut down this allowance almost to half. This it is true may merely have been

1 M. II, 78 (extract from Ham. *tak.*); Ath. (Búláq), VIII, 150, 161–2.

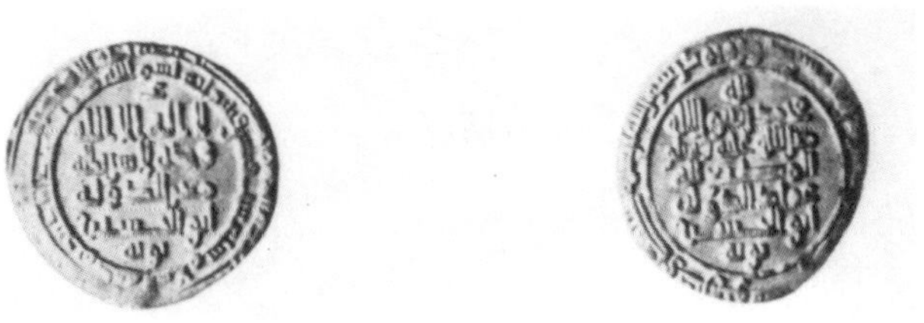

THE COMMANDERS OF THE COMMANDER
OF THE FAITHFUL

dínár (gold) minted at Baghdád in A.H. 336 (A.D. 947–8), showing the joint superscription of the Buvayhids and the Caliph

Legends:

OBVERSE	REVERSE
There is no god but God	*To God*
Alone With him is no Copartner	*Muḥammad is the Apostle of God*
Mu'izz ad-Dawlah	*God bless him and preserve*
Abú'l-Ḥusayn	*Al-Muṭí' li'llah*
Buvayh	*'Imád ad-Dawlah*
	Abú'l-Ḥasan
	Buvayh

Photographed from the cast of a coin in the British Museum

one of the economies that the Mu'izz soon found himself forced to practise. He was so hard pressed for funds wherewith to pay his army, that soon after his arrival in Baghdád, he found that the only means of satisfying his officers was to quarter them in districts from which they might wring what profit they could, without, apparently, having to account for what they received to the Government. Indeed, there was hardly a Government to account to. For the establishment of this system rendered the *díwáns* unnecessary; and before long this was recognised so far that all the branches were amalgamated in one.[1]

The Mu'izz ad-Dawlah had taken Baghdád, but he still had the Ḥamdánids to reckon with, strong and all too close. Some two months after al-Muṭí''s accession, therefore, he resolved to send an expedition against them; but its two commanders quarrelled on the way, and one of them, having looted his colleague's camp, forthwith deserted to the Náṣir. On getting news of this set-back to his plan, the Mu'izz at once sallied forth himself in company with the Caliph. But without waiting for his arrival, the Náṣir, on his side, came down to Sámarrá, eluded the Emir, and made for Baghdád. On the Emir's departure Ibn Shírzád, who had been hiding in fear of his life for having offended him, reappeared. A week later he welcomed the Náṣir and his army at the capital.

At this the Mu'izz retaliated by sacking Sámarrá and Takrít, which he regarded as Ḥamdánid towns. Nevertheless he judged it advisable to return as quickly as possible to Baghdád. On reaching it, he found the west bank clear of the enemy, who had concentrated their forces on the east. He himself, therefore, encamped with the Caliph on the west bank; but soon discovered that the Náṣir had chosen his ground with

1 M. II, 86–7, 96–100; Ath. (Búláq), VIII, 162; Mas. *murúj*, IX, 1.

considerable guile. By watching the river, and patrolling the country lying outside the walls to the west, the Ḥamdánids contrived to institute a strict siege; and before long the inhabitants of the Round City and its suburbs were reduced to the extreme of famine. Houses and estates were sold for food. The want was so frightful that dogs and cats and horses, and even in a few cases children, were devoured; the mortality from starvation and disease was so high that the living were unable to bury the dead.

Across the river, on the other hand, bread was cheaper than it had been for a long time. The Náṣir had every reason to hope for victory. He posed as the champion of legitimacy, and remembering perhaps the provenance of his title, restored the coinage of the year 331 (942–3), with the superscription of al-Muttaqí. He succeeded in setting fire to the Buvayhid boats, and though the advantage of this manœuvre was somewhat discounted by the capture soon after of one of his patrols, the blockade might well have been expected to secure his triumph.

But despair nerved the Mu'izz to make a final attempt against him. He contrived secretly to build a number of rafts on one of the creeks. All was ready by the last day of the year 334 (1st August 946). As soon as night fell, these rafts were hauled to the bank at the narrowest part of the river. The Mu'izz then set forth, with flare of lights and beat of drums, to a point at the northern extremity of the city, hoping to deceive the enemy into supposing that he was attempting a crossing there. The Náṣir's men in fact gathered opposite; but meanwhile the Mu'izz was fast retracing his steps. Aṣ-Ṣaymarí in his absence had already landed unobserved with a small force on the further bank. The Mu'izz now followed with the main part of his army on the rafts. The alarm was given, however, while they were still crossing; and a fierce fight ensued in mid-stream. But aṣ-Ṣaymarí was now able to create a diversion by attacking the Ḥamdánids from their own bank; the Daylamites were in greater strength; and before the Ḥamdánids could sort themselves out, the whole of the eastern bank was in irremediable confusion. The Náṣir was reluctant to make any movement, but when it became clear that the enemy were not to be withstood, he fled with Ibn Shírzád. The Daylamites proceeded to sack these quarters of the city with the utmost fury, and in much less time effected by rapine here the equal of what famine and death had done across the Tigris. The inhabitants of the east bank, who had taunted them in their distress, now received their reward. In wreaking their vengeance the troops threw off all restraint; and it was with the greatest difficulty that the Mu'izz succeeded in checking them.

The Náṣir retreated up-stream to 'Ukbará, whence he opened negotiations for peace. Soon after, however, he discovered that his followers were conspiring against him, and straightway decamped to Mosul. This pre-occupation relieved the Mu'izz of his rivalry. Now he was able to devote his attention to problems of administration and the consolidation of his power. As for the Caliph al-Muṭí', he was soon able to return to what was left of the palace, where he was to reign for many a year, in the ruined capital of his ruined kingdom. Secure in the tutelage of the conqueror from the perils that had assailed his forerunners, he lived on into old age, haunting, like a shade of the great Caliphs that had gone before him, the scenes of their magnificence.[1]

1 Ath. (Búláq), VIII, 162–3, 167; M. II, 89–94, 95–6.

END OF PART FOUR

Conclusion

The night of fury had passed, and the sun of the New Year had risen on the distracted city but a little while, when a messenger from the Vizier aṣ-Ṣaymarí came running to the Mu'izz ad-Dawlah. The Emir was summoned to quell a dispute that had occurred between the minister and one of his chief officers at a house by the river, known as the Garden Gate. The officer, he found, had wished to quarter his men in the place, as many as two hundred; but aṣ-Ṣaymarí had opposed him, saying, "Go away from this house. Your lodging here is not permissible." The officer had refused, and high words, indeed a battle, had ensued.

In the midst of the court stood a coffin, as the Mu'izz could see when he entered. It was the coffin of 'Alí ibn 'Ísà, who had died in the night. After but a day's fever he had died, at the great age of eighty and nine years. His body had been laid out and placed in the coffin. It had been prayed upon and they waited to carry it to the tomb.

"This is not the time for such a scene," the Mu'izz ad-Dawlah expostulated with aṣ-Ṣaymarí. But aṣ-Ṣaymarí was right in acting as he had, on grounds of policy, as he asserted: if they gave way once, they would have to give way altogether. The Emir was persuaded. He took the commander by the hand, and offered to lodge him in his own house. "Surely," he said, "you will not begin by disturbing in their houses and homes the sons and family of this elder, whose memory is famous!"

The history concludes in this way: that owing to the intervention of aṣ-Ṣaymarí, and his reminding the Mu'izz ad-Dawlah of his promise, the house of 'Alí ibn 'Ísà remained to his sons; while that of 'Abd ar-Raḥmán continued in his possession until his death,[1] which occurred thirteen years later, in *sha'bán* 348 (October–November 959).[2] The inmates of the Garden Gate were no more molested; for the wild Persian soldiers, passing it, would say to one another: "This is the house of the good Vizier."[3]

Sulaymán ibn al-Ḥasan had died three years before 'Alí, at the age of seventy-one years, leaving a large family of sons and daughters, none of whom, however, were remarkable.[4] Of 'Alí's two sons, both of whom had entered Government service during his life-time,[5] the elder Ibrahím was made secretary to the Caliph al-Muṭí' in 347 (958–9), and died suddenly in *jumádà'l-úlà* 350 (June–July 961). 'Ísà the younger survived his brother almost half a century. He held the same position under al-Muṭí''s successor,[6] and died in Baghdád at dawn on a Friday of the year 391 (1001), either on 1st *rabí' al-awwal* (29th January) or on 28th *rabí' al-ákhir* (27th March), in his ninetieth year.[7] He came to be noted as a transmitter of Traditions. The assemblies that he held for this purpose were frequented by all the eminent. And he was versed as well in the "Greek" sciences, reading logic with the celebrated authority and translator from the Syriac, the Christian Yaḥyà ibn 'Adí,[8] with whom he was very friendly and from whose learning he derived much profit. 'Ísà himself instructed a number of pupils in

1 Ham. *tak.* fol. 101 a, published in M. II, 107 and H. p. 8 of introduction.

2 Ṣaf. (Paris Arabe 2066), fol. 157 b; Ham. *tak.* fol. 113 b.

3 Yáq. *ud.* V, 279.

4 Ṣaf. (Paris Arabe 2064), fol. 167 b; Ham. *tak.* fol. 89 a.

5 See Yáq. *ud.* II, 123 and M. II, 88.

6 Yáq. *ud.* V, 280; M. II, 184.

7 Dh. *t.* (B.M. Or. 48), fol. 227 b; Ath. (Tornberg), VIII, 119; Qif. 244; H. 424.

8 See O'Leary: *Arabic Thought*, p. 114 for a notice of this learned man.

these subjects. He also annotated in his own hand a translation in ten heavy volumes of the first part of Aristotle's *Physics* from notes taken during his readings with Yaḥyà. His handwriting was as correct and almost as beautiful as Ibn Muqlah's.[1] He had a true passion for learning; and summed it up in lines that Yaḥyà chose for the inscription on his tomb:[2]

Many a dead man has been quickened by learning, and many a one, seemingly alive, has died of ignorance and error.
Therefore acquire learning that you may attain to what is eternal; and account as nothing a life lived in ignorance.

1 Qif. *loc. cit.* and 39.

2 U. I, 235, II, 96.

THE END

INDEX

NOTE: The Arabic article *al-* (*ad-*, *an-* etc., *'l-*, *'d-*, *'n-* etc. after a vowel) is disregarded in the alphabetical arrangement of names and words.

al-'Abbás, Prince, son of al-Muqtadir, 346
al-'Abbás, Prophet's uncle, 274
al-'Abbás ibn al-Ḥasan, Vizier, 63–9, 73, 84–9, 92, 96–7, 102, 114, 170
'Abbásid architecture, 21–3
'Abbásid Caliphate, threatened by Mardávíj, 341; doomed, 357. See also Caliphate
'Abbásid dynasty threatened by Mu'izz ad-Dawlah, 392
'Abbásid force defeated by al-Jannábí, 271
'Abbásid forces, defeat Persian rebels in al-Mu'taḍhid's reign, 43, 45; withstand Carmathian attack on Baghdád, 269
'Abbásid *naqíb*, 74
'Abbásid nobles choose Caliph, 364
'Abbásid system of government changed, 356
'Abbásid throne finally vacated by al-Qáhir, 334
'Abbásid troops in Persia, 307
'Abbásids, 1; triumph over 'Umayyads, 2, 6; favour Mu'tazilites, 3, 51; dupe 'Alids, 6; Zaydite rebellions against, 7; Aghlabids and Ṭáhirids tributary to, 8; regain Ṭabaristán from Zaydites, 9; Persian manners of, 17; mixed descent of, 25; first fear Carmathians, 50–1; cause of Carmathian hostility to, 53; recover Syria and Egypt, 55–6, 168; al-Qásim aims at promoting branch of, other than al-Mu'taḍhid's, 58; connection with, of Ṣúlí family, 80; crises in history of, 84; al-Muqtadir youngest of, 100; jewels of, 100; negotiations between, and Carmathians, 136; lose Ifriqiyyah, 137–8; deny Fáṭimid claims, 138; attacked by Greeks (303), 142; decline of, 177; 'Alí ibn 'Ísà accused of enmity to, 212; Banú Ya'fur acknowledge suzerainty of, 232; family of Ziyád independent of, 232–3; plight of, in 314, 249; eponymous ancestor of, 274; warning verses addressed to, 310; black banner of, 319. See also Caliphate
'Abd Allah, Prince, see Ibn al-Mu'tazz
'Abd Allah ibn 'Alí ibn Muḥammad ibn Dá'úd, 34, 38
'Abd ar-Raḥmán, 'Umayyad Caliph of Spain, 286 note
'Abd ar-Raḥmán ibn 'Ísà, 34, 38, 109–10, 117, 228, 256, 258, 273, 275, 303, 336–8, 352–5, 368, 371, 397
'Abd al-Wahháb, son of 'Alí ibn 'Ísà, 34, 149 note
'Abd al-Wáḥid, Prince, son of al-Muqtadir, 326
'Abdán, Carmathian leader, 53–4
'Abdún ibn Makhlad, 34, 36–7, 79
Abraham, 111, 339
Abú'l-'Abbás, Prince, see ar-Rádhí
Abú 'Abd Allah al-Barídí, 335, 342–4, 358–9, 362, 365–74, 376, 382–3, 385
Abú 'Alí ibn Khayrán, 120–1
Abú 'Amr, friend of 'Alí ibn 'Ísà, 279
Abú Bakr ibn al-'Alláf, 81–2
Abú Bakr Muḥammad ibn Zakariyyá ar-Rází, 185–6
Abú Bakr ash-Sháfi'í, friend of 'Alí ibn 'Ísà, 76–7, 187, 259
Abú Bakr ash-Shiblí, 190–1
Abú Dulaf, dynasty of, 44–5. See also Dulafite Court
Abú'l-Faraj of Iṣfahán, 362 note
Abú Ḥanífah, Imám, 40, 119
Abú'l-Ḥasan, see al-Ash'arí

Abú'l-Hayjá', Ḥamdánid, 237, 264, 269, 281–6, 316, 347
Abú'l-Ḥusayn, son of Abú 'Umar, *qáḍhí*, 76 note, 336, 372
Abú'l-Ḥusayn, son of Ibn Muqlah, 347, 349
Abú'l-Ḥusayn al-Barídí, 342, 370, 374–6, 383–4
Abú'l-Ḥusayn *al-khazzáz* of Wásiṭ, 76
Abú Manṣúr, Prince, son of al-Muttaqí, 374–6
Abú'l-Muthannà, *qáḍhí*, 89, 90, 94–5
Abú'l-Qásim, steward to 'Alí ibn 'Ísà, 82–3
Abú'l-Qásim al-Barídí, son of Abú 'Abd Allah, 383–4
Abú Sahl al-Qaṭṭán, 76–7, 98, 110–11, 256
Abú Sa'íd, see al-Jannábí
Abú'ṣ-Ṣuqr al-Kalwádhí, 185
Abú Ṭáhir, see al-Jannábí
Abú Ṭáhir al-Hudhalí, 77–8
Abú 'Umar, *qáḍhí*, 89, 94–5, 118–20, 165–7, 173, 195–7, 210–12, 258, 276–7, 286, 298, 336, 372
Abú Yúsuf al-Barídí, 342, 374, 383
Abú Zunbúr al-Mádhará'í, 168–71, 208–9, 253–4, 256, 259
Adam, 339
'Aḍhud ad-Dawlah, Buvayhid, 185
'Aḍhudí Hospital, 185, 365
Africa, North, 8; slave trade with, 13; Carmathian propaganda in North, 54
Aghlabids, 8, 137–8
ahl adh-dhimmah, 184. See also "People of Scripture"
Aḥmad, see Ibn Ṭúlún
Aḥmad, see al-Mu'taḍhid
Aḥmad ibn Buvayh, Mu'izz ad-Dawlah, 339, 359, 385–96
Aḥmad ibn al-Furát, 29–32, 43–6, 48, 57, 60–2, 172, 207, 244–5
Aḥmad ibn Kámil, *qáḍhí*, 74
Aḥmad ibn Músà of Ray, *qáḍhí*, 129, 231. See also Muḥammad ibn Músà
Aḥmad ibn Shu'ayb, see an-Nasá'í
al-Ahwáz, 8, 77, 96–7, 146, 174, 176, 226, 258, 268, 342–3, 345
'Ajj ibn Ḥájj, 109, 111
al-Akhfash the Little (*aṣ-ṣaghir*), 278
Aleppo, 66, 316, 377, 380
Alexandria, 139–40
Algebra, aṭ-Ṭabarí versed in, 73
Algeria, 8
'Alí, see Ibn al-Furát
'Alí, see al-Muktafí
'Alí, son of Hishám ibn 'Abd Allah, 117 note
'Alí ibn 'Abd Allah ibn Ḥamdán, Sayf ad-Dawlah, 376–8, 383
'Alí ibn 'Abd al-'Azíz ad-Dúlábí, 74
'Alí ibn Abí Ṭálib, "Orthodox" Caliph, 5–7, 114, 138
'Alí ibn Buvayh, 'Imád ad-Dawlah, 339–45, 358–9
'Alí ibn 'Ísà, employed in *díwán ad-dár*, 32, 43; his birth and early life, family and upbringing, 33–42; chosen to accompany al-Mu'taḍhid to Ámid, 45–6; given *díwán al-maghrib*, 46; his wife, 47; adjudicates on Dimimmá bridge case, and reports on finances of Mosul and Záb districts, 48–9; in ar-Raqqah during Carmathian attack, reports, 57; employs brother Ibrahím and uses influence on his behalf, 60–1; proposed by al-Qásim ibn 'Ubayd Allah and accepted by al-Muktafí as Vizier, but declines office, 63–4; his report on Syria, 65–6; his part in secretaries' war, 67–8; his circle, 71–82; declines to build dyke, 82–3; his books, 75–6, 134; favours Ibn al-Mu'tazz for Caliphate, 84, 86–7; joins in conspiracy, 89–92; his first banishment, to Wásiṭ and Mecca, 95–8; his opinion of al-Muqtadir, 101; travels to Mecca, 108; his life there, 109–12; recalled to Baghdád, 112, 114–15; first becomes Vizier, 116; distributes offices, 116–18; deals strictly with sister, 118; invited to pray at funeral, 120; his opinion of Ibn Khayrán, 120–1; punishes and is tricked by al-Kháqání (I), 121–2; his financial reforms, 122–4; his

'Alí ibn 'Ísà (continued)
administrative reforms, his attitude to bribery, 125–7; improves hospitals, 127–8; his good works at Mecca, 128–9; his secretarial gifts, 129–31; attends false funeral of Ibn al-Furát, 132; his economies, public and private, 132–5; negotiates with the Carmathians, 136–7, 141; takes measures against the Fáṭimids, and gives thanks on their defeat, 139–40; his embarrassments and fall, 142–52; lampooned, 144–5; his deal with Jewish money-lenders, 146; offends Umm Músà, 147–8, 151–2; seeks to resign, 149–50; his letter to Lady, 150–1; fined, 153, 158; defends himself against charge of treason, 154–5; offers Ibn Muqlah employment, 157; compared to *qur'án*, examines list of Viziers, 159; appointed Assistant, 162–4; disapproves Ḥámid's conduct in trial of Ibn al-Furát, 166, 171; remits lying witness's punishment, 167; examines Ibn al-Furát, 167–70; taunted by Ibn al-Furát, 167; refuses Abú Zunbúr's present, 169; reproaches Abú Zunbúr, 171; ousts Ḥámid, 174; opposes Ḥámid's proposal for tax-contract, 175; war between them, 176–7; security restored under his régime, 177; crowd murmurs against him, 179; control of revenue restored to him, 181; draws up budget, 183, 200; interests himself in medical questions, 183–5; his acquaintance with ar-Rází, 185–6; attacked by al-Ash'arí, 186–7; his conflict with the Ḥanbalites, 187–8; turns Ṣúfí (?), 188–9; his relations with Ṣúfís, 189–90, with ash-Shiblí, 190–1, with al-Ḥalláj, 191–5; falls ill, 196; declines Vizierate and suggests appointment of Abú 'Umar, 196–7; implicated in Umm Músà's disgrace, 198–9; economises, 201; his dealings with Háshimites, 201–2; prohibits bribery, 202; his fall, which coincides with Carmathian attack on al-Baṣrah, 204–5; accused of Carmathian sympathies, 206, 210, tried and acquitted, 210–12; imprisoned with Zaydán, 207; his examination by Ibn al-Furát, 207–10; threatened by Naṣr and al-Muḥassin, 213; comes to agreement with Ibn al-Furát, 213–14; suffers enmity of al-Muḥassin, 215–16, who tortures him, 217–19; his final settlement with Ibn al-Furát, 219–21; banished to Mecca, 222; employs 'Abd ar-Raḥmán, 228; his tribulations arouse Mu'nis's sympathy, 229; proceeds to Mecca, attempt on his life frustrated, 231; sent to Ṣan'á', 232–5; his agent dies of fright, 242; compared with Ibn al-Furát, 245–7; Mu'nis advises his recall, 250; leaves Ṣan'á' for Mecca and is appointed Inspector-General of Egypt, 250–1; his visits to Palestine and Pilgrimages, 251; his arrival in Fusṭáṭ, 252; reproaches Abú Zunbúr, 253; accompanied by latter to Mecca, 254; his former relations with Abú Zunbúr, 254 note; refuses to dismiss Ibn Mukram, 255; his unpopularity with Copts, 255–6; his recall, 256; his second Vizierate, 257–75; his distribution of offices, 258–9; humours ash-Sháfi'í, 259; deals with al-Khaṣíbí, 260; produces stolen rosary, 260–1; dismisses dishonest paymaster, 261; attempts to form Arab defence force, 261–3; takes measures against Carmathians, 266–8; makes thank-offering for deliverance, 270; his unpopularity, attempts to resign, 271–2; takes precautions, 273; Ibn Zabr intrigues against him, 273–5; his arrest, 275; compared to 'Umar II, twits Abú 'Umar on his shirt, 276; obeys command of a dream, 276–7; Ibn Durayd's verses on his fall, his attempt to attend prayer when in prison,

'Alí ibn 'Ísà (continued) 277–8; rejects al-Akhfash's claim, 278; his jealousy of Ibn Muqlah, 278–9; suffers enmity of Naṣr, 279–80; set free by Mu'nis, 284; reappointed to Court of Appeal, 287; visits and is well received by Ibn Muqlah, 288; mediates between Caliph and Mu'nis, 292; suggests for Vizierate Sulaymán (who is promoted) and supervises *díwáns*, 293; imposes and remits fine on Ibn Muqlah, 293–4; troops attack his house, 295; Sulaymán seeks refuge with him, 296; sent by Caliph to mollify Mu'nis, 298–9; unable to cope with financial difficulties, 299; offends al-Muqtadir, 300; continues as Supervisor with al-Kalwádhí, 301; banished to aṣ-Ṣáfiyah, 303–4; motto on his signet, 303; rescued by Hárún from malice of al-Ḥusayn, 311, 313, 315; proposed by Mu'nis as Vizier, rejected, but returns to Baghdád, 323–4; insulted by Ibn Muqlah, 324–5; reappointed Inspector of Egypt, but excused, 325–6; made Inspector of Wásiṭ and Euphrates Irrigation, 334–5; assists 'Abd ar-Raḥmán in Vizierate for ar-Rádhí, 336–8; disapproves of Barídís, 342–3; accused of plotting with Ḥamdánids, is banished for a time to aṣ-Ṣáfiyah (Beauty of Baghdád), 347–50; chosen by soldiery as Vizier, assists 'Abd ar-Raḥmán, 352–3; arrested and fined, 354; incurs ar-Rádhí's dislike, 355; given Court of Appeal by al-Muttaqí, 364–5; assists Baghdádís during plague, 368; alarmed at Abú 'Abd Allah's approach, yet greets him, 368–70; takes office under al-Muttaqí, 371; uses device against fatigue in old age, and maintains correctness of manners, 371–2; condoles with Abú'l-Ḥusayn's sons, 372; his alleged encounter with al-Mutanabbí, 378–9; his ruling in case of Edessa image, 380–1; his concern for Muslim prisoners in Greek hands, 381–2; lends money to Ibn Shírzád, 386; visits Mu'izz ad-Dawlah, 388–91; predicts al-Muṭí''s succession, 392; his death, 396–7. Other references: 226, 227, 281, 289, 305, 307, 310

'Alí ibn 'Ísà, see ar-Rummání

'Alí ibn Muḥammad ibn Dá'úd, 34, 38, 118

'Alí ibn Yalbaq, 319, 327–30

'Alid leadership of attacks on Pilgrimage caravans, 140–1

'Alid *naqíb*, 74

'Alid nobles choose Caliph, 364

'Alid plot, pretended, in Ṭabaristán (306), 165

'Alid synonymous with Fáṭimid, 138

'Alids, their claim to Caliphate, 5–6; their rôle in Carmathian teaching, 52. See also Shí'ah

'amid ad-dawlah (title), 313

Ámid, 45–6

amír, provincial governor, 16

amír al-umará', 356 note. See also Emir of Emirs

Ámul, 307–8

al-Anbár, 119, 256, 267–8, 270–1, 273, 384

Anbár Gate (of Baghdád), 268

al-Anmáṭí, 368–9

Anti-Caliphate (Fáṭimid), foundation of, 138. See also Fáṭimids

Antioch, 381

'Aqarqúf, 269 note

Arab battle line, 18

Arab disdain of learning, 128

Arab poets cultivate satire, 81

Arab residue in 'Abbásid blood, 25

Arabia, 1

Arabian Nights, 144–5 note. See also *Thousand and One Nights*

Arabic alphabet still imperfect, 39

Arabic wit, Bachkam puzzled by, 365

Arabs, indifference of, after conversion, 1–2; ousted by Persians, 17; attack Pilgrimage caravans, 69, 140–1; al-Mutanabbí greatest poet of, 377

Aramean Christians, 19
Aramean populations of Syria and al-'Iráq, 18
Architecture of early 'Abbásids, 21–3
Ardabíl, 165–6
'Aríb, historian, 234, 240
Aristotle, 398
Arithmetic, a "Greek" science, 73
Armenia, 154–5
Armenian strain in 'Abbásid blood, 25
Army, organisation of, 17–18
Arraján, 341
As'ad ibn Ibrahím, see Ibn Ya'fur
Asfár ibn Shíravayh, 307–9, 311
al-Ash'arí, 41, 186–7
Asia Minor, 11, 13, 20, 306
'Askar Mukram, 344
Asmá' bint 'Ísà ('Alí ibn 'Ísà's sister), 34, 38, 118
'Ayn at-Tamar, 267
Azarbayján, 27, 154–5, 305, 308

Báb al-Bustán, 71, 82, 116, 190, 275, 326. See also Garden Gate
Báb Ibrahím (in mosque at Mecca), 129
Báb aṭ-Ṭáq, 180
Bachkam, Emir, 358–67, 371, 373
Badr (al-Mu'tadhidí), general, 43–4, 57–8, 61, 119; Hospital of, 184
al-Baghawí, Traditionist, 71–2, 118
Baghdád, 1, 3, 4, 8–10, 17–24, 27, 30, 33, 36, 46, 50, 54, 66, 73–4, 89, 96, 98, 102, 104, 107, 100–11, 117–19, 123–4, 127, 129, 139–43, 147, 165, 168, 174, 176–9, 182, 185, 189, 191, 193, 200–1, 206, 220, 224, 229, 231–3, 236–7, 248–9, 251, 253–8, 262, 266–72, 274, 275 note, 277 note, 280–2, 292, 297, 305–8, 310, 313–15, 317–18, 324, 326, 332, 335, 341, 346–50, 353, 356–7, 359–62, 364–7, 369–70, 372–4, 376, 378–80, 382–6, 388, 391, 393, 397
Baghdádís, 257, 374
al-Baḥrayn, 50, 54, 262, 280
Banú Asad, Arab tribe, 262
Banú'l-Furát, 30, 43, 60–1, 114, 165–6, 222, 300
Banú'l-Jarráḥ, 33–6, 37 note, 43, 60, 62, 68, 104, 354, 371
Banú Shaybán, Arab tribe, 262
Banú Ya'fur, Yemenite dynasty, 232. See also Ibn Ya'fur
al-Baradán, 312, 315
Barídís, 342–3, 362, 365, 370, 374, 376–7, 383–4, 385. See also Abú 'Abd Allah, Abú'l-Ḥusayn, Abú'l-Qásim, Abú Yúsuf
Barqah, 139–40
al-Baṣrah, 8–9, 50, 54, 98, 117, 136–7, 139, 165, 201–2, 205–6, 210–11, 227, 249, 262, 266, 280, 300, 326, 342, 345, 351, 359, 362, 365–6, 377, 382–5
Benghazi, 139
Berbers, 4, 18, 137, 319–21, 344
Black robe (of Vizierate), 174, 196
Black Stone (of Ka'bah), 289
Book of Secretaries, etc. (composition of 'Alí ibn 'Ísà), 76
Boon-Companion (rank of honour), 248, 313, 365
Bribery, attitude of 'Alí ibn 'Ísà to, 125–6, 131, 202
Budget, drawn up by 'Alí ibn 'Ísà, 200
al-Buḥturí, poet, 79
Bukhárá, 43, 307
Bukht-Yishú' ibn Yaḥyà, physician, 183
Bulgarians, 263
Búrán, daughter of al-Ḥasan ibn Sahl, 21
Burton, R. (translation from *Thousand and One Nights* quoted), 145 note
Bushrà the Eunuch, 327
Buvayh, 339
Buvayhid army approaches Baghdád, 386–7
Buvayhid prince ('Adhud ad-Dawlah), 185
Buvayhids, 339, 362
Byzantines, 11, 16–18, 104. See also Greeks
Byzantium, 154, 233

Cairo, 379
Caliph, office of, contrasted with that of Imám, 6; authority of, 14–15; style of, adopted by Spanish 'Umayyad, 286 note

Caliphate, extent of, 1; captured by 'Umayyads and 'Abbásids, 2; decade of anarchy in, 4–5, 7–8; Shí'ite claim to, 5; rescued by al-Muwaffaq, 9; external relations of, 11; slaves imported into, 13; government of, 14–15; at height of its recovery, 60; crises in history of 'Abbásid, 84; splendour of, enhanced by al-Muqtadir, 100; peace between, and Carmathians, 137; menaced by Fáṭimids, 137–8; helpless against Carmathians, 211; plight of, in 314, 249; Greeks take advantage of its enfeeblement, 263; struggle for capture of, 357; the Mu'izz contemplates putting an end to 'Abbásid, and decline of, 392. Other references: 62, 279, 289, 292. See also 'Abbásid, 'Abbásids
Canals of Baghdád, 20–1, 367
Candles, 'Alí ibn 'Ísà economises in, 134; Ibn al-Furát's extravagant use of, 154
Canon, Muslim, 39, 41
Caravans, 108–9
Carmathians, beginnings and doctrine of, 50–5, 138; attack ar-Raqqah, 57; dealings with, of Muḥammad ibn Dá'úd, 69–70; attack al-Baṣrah in 300 and are approached by 'Alí ibn 'Ísà, 136–7, 141; history of, after death of Abú Sa'íd, 205; sack al-Baṣrah (310), 205–6; 'Alí ibn 'Ísà accused of treason with, 206, 210–12, 215; in the Yemen, 233; attack pilgrim caravans (311), 237; sack al-Kúfah (313), 249, 250 note, 254; defence force against, 261–3; Ibn Abí's-Sáj accused of sympathy with, 263; advance on al-Kúfah, and, after defeat of Ibn Abí's-Sáj, on al-Anbár, 266–7; threaten Baghdád, but are driven off, 268–70; retreat, 271; 'Alí ibn 'Ísà accused of favouring, 279–80; Euphrates campaign of (316), 280–2; attack al-Kúfah (319), 302; prevent supplies from reaching Baghdád, 317; captured in Fárs, 333; attack pilgrim caravans (323), 350; decline of, 357–8; employed in body-guard, 374. Other references: 60, 62, 231, 241, 273, 305–6, 318, 328
Caspian Sea, 73, 80, 306, 339
Castle Ghumdán, 235
"Cat", 82
Catholicos, of Jerusalem, 381
Caucasus, slave trade with, 13
Censor (*muḥtasib*), censorship, 296–7, 299
Central Asia, 8; frontier of the Caliphate, 11; slave trade with, 13
"Champion of the Dynasty" (title), 59
Chancellor of Nobility (*naqíb*), 74–5
Chess, aṣ-Ṣúlí's skill at, 80
Chief Eunuch, 88, 103
Chief of Police, 15, 86, 98, 147, 167, 178, 180, 217, 238, 244, 291, 296
Chief *qáḍhí*, 89–90, 119–20, 286, 336, 372
Chosroes, model of the 'Abbásid Caliphs, 17; jewels of, 100
Christian, 'Abdún ibn Makhlad a, 36
Christian, family of Sulaymán ibn Wahb originally, 28, 302
Christian chronicle cited, 255
Christian clerks canvassed by al-Ḥusayn ibn al-Qásim, 302
Christian favourite of al-Muktafí, 59
Christian population of Dayr Qunnà, 35
Christian traitor-friend of Muḥammad ibn Dá'úd, 94–5
Christians, laws against, 4, 101; status of, in Caliphate, 11–12; employment of, in War Office, 170; oppressed by Abú'l-Ḥusayn al-Barídí, 374; of Edessa, 380–2
Cilicia, 58
Citron (building), 261, 285
City of Peace, 1
Climate of Baghdád, 23–4; contrasted with that of Ṣan'á', 233
Coin, with portrait of al-Muqtadir, 101
Coinage, 16–17, 313, 394

Constantine VII, 154, 381. See also Emperor, Byzantine
Constantinople, 197, 381–2
Controls (of *díwáns*), see Registries
Coppersmith, see Ya'qúb ibn al-Layth
Copts, 255
Cordova, 286 note
Correspondence Office (*díwán ar-rasá'il*), 15
Court of Appeal (*díwán an-nadhar fi'l-madhálim*), 15, 287, 303, 364
Court physicians, 58, 101, 145, 183, 191, 327
Crown (palace), 59
"Crown of Baghdád", 367
Ctesiphon, 224, 299, 341, 376
Curcuas, John, Domestic, 380
Custom, of Prophet, 14, 38. See also *sunnah*
Cyrenaica, 139

Dá'í (*ad-dá'í ilà'l-haqq*), 308
Damascus, 1, 10, 54, 57, 251, 253, 256, 274, 280
Daniel, Prophet, 292
ad-Danyálí, 292
Dár al-Qaṭan, 77
Dá'úd ibn 'Ísà, 34, 38, 149
Dá'úd ibn al-Jarráḥ, 33–6, 81
Dawlat, concubine of Ibn al-Furát, 220
Day of Oblation, 105
Daylam, Daylamites, 306–7, 309–11, 339–41, 366, 371, 373, 375, 392, 395
Dayr Qunnà, 33, 35, 303, 313
De Goeje, Orientalist, 205 note, 269
De Slane, Orientalist (translation of, quoted), 121
"Defender of the Dynasty" (title), 376
Dháhirites (Externalists), 191
Dhikrawayh, 54–5, 69–70, 106
Dhú'l-Qarnayn, 305 note
Diar Bekr, 45 note
Dictionary, of Prophet's companions, in two versions, by al-Baghawí, 72; of Traditionists, by aṭ-Ṭabarání, 78
Dictionary of Learned Men, Yáqút's, 78
Dimimmá, 47–8
dínár (coin), 16
Dínavar, 281–2
dirham (coin), 16
díwán al-baríd, 15
díwán al-birr, 129, 210
díwán ad-dár, 32, 37–8, 42, 45–7, 117, 156, 246
díwán al-jaysh, 15, 69
díwán al-kharáj, 15
díwán al-maghrib, 46, 48, 60, 65, 68, 116, 157
díwán al-maráfiq, 153
díwán al-mashriq, 46, 69, 117, 157, 259
díwán an-nadhar fi'l-madhálim, 15. See also Court of Appeal
díwán an-nafaqát, 15
díwán of Estates Confiscated from Ibn al-Furát, 259
díwán of the Harem, 259
díwán ar-rasá'il, 15
díwán as-sawád, 31, 228, 258, 301
díwán at-tawqí', 15, 63
díwáns, 15, 31, 42, 90, 117, 121, 203, 227, 293, 325 note, 371, 393
Diyálá, R., 311, 360, 367, 385, 387
Diyár Bakr, 45
Diyár Rabí'ah, 124, 347
Dome of the Ass (building), 261
Dome of the Rock, 251
Domestic John Curcuas, 380
Drinking, 23; a favourite subject of Ibn al-Mu'tazz, 79–80; al-Muqtadir's propensity for, 101; al-Kháqání (II) given to, 112; al-Khaṣíbí's systematic, 247; Ibn Durayd given to, 277; Názúk indulges in, 285; Ibn Yalbaq elated with, 328; al-Qáhir's hypocritical proscription of, 332–3; Mu'izz incapacitated with, 390
Ducks' food, 'Alí ibn 'Ísà examines, 134, 246
Dujayl, R., 124
ad-Dúlábí, 74
Dulafite Court, 178. See also Abú Dulaf

Edessa, 380, 382
Egypt, 10, 40, 46, 55–6, 60, 65–6, 138–40, 142, 147, 163, 169, 174, 200, 208, 229, 248, 251–2, 254–5, 274, 275 note, 303, 325, 334, 357, 359, 384

Egyptian revenues, 'Alí ibn 'Ísà seeks to enhance yield of, 255
Egyptians, 66, 252
Elephant, 143
Emessa, 379
Emir (title), 286 note
Emir of Emirs (title), 356, 360, 371, 376
Emirate, 373, 382, 385, 388
Emirs, 361, 363, 392
Emperor, Byzantine, 265, 381
Erzinjan, 316
Euclid, 31
Eunuchs, al-Muqtadir's collection of, 100; palace, controlled by Mufliḥ, 197; 'Alí ibn 'Ísà cuts down pay of, 258; flee from palace on al-Muqtadir's second deposition, 283
Euphrates, R., 9, 21, 46, 54–5, 119, 229, 244, 256, 267, 270, 280, 334, 361, 367, 378, 384, 386
Europe, Muslim learning handed on to, 128; ar-Rází known to schoolmen of, as Rhazes, 185
Excellences of the Vizierate, composition of al-Ḥalláj, 195
Expenditure Office, see *díwán an-nafaqát*
Externalists, Ḏháhirites, 191

al-Fadhl, Prince, son of al-Muqtadir, 392. See also al-Muṭí'
al-Fadhl ibn Ja'far ibn al-Furát, 117, 259, 272, 314–15, 317, 324 note, 359, 362 note
faqíhs, 14
Fárs, 35–6, 76, 104, 123–4, 159, 209, 291, 324, 333, 340–1, 344
Fátik, favourite of al-Muktafí, 59
Fáṭimah, Prophet's daughter, 5, 138
Fáṭimids, foundation of their power, 138; their first attack on Egypt repulsed, 139–40, 142, 147; their second attack on Egypt also repulsed, 200–1, 208, 248; Egypt unsettled by invasions of, 251–2; adherent of, executed in Baghdád, 279; take no part in struggle for Caliphate, 357; Mu'izz contemplates acknowledging, 392
Feast, 105–6, 151–2, 230
Feast of Sacrifice, 105 note
Festival of Fire, 342
fihrist, 130
Finance, 15–16; Ibn al-Furát's knowledge of, 30; *díwán ad-dár* specially concerned with, 31
Fines imposed, on dishonest paymaster, 261; on dismissed ministers, 27–9, 36, 57, 61–2, 96, 112–13, 121, 145, 160, 171, 209, 214, 219, 221, 223, 225, 227–8, 241–3, 248, 259, 293–4, 315, 324, 332, 348, 353–5; on millionaire, 146–7
al-firdaws (palace), 59
"Foreign" sciences, aṭ-Ṭabarí's knowledge of, 73; al-Ḥalláj versed in, 193
Foreigner, type of Muslim, 2, 17, 35
Freedmen, status of, 13–14
Friday Mosque, 59
Friday Prayers, 134, 277, 356, 363, 373
Frontier Provinces, 10
Fusṭáṭ, 139, 142, 251–2, 254, 260

Galen, study of, 128
Garden Gate, 71, 284, 303, 352, 368, 396–7. See also Báb al-Bustán
Garden of Záhir, 71
Gharíb, see Uncle
Ghumdán, Ḥimyarite castle, 235
Gílán, 306
Gog and Magog, 305
Grammar, "native" science, 73; Ibn Mujáhid proficient in, 75; Ibn al-Buhlúl a student of, 119
Great Feast, see Feast
Great Seal Office, see *díwán at-tawqí'*
Greece, influence of, on Caliphate, 18
Greek, translations from, 128, 398
Greek fire, 18
Greek (or foreign) sciences, 73, 78
Greek strain in 'Abbásid blood, 25
Greeks, Muslims conquer provinces from, 1; initiation-system of ancient, imitated by Carmathians, 51; attack Caliphate (303), 142; Mu'nis's campaign against (306), 155; raid Muslim

Greeks (continued)
territory (315), 263; are driven back, 265; perennial war with, 305–6; renew raids (320), 316–17; exploits of the Sayf ad-Dawlah against, 377; besiege Edessa, 380; maltreat Muslim captives, 381. See also Byzantines
Gurgán, 43, 80, 309

Ḥabashí ibn Isḥáq the jailer, 98
Ḥajar, 50, 141, 206
ḥajj, see Pilgrimage
Hall of Public Audience, 318
al-Ḥalláj, 190–5
Hamadán, 309–10
Ḥamásah of al-Buḥturí, 79
Ḥamdán Qarmaṭ, 53–4
Ḥamdánids, 316, 347, 349, 351, 375, 380, 383–4, 393, 395. See also Abú'l-Hayjá', al-Ḥasan ibn 'Abd Allah, al-Ḥusayn ibn Ḥamdán, etc.
Ḥámid ibn al-'Abbás, Vizier: 'Alí ibn 'Ísà's opinion of him, 159, 163–4; his early history, 159–60; intrigues for Vizierate, 160–1; found to be unsuitable, is given 'Alí as Assistant, 161–4; prosecutes Ibn al-Furát, 165–71; blamed for misconducting trial, 171; kills Ibn Khalaf and maddens al-Muḥassin with torture, 171–3, 215; ousted by 'Alí ibn 'Ísà, 174; his tax-contract, 174–7, 179–82; at war with 'Alí ibn 'Ísà, 176; in favour with Caliph, 176–7; attacked by people, 180–1; brings about al-Ḥalláj's execution, 195; offends Mufliḥ, 197, who bears him a grudge, 218, and takes revenge, 224; favours Ibn al-Ḥawwárí, 199; lampooned, 202; seeks to regain al-Muqtadir's favour, 203; returns to Wásiṭ, 204; 'Alí ibn 'Ísà seeks refuge behind his authority, 208–9; trapped by Ibn al-Furát, and at first well treated, 223–5; tortured and murdered by al-Muḥassin, 226; huge sum extorted from, 228. Other references: 183, 194, 196, 200, 227, 229, 253, 275 note
ḥammám (bath), 95
Ḥamzah of Iṣfahán, historian, 177, 228, 296
Ḥanafite, Ibn al-Buhlúl a, 119
Ḥanafite school, 40
Ḥanbalite agitation against aṭ-Ṭabarí, 187–8
Ḥanbalite school, 40
Ḥanbalites, 41; 'Alí ibn 'Ísà's antipathy for, 187
Ḥarb Gate, of Baghdád, 270, 383
al-Ḥarbiyyah, 20, 127
Harem, 88, 106, 151, 178, 237, 271, 374
Ḥarrán, 79, 183
Hárún, Prince, son of al-Muqtadir, 149 note, 196
Hárún ibn Gharíb (son of Uncle), 180–1, 241–3, 272, 275, 280–3, 309, 311–13, 315, 317–18, 326, 345–6
Hárún ibn Khumárawayh, Ṭúlúnid, 46, 55–6
Hárún ar-Rashíd, 'Abbásid Caliph, 3, 100
al-Ḥasá, 50
al-Ḥasan, second Imám of Shí'ah, 5–7
al-Ḥasan, son of Ibn al-Furát, 220
al-Ḥasan ibn 'Abd Allah ibn Ḥamdán, Náṣir ad-Dawlah, Emir, 347–50, 361, 369, 375–8, 383, 385–7, 393–5
al-Ḥasan ibn 'Alí, see al-Uṭrúsh
al-Ḥasan ibn Buvayh, Rukn ad-Dawlah, 339, 341, 360, 362, 388
al-Ḥasan ibn Makhlad, Vizier, 34, 36–7, 42, 79, 81, 116, 293 note
al-Ḥasan ibn Muḥammad, see az-Za'faráni
al-Ḥasan ibn al-Qásim, Dá'í, 308
al-Ḥasan ibn Sahl, Vizier, 21
Ḥasaní Palace, 21, 58, 90–1
Háshimite, Umm Músà a, 100 note
Háshimite nobles, 298
Háshimites, 152 note, 184–5, 201–2
"He that shall Appear", Carmathian Imám, 54
"He that takes Vengeance upon the Enemies of God's Religion" (title), 331
Hegira, 1
Hellenistic influences in Carmathian doctrine, 51–2

Hilál (aṣ-Ṣábí), historian, 234, 291
Ḥimyarites, 232, 235
Hishám ibn 'Abd Allah, 117, 121
History of the Viziers, work of Muḥammad ibn Dá'úd, 37
Hít, 256, 280, 386
Hospital, of Badr al-Mu'taḍhidí, 184–5; 'Aḍhudí, founded by Emir Bachkam, 185, 365
Hospitals, 'Alí ibn 'Ísà's care for and foundation of, 127, 183
House of Ṭáhir, 87, 321
al-Hudhalí, 77–8
Ḥufúf, 50
Ḥujarí Guards, 269, 284–5, 290, 333, 351–2, 356, 361
Ḥulwán, 262
ḥuramí (or *ḥaramí*), 88 note
al-Ḥusayn, son of Abú'l-Hayjá', Ḥamdánid, 316
al-Ḥusayn, third Imám of Shí'ah, 5–7
al-Ḥusayn ibn Ḥamdán, 89–91, 142–3, 161, 237
al-Ḥusayn ibn 'Ísà, 34, 38
al-Ḥusayn ibn al-Qásim ibn 'Ubayd Allah, Vizier, 291–3, 301–3, 311–15, 327

Ibn 'Abdún, see Muḥammad
Ibn Abí Dá'úd of Sístán, Traditionist, 72–3
Ibn Abí's-Sáj, 154–6, 158, 160, 165, 200, 236, 262–3, 266–8, 270–2, 305–8, 310, 327
Ibn Abí Uṣaybi'ah, historian, 184, 186
Ibn al-'Alláf, poet, 81–2
Ibn 'Ammár, 37–8
Ibn al-Athír, historian, 92
Ibn Ayyúb, 'Alí ibn 'Ísà's secretary, 216
Ibn Bassám, poet, 81, 144
Ibn Ba'ud Sharr, 241–2
Ibn Bisṭám, 228–9
Ibn al-Buhlúl, *qáḍhí*, 119–20, 165–7, 173, 195, 210–12, 286
Ibn Buvayh, see Aḥmad, 'Alí, al-Ḥasan
Ibn ad-Dáyah, 78
Ibn Durayd, 277
Ibn Farjawayh, 145, 147–8
Ibn Fulayḥah, 210–12
Ibn al-Furát, 'Alí, employed by 'Ubayd Allah ibn Sulaymán, 29–32; engages 'Alí ibn 'Ísà, 32, 42; adjudicates on Dimimmá bridge case, 48; at war with Banú'l-Jarráḥ, 60, 66–9; prosecuted by al-Qásim ibn 'Ubayd Allah, 62; wins al-'Abbás ibn al-Ḥasan's esteem, 68; favours al-Muqtadir for succession, 84–5, 87, 90; made Vizier, 93; his kindness to Muḥammad ibn Dá'úd, 93–5; his treatment of 'Alí ibn 'Ísà and Ibn 'Abdún, 95–8; his influence at Court, 102–4; his first fall, 104–7, 110, 114; tortured by Ibn Thawábah, 112–13; Sulaymán abuses his magnanimity, 117; his kindness to 'Alí ibn 'Ísà's sister, 118; scores off 'Alí ibn 'Ísà, 131; his pretended funeral, 132; intrigues for office, 145–9; his second Vizierate and fall, 153–61, 163; his trial (306), 165–71; pays Caliph, 172–3; faction intrigues for his restoration, 197–9; shows up Ibn al-Ḥawwárí, 199–200; consulted by al-Muqtadir, and restored, 203–4; sends relief force to al-Baṣrah, 206; enlarges Vizierate, 207; examines 'Alí ibn 'Ísà, 207–10, prosecutes him for treasonous dealings with the Carmathians, 210–12, and settles with him, 213–14; loses influence with Caliph to al-Muḥassin, 215–16; his distress at al-Muḥassin's conduct, 218–19; his final settlement with 'Alí ibn 'Ísà, 219–21; his opinion of 'Alí's conduct, 221; banishes 'Alí to Mecca, 222; persecutes enemies, 223–9; his treatment of Ḥámid ibn al-'Abbás, 224–5, of Ibn al-Ḥawwárí, 225–6, of Ibrahím ibn 'Ísà, 227; procures Mu'nis's departure, 229–30; banishes 'Alí ibn 'Ísà to Ṣan'á', 232; his contest with Naṣr, 236–8; relieves Carmathian victims, 237–8; arrested and imprisoned, 239–40; his tactics with Caliph's agents, 240–1; angers al-Muqtadir, 242–3;

Ibn al-Furát, 'Alí (continued) tortured, 243; executed, 244; compared with 'Alí ibn 'Ísà, 245–6; void caused by his death, 247–8; his dealings with Abú Zunbúr, 253–4; avenged, 330; his polite address, 354. Other references: 46, 116, 119, 121, 123, 150–1, 201–2, 250, 255–6, 315, 324 note, 369

Ibn Ḥanbal, Imám, 40, 188

Ibn Ḥawqal, geographer, 65

Ibn al-Ḥawwárí, 156, 159, 162–5, 167, 171, 197, 223, 225–7

Ibn Jání, 'Alí ibn 'Ísà's bailiff, 216

Ibn Jubayr, henchman of Ibn al-Furát, 160, 245–6

Ibn Khalaf, Ibn al-Furát's steward, 171–2

Ibn Khayrán, jurist, 120–1

Ibn al-Kúthání, 222, 231, 234

Ibn Mujáhid, "Reader", 75–6, 133–4, 190–1

Ibn Mukram, qáḍhí, 255

Ibn al-Muktafí, 331. See also Muḥammad son of al-Muktafí

Ibn Muqlah, his early history, 156–7; betrays Ibn al-Furát, 157, and refuses to face him in court, 171; banished to al-Ahwáz, 226–7; employed by 'Alí ibn 'Ísà during second Vizierate, 258; his candidature for Vizierate accepted, 272–3; offended at 'Alí ibn 'Ísà's refusal of his request for al-Akhfash, 278; 'Alí's jealousy of him, 278–9; seeks to mediate between Názúk and Hárún, 281; sent to greet Mu'nis, 282; confirmed as Vizier by al-Qáhir, 284, 286; retained by al-Muqtadir, 287; supervises sales of royal property, and is polite to 'Alí ibn 'Ísà, 288; attacked by troops, 289–90; arouses dislike of al-Muqtadir, 291; arrested, 292; fined, 293–4; persecuted by al-Ḥusayn ibn al-Qásim, 313, 315; restored to Vizierate by al-Qáhir, 324; offends 'Alí ibn 'Ísà, 324–5; appoints him to, but excuses him from taking up, Egyptian inspectorship, 325–6; fears as-

cendancy of Ibn Yáqút, and plots to depose al-Qáhir, 326–8; goes into hiding, 328–9; plots against al-Qáhir, 331, 333; made Vizier to ar-Rádhí, 337–8; patronises Barídís, 343; disappointed over appointment as Chamberlain of Ibn Rá'iq, 345; ousted by Ibn Yáqút, 346, but triumphant, 347; accuses 'Alí ibn 'Ísà of complicity in Ḥamdánid plot, 347–9; leads campaign against Ḥamdánids, 349; obliged to ask 'Alí ibn 'Ísà's help, 350; his embarrassments and fall, 350–2; fined by 'Abd ar-Raḥmán ibn 'Ísà and tortured by al-Khaṣíbí, 353; offends and is killed by Ibn Rá'iq, 359–60; his calligraphy almost equalled by that of 'Ísà ibn 'Alí, 398

Ibn al-Mu'tazz, 79–80, 82, 84–6, 88–93, 97, 114, 118–19, 142, 146, 177, 190

Ibn al-Qáriḥ, historian, 378–9

(Ibn) Qulayjah, or Qalíjah, 210 note

Ibn Rá'iq, see Muḥammad and Ibrahím

Ibn ar-Rúmí, poet, 37–8, 79

Ibn Ṣá'id, Traditionist, 71–2, 118

Ibn Shírzád, Emir, 383–8, 393, 395

Ibn Surayj, jurist, 120

Ibn Thawábah, 112–13, 121

Ibn Ṭ'úlún, 10, 16, 55

Ibn Ṭúmár, naqíb, 74–5, 133, 152 note

Ibn Ya'fur, 232–5, 250

Ibn Yáqút, see Muḥammad and al-Muḍhaffar

Ibn Zabr, qáḍhí, 273–5

Ibrahím, Prince, son of al-Muqtadir, see al-Muttaqí, 364

Ibrahím, son of 'Alí ibn 'Ísà (Abú Naṣr), 34, 47, 368, 388–9, 397

Ibrahím ibn 'Ísà, 34, 38, 60–2, 68, 82, 116, 131, 153, 159, 227

Ibrahím ibn al-Jarráḥ, 34, 81

Ibrahím ibn al-Mahdí, Prince, 25 note

Ibrahím ibn Rá'iq, 291, 299, 311, 318, 326

'íd al-aḍhḥà, al-'íd al-kabír, 105 note

Ifriqiyyah, 8, 137

Ikhshíd, 357, 384
'imád ad-dawlah (title), 388. See 'Alí ibn Buvayh
Imám, Shí'ite theory concerning, 6; bogus Carmathian, 358
Imámate, Fáṭimid claim to, 137–8
Imáms, occult, of the Carmathians, 54
India, form of title used in, 59
Indifferents (early Arab Muslims), 1–2
Inspector-Generalship of Syria and Egypt, 'Alí ibn 'Ísà appointed to, 251; Ibn Muqlah proposes to re-appoint 'Alí to, 325
al-'Iráq, 7, 9–10, 18, 53, 55, 96, 108, 127, 139–40, 183, 233, 309, 379, 380
'Ísà, banker to 'Alí ibn 'Ísà, 209–10
'Ísà, son of 'Alí ibn 'Ísà, 34, 47, 76, 78, 277, 368, 386, 388, 397–8
'Ísà Canal, 269. See also Nahr 'Ísà
'Ísà ibn Dá'úd ibn al-Jarráḥ ('Alí's father), 33–5, 41
'Ísà the Physician, 327, 331–2
Iṣfahán, 165, 174, 199, 262, 310, 340, 358, 362
Islam, 1–2, 129, 137, 212, 235, 289, 306–7, 339
Ismá'íl, son of Ja'far aṣ-Ṣádiq the Imám, 52
Ismá'íl ibn Bulbul, Vizier, 27–9, 31, 36, 131
Ismá'ílí sect of Shí'ah, 7, 52–3, 137, 205
Iṣṭakhr, 341
ithnà 'ashariyyah, sect of Shí'ah, 7. See also Twelver sect

Jabal Nuqum, 235
Jacobite Christians, 11–12
Ja'far, see al-Muqtadir
Ja'far, son of al-Mu'tamid, 25, 27
Ja'far ibn al-Furát, 68
Ja'far ibn Warqá', 354
Ja'far aṣ-Ṣádiq, sixth Imám of Seveners and Twelvers, 52
Ja'far the Barmecide, 21
al-Jannábí, Abú Sa'íd, 50, 54–5, 136–7, 139, 205, 262; Abú Ṭáhir, 205–6, 237–8, 263, 266, 268–71, 279–80, 282, 289, 350, 357–8
al-Jarráḥ, 34–5
al-Jarráḥí, Qaríṣ, 37
al-jarráḥiyyah, well in Mecca, 128
al-Jawharí, Carmathian envoy, 279
Jaysh ibn Khumárawayh, Ṭúlúnid, 55
Jerusalem, 381
Jesters, 258, 365
Jewel Treasury, 260–1
Jewels, Caliphs' collection of, 100–1
Jewish dialectician in 'Alí ibn 'Ísà's circle, 78–9
Jewish moneylenders brought to book by 'Alí ibn 'Ísà, 146
Jews, laws against, 4, 101; status of, in Caliphate, 11–12; purvey learning in Islam, 128; 'Alí ibn 'Ísà's ruling on title of, to medical treatment, 184; oppressed by Abú'l-Ḥusayn al-Barídí, 374
Jibál province, 44–5, 281, 309, 326, 340, 362, 386
Jiddah, 128
John Curcuas, Domestic, 380
John the Baptist, 183
Judges, 14–15. See also Chief *qáḍhí* and *qáḍhís*
Jundí-Shápúr, 128, 165
Jurists (*faqíhs*), 14

Ka'bah, 108–10, 289
al-Kalwádhí, 'Ubayd Allah, Vizier, 247–8, 258, 301–2. See also Abú'ṣ-Ṣuqr
Karach, 340
Karbalá, 6
al-Karkh, 20, 276
al-Karkhí, Vizier, 203, 355
Kárún, R., 124 note
al-khabíth ibn aṭ-ṭayyib, 228
Khafíf, Chamberlain, 66–7
Khajkhaj, commander, 377, 382
khalífah, contrasted with *imám*, 6
al-Kháqání (II), 'Abd Allah ibn Muḥammad, Vizier, 104, 112, 114–15, 121–2, 240–3, 245, 247–51, 259–60
al-Kháqání (I), Muḥammad ibn 'Ubayd Allah, Vizier (father of foregoing), 104–7, 112–16, 121–3, 150, 153, 161, 240, 250–1
kharáj (land tax), 16
al-Khaṣíbí, Vizier, 202, 247–51, 256, 259–62, 305, 314, 332, 334, 353

al-Khaṭíb, historian, 367
al-khazzáz, Abú'l-Ḥusayn, of Wásiṭ, 76
al-Khiḍhr, prophet, 111
Khumárawayh, Ṭúlúnid, 10–11, 55, 147
Khurásán, 9, 18, 43, 54, 267, 274, 308, 310
khuṭbah (public exhortation), 363
Khúzistán, 128, 326, 341–4, 346, 358–9
kitáb al-aghání, 362 note
al-Kúfah, 7, 54, 69, 74, 76, 98, 105–6, 119, 211, 228, 249, 250 note, 254, 262, 266–7, 281, 302, 328, 335, 357
Kúfic writing, 156
Kúrankíj, Emir, 370–1, 373
Kurds, rebellion of, 44
kuttáb, 190

Lady (Shaghab), 13, 99–100, 102, 104, 106, 128, 148, 149 note, 150–2, 154, 160, 174, 178, 194, 198–9, 215, 219, 229, 236–7, 247, 264, 267, 271, 280, 282, 286, 318, 322–3, 346
Land tax (*kharáj*), 16
Law, sacred, 14; schools of, 31, 40; work on, by aṭ-Ṭabarí, 73
Libya, 8
Literalists, favoured by Baghdádís, 3
Logic, 73, 78, 397

Mádhará'ís, 169, 208, 220, 229, 254. See also Abú Zunbúr, Muḥammad ibn 'Alí
Magians, status of, in Caliphate, 11–12. See also Zoroastrianism
al-Mahdí, 'Abbásid Caliph, 124
(al-)Mahdí, first Fáṭimid Anti-Caliph, 137–9, 252, 357
(al-)Mahdí, last Imám and messiah of Twelvers, 53–4
Mákán ibn Kákúy, 307–10, 339, 358
makas (tax), 124
Makhlad ibn al-Jarráḥ, 34, 36–7
Malatia, 316
Málik ibn Anas, Imám, 40
Málikite school, 40, 118
al-Ma'mún, 'Abbásid Caliph, 3, 10, 21, 28, 232
"Man with the Mole", Carmathian Imám, 54–5, 69, 137, 205
"Man with the She-Camel", Carmathian Imám, 54, 57, 137
Manichean system of initiation imitated by Carmathians, 51
al-Manṣúr, 'Abbásid Caliph, 19, 367
Mardávíj ibn Ziyár, 309–11, 317, 339–43, 346, 358, 366
Maryam, daughter of al-Ḥasan ibn Makhlad, 293 note
Maṣáffí infantry, 269, 282, 284, 288–90, 295–6
Massignon, L., Orientalist, 51 note, 379
al-Mas'údí, historian, 26, 33, 102, 206, 334
al-Mattúthah, 77
al-Máwardí, writer, 14
Mecca, 22, 55, 98, 105, 108–10, 114, 124, 128–9, 133, 136, 140, 144, 149, 183, 188–90, 195, 222, 227, 231–2, 234, 237, 249–51, 252 note, 254 note, 260, 289, 350
Medina, 129, 183, 260
Mediterranean coasts, slave trade with, 13
Menagerie, Caliphs', 261
Mesopotamia, 46, 183, 317, 380
Millers' Market, in Mecca, 128
Míná, 255
Minarets, 22, 59
Minbaj, 256
Money-changers, 48, 146
Moral theology, argument on, 187
Morocco, 1, 137 note
Mosque, of the Palace, 59, 180; Friday, 59; at Mecca, 108–11, 129, 289
Mosques, 22; 'Alí ibn 'Ísà's care for, 127; congregational, 134, 234
Mosul, 44–5, 48, 65, 89, 91, 142, 316, 327, 347, 349–50, 367, 369, 374–6, 378, 395
Al-Mu'aḍhḍham, modern suburb of Baghdád, 20 note
mu'adhdhin, 22
al-muḍhaffar (title), 248
al-Muḍhaffar ibn Yáqút, 291, 299, 340, 347, 351–2
Mufliḥ, Negro, 197, 218, 224, 226, 229, 274, 281, 292, 298, 318, 326
Muhájir Ḥasanbas, 34–5

al-Muhallabí, Buvayhid Vizier, 387 note
Muḥammad, Prince, son of al-Muktafí, 322, 327–8
Muḥammad, Prophet, 1, 5–6, 14, 23, 38, 52, 83, 186, 201, 212, 267, 292, 318–19
Muḥammad ibn 'Abdún, 34, 37, 60, 63, 67–9, 84, 88–92, 95–8, 114
Muḥammad ibn 'Alí, see Ibn Muqlah
Muḥammad ibn 'Alí al-Mádhará'í, 254
Muḥammad ibn Baḥr of Iṣfahán, 41, 310
Muḥammad ibn Dá'úd, engaged by Ibn al-Furát, 32; his upbringing and character, 37; his meeting with Ibn 'Ammár, 37–8; appointed to accompany 'Ubayd Allah ibn Sulaymán to Ray, 45; marries 'Ubayd Allah's daughter and is given *díwán al-mashriq*, 46; adjudicates on the Dimimmá bridge case, 48; ringleader in secretaries' war, 60; offers to help Ibrahím ibn 'Ísà, 61; ruled out as possible Vizier, 63; attacks Ibn al-Furát, 67, who retaliates, 69–70; his friendship with Ibn al-Mu'tazz, 80, whom he favours for succession, 84–6, and conspires with, becoming his Vizier, 88–91; his house looted, 92; captured and executed, 93–5; enmity of Sawsan to him, 97; employs 'Abd Allah al-Kháqání, 104; employs Ibn Muqlah, 156; his rivalry with Ibn al-Furát, 245. Other references: 34, 43, 114, 170
Muḥammad ibn al-Ḥasan, see al-Karkhí
Muḥammad ibn 'Ísà, al-'Aramram, 34, 38, 68, 258–9
Muḥammad ibn Ismá'íl, Carmathian Imám, 52–4, 137
Muḥammad ibn Músà, *qáḏhí*, 129. See also Aḥmad ibn Músà
Muḥammad ibn al-Qásim, Vizier, 327, 331–2, 334
Muḥammad ibn Rá'iq, Emir, 291, 299, 311, 318, 326, 345–6, 351–2, 354–62, 373–6
Muḥammad ibn Sulaymán, general, 56, 65–6
Muḥammad ibn Ṭughj, see Ikhshíd
Muḥammad ibn Yáqút, 291, 296–9, 318, 326–7, 345–7, 350–1
Muḥammad ibn Zakariyyá ar-Rází, 185–6
al-Muḥassin, son of Ibn al-Furát, supposed subject of "Cat" elegy, 82; maddened with torture by Ḥámid, 171–2; seeks vengeance on Ḥámid, 197; given robe of honour on his father's restoration (311), 204; persuades 'Alí ibn 'Ísà to pay up, 213, gets him into his power, 215–16, and tortures him, 217–18; censured by father and disapproved by Court, 219; seeks to quarrel again with 'Alí ibn 'Ísà, but desists, 220–1; wishes to kill him, 222; persecutes enemies, 223; Ibn al-Furát threatens Ḥámid ibn al-'Abbás with delivery over to him, 225; has Ḥámid, Ibn al-Ḥawwárí, and Ibrahím ibn 'Ísà murdered, 226–7; tortures 'Ubayd Allah ibn 'Ísà and others, 228; attempts 'Alí ibn 'Ísà's life, 231; attacks Naṣr, 236; in danger from people, 238; hides, 239, but is caught, 241–2, tortured, 242–3, and executed, 244; his widow persecuted by al-Khaṣíbí, 247, 260; tortures Abú Bakr ash-Sháfi'í, 259
Muḥawwal Gate, of Baghdád, 127
al-Muhtadí, 'Abbásid Caliph, 4
muḥtasib, 296. See also Censor
mu'izz ad-dawlah (title), 388. See Aḥmad ibn Buvayh
al-Mukharrim, 20–1, 71, 82, 90, 184
al-Muktafí, 'Abbásid Caliph, 44, 54, 58–60, 62–7, 73, 80, 84–6, 88, 96, 99–100, 118–19, 151, 233, 267, 327, 384
Mu'nis, eunuch, "Victor", supposed to have brought al-Muqtadir to Palace, 88 note; defeats Ibn al-Mu'tazz, 91; Muḥammad ibn Dá'úd relies on him, 95 note; Ibn al-Furát jealous of him, 103–4; supports al-Kháqání, 106;

Mu'nis, eunuch (continued)
guards Vizierate from pillage, 107; favours 'Alí ibn 'Ísà for Vizierate, 113–15; sent against Fáṭimids (302), 139, 142, and against Greeks, and captures Ibn Ḥamdán, 142–3; defends 'Alí ibn 'Ísà, 147–8; defeated by Ibn Abí's-Sáj, 155–6, 160; sent to enquire after 'Alí ibn 'Ísà's health, 196; defeats Ibn Abí's-Sáj and Fáṭimids, 200–1; successful against Greeks, 228; joins in intrigue against Ibn al-Furát, and is sent to ar-Raqqah, 229–30; champions 'Alí ibn 'Ísà, 232; sent for, 238, and returns to Baghdád, 239; supports al-Kháqání (II), 240; Ibn al-Furát blames Caliph for his banishment, 242; debates Ibn al-Furát's fate with al-Kháqání (II), 243; given title *al-mudhaffar*, and becomes all-powerful, 248; sent against Carmathians at al-Kúfah, 249; advises restoration of 'Alí ibn 'Ísà, 249–50; urges appointment of 'Alí ibn 'Ísà to Egypt and Syria, 251; his dislike of Tagín, 252; leaves Baghdád with Abú Zunbúr, 254 note; soothes troops, 261; ordered to proceed against Greeks, 263; fears plot and is estranged from al-Muqtadir, 264; recalled to Baghdád on Carmathian attack, 266; consulted by 'Alí ibn 'Ísà, 267; defends Baghdád, 269–70; has difficulties with troops, 271; consulted by al-Muqtadir about Viziers, 272–3; his co-operation with 'Alí ibn 'Ísà, 272; Naṣr jealous of him, 279; sent after Carmathians, 280; turned against al-Muqtadir, in whose second deposition he takes part, 282–3; releases 'Alí ibn 'Ísà, and sets up al-Qáhir, 284; al-Muqtadir restored from his house, 285–6; influences al-Muqtadir in giving 'Alí ibn 'Ísà Court of Appeal (?), 287; his relations with Caliph worsen, refuses to allow appointment of an-Nayramání, 290–1; objects to dismissal of Ibn Muqlah, 292; his alliance with 'Alí ibn 'Ísà, 293–4; destroys remnant of *Maṣáffis*, 296; insists on dismissal of Ibn Yáqút and his son, 296–9; insists on al-Kalwádhí's being made Vizier, 301; won over to support al-Ḥusayn ibn al-Qásim, 302; befriends 'Alí ibn 'Ísà, 303; offended, decamps from Baghdád, 311–14; goes north, defeats Ḥamdánids, 315–16; gains strength and returns to Baghdád, 316–18; is shown al-Muqtadir's head, 320–1; restores al-Qáhir to Caliphate, 321–2; is persuaded to appoint Ibn Muqlah as Vizier, 323–4; imprisons al-Qáhir in palace, 326–7; plots to depose al-Qáhir, who, however, entraps, imprisons and kills him, 328–30; his dealings with al-Ḥasan ibn Ḥamdán, 347; his palace, 375. Other references: 111, 161, 163 note, 208, 236, 247, 331–2

al-Muntaṣir, 'Abbásid Caliph, 4

al-Muqtadir, 'Abbásid Caliph, objections to his accession, 85–7; his accession, 88; his first deposition, 89–91; his triumph, 92–3; Ibn al-Furát pleads with him for 'Alí ibn 'Ísà and Ibn 'Abdún, 96; Sawsan's dealings with him, 97; disgusts al-Mu'taḍhid with his prodigality, 99–100; his character and appearance, 100–2; Ibn al-Furát takes advantage of his youth, 102–4; refuses Ibn al-Furát a loan, 105, and consents to his arrest, 106; sends letter to Mecca recalling 'Alí ibn 'Ísà, 111; allows torture of Ibn al-Furát, 112–13; disgusted with al-Kháqání (I), decides to make 'Alí ibn 'Ísà Vizier, 113–14; invests him, 115–16; influenced by courtiers, 122; his extravagance, 123; his improvements in Mecca, 128–9; impressed with 'Alí ibn 'Ísà's secretarial skill, 129–30; takes others' advice behind 'Alí ibn 'Ísà's back, 132;

al-Muqtadir (continued)
amused at ‘Alí’s parsimony, 135; despises the Mahdí, 139; orders distribution of largesse on Fáṭimids’ defeat, 140; reconciled with al-Ḥusayn ibn Ḥamdán, 142, whose parade he watches, 143; listens to attacks on ‘Alí ibn ‘Ísà, 145; arrests millionaire, 147; promised allowance by Ibn al-Furát, 148–9; assures ‘Alí ibn ‘Ísà of his good will, 150, but orders his arrest, 152; gradually turned against Ibn al-Furát, 153–9; pleased with ‘Alí ibn ‘Ísà’s defence of his conduct, 155; is advised by Naṣr, 158; persuaded of Ibn al-Furát’s treachery, approaches Ḥámid ibn al-‘Abbás, 161; dissatisfied with Ḥámid, agrees to ‘Alí ibn ‘Ísà’s being made Assistant, 162–4; attends Ibn al-Furát’s trial (306), 165–71; accepts gift from Abú Zunbúr, 169; receives payment from Ibn al-Furát, 172; quashes investigation in return for gift, 174; accepts Ḥámid’s proposal for tax-contract and is pleased with result, 175–7; his first public appearance, 177; recalls Ḥámid, 179; his conduct in famine riots, 180–1; abrogates Ḥámid’s contract, 181–2; his epigram on ash-Shiblí’s physician, 191; attracted to al-Ḥalláj, but persuaded to order his execution, 194–5; honours ‘Alí ibn ‘Ísà and offers him Vizierate (310), but is annoyed by his proposal to elevate Abú ‘Umar, 196–7; favours Mufliḥ, 197; falls ill, 198; disgusted with Ibn al-Ḥawwárí, 199–200; his attitude to Háshimites, 201; Ibn al-Furát regains his favour, 203–4; Carmathian reference to him, 206; hostile to ‘Alí ibn ‘Ísà, 207; ‘Alí accused of acting without his permission, 208–9; persuaded of ‘Alí’s treason, 210; attends ‘Alí’s trial, 210–12; approves Ibn al-Furát’s first settlement with ‘Alí, 214; provoked by al-Muḥassin into ordering ‘Alí’s torture, 215–16, but persuaded by Mufliḥ to order its cessation, 218–19; consents to ‘Alí’s banishment, 221–2; approves al-Muḥassin’s brutality, 223; renews Ḥámid’s contract, 224; Ibn al-Furát doubtful of his intentions, 225; yields to al-Muḥassin’s persuasions, 226; is persuaded to send Mu’nis to ar-Raqqah, 229; Ibn al-Furát denounces Naṣr to him, 236–7; *vice versa*, 238; decides to dismiss Ibn al-Furát, 239; Ibn al-Furát’s bond laid before him, 241; enraged with Ibn al-Furát, 242–3; orders his execution, 244; al-Khaṣíbí attracts him, 247; Naṣr frustrates plot against him, 248; agrees to restore ‘Alí ibn ‘Ísà, 250; persuaded to appoint ‘Alí Inspector of Egypt and Syria, 251; affable to ‘Alí on his restoration, 257, 260; offends him, 258; his first split with Mu’nis, 264; grants ‘Alí help from Privy Purse, 266–7; makes thank-offering for deliverance, 270; grants troops rise in pay, 271; declines ‘Alí’s resignation, 271–2; consults Mu’nis and Naṣr about Viziers, 272–3; favours Ibn Muqlah, 273; deceived by Ibn Zabr, 274–5, orders ‘Alí’s arrest, 275; incensed against ‘Alí, 279–80; his second deposition, 281–4, and restoration, 285–7; sanctions sales of Royal property, 288; resents Mu’nis’s domination, 290–1; relies on Yáqút and his son, 291; attempts to make al-Ḥusayn ibn al-Qásim Vizier, 292, but is obliged to accept Sulaymán, 293–4; forced by Mu’nis to dismiss Yáqút and his sons, 297–9; dismisses Sulaymán, and accepts al-Kalwádhí against his will, 299–301; is offended with ‘Alí, 300; secures appointment of al-Ḥusayn, 302–3; agrees to banishment of ‘Alí ibn ‘Ísà, 303; warned about Daylamites by Ibn Abí’s-Sáj, 305, sends Hárún against them,

al-Muqtadir (continued) 308–9; alarmed at Mardávíj's encroachments, 310–11; relies on al-Ḥusayn and defies Mu'nis, 311–13; disgusted with al-Ḥusayn, 314; dominated by Hárún, 315; loses power to Mu'nis, 316; objects to Mu'nis's approach, 317; after indecision, resolves on war, 318; killed, 319–20; al-Qáhir his opposite, 322; al-Qáhir ill-treats his children, 323; his partisans reconciled with al-Qáhir, 326; gives Fárs to Yáqút, 336; his time looked back to as a Golden Age, 390. Other references: 94, 95, 109, 119, 124, 151, 189, 213, 217, 227, 240, 253, 255, 262, 269, 321, 325, 327, 336, 343, 346, 347

Músà ibn Bughá, Turkish general, 4–5, 10

Músà ibn Khalaf, steward to Ibn al-Furát, 171–2

Music, Muḥammad ibn Dá'úd interested in, 37; Ibn al-Mu'tazz versed in, 80; Muslim discouragement of, 101

Musk, 'Alí ibn 'Ísà proposes to reduce Caliph's allowance of, 135

Muslims, conquests of, 1; relations of, with non-believers, 11–13, 184; attitude of, to slavery, 13–14; shamed by appointment of woman judge, 178; Sasanian example for, 260; most grievous misfortune to befall, 267; consternation of, at Carmathian doings in Mecca (317), 289; perennially at war with Greeks, 306; oppressed by Abú'l-Ḥusayn al-Barídí, 374; attitude of, to Edessa image, 380–2

al-Musta'ín, 'Abbásid Caliph, 4, 19, 21, 33

al-Mustakfí, 'Abbásid Caliph, 385, 387–8, 391–2

al-Mu'taḍhid, 'Abbásid Caliph, 25–31, 36, 43–6, 48, 54–5, 57–61, 63, 85–8, 91, 99–100, 102, 104, 109, 113, 120, 142, 147, 151, 159, 170, 177, 185, 261–2, 267, 291, 306, 323

al-Mu'tamid, 'Abbásid Caliph, 4–5, 7–11, 19, 21, 25, 27–8, 36, 80, 104; a son of, candidate for Caliphate, 86

al-Mutanabbí, poet, 377–9

al-Mu'taṣim, 'Abbásid Caliph, 3, 18

al-Mutawakkil, 'Abbásid Caliph, 3–5, 12, 19, 33, 43, 53, 104; a son of, candidate for Caliphate, 86; *waqf* of his mother's, 184; great-grandson of, suspected of ambitions, 198

Mu'tazilism, 51

Mu'tazilites, 3, 12–13, 40–1, 186–7

al-Mu'tazz, 'Abbásid Caliph, 4, 21, 31, 79

al-Muṭí', 'Abbásid Caliph, 392–3, 395, 397

al-Muttaqí, 'Abbásid Caliph, 335 note, 364, 366–7, 370–1, 373–85, 391, 394

al-Muwaffaq, Prince, 9–11, 18–19, 25, 27–8, 36, 43, 63, 79, 119, 170, 177

Nadhír *al-ḥurami*, 88 note

Nahr 'Ísà, 21, 47. See also 'Ísà Canal

Nahrawán Canal, 21; district of Upper, 30

naqíb al-ashráf, Chancellor of Nobility, 74–5, 152 note

an-Nasá'í, 38–9, 41

náṣir ad-dawlah (title), 376. See al-Ḥasan ibn 'Abd Allah ibn Ḥamdán

Naṣr al-Qushúrí, Chamberlain, captures 'Alid bandit, 140–1; witnesses parade of al-Ḥusayn ibn Ḥamdán, 143; debates with 'Alí and Mu'nis, 147; takes 'Alí's part, 148; opposes Ibn al-Furát, 155–8, and brings about his fall (306), 160–1; persuades 'Alí to become Assistant, 163–4; presides at trial of Ibn al-Furát, 165; disgusted at conduct of trial, 171; stoned by mob, 180; favours al-Ḥalláj, 194–5; al-Muḥassin undertakes to extract money from him, 197; persuades 'Alí to pay up, 213; refuses to assist at his torture, 217; willing, but unable,

Naṣr al-Qushúrí (continued)
to save Ḥámid, 224; hostile to Ibn al-Furát, 229; attacked by Ibn al-Furát, 236–7; retaliates, 238; wishes to arrest him, 239; favours 'Abd Allah al-Kháqání, 240; debates Ibn al-Furát's fate with al-Kháqání, 243; intrigued against by al-Kháqání, supports al-Khaṣíbí, 247; prevents mutiny of officers, 248; consulted by 'Alí on Carmathian attack, 267; aids in defence, 269; has attack of fever, 270; jealous of 'Alí, 271; consulted by Caliph on Vizier question, favours Ibn Muqlah, 272–3; takes charge of 'Abd ar-Raḥmán, 275; hostile to 'Alí, 279; dies, 280, 330
"Native" sciences, 73
an-Nayramání, 263, 266, 272, 291
Názúk, 217, 224, 239, 243–4, 268, 270, 281–6, 291, 330
Negro eunuchs, Mufliḥ chief of, 197
Negro executioners, 227, 244
Negro strain in 'Abbásid blood, 25
Negroes, rebellion of, see Zinj; in Caliphs' army, 18; of the *Maṣáffí* corps spared, 290, but riot subsequently and are destroyed, 295–6
Neo-Platonic elements in Carmathian teaching, 51–2
Nestorian Christians, 11–12
an-Niffarí, 368
Nile, R., 255
Níshápúr, 41
Noah, 111
Non-Muslims, 127–8, 184. See also "People of Scripture"
Non-Pareil, pearl, 100–1

Office for East, see *díwán al-mashriq*
Office for West, see *díwán al-maghrib*
Office of Bribes, 153
Office of Good Works, 129
Office of Private and New-made Estates, 258
Oghuz, Turkmáns, 11
Oratory, 143, 282–3, 387
Orthodox (Sunnís), polemics of, against Carmathians, 51; their terror of Carmathians, 55; Abú Sahl al-Qaṭṭán suspect to, 77; narrow views of, 78; al-Ash'arí revolts at rigidity of, 186; enclave of, at Ṣan'á', 232; influence of, declines in Egypt, 252
"Orthodox" (i.e. first four) Caliphs, 306
Oshroene, 380
Oxus, R., 8

Palace, looted, 283–4; sacked by al-Barídí, 374, see also Ḥasaní Palace; of Round City, 22, 367; of Viziers, 90–1, 107, 207, see also Vizierate
Palestine, 251, 362 note
Parade ground (at ash-Shammásiyyah), 143, 230, 282, 318–19, 330
Paradise (palace), 59
Patriarch, of Antioch, 381
Pentateuch, 78
"People of Scripture", 11–12, 255. See also *ahl adh-dhimmah*
Persia, 7–8, 22 note, 43–4, 59, 108, 119, 163 note, 233, 236, 262, 266, 268, 291, 309–11, 313, 317, 342, 345, 362
Persian, episode of mysterious, 236–8
Persian Gulf, 50, 141, 353
Persian language not that of ceremony, 390
Persian provinces, Muslims conquer, 1
Persian purveyors of learning in Islam, 128
Persian soldiers' good opinion of 'Alí ibn 'Ísà, 397
Persian strain in 'Abbásid blood, 25
Persians, sometimes forge Arab genealogies, 2; in favour with 'Abbásids, 17; in army, but not naturally warlike, 18
Philosophers, in bad odour with Orthodox, 12–13, 51
Philosophy, 51, 193
Physicians, generally infidel, 127–8, 184. See also Court physicians
Physics of Aristotle, 398
Pilgrimage, performed by Ibn al-Mu'tazz, 87; 'Alí ibn 'Ísà takes

Pilgrimage (continued)
part in rites of, 110–12, 251, 254; al-Ḥalláj's mystical substitute for, 195. Other reference: 274
Pilgrimage caravans, 98, 108–9; Dhikrawayh attacks (294), 55, 69; Arabs attack (302), 140–1; Carmathians contemplate attacking, 211; Abú Ṭáhir attacks (311), 237–8, (313), 249, 254, (323), 350; Abú Ṭáhir exacts toll from, 358
Planet (building), 261
Pleiades (palace), 59, 261
Poetry, work on, by Muḥammad ibn Dá'úd, 37; "native" science, 73; Arab addiction to, 'Alí ibn 'Ísà's profound knowledge of, 79; Ibn al-Buhlúl's wide acquaintance with, 120; al-Ḥalláj versed in, 193
Poll-tax (on infidels), 12, 16, 255, 374
Polo-ground, at Baghdád, 89
Poor tax (*ṣadaqah*), 16
Posts, Office of, Shafí' al-Lu'lu'í holds, 231 note. See also *díwán al-baríd*
Prayers, public, recited by aṭ-Ṭabarí at an early age, 73; regularly attended by 'Alí ibn 'Ísà, 134; 'Alí attempts to attend, when in prison, 277–8. See also Friday Prayers
Privy Purse, 26, 67, 105, 113, 145, 150, 153, 209, 248, 260, 266–7, 301
Property tax (*ṣadaqah*), 16
Prophet, see Muḥammad

qádhís, 14, 118
al-Qáhir, 'Abbásid Caliph, 284–6, 322–37, 340, 343, 345, 353, 391
qahramánahs, 100. See also Thumal, Umm Músà, Zaydán
Qaríṣ al-Jarráḥí, 37
Qarluq, Turkmáns, 11
qarmaṭí, 50. See Carmathians
al-Qásim ibn 'Ubayd Allah, Vizier, 45–6, 48, 57–66, 71, 81, 84, 119, 184, 245, 293 note, 295, 313 note
Qaṣr Ibn Hubayrah, 280
al-Qaṭṭán, see Abú Sahl
Qazvín, 165, 309
al-Qazwíní, historian, 189
al-Qudhá'í, historian, 246
Qum, 310
qur'án, Law founded on, 14; supplemented by *sunnah*, 38, 40; controversy on nature of, 41; aṭ-Ṭabarí's early memorisation of, 73; work on, by 'Alí ibn 'Ísà, 75; "Readers" of, 75; versions of, 76; Abú Sahl's familiarity with, 77; Ibn Mujáhid reads, with 'Alí, 134; 'Alí ibn 'Ísà compared to, 159; Ibn al-Buhlúl cites, 166; al-Ash'arí's attitude to, 186; al-Ḥalláj's claim to equal, 193; 'Alí's copy of, 275; al-Muqtadir discovered reading, 283; quoted, 305 note; copies of, carried in procession, and one brandished in battle by al-Muqtadir, 319; al-Muttaqí's predilection for, 364
qur'ánic sciences, 73
Quraysh blood, 25
Quraysh cemetery, 241
al-Qushayrí, 188–9

ar-Rádhí, 'Abbásid Caliph, 143, 149 note, 282, 321, 335–7, 343, 345–9, 351–7, 359–61, 363–4
ar-Raḥbah, or Raḥbat Ibn Málik, 256, 280
ramadhán, fast, 230, 368
ar-Ramlah, 251, 252 note, 280
Raqqádah, 138
al-Raqqah, 46, 57, 63, 229, 248, 282, 383–4
Ra's al-'Ayn, 380
ar-Rashíd, see Hárún
Ray, 44–5, 155, 158, 185, 307–9, 339
ar-Rází (Rhazes), 185–6
Readers, 76, 319
Red Sea, 128
Registries (*zimáms*), 15, 35, 90
Revenue, decline of, 16; shortage of, embarrasses 'Ubayd Allah ibn Sulaymán, 29; of *sawád* enhanced by Aḥmad ibn al-Furát, 31; policy of 'Alí ibn 'Ísà, 49; state of, distresses 'Alí ibn 'Ísà, 123, who increases its yield, 127; farming of, forbidden to statesmen and officers, 182; 'Alí computes deficit in, 200; Ibn al-Furát's energetic measures with, 245; 'Alí attempts to enhance

Revenue (continued)
Egyptian, 255; of eastern provinces recklessly allotted by al-Khaṣíbí, 262; provinces furnish no, 302; of Khúzistán, al-Barídí's profits from, 343; Ibn Rá'iq withholds, dues, 351; shrinkage of, with loss of provinces, 353
Revenue Office, see *díwán al-kharáj*
Rhazes (ar-Rází), 185–6
Roman-Byzantine square, 18
Romanus (Lecapenus), Emperor, 381
Round City of Baghdád, 19–20, 119, 394; Mosque of, 134, 179–80; Palace of, 22, 367
Royal Family, 75, 86, 103, 181
rukn ad-dawlah (title), 388. See al-Ḥasan ibn Buvayh
ar-Rummání, 78, 187
ar-Ruṣáfah, 20; Mosque of, 134, 178–80; Lady's mausoleum at, 178
Russian Central Asia, 8
Russian slave assassinates al-Jannábí, 137

Ṣabárbukht, 34–5
Sabians, status of, in Caliphate, 11–12; religion of, 79, 183
sab'iyyah, sect of Shí'ah (Seveners), 7. See also Ismá'ílí sect
Ṣad'ah, 233
ṣadaqah (property tax), 16
aṣ-Ṣafadí, historian, 35, 133
aṣ-ṣaffár, see Ya'qúb ibn al-Layth
Ṣaffárid rebels, 8–9, 36, 43, 307
Ṣáfí, Chief Eunuch, 88, 94, 99–100, 103
aṣ-Ṣáfiyah, 33, 227, 304, 311, 313, 324, 348, 350
ṣáḥib adh-dhuhúr, Carmathian Imám, 54
ṣáḥib al-khál, Carmathian Imám, 54. See also "Man with the Mole"
ṣáḥib an-náqah, Carmathian Imám, 54. See also "Man with the She-Camel"
Sa'íd, son of al-Jannábí, 137, 205
Sa'íd ibn Ḥamdán, 347–9
Ṣá'id ibn Makhlad, Vizier, 34, 36–8, 42, 79
Sa'íd ibn Ya'qúb of Damascus, physician, 78, 127–8, 183
Saint George, 111
Sájí troops, 327–9, 332–3, 337, 345, 356, 361
Salámah, chamberlain of 'Alí ibn 'Ísà, 251, 295
Sámánids, 9, 43, 306–9, 386
Sámarrá, 3–4, 19, 22, 33, 53, 66–7, 91, 315, 393
Samosata, 263
Ṣan'á', 232–4, 235 note, 250
Sárah, daughter of Abú 'Abd Allah al-Barídí, 362
Sárí, 308
Sasanian architecture, model for 'Abbásid, 21
Sasanian capital (Ctesiphon), 17
Sasanian Court, Nestorians favoured at, 11
Sasanian Court procedure, 'Abbásids take for their model, 14
Sasanian example, 'Alí ibn 'Ísà quotes, 260
Sasanian foundation, medical school at Jundí-Shápúr a, 128
Sasanian House, Buvayhids claim descent from, 339
Sasanian king, Sámánids claim descent from, 9
Sasanian kingdom, Mardávíj dreams of emulating, 341
sawád, 29, 31, 174, 184, 282
sayf ad-dawlah (title), 377. See 'Alí ibn 'Abd Allah ibn Ḥamdán
as-sayyidah, 100. See Lady (Shaghab)
Scholasticism, Muslim, 186
School of Medicine, at Jundí-Shápúr, 128
Schools of the Law, 40; work on, by al-Baghawí, 72
Sevener sect of Shí'ah (*sab'iyyah*), 7. See Ismá'ílí sect
Shafí' al-Lu'lu'í, 219–22, 229, 231, 240–1, 247
Shafí' al-Muqtadirí, 229, 298
ash-Sháfi'í, Imám, 40, 77. See also Abú Bakr ash-Sháfi'í, friend of 'Alí ibn 'Ísà
Sháfi'ite school, 40, 73, 77, 120
Shaghab, see Lady
Sháhriyár, 34–5
ash-Shammásiyyah, 20, 230, 282, 298, 312, 318, 374, 388–9
Shí'ah, 5–7; doctors of, by study of Hellenistic philosophy produce

Shí'ah (continued)
Carmathian teaching, 51–2; hostility of, aroused by tyranny of al-Mutawakkil, 53; deny Fáṭimid claims, 138; in Yemen, 232–3; Mu'izz considers raising prince of, to throne, 392. See also 'Alids, Ismá'ílí sect, Twelver sect, Zaydite sect
Shibám, 233–4
ash-Shiblí, 190–1
"*shí'í*", contemptuous name for (Fáṭimid) Mahdí, 139
Shí'ism, Abú Sahl suspected of, 77
Shí'ite doctrine, al-Uṭrúsh propagates, in Ṭabaristán, 306–7; limiting number of Imáms, origin of, 53
Shí'ite opposition to al-Ḥalláj, 193
Shí'ite plot, pretended, of Ibn al-Furát, 165–6
Shí'ite sympathies, aṭ-Ṭabarí suspected of, 188
Shí'ite theory of Imámate-Caliphate, 6
Shí'ites, see 'Alids, Ismá'ílí sect, Twelver sect, Zaydite sect
Shíráz, 258, 315
Sijilmásah, 137
aṣ-Ṣilḥí, 354–5
Símá, commander, 333, 337, 345
Sinán ibn Thábit, physician, 183–4, 365
Sindh, 1
Ṣíráf, 141
Sístán, 8, 307
Slavery, 13–14
"Son of the Baṣran", contemptuous name for (Fáṭimid) Mahdí, 139
Spain, 1, 286 note
Stewardess (*qahramánah*), 100 note
Ṣúfís, Ṣúfism, 189–93, 276
Sulaymán, 'Umayyad Caliph, 251
Sulaymán ibn Aḥmad aṭ-Ṭabaráni, 77–8
Sulaymán ibn al-Ḥasan, Vizier, 34, 37, 116–17, 159, 226–7, 256, 258, 293–6, 298–301, 332, 336, 353, 355, 364, 397
Sulaymán ibn Wahb, Vizier, 28
aṣ-Ṣúlí, historian and poet, 71, 79–81, 103, 133, 300, 347–8
"Summoner to the Truth" (Dá'í), 308
Sumptuary laws against infidels, revived by al-Mutawakkil, 4, 12; and by al-Muqtadir, 101
sunnah, 14, 38, 40; manual on, by Ibn Ṣá'id, 72
Sunní, 51. See Orthodox
"Support of the Dynasty" (title), 313
Súq al-Ghazal, in modern Baghdád, 59 note
as-Sús, 193, 362
Syria, 10, 18, 22, 46, 54–6, 60, 65–6, 139, 142, 200, 229, 251, 254, 256, 303, 305, 373, 379
Syriac, translations from, 128, 397
Syrian frontier, 283
Syrian revenues, 169
Syrians, purveyors of learning in Islam, 128

ṭabaqát al-aṭibbá', of Ibn Abí Uṣaybi'ah, 184
aṭ-Ṭabaráni, 77–8
aṭ-Ṭabarí, historian, 70, 73–4, 78, 90, 120, 187–8, 306
Ṭabaristán, 7, 165, 306–9, 339
Tagín, governor of Egypt, 139, 252–3, 325, 357
Tagínak, commander, 371
Ṭáhirids, 8–9
aṭ-Ṭá'if, 249
Táj Palace (*at-táj*), 59, 261
takmilah, tax, 124, 130
Takrít, 266, 315, 375, 386, 393
Ṭáliqán, 309
Ṭaríf as-Subkarí, 327–9, 332, 334
Tax-farming, bad effect of, 16, 123; forbidden to statesmen and officers, 182
Taxes, various, 16; *takmilah*, *makas*, etc., 124; Egyptian, on Copts, 255–6; cruel exaction of, by Abú'l-Ḥusayn al-Barídí, 374
Teheran, 44
Thábit ibn Qurrah, 183
Thousand and One Nights, 21. See also *Arabian Nights*
Thumal, *qahramánah*, 178, 198, 240, 247
ath-thuráyá (palace), 59
Tigris, R., 3, 9, 19–21, 58, 91, 96–7, 151, 181, 191, 206, 224, 244 note, 249, 264, 267, 290, 292, 315, 360, 373, 375, 391, 395

Tradition, Traditionists, 14, 38–41, 71–3, 76–8, 118–19, 186, 251, 274, 391, 397
Transoxania, 8–9, 43
Treasury, 61, 67, 103, 122, 146, 208, 229, 251, 290, 299
Treasury of Skulls, 330
Tripoli, 8, 138
Truces between Greeks and Muslims, 154, 265, 380
Ṭúlúnids, 10–11, 46, 55–6, 66, 146, 163, 168. See also Aḥmad, Hárún, Khumárawayh
Tunisia, 8
Turkish monitors of al-Mu'tazz, 31
Turkish strain in 'Abbásid blood, 25
Turkmáns, 11
Turks, 3–4, 17–18, 307, 342, 358, 366–7, 371, 373–4, 376–8, 387
Túzún, Emir, 365, 373, 376–7, 382–6
Twelver sect of the Shí'ah (*ithnà 'ashariyyah*), 7, 52–3, 193

'Ubayd Allah, see al-Kalwádhí
'Ubayd Allah ibn 'Ísà, 34, 38, 109–10, 153, 227–8
'Ubayd Allah ibn Muḥammad, see (al-)Mahdí (Fáṭimid)
'Ubayd Allah ibn Sulaymán ibn Wahb, Vizier, 28–31, 44–6, 48, 57, 60–1, 293 note
'Ukbará, 292, 395
'Umán, 312, 353, 382
'Umar ibn 'Abd al-'Azíz, 'Umayyad Caliph, 12, 276
'Umayyads, 1–2, 5–7, 14, 100, 310
Umm Músà, *qahramánah*, 100, 106, 113, 147–8, 151–2, 197–9, 202, 225, 275 note
umm walad, 13, 99, 104, 106, 323
Uncle, 106, 115, 147–8, 180, 241
ustádh, 43, 246
'Uthmán, "Orthodox Caliph", 76
al-Uṭrúsh, Zaydite Imám, 306–8

Vashmgír ibn Ziyár, 339, 341–2, 359–60, 362
"Victor" (title), 248
Vizier, office of, Vizierate, 14–16, 27–8, 116, 240, 248, 356, 392. See also Palace of Viziers

walí ad-dawlah (title), 59, 313 note
waqf, 184–5
War Office, 15, 69, 116, 170. See also *díwán al-jaysh*
Wásiṭ, 61, 77, 96, 98, 146, 159–60, 165, 170, 181, 194, 204, 224, 226, 262–3, 266, 268, 295, 318, 334–5, 342–3, 345, 351, 356, 358, 362, 365–6, 370, 373, 376–7, 382, 385, 386
al-Wáthiq, 'Abbásid Caliph, 3–4, 19
wazír, see Vizier
Woollen cloak, or shirt, instrument of torture, 113, 216–19

Yaḥyà ibn 'Adí, 397–8
Yájúj and Májúj (Gog and Magog), 305 note
Yalbaq, Mu'nis's chamberlain, 111–12, 114, 239, 270–1, 302, 312, 316, 319, 321, 323–4, 327–30, 337
Ya'qúb ibn al-Layth, 8–9
Yáqút, historian, 78
Yáqút, officer, 291, 296–9, 312, 340–6
al-yatímah, pearl, 100
yawm an-naḥr, Day of Oblation, 105. See also Feast
"Year of Perdition", 223
Yemen, 232–4, 250
Yúsuf ibn Ráfi', see Ibn Abí's-Sáj

Záb rivers, districts of, 48, 60, 65
az-Za'faráni, al-Ḥasan ibn Muḥammad, Traditionist, 38, 40–1, 74
Záhir, Garden of, 71
Zamzam, well at Mecca, 289
Zangí, Ibn al-Furát's secretary, 225, 245–6
Zayd ibn 'Alí, Zaydite Imám, 7
Zaydán, *qahramánah*, 158, 163, 172, 202, 204, 207, 215, 219, 261, 275
Zaydite sect of Shí'ah, 7–9, 43, 53, 233, 306
Zealot, type of Muslim, 1–2, 17
zimáms, 15. See also Registries
Zinj, rebel Negroes, 7–10, 19, 36, 53, 310 note
Ziyád, family of, Yemenite dynasty, 232–3
Ziyárids, 342. See also Mardávíj ibn Ziyár, Vashmgír ibn Ziyár
Zoroastrianism, 35, 37, 306. See also Magians

c